MAKING SENSE OF PENAL CHANGE

Recent titles in this series:

Punishing Persistent Offenders: Exploring Community and Offender Perspections
Roberts

When Children Kill Children: Penal Populism and Political Culture
Green

Criminal Lives: Family Life, Employment, and Offending
Godfrey, Cox, and Farrall

Bar Wars: Contesting the Night in Contemporary British Cities
Hadfield

Bouncers: Violence and Governance in the Night-time Economy
Hobbs, Hadfield, Lister, and Winlow

Making Sense of Penal Change

TOM DAEMS

OXFORD
UNIVERSITY PRESS

OXFORD
UNIVERSITY PRESS

Great Clarendon Street, Oxford OX2 6DP

Oxford University Press is a department of the University of Oxford.
It furthers the University's objective of excellence in research, scholarship,
and education by publishing worldwide in

Oxford New York

Auckland Cape Town Dar es Salaam Hong Kong Karachi
Kuala Lumpur Madrid Melbourne Mexico City Nairobi
New Delhi Shanghai Taipei Toronto

With offices in

Argentina Austria Brazil Chile Czech Republic France Greece
Guatemala Hungary Italy Japan Poland Portugal Singapore
South Korea Switzerland Thailand Turkey Ukraine Vietnam

Oxford is a registered trade mark of Oxford University Press
in the UK and in certain other countries

Published in the United States
by Oxford University Press Inc., New York

First published 2008

British Library Cataloguing in Publication Data

Data available

Library of Congress Cataloging in Publication Data

Daems, Tom.
Making sense of penal change / Tom Daems.
p. cm. — (Clarendon studies in criminology)
Includes bibliographical references and index.
ISBN 978–0–19–955978–7 (hardback: alk. paper) 1. Punishment in crime
deterrence. 2. Punishment—Social aspects. I. Title.
HV8693.D34 2008
364.601—dc22 2008034053

Typeset by Newgen Imaging Systems (P) Ltd., Chennai, India
Printed in Great Britain
on acid-free paper by
Biddles Ltd., King's Lynn

ISBN 978–0–19–955978–7

10 9 8 7 6 5 4 3 2 1

General Editor's Introduction

Clarendon Studies in Criminology aims to provide a forum for outstanding empirical and theoretical work in all aspects of criminology, criminal justice, penology and the wider field of deviant behaviour. The Editors welcome excellent PhD work, as well as submissions from established scholars. The *Series* was inaugurated in 1994, with Roger Hood as its first General Editor, following energetic discussions between Oxford University Press and three Criminology Centres. It is edited under the auspices of these three Criminological Centres: the Cambridge Institute of Criminology, the Mannheim Centre for Criminology at the London School of Economics, and the Oxford Centre for Criminology. Each supplies members of the Editorial Board.

Tom Daems' carefully argued book, *Making Sense of Penal Change*, contributes significantly and originally to a longstanding tradition of key analyses of the sociology of punishment. His analysis includes an account of the socio-political background in which both penal strategies, and our understandings of them, take shape. He, unusually, investigates in detail ('vertically') the intellectual histories and criminological careers of four key analysts of the contemporary sociology of punishment: David Garland, John Pratt, Hans Boutellier, and Loïc Wacquant. In these highly engaging accounts, Daems provides us with a critical summary of the ideas of each, including the key thinkers who influenced each writer, and important changes of direction and emphasis. He delineates their evolution as distinct types of public intellectuals, showing how each is engaged in the project of 'social science with a conscience'. Contemporary cultures of control, intolerance, fragmented and victimalized morality, and urban exclusion, respectively are described and subjected to critical scrutiny. His analysis, and his choice of authors, provides us with a firm reminder of the deep complexity and emotionality of the infliction of punishment in modern democracies. His book pays tribute to the richness (as well as some of the limitations to date) of this much-developed field.

At a time when punishment is an issue of major concern to the public and to policy-makers, and when imprisonment rates are rising steeply, this fresh and careful look at the history of ideas and their effects on penal strategies is both timely and valuable. It will constitute a core textbook for students of the sociology of punishment as well as a contribution in its own right to the debate.

The editors welcome this important addition to the *Series*.

Alison Liebling
University of Cambridge,
May 2008

Acknowledgements

Initial research for this book was made possible by a four-year scholarship awarded by committee G4 'Social, Political and Communication Sciences' of the Fund for Scientific Research—Flanders (October 2003–September 2007). The book was written during a one-year postdoctoral fellowship awarded by the Research Council of the Katholieke Universiteit Leuven (December 2007–November 2008). I am grateful for the financial support provided by both organizations.

I want to thank in particular Kristel Beyens, Marleen Bringmans, Lieven Dupont, Ezzat Fattah, Cyrille Fijnaut, Letizia Paoli, Stephan Parmentier, Tony Peters, Luc Robert and Frank Verbruggen for guidance, assistance, support and feedback throughout and beyond this project. I am grateful to the editors of the *Clarendon Studies in Criminology Series* for welcoming this volume to the *Series* and for providing me with constructive feedback throughout the process of writing the book. I also want to express my gratitude to the team at Oxford University Press—Lindsey Davis, Peter Daniell, Katie Heath, Jodi Towler, and Ruth Munro—for their hard and much appreciated work in order to turn the manuscript into a publishable book.

On a personal level I have enjoyed the company and encouragement of *mi mariposa* Eva. It is to her, to my parents, and to the memory of Carlos González Álvarez that I dedicate this book.

Tom Daems
Leuven
May 2008

Table of Contents

Table of Legislation

1

Making Sense of Penal Change

Introduction

Western democracies seem to punish differently now compared with a few decades ago. A quick look at the tables of contents of scholarly journals in the fields of criminology, sociology and socio-legal studies; the titles in book catalogues of academic publishers; the websites of human rights and penal reform organizations; or even the headlines in periodicals and magazines of the past decade or so would reveal a growing scholarly and wider societal interest in changes in the quantity and the quality (differences) of punishment. Various labels have been used and popularized to describe these developments. Some argue that we have entered a new era. They speak of 'new penology' (Feeley and Simon, 1992), 'new punitiveness' (Pratt *et al*, 2005a), 'new culture of intolerance' (Pratt, 2000e), '*Neue Lust auf Strafen*' (Hassemer, 2000; Rode *et al*, 2005), 'new culture of crime control' (Garland, 2001a), '*nieuwe veiligheidscultuur*' (van Swaaningen, 2004a), '*neopunitivismo*' (Pastor, 2006), and so forth. Others draw attention to how penal practice and thinking changed direction. They write about 'punitive turn' (Frost, 2006), '*Punitive Wende in der Sozialkontrolle*' (Lautmann *et al*, 2004), '*Renaissance des Strafrechts*' (Sack, 2004), 'penal regressions' (Radzinowicz, 1991), '*volonté de punir*' (Salas, 2005), '*populismo punitivo*' (Aranda Ocaña *et al*, 2005); '*La république pénalisée*' (Garapon and Salas 1996), 'gulags western style' (Christie, 2000), '*pénalisation du social*' (Mary, 2003), and so forth. Whatever the merits of these various descriptions, their sheer number and diversity demonstrates how questions about recent penal change have stimulated intellectual activity and creativity.

Most of these writings start from a similar assumption—or better: they accept that another assumption is deeply flawed. The commonsense assumption that is judged to be false tells us that crime and punishment form an inseparable couplet: crime and punishment are tied together as Siamese twins whereby any surgical attempt to separate the one from the other is loaded with life-threatening risks. The Italian criminologist Dario Melossi calls this the 'legal syllogism' which he describes as follows: 'the commonsensical idea, originating in the classical school of criminal law, that punishment is simply the consequence of crime and that, therefore, if there is a need for sociological explanation, such explanation concerns criminal behavior and not the punishment of this behavior' (Melossi, 1989: 311). Decades of historical and sociological research on punishment have demonstrated that crime does not determine the quantity and quality of punishment and that the idea that punishment is merely a means to a certain end belongs in the dustbin. The literature on recent penal change rejects the legal syllogism and starts from a very different assumption: penal change needs to be understood against the background of broader social transformations—either directly or indirectly (that is, mediated through the particulars of policy formation, local political struggles, institutional arrangements, national cultures, and so forth). In turn, social transformations are affected by developments related to punishment and control.

This book is devoted to the burgeoning literature on contemporary punishment and penal change. However, the literature is approached from an unusual vantage point. Readers who hope that they will be presented with yet another explanation for recent penal developments have, unfortunately, bought the wrong book. Those readers who think that they will enter a classical literature review which offers a 'state-of-the-art' in this field of research will also be disappointed. We nevertheless hope that they continue to read because our discussion of the literature is somewhat different, even novel—and, as we hope to demonstrate throughout this volume, also fruitful for the future of thinking about penal change. Instead of offering a new explanation or reviewing the explanations that are on offer on the market of ideas, this book takes an author-oriented approach. We discuss how four leading scholars, over an extended period of scholarly activity and intellectual development, have tried to make sense of penal change. The book's protagonists are David Garland, John Pratt, Hans Boutellier, and Loïc Wacquant. In Chapters 2 to 5 we present and examine their ideas at length, and trace how they have developed over the course of a scholarly career. Chapter 6 closes with a discussion about criminology's public persuasiveness.

The Times they are A-Changin'

According to Ulrich Beck (1994: 26) change is the law of modernity. Change is an inherent feature of living in modern times. In their book *On the Edge* Will Hutton and Anthony Giddens claim that *every* generation believes it is living through great change. Ours is not different in that respect: 'If we believe that information technology and digitalization are likely to transform our lives, earlier generations thought that flight, or electricity, or steam power would do the same for them: and they were right... We are not alone in living through change' (Hutton and Giddens, 2001: vii). Both observations are a warning against chronocentrism, that is, they are meant to make us realize that people in other times and in other places also had to live with—and needed to adapt to—new challenges and pressing problems (or, alternatively, initiate further change to come to terms with previous change). And, arguably, some of these challenges and problems were of a much bigger scale and seemed much more difficult to solve than those we encounter nowadays. Indeed, people of my generation have never lived through wars, oil crises, stock market crashes, revolutions, famine, and so forth. According to the French sociologist Robert Castel (2003) people, at least those who are fortunate to be citizens of developed countries, are living in some of the most 'certain' societies that have ever existed (*des sociétés parmi les plus sûres qui aient jamais existé*). Castel came to this conclusion after highlighting two types of protections: 'civil protections' (guaranteeing fundamental liberties and assuring safety of goods and persons within the framework of an *État de droit*) and 'social protections' (taming the principal risks such as sickness, accident, old age, and so forth). And yet, paradoxically, at the same time we are utterly obsessed with risk and safety issues. How is this possible? Castel asks himself.

Sociologists such as Castel and Bauman (2007) argue that the answer to that question lies in the distinctive nature of the changes that our societies have experienced over the past decades. Indeed, even though change is not an invention of the late twentieth century as Beck, Hutton and Giddens rightly suggest, we have, as they indicate, lived through times that led western societies into a new phase in their development. Social scientists have given different names to this new phase. For instance: postmodernity (Lyotard), late or high modernity (Giddens), second or reflexive modernity (Beck), liquid modernity (Bauman) and hypermodernity (Lipovetsky). Notwithstanding the obvious disagreements on the appropriate label to be used, the bottom line is that there is widespread agreement that we have been (and are) living through a period where profound revisions have been taking place at economic, social, cultural and political levels. These transformations involve developments in capitalism, labour markets and the organization of labour (the shift to post-Fordism); the crises and reforms of welfare states and reorganization of the public sector; processes of globalization and declining influence of the nation-state; changes in youth cultures and leisure activities; the rise of the mass media, developments in popular culture and the reconfiguration of the public sphere; the declining influence of party politics and the crisis of parliamentary democracy; the emancipation of women and changes in the structure of family; ecological developments and growing awareness of risks; a more fluid sense of identity; changes in moral codes and authority; and so forth.

Since crime and punishment are not taking place in a vacuum, it was to be expected that the above listed changes would also impact upon a number of areas of interest to criminologists, and vice versa. Over the past years these transformations have been brought in relation to the changing nature of, and rises in, crime and deviance; to feelings of insecurity, fear of crime, and changing attitudes towards victims and offenders; to a growing acceptance of control measures; and, interesting for this book, to changing responses (punitive and otherwise) to crime and deviance (see e.g. Taylor, 1999; Young, 1999, 2007; Hudson, 2003).

Making Sense of Recent Penal Change

According to Jock Young (2003a) the 'rise in punishment' became 'the new problematic of criminology' in the last decade of the twentieth century. Criminology attempted to come to terms with three related questions: '(1) Why the vast increase in the correctional population—the punitive turn? (2) Why the proliferation of agencies dealing with crime and incivilities? (3) Why the contradictory nature of these responses?' (Young, 2003a: 99). These questions of punitiveness, proliferation and contradiction run as a red thread through much of the recent literature on penal change, on both sides of the Atlantic. At the time of writing that publication stream had far from dried up—and there is no sign that this will happen in the foreseeable future. In this section we will discuss two reasons why sociological questions concerning punishment have risen to the forefront of the criminological agenda: the unpredictability of recent penal change and, related to this, the failure of the classics.

Unpredictable penal change

Back in 1969 *The Annals of the American Academy of Political and Social Science* devoted a special issue to 'The Future of Corrections'. In the introduction John P. Conrad wrote that 'if the state of corrections is any indicator of the condition of civilization, Western man may be prospering better than he knows'. And he continued: 'Although there is much to be done, the present condition of corrections and its prospects for the future give rise to some optimism about the moral progress of man' (Conrad, 1969: xii–xiii). Conrad was hopeful: certainly, from time to time things go wrong, and there is a deep resistance to change in the field of corrections, yet, in general, the American criminal justice system had progressed remarkably. Moreover, at the time he wrote his introduction to the special issue of this prestigious journal, there was no indication that this march forward would soon come to an end.

However, soon after Conrad uttered these optimistic predictions things were changing quite rapidly. In 1976 the court in *Gregg* erased the small success of the 1972 *Furman* case and reinstated the death penalty in the USA. At the same time there was the start of an unprecedented, more than six-fold, increase in the American prison population. The American penal landscape today looks very different from the one Conrad had imagined in the late 1960s: with more than two million people being locked up in American prisons and another five million under judicial control, the future of corrections took a rather unpredictable turn.

As we will see throughout this book, US penal developments have attracted a good deal of attention within the sociology of punishment. In a number of other nations, penal change also took a direction that was hardly foreseen at the time. As late as 1984 Andrew Rutherford could write that 'there are no indications that the prison system in the Netherlands is likely to depart from its reductionist course' (Rutherford, 1984: 145). Six years later the well-respected (ex)criminologist Herman Franke (1990b) speculated that in a few decades it may become clear that the 'tough' 1980s in the Netherlands may actually have resulted in a more humane prison system. His hypothesis went as follows. Over a period of five years the prison capacity in the Netherlands had doubled. This could, eventually, lead to over-capacity and closure of the oldest and most uncomfortable prisons. Dutch prisoners, then, would benefit from the prison-building programme. However, Franke's prediction did not come true.

Constantijn Kelk (2006), a respected expert on the Dutch prison system, recently wrote about the 'regressive movements' in prison policy (*neergaande bewegingen van het algehele penitentiair beleid*) and the general deterioration of living conditions in Dutch prisons (*een algehele verkommering van de detentiesituatie in Nederland*). In his editorial for the Dutch journal of criminal law, Kelk pointed at the budgetary cuts that were affecting the Dutch prison system (a reduction of 17 per cent); the abolition of the principle of 'one inmate per prison cell'; the serious curtailments of activities for foreign drug-smugglers and the creation of 'second-rank' prisoners; the increasing austerity of prison regimes in general; and so forth. Kelk warned about the dangers of current tendencies towards mere incapacitation: the creation of what Pompe once referred to as '*desperados*' and the negative impact upon the mentality of inmates who can no longer benefit from assistance with their reintegration.

Human beings are not 'cultural dopes': there is always an element of choice and, therefore, unpredictability in human behaviour—we do not abide by iron laws that tell us what will happen where and when, how and to whom. Yet, it would be all too easy to attribute the wrong predictions of Conrad, Rutherford and Franke to this basic human unforeseeability. Each of them had good reasons to think that their predictions made sense. Conrad could look back upon a promising history of the gradual 'introduction of professional medical, educational, and social services' which had led to 'the application of social science to penal policy'. Indeed, as he added: 'All signs indicate that this trend is flourishing, and not only in the United States' (Conrad, 1969: xiii). Rutherford thought that Dutch official scepticism towards imprisonment, which had played a crucial role in its reductionist prison policy, was there to stay for much longer. Even the prison-building programme that had been launched in the meantime (in mid-1985) was, so he argued in an updated edition of his book, not an indication of a political willingness to adopt an expansionist course (Rutherford, 1986: 145–151). Finally, when Franke made his predictions, he had just completed a 900-page study on the history of imprisonment in the Netherlands. The bottom line of his Elias-inspired book was that, over a period of two centuries, Dutch inmates had gradually earned more rights and enjoyed better living conditions. Prisoners in the Netherlands became more powerful because, in the eyes of the outside world, their suffering behind bars became increasingly intolerable and increasingly difficult to justify. Against the background of this story it made perfect sense for Franke to predict that Dutch penal policy would continue its slow and painstaking walk on the long road towards further humanizing its prison system. Extra prison capacity could then, as he argued, be used to further ameliorate prison conditions.

Yet despite being firmly grounded in past experience, their predictions did not come true. Many writers on punishment take this sense of unpredictability and 'newness' as the starting point for their descriptions and analyses of recent penal change. The work of the four authors who are at the centre of this book, are exemplary in this sense. On the first page of *The Culture of Control* Garland (2001a: 1) writes that: 'the historical trajectory of British and American crime control over the last three decades has been almost exactly the contrary of that which was anticipated as recently as 1970'. In Chapter 3 we will see how, according to Pratt, it is possible to speak of a new era of 'decivilized' punishment whereby century-old boundaries which used to set limits to modern penality, come to be pushed and make possible previously unthinkable forms and quantities of punishment. In the preface to his book *The Safety Utopia* Boutellier also reflects upon the deep changes crime and punishment had undergone since he started writing on the subject: 'My first encounter with the world of crime and punishment was more than two decades ago, and it has since undergone vast changes. No one could have foreseen that crime-related problems would occupy such a prominent position in cultural awareness' (Boutellier, 2004a: ix). Finally, after summing up a series of wrong predictions being made by scholars in the 1970s Wacquant concludes: 'nothing could have been further from the truth: the US prison was just about to enter an era not of final doom but of startling boom' (Wacquant, 2005b: 5). In spite of their many disagreements (a number of which will be discussed throughout this book) all four share a feeling that significant and unpredictable changes took place, which a few decades ago were hardly foreseeable.

The failure of the classics

Closely related to this unpredictable change there is a shared conviction that established wisdom is unable to account for what is happening. On the one hand, the classical authors were no longer perceived to have the answers to the new questions. Garland, for example, notes the following: 'Not even the most inventive reading of Foucault, Marx, Durkheim, and Elias on punishment could have predicted these recent developments—and certainly no such predictions ever appeared' (Garland, 2001a: 3). Or as Whitman observes: 'The predictions of modernist sociology…turned out to be wrong. History was not tending in the direction in which it seemed to be tending, circa 1965. As a result, we find ourselves in a world we do not understand' (Whitman, 2005: 391).

Durkheim (1969) believed that the shift from mechanical towards organic solidarity would be accompanied by a greater reliance on restitutive law at the expense of repressive law. For Foucault (1977) modern punishment was first and foremost about disciplining and normalizing offenders. Elias-inspired authors such as Franke (1990a) and Spierenburg (1984a) related the long-term trend of the humanization of punishment to changing sensibilities and mentalities. Rusche and Kirchheimer (1968) identified a close relationship between the labour market and punitive practices.

Yet further modernization went hand in hand with more reliance on repressive law not less. Disciplinary power as evinced in rehabilitative programmes and psychological/social work expertise in penal institutions was on the decline while, at the same time, an older sovereign power seemed to reassert itself in the public domain. The deterioration of living conditions in prisons, the revival of shaming sanctions, and the increasing visibility of punishment was difficult to reconcile with a long-term Eliasian trend towards humanizing and privatizing penal practices (that is, the removal of punishment out of sight and behind closed walls). Mechanical economic models that relate changes in punishment to developments on the labour market seemed ill-adapted to the new, post-Fordist methods of producing goods and services under advanced capitalism and the slow build-up of a consumer society. The ideas of the classical authors in the sociology of punishment continued to inspire authors directing themselves at questions related to recent penal change, yet it became clear that they needed to be seriously reworked if they were to be saved from the dustbin.

On the other hand, some of the newer theories were also felt to be inadequate. Blumstein and Cohen's (1973) 'stability of punishment' hypothesis for example, which was supported by evidence showing a remarkable consistency of imprisonment rates from the 1920s until the 1970s would soon be overturned. Some three decades later Blumstein noted that: 'clearly, some fundamental societal and political changes' contributed to the end of an era where 'incarceration policy was largely within the control of functionaries within the criminal justice system' (quoted in Frost, 2006: 29–30). Scull's (1977) hypothesis that the fiscal crisis of the state led to decarceration was refuted by the facts. Soon after the publication of Scull's book the prefix changed significantly and dramatically in scholarly literature: from *de*carceration (Scull, 1977), moving over *trans*carceration (Lowman *et al,* 1987) and *re*incarceration (De Haan, 1995), to end up with *hyper*incarceration (Simon, 2000; Zimring, 2005b). Cohen's (1985) glossary in the appendix of *Visions of Social Control,* designed to help his readers decipher the complexities of 'social control talk', no longer seems to be necessary. In a recent article for a special issue of *Kriminologisches Journal* (with 'Punitivität' as its theme), the German criminologist Fritz Sack stresses the unpredictability of what he refers to as the 'renaissance of criminal law' (*Renaissance des Strafrechts*) and argued that the latter was happening without embellishments (*ungeschminkte Wiedereinsetzung*), without camouflage (*unverhüllt*), and without the (earlier felt) need to provide any special justification (*ohne sonderlichen Begründingsaufwand*) (Sack, 2004: 35–36).

The unpredictability of recent penal change and the related failure of the existing theories have provided a unique stimulus for intellectual activity. It created what Randall Collins might have called a 'hot spot' (see Kurzman and Owens, 2002: 74) or what Rob Stones (1996: 11) might have referred to as an 'imaginative moment'—a window of opportunity for vibrant intellectual activity and scholarly development. Yet the focus on recent and unpredictable change also provides the ingredients for a poisonous and potentially deadly cocktail of errors. It implies that scholars are entering uncertain and unexplored territories; are stepping into a field that is in full transition and addressing changes that are ongoing—that it is, therefore, difficult to separate the more important and lasting developments from the less important and transient ones. Indeed, there is no benefit from hindsight here. Unlike historians who are able to study circumscribed slices of a far-away past (which, in itself, is already an hazardous enterprise), the authors who are addressing themselves to questions related to recent penal change are not dealing with a 'finished' period. In fact, they themselves are living and writing in *these* times—their texts enter, so to speak, in 'real-time' into a world that they aim to reflect upon and interpret. Whitman (2005) exaggerated when he argued that 'we find ourselves in a world we do not understand'. Yet, there is an important message hidden in this statement: it highlights the sheer difficulty of the task at hand, and the multiple risks one runs when embarking upon such a project. And yet, despite these inherent difficulties, academic productivity in this field has been enormous. It provides additional proof of how 'hot' the 'hot spot' is, and how much 'imagination' the 'imaginative moment' is perceived to require.

Life-Course Analysis of Career Criminologists

This book reviews a great deal of published material on punishment and penal change, and might therefore be termed a literature study. But it is important to note that we have approached the available literature in a different and somewhat unusual way. All too often literature reviews go 'horizontal' and are 'problem-oriented'. Available theoretical and empirical studies related to a certain theme are read, presented, discussed and critically examined as indispensable preliminaries for further empirical investigation and theory building. The goal of the review, then, is to arrive at the 'state of the art' in a certain area which enables one to identify theories to be tested, to formulate and fine-tune hypotheses, and to compare the empirical results one derives from one's own study with the ones of predecessors in that specific area of research.

These horizontal, problem-oriented literature studies are also practised in the sociology of punishment. Tonry, for example, brought together and critically examined what, in line with Donald Cressey (1955), one might call a number of 'hypotheses in the recent sociology of punishment'. In a 1999 article, discussing potential explanations for the high incarceration rates in the United States, he identified five such hypotheses: increasing crime rates; punitive public attitudes; cynical politics; single-issue politics; and cycles of tolerance and intolerance (Tonry, 1999). Five years later Tonry added another three to this list: the arrival of a 'risk society'; postmodernist angst; and the role of degradation in American legal culture (Tonry, 2004: 21–61). Voruz (2004) did something similar when she presented a critical overview of what she termed 'the distinct interpretations of penal punitiveness'. In her survey she included work by David Garland, Nikolas Rose, Nils Christie and Zygmunt Bauman dealing with various aspects of culture, politics, economy and human anxieties which are claimed to explain 'penal punitiveness'. In an article discussing recent scholarship on punitiveness, Matthews (2005a) critically reviewed work by David Garland, John Pratt, Loïc Wacquant and Jonathan Simon. Frost (2006: 25–60) similarly devoted a chapter to 'understanding the punitive turn' and reviewed a number of major explanations currently on offer in the sociology of punishment.

These 'horizontal' reviews of the literature are very useful. Stock-taking exercises—especially in a field where so much activity is going on—are indispensable to realize 'what has been done?' and 'what can be done?' They provide us with concise overviews and point us into new directions for future research. However, for this book we have proceeded differently. Indeed, literature reviews can also go 'vertically'; and they can also be 'author-oriented'. This means that instead of putting the problem to be addressed at the centre of one's research, one moves the author who is addressing the problem front-stage. The researcher, then, doesn't merely explore and catalogue plausible explanations for penal change, doesn't just weigh their advantages and disadvantages; in addition, he pays close attention to how an author develops his descriptions and explanations against the background of his own personal development as an author, and the development of the field he is researching. Authors do not think and write in a vacuum: they carry a past with them; they are influenced by new theories and insights in their field of research; they need to take new realities into account; and, in the light of all this, they constantly need to reposition themselves within their own field and the world out there. This is especially the case, one might argue, for authors working in this area who are trying to make sense of a field in full transition. A 'vertical' study, then, is as much about the author as about the story that he brings.

It might be illuminating to draw a parallel with longitudinal studies in developmental criminology and desistance studies. To study criminal careers entails: reconstructing the development of criminals over a life span; identifying their 'risk' factors and various 'needs'; mapping their relational networks and social and familial backgrounds; probing for clues to their desistance from crime; bringing into view those critical 'turning points' in their criminal careers, and so forth. Studying an author runs along remarkably similar lines: authors struggle with their own past and, over the course of a life span, shed bits and pieces of their earlier intellectual identity; they often have tough theoretical choices to make and hard nuts to crack in critical orientation; they have to be able to absorb new developments into their existing interpretations of penal change or, alternatively, adapt them so that the 'new' becomes comprehensible. To conduct life-course analyses of criminologists, therefore, may not be all that different from conducting life-course analyses of criminals. Indeed, throughout this book we aim to demonstrate that it might be interesting and fruitful to shift attention, from time to time, from the criminal to the criminologist, to move from studying 'career-criminals' to studying 'career-criminologists'.

Approaching the research output of authors from a 'vertical' perspective implies that their texts become more than simple text, that is, they also provide context. When authors publish in academic journals or edited volumes, when they write books or reviews, they also leave little traces of their own biographies behind, in footnotes, prefaces or acknowledgement sections. At the most basic level this context makes us sensitive to how fast things change. When reading the books of John Pratt, for example, we learn that he had two Scottish terrier dogs named Binkie and Rosie who gave him company while writing *Punishment in a Perfect Society* (Pratt, 1992a: 6); his dog was Kate when he worked on *Governing the Dangerous* (Pratt, 1997a: v); during his research for *Punishment and Civilization* Kate passed away and Suzie would take her place (Pratt, 2002a: x); and Suzie was still there for him when he completed the manuscript of his latest book *Penal Populism* (Pratt, 2007: xii). As time passes, so dogs come...and they go. But we also learn that Pratt was grateful to somebody for lending a computer to him (Pratt, 1992a: 6). Indeed, we often forget how fast things have changed: in the 1980s and early 1990s computers were not as widely available and used as nowadays; scholars asked for typing advice and borrowed computers from more fortunate colleagues; there was no e-mail to distribute papers amongst colleagues, and no Web of Science to download pdf files of published scientific articles.

Authors live and work in 'times of change'. Sometimes this becomes remarkably clear in one single book volume. In a recent book Loïc Wacquant (2006b), for example, mentioned that more than five million Americans were under control of the criminal justice system (p 92); on another page the number is 6.5 million (p 41); and at yet another page it is 7 million (p 13). It is clear that Wacquant had written the chapters at different points in time (some of them are reworked versions of papers that were earlier published elsewhere) and that the numbers apply to different years, between 1995 and the present. It gives an indication of how fast things can change in this field: in the course of a decade (or in the course of preparing one book manuscript) about 2 million people were added to the American correctional population.[1]

At another level, one may probe footnotes and acknowledgement sections to reconstruct the career shifts of an author. For example, when one browses through the impressive academic output of Hans Boutellier, one can perceive some remarkable shifts. Boutellier's career has always oscillated between academic and policy-oriented positions. And, again, from a 'vertical' perspective, this biographical information becomes indispensable in understanding an author. The fact that Boutellier was always closely involved with policy, that he always had an eye on the practical impact of his work, left a deep imprint upon his thinking and writing and made his trajectory as a 'career criminologist' much more different from, let's say, the career of John Pratt.

A longitudinal author-study can also, and perhaps most interestingly, reveal remarkable shifts in thinking or, on the contrary,

[1] These increasing numbers provide a good example for our purpose here, that is, to illustrate the ever-changing background against which an author writes and thinks. But, of course, a more critical reviewer of Wacquant's book might wonder: Why did he not update (or at least: homogenize) his figures? From an 'author-in-context' perspective, however, to observe these different numbers in one book volume becomes all the more interesting—irrespective of whether the author had this effect in mind or not.

an equally remarkable consistency over many years of intellectual activity. Sometimes we will find contradictory positions. For example, in the work of Pratt we will identify two incompatible depictions of the role of bureaucracy and expertise in punishment: one derived from his early Foucauldian years, the other from his later Eliasian years. Such shifts in perspective only become visible and understandable when an author-oriented methodology is being applied. When read separately, texts often have an immediate attractiveness. The author is able to formulate a challenging hypothesis with supportive evidence or compelling anecdotes. Yet when that same text is placed in a group of texts by the same author and spread out in time 'vertically', one might perceive contradictions with past papers or changes in perspective and position. These contradictions and changes are actually highly interesting.

Finally, the vertical approach makes it possible to explore how an author, on a critical and normative level, relates to his subject, and how such orientations may change over time. Notions such as 'penal regressions', 'mass imprisonment', 'new punitiveness', 'gulags western style', '*die punitive Wende in der Sozialkontrolle*', 'culture of control', 'hyperincarceration', 'killing state', '*pénalisation du social*', '*neue Punitivität*', '*populisme pénal*', '*État pénal*', '*Neue Lust auf Strafen*', and so forth, reveal a sense of unease and, at times, even disgust towards current penal developments. These notions are often deliberately used to expose the profound consequences these changes may have for social life. Against this background it becomes interesting to explore how authors develop their own *public identity*, that is, how they perceive, and give flesh to, the relationship between their intellectual activities on the one hand, and public debate and policy formation on penal issues, on the other.

Indeed, their texts not only provide context (as we discussed above) but they also become part of a context: intellectual products enter—and often are meant to enter—wider public debates on punishment and control. When scholars write about developments which they perceive to be undesirable or disturbing, one can expect that the relationship between their scholarly and public lives moves front-stage. In recent years multiple calls have been launched to engage more directly with the pressing questions and challenges of our times. It has been argued that criminologists should add their voices to those multiple other voices in the public sphere and engage more passionately with issues of crime, unsafety and punishment (see Garland and Sparks, 2000; Chancer and McLaughlin, 2007; Currie, 2007). The author-oriented approach that we adopt in this book provides us with some interesting insights into how Garland, Pratt, Boutellier and Wacquant, in different ways, move back and forth between their social roles of scholars in an academic environment and citizens in a political community.

Selection of Authors

This author-oriented methodology has implications for the selection of authors and the collection of data. In making the selection the following three criteria were taken into account.

The first and most basic criterion was pragmatic in nature: there had to be stuff to work with. The selected authors needed to have produced a substantial amount of work in the form of book-length studies, research articles, chapters in edited volumes, and other published material such as book reviews. Without a considerably large research output a study of this kind is simply impossible. This criterion has been most important for our selection. Indeed, in recent years a large number of scholars have broached questions of penal change, yet there is only a small group which has made it the central focus of its research. A lot of work in this area takes the form of an 'appendix' to empirical studies; commentaries on new laws, policy developments or criminal justice initiatives; critical assessments or programmatic statements. However this means that, notwithstanding the highly interesting and thought-provoking ideas that have thus been introduced into the debate, a sustained treatment of the subject often is missing. The four authors selected for this book have written extensively, and over a long period of time, on the subject at hand.

The two other criteria could only come into play when the first criterion was fulfilled. They are as follows. On the one hand, the authors should have a strong and distinctive opinion on penal change which is grounded in, and further elaborates, the classical perspectives in the sociology of punishment. As we saw earlier, one of the major perceived lacunae that sparked the whole debate was a shared impression that the existing frameworks were no longer adequate to understand recent penal change. This implies that a reworking of classical authors such as Durkheim, Foucault, Elias and Rusche and Kirchheimer became necessary;

or, alternatively, that new interpretative frameworks had to be elaborated to make sense of the recent developments. Each of the four scholars in this book does this: Garland proposes a multidimensional framework which puts culture at the centre of his work; Pratt reworks the classical frameworks of Foucault and, in particular, Elias; Boutellier provides an update of Durkheim by probing for new forms of solidarity centred around victimization and suffering; and Wacquant develops and expands themes in the political economy of punishment that were at the centre of the framework proposed by Rusche and Kirchheimer.

On the other hand, and related to this, it was important that the selected authors could function as 'pegs' onto which authors touching upon similar topics or using similar frameworks could be 'hung'. They needed to be representative of certain strands in contemporary penal thinking. This does not necessarily imply that they are role models or leading figures of different schools in the sociology of punishment—these probably do not even exist (as yet). Yet the themes they touch upon, and the interpretations they offer, should resonate throughout the wider academic community and, therefore, have a broader and more general relevance than what author X at moment Y in place Z had written on topic A. The fruits of the thinking and writing of the four authors in this book are not isolated and closed-off products of solitary intellectual activity but are woven into, and direct contributions to, broader scholarly and public discussions on recent penal change.

To conclude, it is important to note that the author-oriented approach applied in this book should not be confused with writing biographies. Even though we will be looking into the life-courses of four leading scholars, these life-course analyses are largely restricted to their intellectual development. Consequently, the material used to reconstruct our stories is almost exclusively restricted to academic texts. At times some biographical information will be provided such as in Chapter 3, where we briefly touch upon Pratt leaving Great Britain in the mid-1980s and his subsequent settlement in New Zealand. Yet this information is included in the text because it helps us understand a crucial shift in his intellectual development: from that moment onwards Pratt would, for some years at least, devote the major part of his publications to penal developments in New Zealand. In this book we are therefore concerned with intellectual development. Whilst it would be very interesting to write up full-blown biographies of the four authors, paying attention to the small details of their lives by means of exploring personal archives and conducting in-depth interviews, this would be a rather different research project.

A Brief Overview

The next chapter offers an in-depth discussion of the *oeuvre* of David Garland, starting from his work in the early 1980s on the history of the penal welfare strategy in Britain. The bulk of the chapter will be devoted to Garland's book *The Culture of Control* (2001), and the critical discussion that followed its publication. *The Culture of Control* is widely considered to be one of the most important criminological texts of the past decade and has initiated heated and highly interesting debates. A discussion of the book and the critical commentary it provoked, enables us to become familiar with, and critically appraise, an influential account of penal developments in late modernity. The vertical author-oriented methodology applied here will also offer us the possibility to properly situate the study within Garland's intellectual trajectory.

Chapter 3 is devoted to the writings of John Pratt. Pratt has a highly interesting academic trajectory. In the early 1980s he started doing research in the traditions of the sociology of deviance and social control. A decade later he shifted his scholarly gaze to the history of modern punishment. In the 1990s Pratt established himself as a major academic voice in the debate on contemporary penality. The major part of the chapter will discuss Pratt's later work, in particular his books *Punishment and Civilization* (2002), *Penal Populism* (2007) and his work on the 'new punitiveness'. In the latter phase of his career he worked in particular from an Eliasian framework. It is against this background that he launched his hypothesis of the 'decivilization of punishment'. Throughout Chapter 3 we will critically examine his later work in the light of his academic life-course.

Chapter 4 discusses the work of Dutch criminologist Hans Boutellier. Since the early 1980s Boutellier has been interested in broader societal developments, more specifically the transformations of morality and how they impact upon our thinking and acting about crime. The major part of the chapter will be devoted to his two books *Solidariteit en slachtofferschap* (1993) (translated as: *Crime and Morality* (2000)) and *De veiligheidsutopie* (2002) (translated as: *The Safety Utopia* (2004)). Boutellier interprets penal change through a moral lens and applies a Durkheimian framework. His professional life-course is characterized by regular shifts between universities and policy-oriented positions which have left a deep and lasting imprint upon his writing.

In Chapter 5 we will examine the work of French sociologist Loïc Wacquant. In the late 1980s Wacquant, a close collaborator of the late Pierre Bourdieu, did fieldwork in a ghetto in Chicago. It was there that his interest in the transformation of the American penal system originated. Throughout his career Wacquant worked in particular on urban marginality. Since the mid-1990s this line of research was supplemented with the outline of a theory on a distinct neoliberal penality which, in his opinion, forms an indispensable part of a broader America-born neoliberal revolution. We will pay special attention to his books *Les prisons de la misère* (1999), *Punir les pauvres* (2004), *Parias urbains* (2006), and his work on how the ghetto and the prison meet and mesh. Wacquant makes sense of penal change from a perspective that bears resemblances with the political economy of punishment tradition that goes back to Rusche and Kirchheimer. His academic work on punishment needs to be understood against the background of his public role as a staunch critic of the neoliberal revolution.

In Chapter 6 we will pay close attention to the problem of persuasion in criminology. This is an important theme in view of recent calls directed at criminologists to go public—that is, to enter public debate on issues of crime and punishment more directly. We will explore how and towards which ends our four authors aim to persuade their various audiences, and will offer a more general discussion on when criminology is persuasive.

2

Punishment in a Culture of Control

Introduction

In recent decades penal thinking and practice have changed in manifold and, as it turned out, highly unpredictable ways. Indeed, as we saw in the previous chapter, according to many observers, changes since the late 1970s took a turn (a U-turn some would argue) which contemporaries could hardly foresee. This not only implied that new social and penal realities needed to be closely scrutinized in order to come to terms with a puzzling present, but also that some of the older theoretical frameworks for making sense of penal change needed to be subjected to a general re-examination.

Since the early 1980s David Garland has devoted the lion's share of his publications to both topics. Indeed, throughout his *œuvre* we find detailed descriptions and close examinations of the ways in which we (have come to) punish on the one hand, and a never-ending search for adequate theoretical tools to make the present understandable on the other. Garland's career is marked by a continuous dialogue with grand social theorists such as Durkheim, Elias and Foucault and a growing interest in the cultural aspects of punishment. His book *Punishment and Modern Society* (1990) opened an intellectual space for newcomers to the field by sensitizing them to think sociologically about punishment. The interdisciplinary journal *Punishment and Society* that Garland founded in 1999, created an international forum for scholarship on contemporary punishment and recent penal change and played a crucial role in setting up and promoting a research agenda. His latest study *The Culture of Control* (2001) sparked one of the largest debates in the recent history of criminology.

In this chapter we first examine Garland's intellectual life-course, from his first publications dealing with the history of penal-welfare strategies and the birth of criminology to his work on *The Culture of Control*. Next we offer a discussion of some of the defining aspects of his scholarship. The chapter closes with an exploration of how Garland has given flesh to the relationship between his social roles as scholar in an academic environment on the one hand, and as citizen in a political community on the other.

Punishment in a Welfare State

Garland's work in the early 1980s was mainly concerned with the history of penal-welfare strategies in general, and the birth and role of criminology within such strategies, in particular. *Punishment and Welfare* was Garland's very own contribution to the wave of revisionist history-writing. Yet, whereas Rothman (1971), Foucault (1977), Ignatieff (1978), and Melossi and Pavarini (1981) were especially concerned with the late eighteenth and early nineteenth centuries, there Garland directed his attention to the less-researched period of the late nineteenth and early twentieth centuries.[1] His central topic, therefore, was not the birth of the prison, but the birth of the welfare sanction. Like those other revisionists before him, Garland claimed that there was much more going on than 'a "softening" or liberalization of punishment' (Garland, 1981: 42), or a transformation 'that took punishment into its present civilized era' (Garland, 1985a: 248). The origins of the new penal-welfare complex cannot be understood without taking into account the social and penal crises of the late nineteenth century, and need to be interpreted as a set of responses to the problems of social discipline which followed in the wake of the crisis of social and penal regulation in Victorian times. In reality, so he argued, the new penal strategy 'created a more extensive and refined network of control' (Garland, 1985a: 248).

The late Victorian social and penal policies (1865–1895) addressed the lower classes by means of the Poor Law and the prison, and were centred around exclusion and repression. In terms of punishment, deterrence and retribution (and to a lesser extent, reform) were the main objectives. Individuals were treated as free, equal, rational, and responsible. According to Garland

[1] With the major exception of Rothman's *Conscience and Convenience* (1980) (the sequel to *The Discovery of the Asylum* (1971)) which dealt with the same period ('The Progressive Era') for the United States (see also Garland, 1985a: 35, endnote 23).

there was 'an exact symmetry between the legal and the penal which expresses the ideological centrality of legalism in the age of *laissez-faire*. It is bourgeois formal justice in perhaps its purest form' (Garland, 1985a: 18). The late Victorian policies could only survive if two conditions were fulfilled: on the one hand, the enduring importance and viability of the ideology of *laissez-faire* and the free market; on the other hand, the continued disorganization and powerlessness of the repressed class (Garland 1985a: 34). However, these presuppositions of the disciplinary strategy aimed at the poor were increasingly undermined from the 1880s onwards. The Great Depression (1873–1896), the influence of socialist ideas and organizations, the growing unionization amongst labourers, the formation of the Independent Labour Party and the extension of the right to vote were amongst the chief factors which led Britain into a deep social crisis. At the same time, the Victorian penal strategy also came under serious attack. The prison had failed as a disciplinary institution: the problem of recidivism and the over-use of short sentences brought in their wake adverse consequences (in terms of financial cost, overcrowding and the like). The answer to this two-fold crisis would necessarily imply resorting to increased state interventionism and finding an appropriate response to the 'disciplinary deficit' which was no longer tainted by the exclusionary and repressive aspects of Victorian penality (Garland, 1981: 35).

Garland identified four distinctive programmes which elaborated their own paths to resolving the two-fold crisis: the criminological, social work, social security, and eugenic programmes offered 'new ideational materials' which could be used to address the problems at hand. Yet at the same time, these programmes themselves were constantly reworked and rewritten in order to make them acceptable in political and ideological terms. In the case of criminology Garland details these processes at length (Garland, 1985a: 161–202; Garland, 1985c). The idea of a 'science of the criminal' emerged in the late nineteenth century and as it turned out, the early criminologists were willing to sacrifice a great deal of its scientific credentials in order to become politically relevant and ideologically acceptable (Garland, 1985a: 171).

As a result of these anticipatory movements, the radical social aspects—those that emphasized the need for social transformation—quickly disappeared from the criminological discourse. Criminology's commitment to differentiation and individualization, pathology and correctionalism, interventionism and statism made it a highly attractive discourse for policy-makers facing the late nineteenth century penal crisis. Its pertinence lay in 'the *regulatory* and *ideological* possibilities offered by the new programme, possibilities which allowed the extension of effective disciplinary control while doing so in a manner which had strong claims to legitimacy' (Garland, 1985b: 130). Differentiation would no longer happen in terms of the (now politically intolerable) Victorian distinctions such as 'deserving/undeserving' or 'respectable/rough', but 'in terms of a "scientific" discourse which excluded any reference to politics or morality' (Garland, 1985b: 130).

While the social realm came to be reconstituted, allowing for more state interventionism in social and economic policy 'without disturbing the underlying distributions of wealth or the basic relations of power and production' (Garland, 1985a: 246), the penal crisis came to be addressed by a new penal strategy which called into existence a more extensive and refined network of control. The first steps to a welfare state went hand in hand with the birth of the welfare sanction which Garland described, in a language with strong Foucauldian overtones, as 'a sanction which takes as its object not a citizen but a client, activated not by guilt but by abnormality, establishing a relation which is not punitive but normalizing' (Garland, 1981: 40).

Garland's writings in the early 1980s were strongly influenced by Foucault. Like Foucault, Garland drew attention to the role of the prison as a crucial institutional condition for a study of the delinquent: the prison acted as an institutional surface, a kind of 'experimental laboratory' in which criminological knowledge could develop. Moreover, two core concepts of the young human science (individualization and differentiation) were inherently embedded in the architecture of the penal institution: the individual prison cell allowed for individualization, while the prison walls promoted differentiation by drawing a sharp line between the criminal and non-criminal populations (Garland, 1985b: 114–117). Inspired by Foucault, Garland emphasized the 'normalizing' function of the welfare state and the welfare sanction. Crucial for Garland's argument is the intrinsic relationship between criminological knowledge and penal power. In stressing that criminology is inescapably linked to politics, and continuously gives in to a desire for policy-relevance, Garland again agreed with Foucault, who criticized the utility of criminology and questioned its scientific credentials: 'Precisely because criminology's object is a social problem—defined by policies, ideologies and state practices—its "external" origins will always be internal to it.... Criminology's will to truth...has been continually compromised by the will to power' (Garland, 1985c: 3–4).

However, two of the criticisms Garland directed at Foucault deserve special attention. First, the question of timing: Foucault was wrong when he argued that the prison was *from the start* a disciplinary apparatus geared towards transforming criminals. Victorian prisons were characterized by uniform regimes and were keen on treating individuals in a general and equal way. It was only in the late nineteenth century that preoccupations with (non-legal) classification, differentiation and individualization would enter British penal institutions (Garland, 1981: 44, note 4; Garland, 1985a: 31–32). This observation is important because it justifies paying close attention to what exactly has happened in the late nineteenth and early twentieth centuries. Indeed, if one would accept Foucault's timing and situate the birth of modern penality in the late eighteenth century, then there would be hardly any need to pay detailed attention to what happened afterwards. Garland is able to demonstrate, *contra* Foucault, that the major transformation in penality took place *one century later*, and that this can only be understood against a specific socio-political background. For Garland the birth of modern penality is not to be confused with the birth of the prison.

This last remark leads us to Garland's second major critique. In order to grasp the distinctive developments in the late nineteenth and early twentieth centuries one needs to scrutinize closely the historical context: the social and penal crises that undermined the assumptions of the Victorian minimal state with its *laissez-faire* economic and social policies. Unsurprisingly perhaps, in the light of the overall tone of his narrative, Garland avails himself here of a Marxist-inspired vocabulary: notions such as 'bourgeois ideologies', 'strategies of rule', 'Victorian leading classes', 'hegemonic domination', 'bourgeois formal justice', 'ruling bloc', 'bourgeois life', 'dominant class', 'propertyless class', and so forth appear throughout his publications of the early 1980s. Penality, in this early phase of Garland's intellectual development, was first and foremost about controlling the poor and the labouring classes in such a way that the latter would not disrupt existing distributions of wealth and power. This is also why he stressed so much the effect of *depoliticization* of the new penal welfare strategy in general, and criminology in particular: whereas the Victorian penal system displaced social problems to the level of individual morality, so modern penal policy stripped the problem of crime of its social causes and reformulated it, with the help of criminology, as a problem of individual abnormality. Certainly, Victorian *individualism* came to be replaced by, and was utterly different from, the welfare state's *individualization*. Yet the political and ideological effect was the same: they neutralized potential threats to the existing social order.

However, it would be a step too far to infer from this that Garland's early work was squarely neo-Marxist in nature. Foucault was a much bigger influence, something Garland also acknowledged in *Punishment and Modern Society* (Garland, 1990a: 126; see also Cohen, 1986). Moreover, Garland repeatedly stressed that his use of the word 'strategy' is not meant to suggest that there was some kind of pre-existing 'programme' or 'battle-plan'. There was no 'strategist' pulling the strings. The term 'strategy' refers to 'the distinctive and structured pattern of effects which was the *outcome* of these struggles' (Garland, 1981: 36, [emphasis added]; see also Garland, 1985a: 161–162). And it is in this respect that Garland was able to analyse how a strategic solution to the disciplinary problem was 'pieced together' in the late nineteenth and early twentieth centuries. The struggles happened in a particular socio-historical context, yet this does not need to imply that 'economics' or 'class' determined the eventual outcome or that the ideological shifts were mere 'reflections' of an underlying reality.[2]

[2] Prior to the publication of *Punishment and Welfare* Garland had already expressed his doubts about the value of neo-Marxism for the study of penality. In a long review of three Marxist-inspired books he questioned orthodox Marxism's reduction of law and ideology to epiphenomena. Law and ideology, then, are argued to be determined elsewhere, and deemed to lack any effectivity of their own (Garland, 1980). In another review he ridiculed the lack of any practical effect of radical criminology: 'Its declared projects—the global analysis, the Marxist criminology, the "full social theory"—have been of and for the Academy, designed to change not class relations but class exams' (Garland, 1982: 184). A more extensive treatment of Marxism was offered in the opening chapter of *The Power to Punish*—a book that he co-edited with Peter Young (Garland and Young, 1983a). Here both authors concluded a section on 'Marxism and penality' (dealing with work by Rusche and Kirchheimer, Althusser, Poulantzas, and Thompson)

Frameworks for the Sociology of Punishment

Since the early beginnings of his academic career Garland demonstrated a particular interest in theory. While *Punishment and Welfare*, and the related essays on the history of criminology, were primarily historical in nature in which he put theory to work, he was, in other places, concerned with more independent discussions of the advantages and disadvantages of particular theoretical perspectives on punishment and penal change. This would continue throughout the 1980s and, eventually, culminate in the publication of his book *Punishment and Modern Society* (Garland, 1990a). For our discussion in this section it is crucial to keep in mind what Garland and Young identified as 'one crucial problem in establishing a framework for the social analysis of penality':

> how to focus upon the penal realm as a specific object of knowledge, yet also to analyse its relationship to other institutions and types of relationship. One of the problems of employing existing explanatory schemes is that, although they may place the penal in a 'social context', they do so at the expense of destroying its specificity as an object of analysis; *there exists a constant and apparently irredeemable tension between the particular (object) and the general (explanatory form).* (Garland and Young, 1983b: 28, [emphasis added].)

In this section we will trace how Garland, in solving this problem for himself, has unloaded this 'irredeemable tension' by choosing to remain as close as possible to the 'specificity' of his object of analysis (that is, to study punishment in *all* its complexity) while giving up on the idea of a general sociological theory and taking a pragmatic stance towards theory. As we will see, this theoretical choice deeply changed his approach to the work of Foucault, Durkheim, Elias and Marxist-inspired authors. And, as we will see later in this chapter, it would have equally deep consequences for his empirical work on recent penal change. More in particular, and to run a little ahead of the story that will further unfold in this chapter, one cannot fully understand his book *The Culture of Control* if one does not take into account the implications of Garland's response to the 'irredeemable tension' between the 'particular' and the 'general'. Indeed, with a bit of exaggeration, one

as follows: 'the potential of Marxism to provide a framework for the social analysis of penality has yet to be realized' (Garland and Young, 1983b: 29).

could argue that the seeds of all his future work, or at least the parameters in which it would develop, lie in Garland's response to the problem he and Peter Young formulated back in 1983. It is to a clarification of this decisive moment in his intellectual development that we now turn.

Criticizing Foucault

Earlier we saw that, in spite of a number of criticisms, Garland's work on the history of the penal-welfare complex and criminology was strongly inspired by Foucault. Throughout his career, the French philosopher would be a constant source of inspiration but also, and increasingly so, a target for critique. One year after the publication of *Punishment and Welfare* Garland wrote a long paper discussing and criticizing Foucault's *Discipline and Punish*. In this paper we can detect a first glimpse of Garland's answer to the 'crucial problem' that he outlined with Peter Young. Garland stressed that Foucault's power-perspective is of great value in analysis but added that 'it can only ever be a partial and limited basis on which to study punishment or any other social institution' (Garland, 1986a: 868). Indeed, for Garland Foucault's perspective could never stand on its own as an explanatory framework for analysis of punishment and penal change: 'Against the singularity of this analysis in terms of power, I will argue that a wider, more pluralistic vision is necessary' (Garland, 1986a: 868). The question, then, is not whether Foucault is right or wrong (as he emphasized repeatedly and as he demonstrated in *Punishment and Welfare*, there clearly is a lot to gain from Foucault) but whether he provides us with a perspective on punishment and penal change that enables us to understand the full picture; or, as Garland and Young (1983b: 12) put it, that would pay full respect to 'the integrity of the empirical object'. The answer to that problem was clearly negative.

His choice for theoretical pluralism also implies that the nature of his critique would change. Garland started to highlight those aspects of punishment and penal change that remained a 'blind spot' when approached from Foucault's power-perspective, or that were too quickly 'reduced' to matters of control. One of Garland's goals became to expose Foucault's 'one-sided understanding of punishment and penal institutions' (Garland, 1986a: 872). In addition, his newly adopted pluralist position made him worry about the future of the sociology of punishment which, at that time, was so much influenced by the work of Foucault. There was 'a danger that the influence of one powerful perspective can dominate thinking in a way which is intellectually constraining and ultimately counterproductive' (Garland, 1990b: 3). This counterproductivity, so he argued, flowed from a tendency 'to transform the sociology of punishment into a rather one-sided analytics of control and domination' (Garland, 1990b: 3).

Rehabilitating Durkheim

One author who could assist Garland in exposing the limits of Foucault was, of course, Durkheim. In many respects Durkheim's treatment of punishment was almost the opposite of Foucault's. For Durkheim punishment is not about rationality or instrumental control; rather, it is about irrational emotions and passions. Punishment is expressive and non-utilitarian. It is provoked by the violation of certain widely-shared collective sentiments. Through punishment, social solidarity is re-affirmed. These are all aspects that escape from Foucault's particular viewpoint. But, of course, the critique worked both ways: what Foucault *did* address and bring to light was conspicuously absent in Durkheim's account. Using Durkheim to expose some misgivings and gaps in Foucault was therefore not meant to give priority to Durkheim over Foucault. Indeed, as a pluralist Garland needed both: 'any analytical approach should look for the pattern of cultural expression as well as the logic of social control' (Garland, 1990b: 10).

His new pluralist position also allowed Garland to treat Durkheim in much more positive terms than he did before. In a 1983 paper he delivered a hard-hitting and thorough critique of Durkheim's sociology in general, and his theory of punishment in particular. It is crucial to understand, however, that the critique was so sharp because Garland judged Durkheim's theoretical system 'on its own terms' (Garland, 1983: 40). It is in that sense that he could conclude that there was 'little prospect of a reformed Durkheimian sociology' (Garland, 1983: 58). Yet, as soon as Garland moved to an explicitly pluralist position he no longer needed to discuss Durkheim's sociology exclusively 'on its own terms'. Indeed, now Garland's own project of understanding punishment in all its complexity moved to the centre, pushing Durkheim's speculative explorations of the role of punishment in safeguarding the *conscience collective* into the background. This implied that he could more easily look for the positive openings Durkheim's work provided for the study of punishment—and, related to this, he could justify this movement on theoretically sound grounds.[3] In sum, the question was no longer to save or abandon the theory *in itself* but to use it as a 'resource' for *his* larger project, that is, what Durkheim could contribute to *his* multidimensional project took priority in his re-reading of the sociologist.

Discovering Elias

While Foucault and Durkheim were well-known and often-discussed authors in the 1970s and early 1980s this was hardly the case for Elias. One of the major contributions of Spierenburg (1984a) to the debate was to demonstrate the potential of Eliasian sociology for understanding penal change. Moreover, it seems that the timing of the publication of his book *The Spectacle of Suffering* was perfect for Garland's pluralist project which at that time was still in its embryonic phase. Indeed, Spierenburg not only (like Garland) criticized the 'idiom of control' (Spierenburg, 1984b: 6) in prevailing discussions on punishment but he was, in addition, able to point at a new set of questions and to present an unexplored and promising new perspective. This would only add extra weight to the need for a wider and multidimensional framework, as Garland envisaged it from the mid-1980s onwards.

It should not come as a surprise, then, that Garland welcomed Spierenburg's contribution (Garland, 1986b; see also Garland, 1994b). Spierenburg highlighted the role of long-term transformations in sensibilities and mentalities and, therefore, emphasized that punishment must always operate within certain morally and culturally defined boundaries. Spierenburg (1984a: ix) presented his book as a 'counter-paradigm' to the approach of Foucault.

[3] From a pluralist position Garland's more benign judgement of Durkheim made perfect sense. Yet, for readers who were sceptical about his project of a multidimensional sociology of punishment, this re-evaluation of Durkheim provided easy ammunition: in the light of his early damaging critique, how could Durkheim ever be rehabilitated? Adrian Howe argues that Garland's rehabilitation of Durkheim is a 'strange rehabilitation': 'Durkheim is accorded legendary status, but in a manner which appears to contradict Garland's earlier assessment of this founding father's failure to take punishment as a serious object of analysis' (Howe, 1994: 8).

Yet, unsurprisingly, Garland-as-pluralist was quick to correct him: 'there is no question of "paradigm", "counter-paradigm" and a choice between them...the aim should be to bring these separate studies—which are differently focused but far from incommensurable—into a complementary relationship in which each sheds light on the other' (Garland, 1986b: 315). For Garland there was no need for an 'either/or' discourse in the sociology of punishment. On the contrary, a 'mature sociology of punishment', so he argued, needs to approach punishment as 'a complex, multi-layered phenomenon, shaped by psychic, cultural and socio-political forces' and should strive for 'integrated, pluralistic interpretations' (Garland, 1986b: 318).

The multidimensional approach

By the end of the 1980s Garland had laid the foundations for *Punishment and Modern Society*. His dispersed discussions of work by Foucault, Durkheim and Elias could now be brought together into a coherent manuscript and further expanded to include other perspectives, that is, an elaboration of his earlier critique of Marxist themes in the sociology of punishment and an exploration of the value of Clifford Geertz's work for a cultural perspective on punishment. Garland refers to his book as a 'textbook of sorts' (Garland, 1990a: 1) and, indeed, it can be (and is) used like that. However, it does (and is) intended to do much more.

The book is first and foremost a plea for a particular way of practising the sociology of punishment. The starting point for Garland's sociology of punishment is, as we have seen, the recognition of the deep complexity of punishment and an eagerness to understand it accordingly. He argues that this is only possible if we abandon the belief that one perspective can provide us with all the answers. For Garland only pluralism will prevent us from making the mistakes of Foucault, Durkheim, Marx and Elias whose theories will always and unavoidably be partial, because they do not place 'the integrity of the empirical object' (punishment) in the centre of their projects. Their theories, then, become 'sources' of specific interpretations of penality upon which the pluralist can rely selectively, instead of having to follow slavishly one single interpretation (Garland, 1990a: 278).

Moreover, theory needs to be pragmatic, adaptive, flexible. Theories become 'tools' which the sociologist of punishment can 'use' whenever the sociologist needs them to solve a particular problem.[4] And like the handyman who sometimes needs a hammer or a spade, and at other times a saw or a screwdriver, so the analyst of punishment needs to look closely which 'tool' or 'set of tools' is best suited to answer the questions posed:

> each of the different traditions of social theory provides a specific set of tools in the form of a specially adapted conceptual vocabulary, designed to explicate a particular aspect or dimension of social life...each of these interpretive vocabularies has its uses in understanding punishment, and becomes more or less useful *depending upon the questions asked and the characteristics being explained.* (Garland, 1990a: 286, [emphasis added].)

Such a pragmatic orientation to theory also forecloses the prospect of a new general theory of punishment based upon a grand synthesis of the existing frameworks. Theory, in Garland's view, comes in second place; it needs to be subordinated to the particular questions one aims to address and should therefore never be a substitute for empirical enquiry.

Living and Punishing in a Culture of Control

At the start of the 1990s Garland had drawn up his multidimensional framework—a framework which he could now apply. Indeed, its theoretical propositions would, eventually, guide his empirical work for *The Culture of Control* (Garland, 2001a). At the time when he wrote *Punishment and Welfare* Garland already indicated that the penal-welfare strategy was increasingly questioned. Five years later he would refer to this 'crisis of self-definition' as a motivation for writing *Punishment and Modern Society.* If we want to come to terms with the 'crisis of penological modernism', so he argued, we need to understand better 'the social foundations of punishment, its characteristic modern forms, and its social significance' (Garland, 1990a: 9). Throughout the 1990s he started to focus more directly and empirically on the crisis of penal-welfarism, that is, to the 'what' and 'how' of recent penal change. His various explorations would culminate in *The Culture*

[4] Garland's pragmatic *use* of theory resembles the approach Cohen adopted in *Visions of Social Control.* As he wrote: 'This is a book which uses theory rather than being about theory...I have raided certain theoretical perspectives and adapted them for my own purposes. Ideas are part of the market place and not commodities to be fetishized by the privileged few' (Cohen, 1985: 9–10).

of Control, a book that would complete the trilogy 'by bringing *Punishment and Welfare*'s historical account up to the present, and by using the theory developed in *Punishment and Modern Society* to interpret and explain a concrete set of institutions and ideas' (Garland, 2001a: x). But before we discuss *The Culture of Control* we have to devote a few lines to Garland's ideas about postmodern penality and governmentality.

Cautionary notes about postmodern penality and governmentality

Throughout the 1990s the debate in the social sciences on whether or not we had entered into a distinctively 'new' postmodern phase of development also came to inspire discussions on crime and punishment. For some observers recent penal developments departed so sharply from the ways in which modern societies used to respond to crime that they formed an integral part of, and were indicative of, the start of a new postmodern era. In his contribution to this 'postmodern penality' debate Garland (1995a) explained why he was not convinced by this line of thinking. The developments within the penal realm, which some criminologists had placed under the heading of 'postmodernity', were better understood in terms of concepts derived from the sociology of modernity. Garland referred to the collapse of the grand narrative of penal reform, the relativization of morals in the penal realm, the amoral and demoralized character of contemporary crime control, the commercialization of the penal realm, the politicization of crime and punishment and the emphasis on signs and symbols of punishment within philosophical writings. These changes, he wrote, were 'the outcome of certain long-term modernizing dynamics operating in combination with a set of conjunctural political and cultural shifts' (Garland, 1995a: 184).

In a second theoretical essay Garland added his voice to the then burgeoning literature of governmentality studies. Throughout the 1990s there was a remarkable revival of interest in Foucault. Some of his later papers gave rise to what has been termed a second 'Foucault effect' in theoretical criminology. Whereas the centrepiece of the first 'Foucault effect'—*Discipline and Punish*—tended to characterize individuals as 'docile bodies' which were brought to conformity by disciplinary power, the latter Foucault would pay more attention to individuals as active subjects whose choices come to be linked up with the aims of governing authorities. Within the social sciences in general, and criminology in particular, Foucault's scattered (and unfinished) ideas were picked up and reworked in order to analyse how people are 'made up' so that they can exercise a kind of regulated freedom, e.g. by means of making private citizens responsible for their own security.[5] In his paper Garland (1997a) pointed at some problems with governmentality studies (such as the terminological confusion; the parallels with conventional sociological wisdom, and the need for close empirical analysis of the 'rationalities' and implementation of the 'programmes'). In addition he formulated a critique that we have encountered earlier in this chapter. For Garland governmentality studies had a great deal to offer in terms of analysing technical and knowledge-based rationalities but they tend 'to neglect the expressive, emotionally-driven and morally-toned currents that play such a large part in the shaping of penal policy' (Garland, 1997a: 202). This is again Garland who speaks from the angle of analytical pluralism. And, indeed, Garland advised that governmentality research should not be viewed as 'an autonomous mode of enquiry' but rather it needed to be developed 'in conjunction with the sociological tools necessary to it' (Garland, 1997a: 204).

The Culture of Control: closing the trilogy

The Culture of Control is about developments in crime control and criminal justice in the UK and the USA. Yet, the book is not a comparative study. Garland aimed to detect similar crime control responses in both countries and to demonstrate that these are not the result of political imitation or policy transfer, but of a similar process of social and cultural change which has had, since the early 1970s, a tremendous impact on social organization and crime control in both nations. Garland referred to these changes as 'the coming of late modernity'. This also implies, so he suggested, that the analysis he offers is important for other societies that are

[5] There is no space here to discuss these governmentality studies. For useful introductions see Burchell *et al* (1991) (this volume also contains Foucault's essay 'Governmentality'), Rose and Miller (1992), Dean (1999), and Rose (1999). For applications in criminology, see e.g. O'Malley (1992), Garland (1997a), and Smandych (1999). In the next chapter we will devote more attention to Pratt's study *Governing the Dangerous* which was deeply inspired by the governmentality literature.

experiencing the coming of late modernity. The fact that his book has been translated into a number of languages (such as Italian, Spanish, Chinese and Portuguese) flows from Garland's conviction that the book, because of its wider relevance, deserves a readership which crosses the borders of the Anglo-Saxon world. In his preface to the Spanish edition he re-emphasized and rejustified his focus on similarities. There he observed that there are clearly differences in Germany, Scandinavian countries, and Southern Europe which are important, yet these differences are the product of 'politics'. While 'politics' matters, he warned his (Spanish) readers they should not overestimate the extent to which political actors can determine future developments—political decisions are always structured by social and cultural conditions. To the extent that other societies have also become late modern, they will experience a similar set of problems and challenges as he described and analysed for the two Anglo-Saxon nations that are at the centre of his book (Garland, 2005a: 25–28).

We dwelled a little longer on Garland's focus on similarities because, as we will see later in this chapter, this has been one of the most controversial aspects of the book. Let us now turn to the story being told in *The Culture of Control*. The book grew out of a sense of bewilderment. In the introduction twelve indices of change are listed which offer an indication of the deep transformations that have taken place with respect to punishment and control in the USA and the UK over the last three decades: the decline of the rehabilitative ideal; the re-emergence of punitive sanctions and expressive justice; changes in the emotional tone of crime policy; the return of the victim; the protection of the public; politicization and new populism; the reinvention of the prison; the transformation of criminological thought; the expanding infrastructure of crime prevention and community safety; the role of civil society and the commercialization of crime control; new management styles and working practices; and a perpetual sense of crisis (Garland, 2001a: 6–20). These 'indices of change' come as a surprise to Garland because nobody seemed to have expected them. Until the 1970s nothing seemed to indicate that the existing hybrid 'penal-welfare' structure—with its attention to due process and proportionate punishment on the one hand, and its commitment to rehabilitation, welfare, and criminological expertise on the other, would soon lose its hegemonic status. On the contrary, until then, the system could rely on a broad-based professional and political support and it was, moreover, embedded in the post-war welfare state and its social democratic politics. To contemporary observers the status quo on punishment seemed to be quite solid.

Yet, from the mid-1970s things changed very quickly. Garland rejects the 'standard account' which argues that sharp critiques targeted at the assumptions and practices of penal welfarism (such as the empirical 'nothing works' critique and various objections related to paternalism, determinism, positivism, discretionism and the like) were responsible for the breakdown of the status quo. Neither failure nor critique suffices as an explanation. Negative research findings have been produced since the 1930s so were far from new; the 'nothing works' critique was an overreaction and overstatement; and social institutions always have a margin in which failure can be tolerated and defined as a problem of implementation (as opposed to theory-failure) without having to question the penal-welfare structure itself. The answer to the 'why' question, therefore, does not lie in the critiques or reform proposals, but rather in deeper social and cultural changes, that is, 'the character of late twentieth-century society, its problems, its culture and its technologies of power' (Garland, 2001a: 72). This new field of crime control, moreover, did not resemble the plans of the reformers: just deserts and proportionality in punishment gave way to a much harsher penal politics of deterrence, incapacitation and, in the end, mass imprisonment and expressive punishments.

Garland distinguishes two sets of transformative forces. On the one hand, the social, economic, and cultural changes that came to characterize late modern societies. These changes deeply impacted upon the welfare state and criminal justice institutions and policies, as they were tuned in the older 'penal-welfare key'. Important for our understanding of the reconfiguration of the field of crime control is that late-modern societies, in Garland's opinion, tend to develop high crime rates as a by-product: they are 'high crime societies' (Garland, 2000c). The coming of late modernity resulted in more opportunities to commit crime; reduced situational controls; an increase in the population 'at risk'; and a reduced efficacy of social and self controls. Garland suggests that there is a causal link between the coming of late modernity and a society's increased susceptibility to crime. The second set of transformations relates to the political realignments and policy initiatives that were developed in response to the first set of transformations. These answers were reactionary in nature: the attitude towards late-modern change was filled with regret and a firm determination to rewind the clock. This reactionary attitude came to be translated into the neo-conservative politics of Thatcher in Britain, and Reagan and Bush in the United States. Garland writes about 'a strikingly *anti-modern* concern for the themes of tradition, order, hierarchy, and authority' (Garland, 2001a: 99).

Policy makers, therefore, came to be confronted with a nagging predicament. High crime rates became a normal 'social fact'[6]; the limits and failures of the criminal justice system were more and more acknowledged; and the myth of the sovereign state and its monopoly of crime control eroded irreversibly. The answers to this predicament were intensely ambivalent. On the one hand Garland identifies a range of *adaptation* strategies which attempt to face up to the predicament: the professionalization and rationalization of the criminal justice system; the commercialization of justice; 'defining deviance down' (that is, limiting the demands placed upon criminal justice agencies); the redefinition of success indicators; the concentration upon the consequences (rather than the causes) of crime; and a relocation and redefinition of responsibilities. On the other hand, he perceives highly politicized strategies of *denial* and *acting out*: the first denies the predicament and aims to reassert the old myth of the sovereign state; the second limits itself to expressing the anger and outrage provoked by crime. The combined result of these seemingly contradictory responses is a highly volatile and ambivalent pattern of policy development.

Both sets of strategies are accompanied by different criminologies. The 'new criminologies of everyday life' (which include: routine activity theory, crime as opportunity, lifestyle analysis, situational crime prevention, and rational choice theory) align themselves with the strategy of adaptation. Garland also speaks of 'criminologies of the self' because in these criminologies criminals

[6] As Garland clarified in an earlier paper, the 'normality' of high crime rates needs to be understood in 'the technical sociological sense': 'They are a feature of all similar societies at a similar stage of their development'. In this reasoning Garland follows Durkheim's notion of 'normal social facts', as set out in *The Rules of Sociological Method* (see Garland, 1997b: 185).

stop being the poorly socialized misfits of welfarist criminology—in a significant way they are like all of us. The 'criminology of the other', on the other hand, turns criminals into 'aliens', 'monsters', 'superpredators', that is, their 'otherness' comes to be emphasized and their conduct is seen to escape all human understanding. This criminology goes hand in hand with the strategies of denial and acting out. The 'excluded middle ground', as Garland observes, is the once dominant welfarist criminology (Garland, 1999b; 2000a).

It is important to note that Garland explicity refuses to understand this set of strategies in terms of a policy of bifurcation. The concept of 'bifurcation' refers to a 'twin-track approach', that is, it implies that governments simultaneously increase the penalties for serious offenders while decreasing them for offences of a less serious nature (Bottoms, 1977). Yet, when one tries to grasp the strategies of adaptation and denial in terms of bifurcation one risks missing the underlying political ambivalence (Garland, 1996: 462–463). Garland's use of Freudian language (strategies of 'denial' and 'acting out') highlights the fact that, in his opinion, bifurcation is not well suited to capture the core issue at stake, that is, that we are dealing with a set of contradictory responses provoked by the inability of the (formerly) sovereign state to wipe out the social fact of high crime rates and the limits and failures of the criminal justice system (see also Matravers and Maruna, 2004). As he argues at another occasion: 'What we have seen in recent years has been conflict and doublethink, not carefully differentiated reasoning' (Garland, 1997b: 196).

But what has made these strategies possible and desirable? Throughout the book (and elsewhere) Garland avoids blaming 'bad media' or 'opportunistic politicians': the success of the ambivalent policy options cannot simply be attributed to media representations or politicians who use the crime issue for personal gain. Instead he argues that the ensuing policies were conditioned by a 'new collective experience of crime and insecurity'—the so-called 'crime complex'. They depend upon the pre-existence of widespread 'extra-political' social routines and cultural sensibilities that came into existence over the past few decades. At this point Garland weaves culture into his explanation. Indeed, in an earlier article he outlined a 'theory of cultural adaptation' (Garland, 2000c) to answer his self-imposed puzzle. In their daily lives people were increasingly confronted by crime and it was their multiple adaptations to this 'social fact' that gave rise to a new collective experience of crime which, in turn, provided support for the strategies that came to be adopted. The high crime rates and the routine responses of late-modern citizens brought *cultural* effects in their wake: 'They changed how people think and feel, what they talk about and how they talk about it, their values and priorities, how they teach their children or advise newcomers to the neighbourhood. The fear of crime—or rather a collectively raised consciousness of crime—has gradually become institutionalized' (Garland, 2001a: 163).

This new experience of crime is important to explain the adaptations of the professional middle classes. It was this group that had profited from the generous education system of the welfare state; that worked within the public sector; and that had supported and defended the assumptions and practices of penal welfarism. Yet, the developments of the past decades also changed their experience with crime: crime no longer was a 'far-away' show, but became an undeniable part of everyday reality: 'From being a problem that mostly affected the poor, crime and incivility became a daily consideration for anyone who owned a car, used the subway, left their house unguarded during the day, or walked the city streets at night' (Garland, 2001a: 152). As a result, so Garland argues, the new policies he documents in his book happened because the liberal elites *allowed* them to happen—they were the dog that did not bark. As such, a new culture of crime control comes into existence which may, eventually, lock us into a new Weberian iron cage. Moreover, because the most significant change has happened at the level of *culture*, it is to be expected that the culture of control, as it stands at the moment, will not change overnight. Indeed, the very originality of Garland's cultural explanation also implies, inevitably, that the prospects of an easy escape out of the current 'crime complex' are grim indeed.

Discussion

It is difficult to underestimate Garland's distinctive contribution to our thinking about punishment. Seldom has one single author put such a decisive stamp on a field which he, as one reviewer argued, 'has done so much to develop' (Morgan, 1991: 431). According to Stanley Cohen (1986: 410) his first book was 'one of the most important pieces of work ever to emerge in British criminology'.

Adolfo Ceretti, who (with Francesca Gibellini) translated two of Garland's books into Italian, argued that Garland helped to change the way we think about punishment and control (Ceretti, 2005b: vii). Or what to think of the fact that 76-year-old Fritz Sack, one of Germany's most respected criminologists, devoted in June 2007 a five-day intensive seminar '*Kriminalität und Gesellschaft*' to Garland's work, at the Institut Für Strafrecht und Kriminologie at the University of Bern in Switzerland?

Jonathan Simon features on the cover of the *The Culture of Control* with the following significant oneliner: 'The most important book on the sociology of punishment and social control since Foucault's *Discipline and Punish*'. Taking Simon's comment seriously (as we will be doing here) has two beneficial consequences for the remainder of this chapter: on the one hand, it implies that by discussing Garland's work a perspective on penal change is being presented that stands in high regard throughout the academic world; yet, on the other hand, it also means that, like Foucault, Garland's particular way of making sense of penal change may, in fact, turn out to be much more controversial then one might infer from the above-mentioned acclaim for his work.

Indeed, as we will see in this chapter, his latest book *The Culture of Control* has sparked one of the largest debates in the recent history of criminology. Far from closing the discussions on recent penal change with a definite 'take-it-or-leave-it' analysis Garland, like Foucault before him, is able to open the debate. This was also Garland's explicit aim. In the opening pages of *The Culture of Control* he challenges his readers and writes provocatively: 'attempts to delineate patterns of structural change will tend, whether or not their claims can be sustained, to have a productive effect in stimulating further empirical studies and energetic critical response' (Garland, 2001a: ix). It is especially at this last point that Garland shares common ground with Foucault. As Foucault once mused in an interview: 'I like to open up a space of research...What I say ought to be taken as "propositions", "game openings" where those who may be interested are invited to join in—they are not meant as dogmatic assertions that have to be taken or left en bloc' (Foucault, 2002: 223–224).

Institutionalizing the sociology of punishment

Back in 1990 Garland argued that the sociology of punishment was an underdeveloped area of social thought: 'the corpus of works is disparate and uneven in quality, and lacks any settled research agenda which can command widespread assent and promote a sense of collective endeavour' (Garland, 1990a: 11). In 2001 this sounded much different. In the preface to *The Culture of Control* he speaks in terms of 'collective effort', 'communal endeavour', and 'collective work' (Garland, 2001a: xii). More recently he referred to the large scholarly interest and academic production in this field as a 'collective project' (Garland, 2004a: 160). Richard Sparks, the former editor-in-chief of *Punishment and Society*, also seems to hint at this when he wrote that the journal is an 'intellectual project and not just another journal'. For him Garland's programmatic statement in the inaugural issue of the journal (Garland, 1999a) needs to be understood as a 'manifesto' (Sparks, 2004: 355).

Punishment and Society has undoubtedly played a key role in opening an intellectual and institutional space to think about questions related to penal change. From 1999 until 2001 Garland acted as editor-in-chief of the journal which he founded in order to 'provide a new focus for penological scholarship, and to foster the field's development by encouraging interdisciplinary and international exchange, highlighting new and innovative work, and providing a dedicated forum for all those whose interests center upon penal matters' (Garland, 1999a: 10). Such an institutional space within the world of criminology is important; to recognize a certain topic as worthy for further inquiry and to build a sense of professional identity amongst social scientists who share the same interests. It also provides a reference point for newcomers to the field and assists in networking. James Whitman, for example, is a legal historian whose work was quickly picked up in the journal (Savelsberg, 2005; Whitman, 2005). The same applies to Loïc Wacquant whose work we will discuss at length in Chapter 5. As a sociologist interested in urban marginality, Wacquant developed an impressive body of research on punishment which in the late 1990s, seemed to have earned him a ticket to the network with regular contributions in *Punishment and Society* and various chapters in volumes edited by leading scholars in this field.

The remarkable academic output generated in the wake of the publication of *The Culture of Control* testifies to how a shared research agenda that seemed to be absent two decades ago is attracting the attention of scholars from different corners of the globe. Few books in the recent history of criminology have sparked so much discussion, critique, and are in the process of furthering empirical research as *The Culture of Control*. Next to the countless reviews published in various academic journals there are the thematic issues in journals such as *The Cambrian Law Review* (Kilcommings and Vaughan, 2004a), *Justitiële Verkenningen* (Van Swaaningen, 2004a), the *Critical Review of International Social and Political Philosophy* (Matravers, 2004) and *Kriminologisches Journal* (Hess *et al*, 2007). Special conferences were convened in York, Milan and Frankfurt (see also Ceretti, 2005a). The fact that so many of Garland's readers have been willing to add their voices to this grand interchange of ideas, opinion and research is an indication, we would argue, of the richness of current debate in this branch of criminology. Garland's lasting contribution to the intellectual and institutional maturation of this field of inquiry, therefore, is difficult to underestimate.

Against reductionism: pluralism and the legacy of Durkheim

The defining feature of Garland's scholarship from the mid-1980s onwards is a disavowal of reductionism. This has translated itself into two key aspects of how he approaches questions of penal change: pluralism and a pragmatic orientation towards theory on the one hand, and a faithfulness to the old Durkheimian position that we first need to understand punishment before we can think about it in normative terms on the other. Both are closely interconnected in Garland's thinking.

For theoretical purists it can be frustrating to 'pin' Garland down in theoretical boxes. For example, throughout *The Culture of Control* Garland uses concepts as 'field' and 'habitus' which he borrows from Pierre Bourdieu; he continues his life-long dialogue with the legacy of Michel Foucault, proclaiming to adopt a genealogical analysis, and refers to 'governing-at-a-distance' when he discusses the responsabilization strategy, a key notion derived from Foucault-inspired governmentality studies; his use of notions such as 'ontological insecurity' and 'time-space distanciation' seems to be inspired by the work of Anthony Giddens; when he writes in terms of 'social facts' and 'collective experiences' it seems as if the Durkheim-inspired Garland is speaking which, again, should hardly surprise us because over the years he has invested a lot of intellectual energy in rescuing and rehabilitating Durkheim for the sociology of punishment; concepts such as 'mentalities' and 'sensibilities' bear the imprint of the work of Norbert Elias, an author Garland discovered in the mid-1980s and whose theory of civilization features prominently in *Punishment and Modern Society*; there are the multiple uses of Freudian terms (such as 'repression', 'acting out', 'denial', 'hysteria', 'reality principle') throughout his book and papers of the late 1990s which suggest that he is influenced by psychoanalysis (see also Matravers and Maruna, 2004).

In the light of his choice for pluralism Garland's reliance on a number of authors and perspectives in *The Culture of Control* becomes more intelligible (see also Garland, 2006a). His pluralist position may also explain why he was not persuaded by the 'post-modern penality' hypothesis (Garland, 1995a), or why he demonstrated such a deep reluctance to let the second 'Foucault effect' impact upon his thinking (Garland, 1997a). Indeed, one might argue that his theoretical pluralism came to function as a 'safety valve': an ingrained scepticism towards hypotheses and frameworks that, from his pluralistic position, run a huge risk of missing crucial aspects. Or to put it somewhat differently: when the choice for pluralism has been made and when this has fermented over a longer period of time, it may turn into a little voice whispering warning messages into the ear of an author. In Garland's case these messages may, for example, sound like this: '*Beware David, however interesting the postmodern penality-hypothesis may sound or however attractive the governmentality perspective may seem, there are always some crucial aspects—such as the obvious continuities with penal modernism in the first case, or questions related to social solidarity in the second—that will fall out of the grand picture. You will miss them!*'

This pluralist position is closely related to how he uses theory. In two recent essays Garland (2004a; 2004b) further elaborated on how theory features in his work. Theory operates as a 'learned disposition', that is, 'a set of intellectual reflexes that come to define an author's distinctive way of looking at the world' (Garland, 2004b: 5). Garland provided a list of his 'exemplary theorists' which includes Marx, Hirst, Freud, Foucault, Weber, Durkheim, Geertz, Elias, and Bourdieu. Throughout his discussion Garland used terms as 'habitus', 'instinct', 'theoretical reflex', 'ingrained disposition' all of which point, in a way, to how theory becomes like a second voice, a part of a writer's intellectual self. Indeed, as he explained, developing a theoretical habitus means 'finding one's own voice' without, however, losing sight of a permanent need for self-reflexivity. Important to note is that for Garland theory is not an end in itself, it needs to be put to work: 'The task of "theory-building" ought to be a provisional stock-taking between projects, rather than an end in itself...theoretical concepts function as means rather than ends, as tools for analysing rather than as topics of analysis' (Garland, 2004b: 19–20). Theory, therefore, has to be dynamic, adaptive, and pragmatic: it must be responsive to the nature of the phenomena being studied (Garland, 2004a: 166; see also Garland, 2007b: 439). This also explains why in a recent paper on the history of lynching in the United States—a history that seems to be at odds with conventional stories that forge an automatic link between modernization and civilized sensibilities—he added that 'we need to be more flexible in the way we understand theoretical generalizations and historical periodization' (Garland, 2006c: 31).

These theoretical options need to be understood against the background of his *Leitmotiv*: 'we need to know what punishment is in order to think what it can and should be' (Garland, 1990a: 10). There is a definite sequence here—first analysis, then critique—which comes close to Durkheim's plea for the separation of 'value judgements' from 'reality judgements', the latter being the province of the sociologist (Durkheim, 1996). This explains why in *The Culture of Control* Garland aimed to subdue his normative voice until *completing* his analysis (Garland, 2001a: 3). This also returns in his most recent work devoted to capital punishment in the USA. Here Garland is on his guard for 'the polarizing rhetoric of normative debate' and argues that 'there are analytical benefits to be had from abjuring the normatively engaged rhetoric of "us" and "them", "retention" and "abolition"' (Garland, 2007b: 437, 440; see also Garland, 2007d: 136–137). In the death penalty literature 'critical thought' tends to dominate over 'analytical precision' (Garland, 2007a: 126). This should not come as a surprise: capital punishment is, after all, a deeply problematic sanction. Yet, this eagerness to criticize a problematic penal practice such as capital punishment in the USA, may hamper our understanding of its deep complexity. As he wrote: 'In their eagerness to criticize an institution that is deeply controversial, commentators may be too quick to reduce a complex network of actors and system of practices to a singular "symbolic" dimension; too ready to ignore the instrumental uses to which capital punishment laws can be put, whether or not anyone is actually executed; too one-dimensional and unempirical in their discussion of symbolic communication and too casual in their use of the term "symbolic" to effectively address what is at stake in this description' (Garland, 2007a: 112).

It does not make a difference if we talk about punishment in general, capital punishment in particular, or about the field of crime control *en globo*, Garland's *Leitmotiv* always remains the same: a firm description is needed *before* we should start the project of critique and normative reflection. Critique should be postponed, so to speak, until the institution is analysed in all its complexity. Pluralism and the Durkheimian legacy, then, are jointly mobilized in an academic project that is directed against reductionism.

Sociology of late modernity

Garland is more interested in similarities than in differences. In his inaugural editorial for *Punishment and Society* he stressed that the 'current American scene' is by no means 'an isolated one' and that the same kind of issues manifest themselves elsewhere. There is an 'internationalization in penal matters' and 'similar social demands and institutional problems reappear in different national contexts, prompting policy-makers to act in ways that resemble the responses of other jurisdictions' (Garland, 1999a: 6–7). Earlier in this chapter we devoted a little more attention to Garland's choice in *The Culture of Control* to abstain from a study in comparative criminology: the USA and the UK were put on an equal footing because of this enduring interest in their similarities. In addition, as we have seen, he suggests that his analysis might also apply to other societies that have experienced the coming of late modernity. This is also illustrated by the titles of his publications which refer to 'contemporary society' (Garland, 1996; Garland 2001a) and 'high-crime societies' (Garland, 2000c), and not simply to the USA and the UK. In a response to his critics Garland repeated that the book aims 'to develop a critical understanding of the practices and discourses of crime control that have recently come to characterize *a number of contemporary societies*—notably the USA and the UK' (Garland, 2004a: 160, [emphasis added]). His formulation is, as always, careful: while the book discusses the American and British cases and draws upon research conducted in both countries, he is convinced that the insights he offers have a much wider relevance.

Garland is well aware that there are obvious differences between the USA and the UK. In the preface to *The Culture of Control* he refers to America's distinctive combination of racial division, economic inequality, and lethal violence that have clearly impacted upon the scale and intensity of its penal responses—most notably the death penalty and the phenomenon of mass imprisonment. Yet, so he argues, for a study which seeks to reveal structural patterns, questions of size and degree can be suspended, because the similarities move into the spotlights. Moreover, in an obvious anticipation of critical comment, Garland cleverly attempts to immunize his study against empirical falsification by arguing that the high level of abstraction of his argument makes it *inevitable* that certain facts don't fit on the big picture. This follows from an inescapable tension between 'broad generalization' and 'the specification of empirical particulars' (Garland, 2001a: vii).

Despite these reservations and immunizations Garland has not been able to appease his readers. His focus on similarities, his claim that the analysis applies 'elsewhere' and his attempt to seek shelter against 'local' critique behind the ongoing dialectic between 'big picture' and 'local detail' are amongst the most controversial aspects of his study. To what extent are the USA and the UK similar? To what extent are they similar to other Anglo-Saxon countries, or continental-European countries? How far can the focus on similarities be pushed? Is it possible that some differences are so big that they simply don't fit and may call into question (some aspects) of the generalized 'big picture'? Such questions may not only raise problems for Garland's particular approach to making sense of penal change, but also for resistance and things to be/become different. If all western (or better: late modern) societies can be characterized in the same terms as the 'worse case' (read: the USA) where does this leave those other nations? Are they merely lagging behind and in the process of catching up? If the culture of control came to be shaped out of the challenges of late modernity in general, as Garland suggests, then the future of those other countries may be grim indeed.

The challenge of comparative criminology

The first and most basic critique coming from a comparative perspective is the following: Garland should have selected neither the USA nor the UK to explore the culture of control in contemporary or late modern societies. If his goal is to arrive at a broad and general account of *the* culture of control his selection of two rather 'atypical' cases seems somewhat awkward: 'Garland may have explicated the exception of an as-yet unexamined norm' (Feeley, 2003: 126). The selection of two extreme cases or outliers would do well for a 'deviant case analysis' but is more difficult to justify when the goal is to discuss and analyse control cultures in late modern societies *in general*. His selection, therefore, should have been more representative, more 'close to the norm' (Feeley, 2003; see also Savelsberg, 2002: 687).

The second type of critique is different in nature: in some crucial respects the differences between the UK and the USA are more important than the similarities. Such differences cannot that easily be suspended. These include both aspects related to crime and punishment (such as the USA's rates of (lethal) violence, the death penalty, the extremely high imprisonment rates, and racialized aspects of penal control) and the social, economic, and cultural conditions (such as high levels of social inequality, the predominance of the free market, the cultural ideal of the American Dream, a history of racial segregation, the gun culture, its poor welfare state tradition, and so forth). Moreover, in view of the large interstate differences in terms of imprisonment, and the use of capital punishment, it can also be argued that the USA should not be treated as an undifferentiated whole. Indeed, the most conspicuous penal developments are restricted to the Southern states and California (see e.g. O'Donnell, 2004; Zimring, 2003).

At times Garland presents examples in his book which only apply to the USA: the death penalty, 'truth in sentencing' laws, the reintroduction of chain gangs, community notification schemes, sexual predator laws, boot camps, supermax prisons, and so forth are not or hardly present in the UK. This 'undiscriminating equation of US and UK policies', as one reviewer has put it (Rumgay, 2003: 441), seems hard to justify. One might even argue that, because some of these differences are of such a scale that they should have been moved to the centre of attention, not the similarities (see e.g. Currie, 1997: 148–150; Zimring and Hawkins, 1998). As Jock Young remarks: 'It is as if we were to study violence by comparing the similarities between men and women: we would undoubtedly find common profiles in terms of age, class and ethnicity yet we would lose sight of the most obvious factor: gender' (Young, 2003b: 232).

Moreover, in a thematic issue of *Punishment and Society* Garland suggested in quite strong terms that mass imprisonment in the USA is 'pathological', 'extraordinary', in need of 'a name of its own': 'This is a phenomenon—Emile Durkheim (1933) would say a pathological phenomenon—that has no parallel in the western world... Because it is so extraordinary, this phenomenon should be differentiated from imprisonment as it occurs in other comparable nations. An extraordinary phenomenon of this kind deserves a name of its own' (Garland, 2001c: 5). Many would probably agree that locking away more than 2 million people is, indeed, a phenomenon that deserves 'a name of its own'.

Moreover, there is not only the quantitative aspect that sets US mass imprisonment apart: 'Imprisonment becomes *mass imprisonment* when it ceases to be the incarceration of individual offenders and becomes the systematic imprisonment of whole groups of the population' (Garland, 2001c: 6). The groups Garland was referring to were young black males residing in large urban centres. Against the background of Garland's definition one may feel safe to label mass imprisonment a distinctively *American* phenomenon. Yet this makes it more difficult to put it on the same footing with rising imprisonment rates in the UK (or other western countries).[7] If mass imprisonment needs to be differentiated from imprisonment in other nations would it then not be more plausible to explore what differentiates the USA from the rest of the world—instead of what binds us together?

The third type of critique relates to Garland's contention that the analysis he presents in *The Culture of Control* also applies elsewhere: that is, late modern societies other than the USA and the UK. The German criminologist Hans-Jörg Albrecht (2001) was a little irritated by Garland's use of the phrase 'and elsewhere'

[7] The quote from his introduction to the thematic issue of *Punishment and Society* stands in sharp contrast with the following passage from *The Culture of Control*: 'There has thus been a shift—*more pronounced in the USA than in the UK but present in both countries*—toward a much greater and more intensive use of custody' (Garland, 2001a: 168, [emphasis added]). Whereas the discussion on 'mass imprisonment' suggests that imprisonment in the USA is *qualitatively* different and in need of its own name, there his discussion of imprisonment in *The Culture of Control* suggests a continuity, that is, a mere *quantitative* difference. However, by reducing the difference to a question of 'numbers' Garland seems to leave out of sight a crucial aspect of his own definition of mass imprisonment. It seems as if mass imprisonment needs to lose its distinctiveness in light of Garland's probing for similarities between both jurisdictions.

in his 1996 article (Garland, 1996). At first the 'elsewhere' seemed to refer to Australia and the United States. Then, after conceding that the British trends outlined in the article can also be observed in Australia and North America, Garland added another 'and elsewhere, too'. Yet, there was no further discussion of the 'elsewhere' (Albrecht, 2001: 294). More generally, Lesley McAra is critical of a tendency in recent literature to treat transformations in the penal systems of the USA and England and Wales 'as if they were paradigmatic of western systems as a whole' (McAra, 1999: 355). Both authors point at a similar problem, probably shared by a number of continental-European criminologists: in an academic world where English is the *lingua franca*, it being the working language in the major international fora and scholarly journals, penal developments observed and analysed in the UK and the USA are, at times, too readily assumed to occur 'elsewhere'.

A number of scholars have explored to what extent the ideas developed in *The Culture of Control* also apply to crime control developments in their backyards *inter alia* in the Republic of Ireland (Kilcommins and Vaughan, 2004b; O'Sullivan and O'Donnell, 2007), Northern Ireland (Dwyer, 2004), Scotland (McAra, 2004), Germany (Eick, 2007; Köllisch, 2007; Kreissl and Ostermeier, 2007; Lehne and Schlepper, 2007); and the Netherlands (Van Swaaningen, 2004b; Downes and Van Swaaningen, 2007; Downes, 2007; De Haan, 2007). There is no space here to enter into a detailed discussion of these various country reports. Taken together they can be summarized as follows: whereas the hypothesis of the culture of control seems to apply to *some* extent in those other countries most authors are quick to identify crucial differences in crime and control patterns, as well as in the political, socio-cultural and institutional dynamics. In general, they warn of an all-too-easy transfer of the hypothesis to other settings and are prudent not to embrace the culture of control-thesis in an unqualified way.

The challenge of American exceptionalism

It is remarkable how often the words 'exceptional' and 'exceptionalism' are used in the literature on crime and punishment in the USA. Tonry (1999: 420) suggested that the high imprisonment rates in the USA are 'exceptional' in relation to other western countries; Western (2004) argued that America is 'exceptional' in terms of its unique history of race relations and racial disparities in incarceration; Monkkonen (2006) referred to America's 'exceptionalism' when discussing its remarkable increase in homicide rates at the same time as they decreased in western Europe; Stern (2006: 44–7, 140–1) argued that America's harsh penal policy in general, and its treatment of drug offenders in particular, justifies the use of the label 'exceptional'; Poveda (2000), Steiker (2002) and Zimring (2005b) used the notion 'American Exceptionalism' in their discussions on capital punishment; Frase (2004) wrote about the 'exceptional' severity of sentencing in the USA; and so forth.

These recurring references to American exceptionalism point to developments that are judged to be so extreme that the USA comes to be seen as an 'aberration', as if it no longer shares a common tradition with other western societies. If this is true, then this has serious implications for how we try to make sense of penal change: it then poses a tremendous challenge to *generalized* accounts (such as Garland's) which tend to put the USA on the same footing as other western societies. Indeed, as Sparks wondered, when he reflected on this topic: 'Can the penology of Europe and the penology of the United States make use of the same conceptual resources?' (Sparks, 2001: 165).

The notion of 'American exceptionalism' has a long history which dates back to Alexis de Tocqueville's *Democracy in America*. Tocqueville (1988) identified five values that he judged to be crucial to America's success as a democratic republic: liberty, egalitarianism, individualism, populism and *laissez-faire*. They are also known as the 'American Creed'. Lipset (1996) followed in Tocqueville's footsteps when he suggested that America's organizing principles and founding political institutions are 'exceptional, qualitatively different from those of other Western nations', and concluded that therefore 'the United States has developed as an outlier' (Lipset, 1996: 13). For Lipset American exceptionalism is a double-edged sword, turning his home country into both the *worst* and the *best* nation on the globe. Seen from this perspective, it can be hypothesized that the above-mentioned references to mass imprisonment, high rates of homicide, capital punishment, racialized crime control and repressive control of drugs offences are an expression of the dark side of American exceptionalism.

To raise such an hypothesis is also important for discussions on (the future of) punishment in Europe. European criminologists and criminal justice specialists often are worried about the

'Americanization' of continental criminal justice systems. There is a fear that European ways of responding to crime may get infected by the American virus (see e.g. Van Stokkom and Ter Veer, 1995; Kuhn, 1996; Lagrange, 2003). As Sim (2002: 314) has put it recently, the 'penal atavism' (the term is Sim's) that underpins crime control policy in the USA 'provides those of us in other countries with a glimpse of a brutal and bleak future unless direct action is taken to construct and mobilize alternative strategies for dealing with offenders'. Related to this, a need has been felt to specify our own European penal identity, to probe deeper for what European values may underpin a more humane response to crime (see e.g. Snacken, 2006; Van Zyl Smit, 2006). Seen from such an angle, the 'American exceptionalism' debate becomes utterly relevant for European criminologists: if the hypothesis of American exceptionalism can be accepted, then this is comfortable news for Europeans (the problem, then, is an American one, not ours); if not, then it might mean that Europeans need to be more closely on their guard (the problem, then, can become, or is already embryonically, ours).

James Whitman (2003) has been at the centre of this debate. His book *Harsh Justice* is a large-scale historical study which compares criminal punishment in the USA on the one hand, and Germany and France on the other. Whitman's explanation entails two counter-intuitive insights. The first part of his explanation points at the different traditions in social hierarchy on both sides of the Atlantic. The USA misses the 'aristocratic element' that has played such a crucial role in continental European history: status equality is more important than status differences. According to Whitman, we need to understand punishment within such hierarchical traditions because punishment is all about 'degradation': to punish is to reduce a person in status; punishment means treating another person as inferior. The USA is much more susceptible to processes of status degradation (and thus more inclined to punish harsher) than Europe because this 'aristocratic element' has not been present in its history. This has led to two directly opposing patterns of development: *levelling up* in France and Germany, *levelling down* in the United States.

The hierarchical societies of Germany and France made a sharp distinction between low status and high status and, related to this, between low status and high status forms of punishment. Offenders of high status, for example, were imprisoned in quite comfortable cells where, shielded from public exposure, they could buy food of decent quality, continue their intellectual activities, have visitors, and so forth. For low status criminals, life behind bars was much less pleasant: they were subjected to forced labour and corporal punishment. But more frequently they were condemned to painful public humiliation (such as flogging, branding, mutilations, pillory, and so forth). The same status distinction applied with respect to the death penalty: (honourable) decapitation was reserved for criminals of high status, whereas (disgraceful) hanging was applied to low status offenders. The historical pattern in France and Germany is characterized by a gradual abolition of low status treatment. This is why Whitman speaks of a 'levelling up egalitarianism': the old privileged high status punishments gradually came to be applied to everyone. In the USA Whitman observes the opposite: not a generalization of high status treatment, but rather its abolishment. The American striving for equality gave rise to a pattern of 'levelling down': eventually everyone, irrespective of rank or status, would be subjected to the low status punishments. It is not so difficult to see why Whitman's historical narrative is counter-intuitive: indeed, hierarchical and fundamentally unequal societal structures formed the highly unattractive basis upon which France and Germany could build their relatively mild punishment tradition.

But also Whitman's second part of the explanation is counter-intuitive. Here he points at the role of, and attitudes towards, state power. According to Whitman, strong states tend to punish less harshly. Strong states have two characteristics: they are

> relatively *powerful* and relatively *autonomous*. They are powerful in the sense that they are relatively free to intervene in civil society without losing political legitimacy. They are autonomous in the sense that they are steered by bureaucracies that are relatively immune to the vagaries of public opinion. (Whitman, 2003: 13–14.)

Powerful and autonomous states can more easily show mercy. Mercy, moreover, presupposes a social hierarchy: when showing mercy to an offender, we implicitly confirm his inferior status. 'A society with a strong tradition of acknowledging and enforcing status differences will thus often be a society with a tradition of mercy' (Whitman, 2003: 12). The strong states of France and Germany can exercise mercy more systematically and function more independently from public opinion. In the USA, on the other hand, there is a long and deep tradition of resistance against state power and a much stronger emphasis on formal equality: the principle 'everyone is the same in front of the law' is difficult to reconcile with a free assessment of individual cases. Whitman, therefore, introduces another counter-intuitive line of thinking in his narrative: the American distrust towards the state paradoxically paves the way for a much harsher repression of crime by that very same state. It is not the continental despotic and absolutist state that punishes harshly (as Montesquieu and Durkheim believed), but the distrusted and weaker state from the American tradition.

Whitman does what Garland does not: his study is a comparative analysis which, moreover, traces current diverging patterns in punishment on both sides of the Atlantic to deep cultural differences that have their roots in the eighteenth century. For Whitman understanding American punishment is impossible without understanding America: 'there is something in the American idiom, something in American culture, that is driving us toward harsh punishment' (Whitman, 2003: 6). Such a hypothesis poses a direct challenge for Garland's argument which, as we have seen, stresses the similarities at the expense of the differences. Garland is well aware of this and has, over the years and on various occasions, rejected thinking in exceptionalist terms.

A decade ago Garland already expressed serious doubts about explanations that might be classified as 'exceptionalist' in nature. This happened at the 1998 University of Colorado Law Review Symposium devoted to the book *Crime is Not the Problem* by Zimring and Hawkins (1997). Zimring and Hawkins argued that general crime rates in the USA are broadly comparable to crime rates in other western societies. Yet, in terms of lethal violence it stands out—lethal violence sets the USA apart from other developed countries. To highlight this observation they coined the phrase the 'American Difference'. For Garland (1998a) this focus on lethal violence was somewhat misplaced and missed out the crucial importance of low-level crime control. The observation that property crimes have increased in most countries, including the USA, leads Zimring and Hawkins to focus on what makes the USA special, that is, its exceptionally high rates of lethal violence. Yet, according to Garland those increases in property crime matter much more than Zimring and Hawkins are willing to acknowledge: they put the much larger group of property crimes too quickly aside and thereby ignore the deep social impact they have had. Indeed, the title of their book (*Crime is Not the*

Problem) suggests that these increases are only of minor importance. Garland disagreed with this:

> the British public—despite its comparatively benign rates of lethal violence—relates to crime in ways that are *very similar to those that characterize America*... Zimring and Hawkins's claim that '(h)igher rates of theft change social life in many small ways, but no big ones' is an empirical mistake grounded in a theoretical fallacy. The theoretical fallacy is that large-scale social changes require equally large-scale social causes. In fact, multiple, incremental adjustments, accumulating over time, and generalized throughout the population, are much more typical of the way in which important social changes occur. (Garland, 1998a: 1152–3, [emphasis added].)

In this quote resonates what three years later became the backbone of *The Culture of Control*: the multiple, everyday, low-level adaptations to high crime rates of people living in late modern times, and the cultural effects these bring in their wake, are for Garland much more important. And in this respect, Britain and the USA (and other late modern societies) are more similar than different.

In a long review article criticizing Whitman's book (and also Zimring's (2003) which we leave out of the discussion here) Garland summarizes his deep scepticism about the notion 'American exceptionalism' in the following words:

> In my view, the theory of 'American exceptionalism'—and especially the *culturalist* versions of the theory that Zimring and Whitman develop—is an inappropriately deep and deterministic way to understand a difference in penal policy that is actually much more recent and much more contingent than this literature suggests... such an approach directs attention to the wrong historical period and the wrong historical processes. (Garland, 2005b: 349; see also Garland, 2007b: 438–9.)

Garland's critique is two-fold. First, how can long-standing cultural differences explain the fact that the death penalty only returned in 1976? For Garland going one or two centuries back in time is to miss out the crucial historical processes since 1972 (the year of the *Furman* arrest) which have led to a reinstatement of the death penalty. Moreover, Whitman's historical narrative ignores the (more or less) 80-year period of the hegemony of penal welfarism in the USA which (*contra* Whitman's insistence on formal equality in American penal culture) embraced individualization and respect for the dignity of the offender (see also Tonry, 2004: 59). Second, political choices and legal decisions of a contingent nature are much more important to explain American's retention of the death penalty than some deep-seated cultural values. As Garland (2005c: 301) wrote in a sharp review of another 'culturalist' book: 'you can't explain variation by a constant'.[8] Understanding capital punishment calls for detailed research into the 'particular historical conjuncture' which made it possible. In this restricted 'conjunctural' sense the USA is distinctive, but this is not a distinctiveness that needs to be traced back to a deep 'cultural trait'—rather: it has to do with institutional structure, legislation, criminal procedure and case law.

There is neither space nor need to further explore this debate. The most important thing for our discussion here is that Garland's deep aversion to exceptionalism needs to be understood against the particular background of how he has developed his distinctive approach of penal change. He even somehow caricatured the exceptionalist claims of Whitman (and Zimring). Indeed, both authors were not happy at being labelled exceptionalist. For Whitman, speaking in terms of 'American exceptionalism' has little social scientific value. The notion assumes that there is a 'normal' path of development, from which the USA has deviated. Whitman is sceptical that such 'normal' path can be identified (Whitman, 2005). Also Zimring was not pleased with the 'exceptionalist' label and argues that the analysis offered in his book, which pays a great deal of attention to inter-state variation in the history of lynching and execution patterns, testifies to a '... rather forceful debunking of any theory of monolithic American exceptionalism' (Zimring, 2005a: 378). It seems as if all three authors, despite their obvious differences in opinion, can agree that thinking in terms of 'American exceptionalism' is not very helpful to advance the cause of coming to terms with recent penal change in the USA. Despite their obvious disagreements the proper conclusion for now might be that cultural elements are important (as

[8] See also Garland's elaborated review essay of *The Killing State* by Austin Sarat (2002). Here Garland writes that cultural conditions are not 'invariants of the American landscape' and formulates the research question that needs to be addressed as follows: 'What needs to be addressed is how, *in the period since 1972*, a newly vigorous killing state has come into being, together with a political establishment and a popular culture that appear to support it' (Garland, 2002: 478, [emphasis added]).

Whitman and Zimring suggest) but that we should not fall into the trap of cultural essentialism (as Garland warns).

Paradoxical closures

Even though Garland's scholarship is marked by his struggle against all forms of reductionism there are nevertheless some paradoxical closures which follow from his approach towards questions of penal change. In this section we discuss how his Foucauldian treatment of criminology and the methodological and descriptive choices he made in *The Culture of Control* have created a number of blind spots.

The Foucauldian legacy: power/knowledge

Throughout his career Garland's understanding of criminology remains remarkably consistent and inspired by a Foucauldian power/knowledge logic. As we saw earlier in this chapter, in *Punishment and Welfare* and related papers Garland described and analyzed in close detail how the emergence and successful development of criminology needs to be understood against the background of it being tied into the disciplinary strategy of the welfare state: 'a discourse fixed in a socio-political space, a technical auxiliary of the welfare state, which endlessly reproduces itself and the policies it supports' (Garland, 1985c: 30, note 33). We also discussed how in *The Culture of Control* the strategies of adaptation and denial are accompanied by two different criminologies: the 'new criminologies of everyday life' and the 'criminology of the other'.[9] These criminologies, like the welfarist criminology before them, are again closely connected to broader control strategies. As he argued with respect to the new criminologies of everyday life and their relation to the strategy of responsabilization:

> a new form of knowledge is being assembled which will support and extend this strategy in the same way that positivist criminology once

[9] The 'criminology of the other' is not really a criminology (that is, it is not aimed at a scientific understanding of crime and its control) but rather groups various writings which tend to dramatize crime and demonize offenders. In a 1999 review essay Garland used the book *Body Count: Moral Poverty…and How to Win America's War Against Crime and Drugs* (by Bennett, DiIulio, and Walters) as an illustration. Here juvenile offenders are characterized as 'super-predators' with 'fewer moral restraints than any such group in American history' (see Garland, 1999b: 363).

supported strategies of rehabilitation and individual correction. And, like that earlier knowledge of the criminal individual, which grew up quietly in the routines of institutional practice, this new knowledge is developing in out of the way reports and research studies which receive little public attention or scrutiny. (Garland, 1996: 455.)

In his treatment of criminology Garland continues to think in a Foucauldian 'power/knowledge' framework. Garland explained his view of criminology at length in his inaugural lecture of the Chair of Penology which he delivered on 24 May 1995 at the University of Edinburgh. In a skilful attempt to break with the view that penology is merely an applied sub-discipline of criminology[10], he argued that it should be the other way around, that penology is 'the more basic discipline', 'the study of the social processes of punishment and penal control, which is to say, of the whole complex of laws, ideas and institutions which regulate criminal conduct' (Garland, 1997b: 181). In this more expansive sense penology *includes* the study of criminology:

This seems to me to be the right way to think about criminology: not as an academic subject—though it has certainly become one—but rather as a *practical* ingredient in the modern system of penal control. A penologist does not 'do' criminology. Instead, he or she *observes* it in operation, studying how criminological ideas have insinuated themselves in our penal institutions, shaping and legitimating our practices of punishment. For penologists, criminology is one of the discourses upon which penal practice is based, one of the knowledges that combines with penal power to create our modern system of penal control. (Garland, 1997b: 182.)

Garland (as penologist) *observes* criminology 'in action' and the ideas he sees 'at work' in contemporary crime control strategies, are the criminologies of the self and the other—they are the *practical* ingredients of crime control strategies in a culture of control.[11]

[10] As a *fait divers* it is interesting to observe how Garland is departing here from his earlier definition of penology. For Garland penology was, until then, limited to the application of positivist scientific knowledge in the practical sphere, and it was firmly anchored within penal institutions (see e.g. Garland and Young, 1983b; Garland, 1985a; Garland, 1985b; Garland, 1990a). As a sociologist of punishment who was now awarded a Chair of Penology at the University of Edinburgh Garland must have felt a compelling need to adapt his earlier definition of 'penology' so that it could include his very own research agenda.

[11] Garland is well aware that there are also other criminologies 'which bear little or no relation to power' but he quickly adds that 'for most of its history, criminology has been a knowledge for power—a subject which is primarily useful rather

This also implies that criminology enters his story in a selective way. Indeed, his goal was to write a history of the present—not a history of the past. His genealogical aims made him focus on *certain* aspects of the past which can make that very present more intelligible.[12] Since Garland is interested in the *practical* effects of criminology in the *constitution* of the culture of control he leaves those that have only played a marginal role in this respect, out of the picture. Again, and not surprisingly in the light of Garland's proclaimed genealogical analysis, this selective treatment of criminology's history is very similar to Foucault's approach to criminology: because Foucault wanted to come to terms with the modern-day prison as a disciplinary institution he focused on the birth of a specific clinical, treatment-oriented criminology in nineteenth century prisons. However, at the same time there were also various other and incompatible strands in criminology that were much more concerned with statistical and sociological aspects of crime (such as the work by Quetelet and Guerry).[13] In the same sense as Foucault's genealogical aims in *Discipline and Punish* narrowed his focus on a clinical criminology, so Garland's genealogical aims in *The Culture of Control* directed him to the criminologies of everyday life.

This genealogical narrowing down jeopardizes a proper understanding of recent penal change. Many of his readers (often with a training in criminology) take issue with how he treats crime and

than true' (Garland, 1997b: 182). This comes very close to how Foucault characterized criminology: 'One has the impression that it is of such utility, is needed so urgently and rendered so vital for the working of the system, that it does not even need to seek a theoretical justification for itself, or even simply a coherent framework. It is entirely utilitarian' (Foucault, 1980: 47). In a 1992-paper Garland criticized Foucault for generalizing his observations on the specific disciplinary origins of criminology in nineteenth century prisons to how criminology functions today (see Garland, 1992: 405–412). Yet, by 1997, Garland seems to have reverted to the Foucauldian position and leaves the possibility of critique to penology: penology, so he suggests, is the only discipline that is equipped to *observe* criminology's *practical* contributions to penal control.

12 As Garland explains: 'In describing this work as a "history of the present" I hope to distance myself from the conventions of narrative history *and above all from any expectation of a comprehensive history of the recent period*. My primary concern is analytical rather than archival' (Garland, 2001a: 2, [emphasis added]).

13 Indeed, as Garland argued: 'Foucault's analysis of criminology should be viewed not as a history of criminology but instead as a genealogy of one of its elements' (Garland, 1992: 412).

with the prominent place he gives to the criminologies of everyday life. First, it has been argued that Garland overstates the reality of crime. He relies too heavily and too uncritically on official police data and ignores a large body of evidence that questions, or at least qualifies, the idea of high crimes being a 'social fact' (Beckett, 2001; Lynch, 2002; O'Malley, 2002; Matthews, 2002; Zedner, 2002; Köllisch, 2007). Second, and related to this, the mass media, moral entrepreneurs and politics may have played a much larger and more significant role in the salience of crime than Garland is willing to acknowledge (O'Malley, 1999; Beckett, 2001; Feeley, 2003; Western, 2004; Cavender, 2004; Reuband, 2007; Lehne and Schlepper, 2007; Kreissl and Ostermeier, 2007; Quensel, 2007). Third, the explanation he offers for the high crime rates is too much attuned to the 'criminologies of everyday life' and misses a great deal of the reality of crime as it has been exposed by other criminologies (such as critical, feminist and cultural criminology) (Young, 2003b; Hagan, 2004). Fourth, his hypothesis on the crucial role of the middle classes and their fears and adaptations to the predicament has been questioned (Young, 2002; Young, 2003b; Brown, 2006). Fifth, his observation that governments increasingly accept the social fact of high crimes is slightly exaggerated: the remarkable boom of a government-sponsored evidence-based criminology (and evidence-led initiatives) suggests that those in power still believe they can reduce levels of crime (Hughes, 2004a; Hughes, 2004b; McAra, 2004; Daems, 2005).

In sum, his treatment of criminology and crime is reductive in two ways. First, he only sees criminology in relation to power thereby failing to examine how criminology challenges power or how knowledge can be unrelated to power. Victimology offers another example. For sure, certain strands of victimology are inspired by the 'new criminologies of everyday life' (e.g. life-style analysis and routine activity theory) and are, therefore, closely connected to crime control strategies. Yet these do not exhaust the 'science of the victim'. Many aspects of victimology (such as the psychological and psychiatric branches that have mapped the mental-health aspects of victimization), and their potential impact upon penal developments, escape from Garland's view because victimology is, to a large extent, not a 'practical ingredient' in control strategies. Yet, again, the fact that victimology is often not 'useful' in terms of crime control does not necessarily imply that it had no impact on penal change. The problem is that Garland's conception of criminology forecloses a discussion of criminologies that are further away, or even disconnected, from 'penal control'. The focus on 'control criminologies' obscures how various knowledges may have impacted in different ways—less related or even unrelated to control—on punishment itself. Second, Garland's uncritical acceptance of high crime rates or, as he recently put it, his suspension of 'epistemological doubts' about crime (Garland, 2007c: 238) fails to interrogate the roots of this prominence of crime. Crime may, indeed, be operative in structuring social action and shaping outcomes but this leaves the processes of making crime such a salient feature of contemporary culture, out of the picture. Both of these problems have implications for how Garland can think about ways in which things could be different. We turn to this issue in the next section.

Consequences of methodological and descriptive choices: locked in the iron cage

The Culture of Control was met by a number of telling descriptions which do not need much further comment: 'a depressing book' that 'offers little hope' (Adams, 2001); a 'disturbing' book (Bruner, 2003); a 'depressive analysis' in which 'all things seem to conspire to the same regrettable ends' (Rumgay, 2003: 444); 'Like Weber, he remorselessly analyses trends about which he is clearly unhappy at an ethical level' (Reiner, 2002: 4); 'Heavy on analysis but light on strategy, heavy on explanation yet light on prescription (despite his own insistence that "the future is not inevitable")' (Sarat, 2001); the analysis is 'too dark' (*zu dunkel*) and 'too negative' (*zu negativ*) (Kaiser, 2003: 239); the book exhibits an 'undue pessimism' and 'a sense of inevitability' (Matthews, 2002: 220); Garland's vision is one of a 'catastrophic rupture in "penal modernity"' (Hutchinson, 2006: 446); and so forth.

The gloomy picture that is painted of the culture of control stands in sharp contrast to Garland's benign depiction of the post-war period when penal welfarism was assumed to be hegemonic. However, such a presentation runs the risk of romanticizing the past (Rumgay, 2003: 444; Zedner, 2002: 344–346). Indeed, as Loader and Sparks note: 'such histories of the present run the risk of doing violence to the past, of underplaying its tensions and conflicts, of inadvertently reproducing one-dimensional—implicitly rose-tinted—accounts of both the history and politics of penal modernism, and the reasons for its (apparent) demise' (Loader and Sparks, 2004: 14–15). Moreover, one wonders whether the young Garland of the early 1980s would have agreed with the middle-aged Garland of 2001. In the opening pages of *The Culture of Control* Garland refers to his first book *Punishment and Welfare* as the first part in a trilogy. However, as we have seen at the beginning of this chapter, in that book he was much tougher on penal welfarism, it being a new strategy of control aimed at solving a problem of social discipline that followed from the crisis of Victorian penality. In fact, a lot of the revisionist history-writing of the 1970s and early 1980s, including Garland's, was opposed to the assumed benevolence and humanitarianism of penal welfarism.

But why this dark picture of the culture of control? We argue that this follows from a number of Garland's methodological and descriptive choices. First, Garland's focus on similarities has as a result that diverging tendencies are pushed into the background. It does not allow Garland to probe for those differences that can make a difference. Moreover, the effect of this methodological choice is even stronger because of his selection of two rather atypical cases—the USA and the UK—for his study of crime control in late modern societies. Second, his Foucauldian approach to criminology and his acceptance of high crime rates as given, leaves other criminologies in the dark and makes it impossible to explore in more depth the role of media, politics, and various moral entrepreneurs in the construction of social problems.

Third, even though Garland regularly argues that things could have been different there seems to be a lack of space to make other choices. The social, political and cultural changes outlined in the book, seem to have had such a deep impact upon the characters of his late-modern play that one might wonder: *How* could they have acted differently? *Why* should they have acted differently? *Who* should have acted differently? (Beckett, 2001). Garland argues that the changes associated with the coming of late modernity have not 'determined' political decisions and policies; instead the latter are 'conditioned' by these changes and the 'probability' that they will occur increases because of them (see e.g. Garland, 2000c: 347; Garland, 2001a: 139, 158). Yet it remains difficult to see how the build-up of the 'new iron cage' could have been slowed down or stopped and, related to this, how its bars can be bent or broken to provide openings for acting otherwise in the future. Garland's explanation involves two kinds of accounts: a *structural* account 'that points to the general characteristics of a certain kind of social organization', and a *conjunctural* account 'that identifies the choices and contingencies that shaped how particular social groups adapted to these structures and mediated their social consequences' (Garland, 2001a: 201). Yet, how can the second ever overrule the first? The fact that Garland is not able to point at significant counter-developments, one might argue, further decreases the importance of the 'conjunctural' moment and increases the overpowering influence of the 'structural'.

Fourth, there are a number of untold stories and contrary trends that either do not appear in Garland's overall story of crime control in late modernity, or that are quickly set aside as of lesser significance. It is not a coincidence that restorative justice has often been named as one of the major 'blank spots' on Garland's big picture (see e.g. Matthews, 2002: 223; Vaughan, 2002: 361; Young, 2002: 147; Zedner, 2002: 355–6; Daems, 2004; Rumgay, 2003: 442). Restorative justice is mentioned several times but either it is quickly set aside as operating 'on the margins of criminal justice' and playing 'a tiny role at the shallow end of the system', or it is relegated to the endnote section of the book (see e.g. Garland, 2001a: 104, 169, 271, endnote 41). But why should the reintroduction of chain gangs and corporal punishments, for example, have left a more 'emblematic mark on the culture of punishment' than innovations such as restorative justice? (see Garland, 2001a: 104) The first are only very marginal penal developments, restricted to certain geographical areas in the south of the USA, while the second has a worldwide boost, gaining attraction from local, national and supranational policymakers.

The remarkable boom of restorative justice literature prompted Daly (2004) to make the following observation: 'An important question for the sociology of knowledge is to ask not only what conditions have facilitated its popularity, but also why so many feel compelled to say something about it' (Daly, 2004: 500). Part of the answer, for sure, is that in the eyes of many scholars and practitioners working in this field restorative justice may offer *some* answers to the problems and challenges of late modern crime developments. Seen from this angle, Garland's *The Culture of Control* attracts so much attention because we want to know what exactly is going on in our disturbing times; and restorative justice does the same for a related set of reasons, that is, because we want to arrive at an answer to that ever-recurring and ineradicable question 'What is to be done?' (see Cohen, 1985: 236–272). The disappointment of some of his readers, then, needs to be understood as follows: while Garland's analysis makes the 'What is to be done?' question more pressing and timely, he retreats from giving indications where we should look for answers. In this sense, *The Culture of Control* may come to share similar ground with Foucault's *Discipline and Punish*, that is, there is a real possibility of a repetition of the 'anaesthetizing effect' which leads to the impression that there is 'no possible room for initiative' (see Foucault, 2002: 234–236).

Because of his two-fold description of crime control developments—adaptation or denial—Garland leaves us with only two options for the future which are not very attractive. The few concrete suggestions he has to offer, therefore, point in the direction of an enhancement of the 'criminologies of everyday life': 'Efforts to share responsibility for crime control, to embed social control into the fabric of everyday life, to reduce the criminogenic effects of economic transactions, to protect repeat victims' (Garland, 2001a: 202). This probably explains why Jock Young, in his latest book *The Vertigo of Late Modernity*, somewhat provocatively referred to Garland when he wrote about a 'neoliberal criminology' (Young, 2007: 54; see also Young, 2003b). It also helps explain why Stephan Quensel spoke of a criminology that seems to be oriented towards conserving the status quo (Quensel, 2007: 200). Indeed, these crime control strategies are compatible with the neoliberal, individualist ethos of late modernity, as Garland himself argued in his writings on situational crime prevention (see e.g. Garland, 2000b: 11). Moreover, earlier he pointed at the social costs and inequalities these bring in their wake (see Garland, 1996: 463–4; Garland, 2001a: 131). His (reluctant) support for these criminologies, therefore, feels somewhat awkward and, arguably, fundamental change can hardly be expected from those proposals. It seems as if Garland, when having to choose between the strategies of punitive segregation and adaptation, opts for the latter—as a lesser kind of evil. Indeed, it may be, as we will try to demonstrate in the next section, that this is Garland's very own *personal* strategy of adaptation, that is, *his* adaptive strategy which probes for a progressive reading of those criminologies that are such a firm and undeniable part of late modern social organization.

The analysis of Garland is pitched at a high level of abstraction that makes it difficult to grasp counter-trends or to identify sources of conflict or tension. In 2004 he acknowledged this: 'A greater emphasis upon those ongoing "counter-doxic" struggles, and upon the distributions of power and prestige that sustain them, would have provided not just a fuller sense of the present, but also a more adequate basis for thinking about future possibilities' (Garland, 2004b: 167–8). Alternative methodologies which are more 'down-to-earth' and closer to human action, may leave more room to identify conflict and contestation. Loader and Sparks eloquently capture the impact of analytical procedures for praxis in the following quote: 'By attuning analysis to the significance and dynamics of political and cultural struggles about crime and social order, and the ideas that are contested therein, we may begin to pay fuller attention to the competing—"dominant", "residual" and "emergent"—elements of contemporary culture, and hence to possibilities of making the world otherwise that lie immanent within the present' (Loader and Sparks, 2004: 27).

This also explains why a number of his readers have pleaded for different methodologies: not a history of the present but a history of the past (Braithwaite, 2003); a 'historically situated hermeneutics' which takes politics seriously and is attentive to political and intellectual struggles (Loader and Sparks, 2004); the detailed study of particular nation states in late modernity, that is, *cultures* of control in contemporary *societies*, in order to grasp cross-national differences (Savelsberg, 2002); a closer analysis of policy formation and transfer, with attention to the difference between symbolic and substantive levels (Jones and Newburn, 2002); a 'situated problem-solving action' approach which pays due attention to the 'sheer messiness and the contradictory character of crime control practices on the ground' (Hughes, 2004b); a 'systems analytical framework' which institutes a relational, multi-level approach that can cut across the macro/micro divide (McAra, 2005), and so forth. There is no space here to discuss these various methodological suggestions. The point we want to make is the following: all of them, in different ways, point to the need for a kind of 'middle range' methodology to deal with what is perceived to be missing in Garland's 'grand theorizing', to re-introduce agency in a history that is written at too abstract and structuralist a level.

Garland as a Public Intellectual

In the previous chapter we suggested that a 'vertical' author-oriented study enables us to chart how an author's scholarly activities relate to the development of a public identity, and how such a relationship might change over time. Indeed, particularly when questions are formulated on topics that tend to provoke a sense of unease in the person addressing them, one might expect that authors move back and forth between their social roles of scholars in an academic milieu and citizens in a political community. In this last section we will discuss how Garland has given flesh to his public role. We will first trace the changes in Garland's critical position. Then we briefly return to the lack of clear-cut exit scenarios in his work and how this follows from his particular way of making sense of penal change. We conclude with discussing Garland's very own 'personal' adaptation strategy.

Changes in Garland's critical position

Garland's early writings were, like the writings of many of his contemporaries, openly politically inspired. In 1982 he concluded a book review with the following 'call for action':

> it becomes crucial to construct alternative strategies of control, drawing upon ideologies of collective and social responsibility, popular participation, democratic regulation and the accountability of expertise while recognising and limiting the oppressive (and sometimes reactionary) potential these policies represent. A task not for the future, but for now (Garland, 1982: 185).

A year later, in the opening chapter of *The Power to Punish*, Garland and Young were highly explicit about the purpose of the social analysis of penality, that is, 'the very purpose of producing knowledge about the social world is to change it' (Garland and Young, 1983b: 32). And this change, so they argued at the time, revolved around the question 'how to construct alternative forms of penality which are more socialist, more popular, more democratic—which aspire to the paradox of a liberative penality' (Garland and Young, 1983b: 33). By the time of the publication of *Punishment and Modern Society* this critical voice had become more tempered and there were no longer any explicit political statements in the text. On the one hand, Garland continued believing (as he has done throughout his career) that theory may, in itself, contribute to bringing about change (see e.g. Garland, 1990a: 277–8), yet, on the other hand, there is no longer any explicit guidance on how we have to think differently about punishment. At the end of the book there are some vague suggestions that social justice and moral education are better suited for socializing and integrating young citizens than penal policy and that, in case punishment is unavoidable, it should be viewed as a morally expressive rather than a purely instrumental undertaking (Garland, 1990a: 292). The 'pedagogical role of analysis' (Garland and Young, 1983b: 34) is still present but it seems as if the teacher is no longer willing or able to offer clear 'lessons to be drawn' from his classes. His role changes to promoting a 'critical self-consciousness about our own questions and assumptions' (Garland, 1994a: 24) in his pupils in the hope that they, packed with better insight about the contingent historical origins of current practice and thinking, will work out their own solutions.

The Culture of Control was written with a larger audience in mind than only academic criminologists. This is why Garland aimed to maintain a 'lightness of touch where theoretical matters are concerned' so that 'the general reader' would be able to follow his argument 'without undue effort'. For the same reason footnotes were omitted and relegated to the lengthy endnote section so that the (non-professional) reader would not be disturbed by their intrusion in the text (see Garland, 2001a: ix–x). Clearly, Garland aimed to attract a much wider readership than his fellow academics but, as we discussed earlier, he could hardly offer any guidelines for those who want to break free from the new iron cage. His modest plea for enhancing the 'criminologies of everyday life' seems to be miles removed from the construction of 'an alternative socialist programme and ideology of penality' as he put it with Peter Young at the start of his scholarly career (Garland and Young, 1983b: 34). Nowadays Garland describes himself as a 'dispassionate observer', 'the aim being to investigate issues with which one is passionately involved, but with a detachment that permits one to grasp complexities and to minimize the projection of one's own wishes and fears onto the phenomenon' (Garland, 2004a: 163; see also Garland, 2006b: 1).

The reason for highlighting these changes in critical position is not to stir the consciousness of Garland (or, for that matter, of any other writer who went through a similar process of intellectual development) but because they reveal some crucial shifts in the sociology of punishment. 'Thinking differently' is the flipside of 'thinking sociologically' about punishment because penal practices are not carved in Moses-like stone tablets but are susceptible to human choices. Punishment is part of the 'human-made' world and (to use a phrase from Zygmunt Bauman's textbook on sociology) it therefore 'bears an imprint of human activity, which would not exist at all but for the actions of human beings' (Bauman, 1990: 3). What we observe, however, is that authors such as Garland (and, as we will see in the next chapter, John Pratt) have started to think differently about 'thinking differently' itself. This is, for sure, partly due to changing theoretical preferences, but it also has to do with developments in sociology in general; with the growing scepticism towards penal reform in the light of the failing alternatives in the 1980s; with the declining prospects of any 'real' change in the penal system in the foreseeable future; and so forth.

The inevitable lack of clear 'exit scenarios'

Many of Garland's readers were disappointed by the lack of any clear-cut 'exit scenarios' that may lead us out of the culture of control. There are at least two reasons why Garland, if he wants to remain honest to his own project (and there is thus far no indication that he will stray from his own theoretical starting points), cannot respond in a straightforward way to the question 'What is to be done?' The first reason relates to his choice for a multidimensional sociology of punishment. Since the mid-1980s Garland started to build up a multidimensional framework for the sociology of punishment which puts punishment, in all its complexity, at the centre of his research agenda. This theoretical choice was recently reaffirmed (Garland, 2006a). The implication, however, is that his willingness to attend to the inherent complexities of his object of research makes it more difficult to come up with clear-cut proposals for reform. Indeed, the 'tragic quality of punishment', it being always 'beset by irresolvable tensions' and 'inescapably marked by moral contradiction and unwanted irony' (Garland, 1990a: 292) reduces the critical edge of any analysis that wants to come as close as possible to 'the integrity of the empirical object'.

The second reason is more important and follows from his analysis in *The Culture of Control.* As we have seen, Garland has to be cautious about optimism or quick solutions. According to Garland, the most significant change took place at the level of culture and it is, by definition, much more difficult to alter how we think, feel and act about punishment. The new collective experience of crime is 'slow to change and resistant to deliberate alteration' (Garland, 2000c: 355). Blaming politics or mass media is, for Garland, like shooting the messenger: in the end, we *all* are to blame. Changing the cultural underpinnings of contemporary punishment and control arrangements then calls for a kind of 'collective' change since we all are implicated (see e.g. Garland, 2004b: 185).

This may sound disappointing in the ears of many of his readers but, again, it is the only possible option one has if one accepts Garland's methodological choices in *The Culture of Control.* Given the remarkable success of the book it may be that these choices in a way also 'pay off'. In a short period of time his study has become a 'culture product' itself, appearing on numerous reading lists of criminology and criminal justice courses all over the globe. For many people who are currently working in the criminal justice system or who will hold key positions in the future, the book will become part of their 'cultural repertoire'. Indeed, a book that attracts so much attention and sparks so much debate has, arguably, a deeper impact and reaches more people than some government-sponsored research report with clear policy recommendations which (as it is, unfortunately, often the case with criminological research) ends up in a dark closet on the Xth floor of the penal bureaucracy. The fact that Garland has been able to write a book that is so widely read and discussed is, therefore, an achievement in itself. This does not mean, however, that readers have to accept the methodological and descriptive choices that he made: making other analytical choices, as we aimed to demonstrate, leads to different accounts of recent developments and may open more space for the exit-scenarios that many of Garland's readers are missing in his work (Daems, 2007b).

Garland's personal adaptation strategy

Next to the changes in critical position that we touched upon earlier in this section it might be that there is nowadays also a sober pragmatism at work in his thinking, that is, a genuine (personal) strategy of adaptation of Garland, as an author and critical thinker, to a new reality. Many of his readers who focus on the darker spots in *The Culture of Control* may not have noticed this. In his review of Crawford's *The Local Governance of Crime* (1997), a book which in many respects can be read as a critical discussion of the strategies of adaptation, Garland argued that Crawford tends to give an 'overwhelmingly negative impression of the new strategies' which leads Crawford 'to underplay the positive, progressive possibilities that could follow the break-up of the criminal justice state and its punitive monopoly of crime control' (Garland, 1998c: 518). Garland's adaptation to the new reality can be illustrated by means of the 'if'/'then' way of phrasing his argument in the following quote:

> *If* the social morphology of late modern societies is shifting away from the liberal terrain of state/individual relations towards a more complex set of relations between highly individuated citizens, networks of intermediate associations and a pluralist state, *then* the question is how to harness these structures to progressive values and render them accountable to democratic processes. (Garland, 1998c: 519, [emphasis added].)

Garland's stance, therefore, is far removed from an old radical position which, in one significant formulation, argued that 'tinkering around with the criminal justice system in a radically unjust society is unlikely to advance us very far toward justice, equity or, come to that, efficacy' (Scull, 1983: 165). His position is more modest, taking the 'social morphology of late modern societies' *as it is*, adapting (which is not necessarily the same as accepting), so to speak, to the new social facts that he perceives to be firmly ingrained in contemporary late modern societies. This may be termed Garland's very own adaptive strategy. A recognition, based on his own analysis of late modern society, of the necessity to think differently about control in a deeply changed and, for the time being, difficult to change social and cultural context.

Moreover, since for Garland the new control landscape has not been designed by 'malicious politicians' or 'bad media' but is the result of *our* own social routines and cultural sensibilities, the choice is, to put it in somewhat populist terms, 'to the people'. In the end, Garland's cultural analysis spreads the responsibility for the current state of affairs over all those people who live, work, entertain, travel, and so forth day-in day-out in those late modern societies. As he writes in the concluding lines of his review of Crawford's book: 'how we govern crime is related to how we govern ourselves' (Garland, 1998c: 519). Seen from this angle, Garland's adaptive strategy clearly makes sense: as long as we continue 'governing ourselves' as we currently do, we might better find ways to 'govern crime' that are adapted to it in the best possible way.

There is therefore a clear and conscious move away from 1970s and 1980s discussions on social control (which were infused, as Garland puts it, by a 'libertarian paranoia'), and an attempt, as he argued in another book review, to think 'positively and progressively' about the problem of control (Garland, 1998b: 323–4; see also Garland, 1995b: 4). And, one might add: less state-centred, more local, more embedded, that is, more in line with the original sociological usage of the term 'social control'. Many readers of *The Culture of Control* (including myself (Daems, 2004)) have wrongly argued that the book is primarily about the 'punitive turn' or about punitiveness. In fact, Garland emphasized at several places that, in his opinion, the lower-level and less eye-catching adaptive strategies are the most profound changes in terms of crime control, they are the 'most significant development' (Garland, 2001a: 170; see also Garland, 2005a: 22–3). With respect to the adaptive strategies Garland is far from pessimistic, and maybe even too optimistic (see Hughes, 2004b). Indeed, while many reviewers criticize him for not showing 'other paths' or 'exit scenarios' one must conclude that his critics are mainly referring to the strategy of denial and the most salient and abhorring aspects of the culture of control.

Towards the end of the next chapter we will see that Pratt's way of relating thinking sociologically to thinking differently is very different from Garland's. But before we can illustrate this, we need to examine more closely his intellectual life-course.

3

The Decivilization of Punishment

Introduction

The infliction of punishment in modern democracies always takes place within certain boundaries, which set limits to the forms and quantities of punishment that are acceptable in a particular time and place. However, such boundaries are far from fixed. A crucial question in the debate on recent penal change, then, is to consider to what extent those boundaries are moving, what kind of forces are at work, and how this affects the ways in which we punish. Elias-inspired authors such as Spierenburg and Franke were concerned with the historical processes which resulted in certain forms of punishment becoming unacceptable. Spierenburg (1984a) detailed this at length with regard to the decline of public executions on the European continent. Franke (1990a) highlighted how, over a period of two centuries, the prison experience of Dutch inmates changed significantly: living conditions improved greatly and ultimately, prisoners were granted a set of rights.

One observation that often returns in discussions on recent penal change is that formerly 'unacceptable' and 'unthinkable' forms and quantities of punishment have, again, become 'acceptable' and 'thinkable'. By way of example authors refer to high imprisonment rates which are no longer perceived to be a disgrace; the deterioration of prison conditions; the return or reinvention of old sanctions that aim to name, shame and stigmatize offenders; the appearance of new sanctions that provide room for the release of emotions; and so forth. John Pratt has been at the forefront in exploring such developments. According to Pratt 'the boundaries of punishment in the civilized world' came to be pushed into 'new, uncharted regions' (Pratt, 2002a: 166). For Pratt we are not dealing with a 'new culture of control', as Garland argues, but rather with a 'new culture of intolerance' (Pratt, 2000a: 136) that opens new possibilities for punishing which signal a significant departure from earlier penal patterns. The conditions in which punishment took a distinctively 'modern' character, that is, it being state-controlled, expert-driven, closed-off from the public, administered by professional bureaucracies, guided by scientific knowledge and goal-oriented, have crumbled and made possible previously 'unthinkable' penal sanctions.

This chapter discusses how Pratt came to address the above-mentioned issues in his research. We begin with an exploration of Pratt's intellectual life-course, starting in the early 1980s with his writings on controlling youth delinquency and finishing with his research on the history of the modern prison. We then examine his work on recent penal change, that is, the place of punishment in a culture of intolerance captured in his phrases 'the decivilization of punishment' and the 'new punitiveness'. Next we offer a critical discussion of Pratt's way of making sense of penal change. Finally we will discuss Pratt's evolution as a public intellectual.

From the Sociology of Deviance to the Sociology of Punishment

'[T]o talk now about "the sociology of punishment" is likely to bring quizzical looks from more than a few criminologists, not to say sociologists themselves. "Punishment? It's all part of the sociology of deviance isn't it?", a senior lecturer in that discipline once asked me' (Pratt, 1994: 213). Pratt used this small anecdote in the introduction to his review essay of Garland's *Punishment and Modern Society,* to highlight how difficult it was at that time to imagine that punishment is a topic that deserves to be researched *on its own*—not simply as part of a larger sociology of deviance. This might explain, so Pratt argued, the dearth of literature on the sociology of punishment at that time—a state of affairs that he openly bemoaned.

If there is one person who should be able to 'feel' the differences between the sociologies of deviance and control, crime and punishment, it should be John Pratt. Indeed, as we will see in this section, before he turned to the subject of punishment Pratt had written an impressive amount of work on a broad range of topics within those other sociologies *inter alia* on sexuality, truancy, intermediate treatment, law and order politics, and so forth. It is essential that we first touch upon this earlier body of research, because even though Pratt's little anecdote seems to suggest that the one has nothing to do with the other, it does.

Much sociological literature on punishment stems from, and reacts against, an older tradition that was devoted to the study of social control. Throughout the 1980s Pratt shared a lot of the assumptions and theoretical preferences of this strand of sociological thought and played an important role in its development. A proper understanding of how Pratt, in the 1990s and 2000s approached (and still approaches) questions related to punishment needs to start with his understanding of social control developments in the 1980s.

Controlling youth delinquency

A major part of Pratt's early publications was devoted to different aspects of juvenile justice. Pratt was not so much interested in why youngsters deviate from societal norms (that is, the aetiology of their delinquency) but rather in the forces that shape the social and criminal justice responses to their deviance. To put it differently: not why they *acted* in certain ways, but rather why the surrounding environment *re-acted* in particular ways became his central topic of research. In the early 1980s Pratt participated in a research project on school attendance and the use of legal action at Sheffield University. The empirical observations derived from this project formed the background against which he tried to make sense of the panoply of reactions to a perceived problem of truancy, that is, young British people unwilling to attend school. His approach to truancy reveals how deeply he was immersed, at this early stage in his academic career, in the sociology of social control.

At the time of the research project there was a perceived crisis in the education system of England and Wales; and truancy came to be seen as a major social problem that was being addressed by a growing array of interventions, formal and informal, ranging from home visits by education welfare officers to interventions by the courts, such as care and supervision orders. Staff numbers were increasing as well. What was going on here? Interestingly for our understanding of how the young Pratt made sense of the world, we see him adopting a Foucauldian approach. This whole apparatus designed to deal with deviant youngsters needed to be interpreted as a way to police unemployed youth, set against a background of a more general 'crisis in the *normalization* of young people' (Pratt, 1983b: 233). This crisis, he argued, had its roots in 'the growing contradiction between the alleged purposes of schooling and the growing likelihood of unemployment' (Pratt, 1983a: 349). Indeed, the traditional pathway to their 'normalization'—years of schooling preparing them for a certain job waiting to be taken up—was no longer that self-evident. The prospect of unemployment was undermining the legitimate expectation underpinning the whole educational system, that is, the central idea of a 'normal life' that it helped in reproducing: 'Behave well, work hard, obtain good results, and you'll get a decent job'. Youngsters, so Pratt argued, were questioning the value of their education and importantly, they were doing this for good reasons.

This implied that, instead of blaming and punishing truants for not attending school, it may be more fruitful to listen to them. If particular sections of the school population drop out because they anticipate unemployment there is much to gain in taking their arguments seriously and in situating the so-called truancy problem within a broader economic context (Pratt, 1983c). In that respect he advised youth workers to stop using treatment language that only helped to perpetuate the existing conceptualization of youth crime. Instead he invited them to make an epistemological move from socio-psychological positivism to a phenomenology of the client, which emphasizes an 'accurate reconstruction of event rather than positivistic explanation' (Pratt, 1985c: 15), 'a more innovative style of reporting' (Grimshaw and Pratt, 1985: 338). These proposals for changing work practices of youth workers reveal his eagerness to move away from a reigning positivistic approach in truancy research:

> The concern is usually to establish the local truancy 'rate', and from there go on to isolate a cluster of 'facts' taken from the family and immediate social circumstances of the truants, which are then represented as various pathological features of their backgrounds. (Pratt, 1983b: 224.)

However, if the truancy crisis is a symptom of a crisis in the value put on the educational system by young people then a wrong diagnosis was being made (Pratt, 1983c: 351).

Moreover, an all-too-easy link was being forged between truancy and delinquency, a link that was the product of the 'evil breeds evil' logic (Pratt, 1983c: 350) which 'only leads to further justification for the range of measures that can now be brought into action' (Pratt, 1983b: 234–5). Pratt's truancy papers, therefore, make the classical move of sociology of deviance studies against the individualized focus of positivistic research: shifting the analytic focus from the (individual) youngsters to the (social) institutions, that is, the educational system and the 'missing link' with a labour market that is unable, or unwilling, to provide enough jobs for school-leavers. In the light of this critique his advice to adopt a Matza-inspired naturalistic approach which draws attention to the ways actors themselves make sense of their own situations, becomes all the more understandable (Pratt, 1983c: 350; see also Matza, 1969).

Some of the truants in his early research became involved in intermediate treatment (IT) packages (Pratt, 1983b: 226–7) and this probably made his move to investigate and reflect upon these measures more obvious. Indeed, in the mid-1980s Pratt became a senior research associate on the Intermediate Treatment Evaluation Project at the Institute of Criminology of the University of Cambridge. The, by definition, intermediate position of IT made such interventions especially vulnerable to become a first step towards more intensive regulation, an (at first-sight) benevolent form of treatment that might pave the way for more intense formal reactions and, possibly, the ultimate incarceration of young people (Pratt, 1983d: 20). Because of this vulnerability, the study of IT proved to be highly interesting in the wake of the then burgeoning literature on social control in general, and Stanley Cohen's important and thought-provoking contributions to this literature in particular. Indeed, Pratt wrote in Cohenian terms when he argued that 'the *widening* of IT practices has coincided with a trend towards the *intensification* of IT programmes' (Pratt, 1983d: 29, [emphasis added]). IT did not turn out to be the alternative to incarceration as many had envisaged and hoped it to be. The story of IT seemed to be yet another story of 'good intentions' being turned into 'bad consequences'.

But in his reflections on IT Pratt went one step further which, again, demonstrates how well he was socialized into the intellectual currents of his time. In a 1987 paper he challenged conventional histories of IT and came to question the 'good intentions' themselves. The history of IT, so he argued, is not the story of a long and painstaking battle against the incarceration of young people which was eventually lost. IT does not have such an 'essential quality and purpose' (Pratt, 1987b: 423). Rather it formed part of a range of interventions designed to respond to a series of successive crises in the normalization of the young. The problem that IT aimed to address, therefore, was more one of 'youth management' than one of reducing the use of incarceration. It is not a coincidence that Pratt gave his 1987 article the title 'A revisionist history of intermediate treatment'. The revisionist histories of Rothman (1971), Foucault (1977) and Ignatieff (1978) critically re-examined conventional history writing which, in their opinion, too quickly and too superficially, depicted the history of criminal justice as an evolution from the 'barbaric' Dark Ages to our 'humane' Enlightened times. This revisionism of the 1970s had a tremendous impact on subsequent research(ers) in this field—including, so it seems, the young John Pratt who started publishing in those, for criminologists interested in social control developments, highly exciting and vibrant times. Indeed, Pratt shared its typical suspicion towards the (good) intentions of reformers, and by revealing some deeper rationale for IT, his own re-examination of its history contributed to this larger body of research.

Pratt supplemented his writings on particular topics such as truancy and IT with more general papers on wider developments in juvenile justice policy and practice. In two of them he openly adopted a typical Foucauldian functionalist position. In a 1985 paper Pratt speculated on the interesting idea of what would happen if youth delinquency were to 'dry up', that is, if the number of young offenders would significantly decline in the wake of demographic change. The implications for the existing infrastructure might only be minimal, so he suggested, because many have 'a vested interest in the delinquency business' (Pratt, 1985d: 94). Moreover, and similar to what Foucault wrote about the failure of the prison, Pratt argued that the apparent failure of diversionary measures such as police cautioning (that is, their inadequacy to reduce the use of incarceration) in fact constituted its success. Seen from this functionalist perspective which, as he acknowledged, had perhaps 'too conspirational an overtone for some', Pratt rephrased the question to be asked as follows: 'Rather than querying the extent to which it should be modified to bring it into line with the aims set out for it, the question is *what purpose does this policy have*?' (Pratt, 1986a: 214, [emphasis added]). We need to look at 'the functions of this practice' (Pratt, 1986a: 214), the 'functionality of this supposed failure' (Pratt, 1986a: 229) which, unsurprisingly for the Pratt of the 1980s, had to be seen against the backdrop of the production of a 'new regulatory field over minor delinquency'.

This new way of regulating youth delinquency could not be understood in terms of the 'welfare' and 'justice' models. With the 1908 Children Act a welfare model gained ascendancy in

England and Wales. Yet from the mid-1970s onwards, so the argument went, a 'justice' model with emphasis upon certainty, due process, visibility, accountability, less restrictive intervention made its inroads in the British justice system and eventually became (again) ideologically dominant. But in practice something totally different took place. The major trends and developments corresponded to what Pratt called 'corporatism'. This third model was characterized by 'an increase in administrative decision-making, greater sentencing diversity, centralization of authority and coordination of policy, growing involvement of non-juridical agencies, and high levels of containment and control in some sentencing programmes' (Pratt, 1989: 245). Corporatism, therefore, was the name Pratt reserved for that whole apparatus that came into existence to deal with recalcitrant and delinquent youth and that was far removed from all the 'justice model talk'.

Lastly, during the 1980s Pratt wrote a handful of papers on sex. It might seem strange, at first sight, to see Pratt devoting quite some academic energy to a topic that seems to be far removed from his research interests throughout the decade. Yet, his approach again, testifies to his deep immersion in the critical social control tradition of his time. In a 1981 piece he reflected on political relationships in the United Kingdom where, at that time, Thatcher and her Conservative Party had shaken up the political landscape. Pratt was critical of Stuart Hall's analysis of the New Right when he argued that there was a kind of return to a traditionalist morality—in Hall's words a 'regression to a stone-age morality'. With respect to sexuality, so Pratt argued, there was rather a continuation of the permissive tendency of the 1960s: the attack from the Right was not directed at permissiveness (there were no full-blown moral crusades from the Right against the permissiveness of the 1960s) but at the economic and social policies of welfarism which were held responsible for letting the 'unworthy' enjoy the fruits of permissiveness at the expense of the hard working and enterprising 'worthy'. According to Pratt it was crucial to properly understand the popular appeal of the New Right in this respect—analyses which refer to the imposition of a traditional social-moral order were wrong and were oversimplifying the nature and appeal of its populism (Pratt, 1981, see also, and similarly, Pratt and Sparks, 1987).

In other papers Pratt (1982; 1983e; 1986b) further elaborated on the topic of sexuality where, unsurprisingly in light of his theoretical preferences during the 1980s, he fully endorsed Foucault's revisionist reading of the history of sexuality. Following Foucault, Pratt called upon his readers to abandon the categories of repression/freedom and challenged the historical trajectory as evoked by the 'repressive hypothesis' which depicts the history of sexuality as a long march towards sexual freedom, a gradual liberation of our sexuality from the shackles of Victorian times. The sociology of Stuart Hall and others proved to be unfruitful to Pratt because it was wedded to a similar scheme of thought: interpretations that refer to a return of moral orthodoxy and sexual repression in the 1970s equally make use of the inadequate concepts of repression/freedom and miss out a whole lot of stuff going on in talk about sex and display of nudity (Pratt, 1986b). Indeed, Pratt wanted to draw attention to a power that 'produces' rather than 'prohibits', a positive rather than a negative concept of power, which is, of course, one of the hallmarks of Foucauldian social thought (see Pratt, 1982: 65).

To conclude this first section it is not so difficult to draw a picture of the author behind all this published work. Pratt inscribed himself in, and contributed to, a stream of thought which was highly influential throughout the 1980s. It is fair to say that Michel Foucault was his main theoretical source in this first phase of his academic career. Pratt's studies are characterized by a typical Foucauldian approach and impregnated by its concomitant vocabulary of 'normalization', 'disciplinary control', 'regulation', 'surveillance', and the notion of 'genealogy' (which Foucault himself borrowed from Nietzsche). As we have seen, some of Pratt's papers carry the stamp of Foucault's functionalism and Pratt equally adopted a 'hermeneutics of suspicion' when he critically examined conceptual pairs such as repression/freedom, failure/success, good intentions/bad consequences and welfare/justice. In addition, and related to this, Pratt's work was strongly inspired by the then burgeoning social control literature and revisionist history writing. Moreover, he shared the sociologist of deviance's critique of positivist criminology and he flirted with Matza's naturalism. In short, the young Pratt was a textbook example of an author shaped by (and himself further shaping) a certain strand in sociological criminology.

This is important for our study. As we will see later in this chapter, Pratt gradually moved away from his early interest in juvenile justice and started focusing on punishment more directly. He also began to reconsider his theoretical framework. Like

Garland, as we discussed in Chapter 2, he needed to 'shed off' his 1980s 'social control clothes' which came to be felt more like a straitjacket than a comfortable suit from which to explore a world which itself was in the process of deep change. Yet, as we will see, the choices he made were to a large extent different from those of Garland and resulted in another way of making sense of penal change.

History of (modern) punishment: the case of New Zealand

In the late 1980s it seems as if Pratt was entering an important transition period. First, even though there are some scattered remarks on (the sociology of) punishment in his work throughout the 1980s (see e.g. Pratt, 1983d: 30; Pratt, 1985a: 292; Pratt, 1987c), he did not systematically address the 'hard end' himself: Pratt's focus was more on the 'soft end', that is, different kinds of (youth) deviance such as truancy, hooliganism, sexual deviance, and so forth and the different ways the (juvenile) justice system was reacting to it. This started to change and by the early 1990s Pratt had made a definite turn towards the topic of punishment. Second, while his work of the 1980s almost exclusively dealt with developments in Britain we can observe how Pratt starts to redirect himself geographically. In fact, most of his writings in the late 1980s and early 1990s—including his book-length study *Punishment in a Perfect Society*—concerned New Zealand. This was related to his career move: in 1986 Pratt found a new home in New Zealand where he became lecturer at Massey University and, later, took up a position at Victoria University of Wellington—where he is nowadays a professor in criminology. Third, Pratt also widened his gaze in another way: from now onwards, historical questions entered, more explicitly than before, his research agenda. These three moves had a significant impact upon his thinking and writing.

Moving to New Zealand, moving away from Foucault

In the late 1980s Pratt directed his attention to penal practices in New Zealand and he also started publishing in the *Australian and New Zealand Journal of Criminology*—a journal of which he later, from 1997 until 2005, would be editor-in-chief. The themes he explored in his first years in New Zealand were broadly the same as in his early British papers. Pratt touched upon the dilemmas of thinking in terms of 'alternatives to custody' for New Zealand practice—and this against the background of the failure of decarcerative projects and programmes elsewhere in the western world (Pratt, 1987a). He also wrote a paper on the future of probation in New Zealand wherein he pleaded for rethinking its aims and objectives—to move away from the outmoded therapeutic casework approach and toward 'reducing the prison population through the use of probation resources and related facilities' (Pratt, 1990b: 111). Also his way of making sense of the developments in New Zealand was largely similar. Foucault and the critical social control literature were mobilized on the one hand, while his paper on the future of probation contained, again, naturalistic proposals (an attempt to 'let the client speak') inspired by the work of David Matza.

It seems as if Pratt was applying the wisdom he accumulated in Britain to the New Zealand situation, as if he was trying to offer a fresh look from a neophyte to the country to developments that were in line with what was happening elsewhere (see also Pratt, 1988; Pratt and Treacher, 1988). Indeed, as he argued, '[D]uring the last two decades, the course of New Zealand penal policy has followed a similar route to that of many other western-based societies' (Pratt, 1987a: 148). The shift in these papers, therefore, was mainly geographical: on the one hand, the attention for New Zealand but, on the other hand, also for cross-national developments. Indeed, from now onwards his observations would increasingly cover a larger territory. Pratt wrote about 'the map of penal control *in many western societies*' and described his work as 'a general commentary on current trends *in western penal systems*' (Pratt, 1987a: 158, [emphasis added]). Pratt seemed to be confident enough to make more general and, therefore, more abstract observations on 'modern society' (Pratt, 1987a: 150).

But he also started to feel comfortable enough to commit—tentatively but surely—the proverbial patricide. Indeed, we see the first breaks and fissures in his 1980s intellectual outlook. This happened in 1990 in his (last) paper on developments in the social control of youth crime and delinquency in England and Wales. Pratt distanced himself explicitly from what he called 'the Foucault, Cohen bloc' (Pratt, 1990a: 219). The trends and developments he outlined in the paper were too different and too complex: 'it is as if interpretations of Foucault that emphasize the resurgence of the disciplinary mode of social control have simply been overtaken by events' (Pratt, 1990a: 233). This implied that in this last paper dealing with delinquency and juvenile justice—at a time when he was turning to his history writing on punishment—he 'became clean'. There is a great deal of symbolism in this: instead of entering the 1990s with a final endorsement of his intellectual inspirators, we see him taking a first step towards looking for something new. With a bit of exaggeration, one might argue that he was making *tabula rasa*, clearing his writing table, putting Foucault back on the shelves (temporarily though, as we will see) and closing the 'juvenile justice' chapter in his academic trajectory. With the publication of this last article Pratt had turned a page and was ready to start a new chapter.

Punishment in a perfect society

At the beginning of his book *Punishment in a Perfect Society* Pratt reflected on how he came to research the history of punishment in New Zealand: 'Imagine the surprise...when I came to New Zealand in 1986, to find that there was not only none of the debate with which I had become so familiar, but that there was virtually no penal history' (Pratt, 1992a: 9). The 'debate' he was referring to in this quote related to the immense influence of Foucault on British criminology. Pratt made it his task to fill up this gap in penal history writing. As he acknowledged in the introduction to his book, Pratt had the advantage that he could build upon the shoulders of Spierenburg (1984a) and Garland (1985a), while continuing his critical dialogue with the legacy of Foucault. Yet, he was also able to add something distinctively new, that is, the impact of colonization on penal history, and the need to move away from a perceived 'Eurocentrism in most if not all of the sociology of punishment' (Pratt, 1992a: 9).

According to Pratt the history of modern penality in New Zealand contains two inter-related histories. On the one hand, there is a story of 'silencing', that is, a long process whereby the existing indigenous (Maori) ways of conflict resolution came to be 'silenced' by the settlers. Pratt's book starts in 1840, a date which marks the introduction of a western-based system of justice, with the declaration of New Zealand as a British Crown Colony. This silencing, however, did not occur overnight. Indeed, initially there was some recognition and even room for coexistence of the 'old' and the 'new'. It was only in 1893 that the Magistrates Court Act abolished the remaining special provisions for Maoris and that the assimilation was expected to be completed. This means that it took more or less half a century for the gradual extinction of indigenous conflict handling to come to its final conclusion: one (British) justice system for all. This story of silencing cannot be separated from the British colonist's eagerness to 'civilize' the Maori, that is, to introduce them into the supposedly superior British way of life. This 'gift' of civilization meant the dismantling of Maori culture, values and practices. Inevitably this included giving up traditional ways of conflict resolution for a superior European punishment tradition. 'In return for being granted British citizenship and imperial protection, Maori people would have to give up "being Maori", irrespective of whether they wanted this to happen, and irrespective of treaties to the contrary' (Pratt, 1991b: 294).

On the other hand, there is what Pratt refers to as a 'history of failure' which, actually, is a history of how a modern punishment system came to be established into New Zealand. The content of this story is, at its core, very similar to David Garland's exposé in *Punishment and Welfare*. Indeed, both authors paid a great deal of attention to the role of (criminological) science and the treatment ideal with its concomitant assumptions of human nature in the making of modern penality (see Pratt, 1990c). For New Zealand 'the new era' was heralded with the *Crimes Act Amendment Act* of 1910 which introduced the sentence of reformative detention and which symbolized a major break with classical penology and a turn to positivism. Yet, colonization made a difference. In that sense it is interesting to read both books together. Seen from Pratt's perspective, Garland is telling a story of how penal welfarism came into existence in Britain which, in turn, acted as an example after which the criminal justice system in New Zealand could be modelled. British reformers designed a legal system that could be imported (at least, so it was thought at the time) into that small colony at the other side of the world.

Yet there was no direct policy transfer—ideas and practices are not that easily transplanted from one jurisdiction into another. This meant that some important differences emerged: the retention of 'public works' programmes and the 'march of shame' (until 1915); the limited use of probation; and the development of work camps and prison farms where, by 1934, more than half of the prisoners were employed. The latter had to be seen in light of the utility of convict labour in a country with a small population such as New Zealand. Yet, next to that, the 'perfect society' also struggled with a set of problems (lack of resources, lack of training, organizational deficiencies, institutional resistance, and so forth) that caused 'a major gulf between commitment to the theoretical principles of the new penology and the practice of punishment' (Pratt, 1992a: 237).

From a theoretical point of view Pratt continued and expanded his critique directed at Foucault in a three-fold way. First, the fact that in a country such as New Zealand, which was so far removed and so different from Britain and which had none of its fears of the 'criminal classes' came to be implemented a penal system based on broadly similar terms, challenges the functionalist argument. Indeed, as Pratt argued: 'The differing nature of crime problems and related anxieties would seem to challenge the instrumentalist argument that all along there has been some implicit rationality, some hidden function underlying the development of the punishment system to the effect it thus "made sense" to replicate the British punishment system in this particular new colony' (Pratt, 1991a: 132). The colonial links tied New Zealand almost inextricably to a foreign punishment system that 'was neither necessary (in view of the population levels and extent of crime) nor possible to resource' (Pratt, 1991a: 134). Questions of national identity—the multiple bonds to the 'mother country' and the creation of a Britain in the South Pacific—mattered more in explaining the particular developments in New Zealand (Pratt, 1992a: 38).

Second, Pratt insisted on the importance of the legacy of Victorian political economy, that is, the impact of the principle of less eligibility[1] on modern penality. This implies, so he argued, that Pentonville Prison, which was opened in London in 1842, offers a much better model to think of subsequent developments than the Panopticon. Indeed, while Foucault used Bentham's Panopticon to draw attention to the dark side of our supposedly

[1] Pratt defined it as follows: 'the idea that those who would become a burden on the state in whatever capacity, would endure worse conditions than those of the poorest non-dependents' (Pratt, 1993: 375). Originally this principle aimed to regulate provision for the poor in Victorian Britain. As Sidney and Beatrice Webb wrote in 1910: 'The principle of "Less Eligibility"... that is, that the condition of the pauper should be "less eligible" than that of the lowest grade of independent labourer—is often regarded as a root principle of the reforms of 1834' (cited in Mannheim, 1939: 56).

enlightened times, to highlight strategies of discipline and surveillance operating throughout modern society thereby constituting a 'carceral archipelago', it is Pentonville that gives a more accurate description of what really happened: secrecy, silence, and pointless labour were the hallmarks of the prison, not inescapable visibility and useful training directed at making 'obedient and productive' bodies. Here the principle of less eligibility was ever-present and operative: 'those confined had to suffer more than those who were free and non-burdensome, they had to be *actively* penalized' (Pratt, 1993: 386, [emphasis added], see also Pratt, 1992b: 104–8).

Third, we can see how Pratt, like other scholars working in this field, started to turn to an Eliasian perspective for answers to his questions related to penal change—more, in particular to the work of Spierenburg. Pratt drew attention to the observation that the prison became a highly secretive, closed-off institution. The infliction of punishment, gradually came to be 'privatized', that is, to be hidden away behind high walls, out of sight of the public at large, and to be executed by a new army of experts (Pratt, 1992a: 19). Yet, this did not mean that Pratt shifted completely to an Eliasian reading of penal history. Discontinuities and short-term breaks in penal developments (as thematized by Foucault) needed to be seen in tandem with long-term developments in penal sensibilities (as Spierenburg claimed). The 'complete change' (from classical to new penology) needed to be seen against the backdrop of a slow, continuing tendency to 'close off' punishment from public involvement (Pratt, 1992a: 23). Pratt suggests that both developments are not incompatible: it is as if the perceived break enveloped within Eliasian parameters. And in fact, as he argued, by attaching so much importance to criminological expertise 'the new penology lent itself to the view that there should be a greater distance between the public and the dispensation of punishment' (Pratt, 1992a: 177). In other words: the break in criminological thought and penological practice may have contributed to a further closing off of penal affairs. Foucault and Elias might therefore have been marching hand in hand.

It seems as if Pratt was sharing Garland's view of the need for a multidimensional sociology of punishment, that is, that the combination of different frameworks can provide us with a fuller picture of an inherently complex object of research. Yet, as we will see, this impression is false. After *Punishment in a Perfect Society* Pratt returned to a position of theoretical exclusivity.

Punishment and dangerousness

In his review essay of *Punishment and Modern Society* Pratt offered the following reflection on Garland's multidimensional approach: 'it is not his intention to present "the field" in such a way that, ultimately, one theorist in particular is seen as having "the answer" while all the rest fail for one reason or another (although, from the range and strength of expositions in the book, *I suppose that it would be possible to do that*)' (Pratt, 1994: 214, [emphasis added]). A little further in the same essay Pratt devoted most of the available space to Elias[2] and he welcomed attention for the link between punishment and culture as 'a major breakthrough in our understanding of punishment' (Pratt, 1994: 217). Based on the combination of these two observations, that is, the possibility of theoretical purism on the one hand, and an uncritical endorsement of the approach of Elias on the other, one might have predicted that Pratt would ally himself to Elias. Indeed, this would also seem logical in view of his intellectual trajectory which, thus far, had been marked by a gradual moving away from a straightforward Foucauldian theoretical position. And yet something completely different happened when Pratt embarked on his next research project, that is, the history and present of dealing with dangerous offenders. For the next couple of years Elias was temporarily banished from his writing table. In fact, Elias did not appear in the list of references of his book *Governing the Dangerous* nor in the major part of the research articles that he wrote at this time.[3]

What had happened? As we saw in the previous chapter, during the 1990s there was a remarkable revival of interest in Foucault's later publications which inspired so-called 'governmentality studies' in the social sciences in general, and in criminology in particular. Pratt's work on dangerousness firmly established itself within this research tradition, at the expense of Elias, so it seemed. His vocabulary changed in its wake: Pratt no longer talked about 'sensibilities' and 'sensitivities' but about 'political rationalities',

[2] Elias received almost two pages while he devoted approximately half a page to each of the other authors (Durkheim, Marxism and the political economy of punishment, Foucault, and Weber) (see Pratt, 1994: 214–18).

[3] There was only one reference to Elias in one paper. However, this was *not* with respect to punishment, but rather related to the growing sensitivity to behaviour threatening the integrity of the body (Pratt, 1996b: 30).

'liberalism', 'welfarism', 'neoliberalism', 'programmes', 'risk management', and so forth. From an 'author-in-perspective' point of view two significant things are happening here. First, while the theoretical framework used in *Punishment in a Perfect Society* seemed to suggest that Pratt, like Garland, was moving to a more pluralist position (integrating Foucault and Elias) he now seemed to return to a purist position indicating, against Garland, that one perspective might have all the 'tools' to answer his questions. Second, his return to a Foucault-inspired theoretical framework, and the concomitant temporary 'amnesia' about Elias, is the first reason why we will term his theoretical position later in this book 'volatile'. Indeed, for his next project he would again return to Elias and forget about Foucault. We will discuss Pratt's volatile scholarship at length later on in this chapter. Let us now turn to the content of his work on dangerous offenders.

In *Governing the Dangerous* and related papers Pratt offered a splendid example of the 'defamiliarization' of punishment, that is, of making 'evident things into puzzles' (Bauman, 1990: 15). The desire to protect ourselves from dangerous persons seems to be so obvious, and so deeply ingrained in human nature, that most of the time it hardly prompts any questions. Yet, as Pratt demonstrates, our ways of dealing with dangerous offenders are far from self-evident: both the persons who are judged to be dangerous and the policy instruments to deal with them, have changed remarkably since the birth of the concept in the nineteenth century. What we term 'dangerous' does not simply refer to some inherent quality in a person's constitution: 'It does not exist...as some pre-given entity' (Pratt, 1995: 7). Dangerousness is 'a constantly shifting phenomenon' (Pratt, 1998a: 26). As soon as we are willing to realize this it becomes possible to trace the history of how the concept came to be applied to different groups of people, and how the responses changed over time.

At the end of the nineteenth century dangerous offenders were almost exclusively professional/habitual property offenders and small-time fraudsters. Property crime was perceived to be the real threat and attracted almost all the attention at a time when there was not yet a consumer society with abundant consumer goods and generalized private insurance schemes against property losses. Between the 1930s and the mid-1950s a new risk category was added: sexual offenders joined the habitual criminals in the dangerousness framework. Because of this sexualization of risk, which was stimulated by developments in psychology, the modern state not only acted as the guardian of property but also as the guardian of morals. Towards the mid-1960s another shift took place: the older habitual criminals, as well as a good deal of sexual deviants, almost disappeared from view. On the one hand, property crime was no longer perceived to be such a threat in an increasingly affluent society with a greater spread of ownership. Habitual criminals came to be seen as 'inadequate and in need of assistance, rather than dangerous and in need of indefinite confinement' (Pratt, 1997a: 100). For this group preventive detention lost its purpose and alternative ways to govern them which corresponded better to their new 'inadequacy' status, came into existence: the hostel and the mental institution. On the other hand, sexual offences became more focused. This was made possible by the deregulation of morals and a growing recognition that certain forms of sexual behaviour (such as homosexuality) were no longer carrying any risk for the rest of the population. In light of the post-war baby boom, for example, homosexuality was no longer perceived to be a threat for population decline.

These various groups became objects for government—they became a 'risk' to be acted upon in order to protect the well-being of the norm-conforming population. Indeed, as soon as political rationalities moved from 'classical liberalism' to 'welfarism' the role of the modern state changed significantly: in return for protection and insurance against a number of risks citizens were prepared to allow for greater state intervention in their lives. To make them governable the indeterminate prison sentence (or, hostels and mental institutions) came to be included in the penal armoury as a form of social defence and risk management. For Pratt the concept of 'public protection' which was used to justify new ways of governing the dangerous, could only be written into law because of the shift in political rationalities: 'it was...only when risk management in a broader sense became part of the general programme of government of modern societies that we begin to see this concept being written into criminal law in the early part of this century' (Pratt, 1997a: 53). The right to protection that the welfare state promised on a number of levels, therefore, extended to the presumed risks posed by the dangerous. The people judged to be 'dangerous' changed over time—due to economic prosperity, developments in psychology, various changes in perceived threats, and so forth—yet these various 'risks' were all addressed within the welfarist programme of government.

From the early 1970s, however, welfarism as political rationality increasingly came under attack and, eventually, had to make room for neoliberalism, that is, '...a programme of government which shifts the general burden of risk management away from the state and its agencies and onto the self, in partnership with non-state forms of expertise and governance' (Pratt, 1997a: 133). During the 1960s, as we saw, the concept of dangerousness experienced 'something of a quietude': 'no-risk welfare societies had considerably eroded its base and narrowed it down' (Pratt, 1997a: 132). Yet, with the shift to neoliberalism dangerousness would enjoy a renaissance and it again changed form: after 1970, violent and sex offenders came to the foreground mirroring the growing preoccupation with human (especially female) bodies (Pratt, 1997a: 139).

The neoliberal state, then, continued to protect its citizens from the dangerous. The discontinuities with the past had to do with deciding 'in advance' who is dangerous and who is not. This was done in two ways: (1) new dangerousness laws were much more narrowly drawn and discretionary powers of the judiciary were curtailed; (2) and, similarly, the powers of the 'psy-professionals' were curbed. In addition, there was a growing interest in the management of future risk and actuarialism. However, according to Pratt another shift was already underway in the mid-1990s. He referred to the reaffirmation of the viability of the indeterminate sentences (e.g. 'three strikes and you're out' laws), the widening of the boundaries of dangerousness (which again started to include property crime), and a general relegitimization of the prison. Pratt interpreted this as being a retreat from the principle of bifurcation that held sway until the early 1990s: 'With these new initiatives...it seems clear that prison is intended to be much more generally available rather than confined to a "serious" or "dangerous" few' (Pratt, 1996a: 245).

The influence of the second Foucault-effect on Pratt at this stage in his scholarly career is difficult to underestimate. His vocabulary was strongly inspired by Foucault's work on the history of sexuality and governmentality: biopolitics, the population and the individual as target (Foucault's '*Omnes et singulatim*'), the role of the human sciences, rationalities, programmes, welfarism, neoliberalism, and so forth. Chapter 7 of his book was named 'The care of the self' which is an implicit reference to the third volume of Foucault's trilogy on the history of sexuality (Foucault, 1986). Even though direct references to Foucault are rather sparse (see e.g. Pratt, 1997a: 1, 4–5, 32) it is clear that Pratt's research on dangerous offenders was fully immersed in the 1990s Foucault-revival in theoretical criminology that took place under the umbrella of 'governmentality'. Pratt appropriated the language and the concepts without always acknowledging his debt to Foucault but it was there, for sure, on almost every page he wrote at this stage in his career.

The civilization of punishment

Soon after the publication of *Governing the Dangerous* Pratt returned to Elias as the guide for his next research project. In a number of papers that preceded the publication of his book *Punishment and Civilization* Pratt explained why the ideas of the German sociologist were particularly helpful for his study on how modern penal systems, over the course of two centuries, came to be seen as 'civilized' and how these 'civilized' penal arrangements, in turn, came under increasing attack from the 1970s onwards leading to a 'decivilization' of punishment (Pratt, 1998b; Pratt, 1999b; Pratt, 2000b).

Pratt was not the first to apply an Eliasian framework to questions of penal change. Yet, whereas Franke (1990a), Spierenburg (1984a), and Pratt (1992a) himself were concerned with penal change in a more or less far-away past, Pratt's research for *Punishment and Civilization* and related papers would take us straight into the present. The originality of his work, therefore, needs to be situated in making Elias' theory in general, and the concept of decivilization in particular, relevant for discussions on recent penal change. There is also a second point that makes his study stand out. Pratt drew attention to the idea that civilizing processes can bring uncivilized consequences with them: the hiding of punishment, bureaucratic rationalism, scientific expertise, and so forth can lead us 'instead into the commission of monstrous incivilities, conduct that we would think had no place in the "civilized" world' (Pratt, 2002a: 2). In order to expand on this he built upon the shoulders of Bauman (1989) and Christie (2000) who both rejected the idea that 'civilization' naturally would lead to more humane treatment and that inhumanity is a mere aberration of an otherwise perfect functioning society. Pratt acknowledges the dark side of modernizing and civilizing processes and, therefore, presents us with a more complicated, and inevitably ambivalent, account of the 'civilizing' of punishment.

Pratt's study covers five English-based jurisdictions (England, Australia, New Zealand, Canada, and the United States) and starts off in the late eighteenth century. Public executions were in decline and lost much of the earlier 'spectacle of suffering'. They were increasingly screened off from public view and came to be administered behind the walls of the prison. At the same time the prison started to play an important role in closing off punishment from public scrutiny. In a first step the prison would hide away punishment behind its high walls thereby establishing a clear barrier between life in prison and public life. But, eventually, also the prison would disappear out of view: whereas the old prisons were deliberately built in city centres new ones were more likely to be constructed in outlying, elevated sites, far removed from daily life. Moreover, prison architecture changed over time: unlike the first prisons which were imposing gothic buildings, the newer ones were designed in such a way that they were much more anonymous and invisible, almost unrecognizable to people passing by. In addition, also the contact between prisoners and the public decreased, e.g. by making public access to prisons more difficult and preventing prisoners from working beyond the prison walls.

This 'disappearance of prisons' was accompanied by an amelioration of life behind bars. Pratt refers to changes in prison conditions regarding food, clothing and hygiene to illustrate how this took place. This tendency towards improving living conditions was, at times, interrupted by the power of the less eligibility principle. Yet such interruptions were only temporary and could not prevent a general process of 'normalization' taking place in due course (Pratt, 2002a: 79). Next to these material changes official discourse came to be sanitized. Penal language transformed: 'from emotive, moralistic denunciation to that of scientific, rationalistic objectivity' (Pratt, 2002a: 95).

Yet, this gradual amelioration of prison conditions was not always perceived like that by prisoners themselves. Their stories, as Pratt illustrates, departed in significant ways from the 'official truth' about the modern prison. In that sense the book is not only about the 'civilization' of punishment but also, and importantly so, about how punishment came to be represented and viewed as 'civilized'—how one story (the official) came to dominate and silence the story that prisoners themselves had to tell. Unlike the official version which told a story about the decline of physical punishment; better food, hygiene, clothing; regimes shaped for rehabilitative and educational opportunities, and so forth, the accounts of the prisoners were pointing at continuing deprivation and degradation.

The success of the prison authorities to turn their version of the truth into the more or less unchallenged truth, as well as the improvements that actually took place, were the product of the two forces that made the 'civilized' prison possible: bureaucratization and public indifference. The process of centralization and the further strengthening of state bureaucracies further turned the administration of punishment into a 'privatized' affair: a centrally organized bureaucracy would do the 'dirty job' of punishing law breakers, out of view of the public. This centralized, professionalized, and unified penal bureaucracy made it easier to speak with 'one voice' and was powerful enough to draw 'a veil of silence' across other versions of the truth of the modern prison. This bureaucratization went hand in hand with, and contributed to, the generation of a sense of moral indifference in the public. Over the course of two centuries the general public had been progressively excluded from the punishment process. But this was not only the result of the distancing that was caused by bureaucratization: 'Self-restraint and a desire not to become involved began to repress any inclination for such participation. The sight of prisoners began to provoke feelings of disgust and revulsion' (Pratt, 2002a: 138). The two developments, which are characteristic of the civilizing process, mutually reinforced and supported each other. This process of civilizing punishment reached its highpoint around 1970. Thereafter, however, a breakdown of these civilized penal arrangements began to take place. These post-1970 developments and their consequences will be discussed in the next section.

Punishment in a New Culture of Intolerance

In the introduction to this chapter we argued that state punishment, at least as long as it is claimed to be legitimate, always takes place within certain boundaries which set limits to which forms and what quantities of punishment are acceptable—and the quantities and forms that are not. For Pratt, recent penal change needs to be understood against the backdrop of a shift taking place in those boundaries (Pratt, 2002a: 3). It is not so much a 'new culture of control', then, but rather a 'new culture of intolerance' that explains why recent penal developments tended to depart from the 'civilized' penal arrangements of the past. In the previous chapter we saw how Garland emphasized the multiple adaptations of late modern citizens to the new 'social fact' of high crime rates which, in turn, provided support for the contradictory strategies of adaptation and denial. For Pratt something rather different took place: a new axis of penal power came to be established between the state and the general public. This diminished, to a considerable extent, the control the once dominant penal bureaucracy exercised over the process of punishment.

The new axis of penal power

During the 1960s and 1970s 'something like a breakdown in civilization' began to take place (Pratt, 2002a: 145). The penal arrangements that had been slowly built up over the course of almost two centuries started to crumble under the weight of a number of developments. First, the 'civilized' prison became a prominent site of disorder and disruption: riots, strikes, escapes, scandals and the like brought the prison back into the spotlights—though in a rather negative way which, eventually, called into question the authority and expertise of the penal bureaucracy. Second, prison numbers started to increase and living conditions behind bars were deteriorating because of overcrowding and insufficient investment in the prison system. Third, the unified penal bureaucracy became an 'increasingly fragmented and despairing body' (Pratt, 2002a: 159). Prison authorities were no longer able to conceal the deficiencies of the system and were more prepared to acknowledge the difficulties they faced and the failures they encountered.

According to Pratt public indifference gave way to 'increasing anxiety and alarm' and 'the public's threshold of tolerance and self-restraint was being progressively lowered' (Pratt, 2002a: 162). Whereas previously the public was kept away from the process of punishment by a powerful penal bureaucracy and, in addition, was itself not keen on being involved in the shameful business of punishing offenders, it now became more and more involved in penal affairs. These developments would eventually lead to the establishment of a new axis of penal power between the central state and the general public. While the penal bureaucracy used to dominate the old axis, it now was progressively excluded from setting and policing the boundaries in which punishment should take place: 'instead of the central state educating the public and leading them along a rational, reasoned path of development, it is as if the position comes to be reversed, with the axis of penal power significantly shifted away from the dominant bureaucratic rationalism of the state and towards the emotive punitiveness of the general public' (Pratt, 2002a: 182). Pratt emphasizes that this reconfiguration of penal power does not mean a full reversal of the effects of the civilizing process. Yet, what seems to interest him most, is the ways in which the boundaries of punishment came to be pushed into new and unfamiliar regions.

The decivilization of punishment: towards a new punitiveness

As a result of this reconfiguration of penal power 'the options for punishment are increasingly stepping outside its modernist framework and cultural parameters' (Pratt, 1998b: 511). The existing boundaries of punishment are pushed back and conjure up 'new possibilities of punishing which previously seemed to have no place in the civilized world' (Pratt, 2002a: 177). According to Pratt this happened (and is happening) for both the quantity (more and longer) and the quality (different) of punishment. In terms of the quantity of punishment the earlier efforts to restrict and stabilize prison populations came to an end. The USA stands out in its unprecedented prison growth but also other countries have experienced significant increases in imprisonment (Pratt, 2002a). High imprisonment rates no longer provoke feelings of shame: 'Instead of high levels of incarceration being seen as a sign of shame, they now are more likely to be regarded as an indicator of political virility, something to be proclaimed rather than embarrassed about' (Pratt, 2002c: 64). At the same time the rationale of imprisonment more and more veers towards incapacitation: prison 'works', it is argued, by keeping law breakers away from the rest of society. Pratt repeatedly refers to the introduction of laws that allow for long or indefinite (mandatory) periods of incarceration (such as 'three strikes and you're out' laws and sexual predator laws) to illustrate how imprisonment moves frontstage in contemporary penality (see e.g. Pratt, 1998b).

But also the quality of punishment changes under these conditions. Pratt points in particular at sanctions that privilege or presume public participation in the administration and delivery of punishment and that allow for emotive expression. Both aspects run counter to the bureaucratic, rational way of punishing law-breakers that came to characterize, as we have seen, penal modernity (Pratt, 2000d). The resurgence of shame—both in its humiliating, degrading and brutalizing variant as well as in its more productive version—is emblematic for these developments. On the one hand, penal practices from previous eras that were thought to have died out, are being reintroduced: chain gangs, shaming penalties aimed at stigmatizing offenders, laws that proscribe the notification of released sex offenders. On the other hand, restorative sanctions provide for a form of reintegrative shaming and offer possibilities, and deliberately so, for the expression of emotions that were for a long time deemed to have no place in the civilized penal arrangements (Pratt, 2003). Pratt also refers to the resurgence of curfews for youngsters and the growth of vigilante groups and angry mobs (e.g. in response to paedophiles settling in residential areas) as examples of how the public has become more involved in criminal justice policy—or (in the case of vigilantism) is increasingly willing to take the law into its own hands when criminal justice agencies are felt not to be responsive enough. These various developments provide evidence, so he argues, 'of a resurgent trend in penal outlets providing for, often approving of, emotional release and which "send messages" through their ostentatious display' (Pratt, 2000d: 420).

For Pratt these various developments in the quantity and quality of punishment add up to a 'decivilizing' of punishment (Pratt, 1998b) and the emergence of a 'new punitiveness' (see e.g. Pratt, 1998b: 510; Pratt, 2000a; Pratt, 2000c: 131–4; Pratt, 2002c: 65; Pratt, 2002a: 177–181; Pratt *et al,* 2005b). The latter notion reappears throughout his writings since the late 1990s and, eventually, led to the publication of a co-edited volume *The New Punitiveness* (Pratt *et al,* 2005a). This punitiveness is new, so he argues, 'because it seems in some ways to reverse longstanding traditions that had become the hallmark of modern penal culture, it introduces sanctions that seem to have their roots in the non-modern world, it significantly reorders the modernist penal configuration, and it obeys a different set of values and cultural expectations from those that had erstwhile provided frames of reference for the development of modern punishment' (Pratt, 2000c: 133–4).

Challenging four influential accounts of penal change

Pratt not only developed his interpretation of (recent) penal change solely on the basis of his own research but he also directly contrasted his version with the interpretations offered by others. For readers of his work this has a clear and intellectually rewarding advantage: it sharpens our understanding of his way of making sense and helps us to position Pratt in various debates and in relation to the work of other authors. His interlocutors were David Garland, Nils Christie, Stanley Cohen and Anthony Bottoms. The topics being addressed were postmodern penality, gulags western style, visions of social control, and penal populism.

Against Garland: postmodern penality

In the previous chapter we briefly saw how Garland rejected the idea that recent penal change needed to be captured in terms of a 'postmodern penality'. He concluded his essay with the following words: 'Other theorists may subsequently construct a different and more persuasive account, in which case my conclusions will need to be revised' (Garland, 1995a: 193). In a paper that was published five years later Pratt would take up the challenge. His position, as he argued, 'is informed by but ultimately reverses that taken by Garland (1995) in his authoritative contribution to this debate' (Pratt, 2000c: 127).

Pratt's paper was prompted by a passage from Louis Masur's (1989) book *The Rites of Execution*. Here he found a reference to a Pennsylvania law of 1786 which provided for punishment by 'continued hard labour, publicly and disgracefully imposed... in streets of cities and towns, and upon the highways of the open country' (Masur, 1989: 78, quoted in Pratt 2000c: 128). These criminals were known as 'Wheelbarrow Men'. For Pratt, the punishment of the Wheelbarrow Men belonged to a world that was utterly different from that of the era of modern penality.

Yet, as the title of Pratt's paper suggests (*The Return of the Wheelbarrow Men*) penal modernity was not to stay with us forever. Pratt saw a clear parallel between the Wheelbarrow Men and the Punitive Work Order that was introduced in 1996 in the Northern Territory (Australia). Offenders punished by such orders needed to wear special conspicuous uniforms, which were deliberately intended to shame the convicts. For Pratt this recent Australian penal development illustrates how 'some of the penal qualities associated with that earlier modality of punishing seem to have resurfaced in the new sanction' (Pratt, 2000c: 130). It offers one example of how deliberate shaming, again, becomes an acceptable penal option.

The crucial question to be addressed, of course, was whether this 'return of the Wheelbarrow Men' and related penal developments (see Pratt, 2000c: 131–4) could be understood as a continuity of penal modernism or, alternatively, as a discontinuity which had led us into an age of postmodern penality. It is here that Pratt departed from Garland's position. Whereas Garland's survey of recent penal developments led him to conclude that these various changes have taken place within a modernist framework, Pratt argued the opposite: 'The various features of the new punitiveness . . . represent discontinuities from, rather than exemplifications of, modernity and can . . . be seen as displaying characteristics that we would associate with postmodernist themes' (Pratt, 2000c: 137). New managerialist developments, the decline of expertise, the growing emphasis on the signs and symbols of punishment, the intrusion of actuarialism and risk management at the expense of the grand narrative of reform and progress, the spread of shaming punishment and the increasing visibility of punishment—all of these are, so Pratt argues, indicators of an emergent postmodern penality. As a result, we enter into an era packed with uncertainty where past experience (including the accumulated wisdom of the sociology of punishment itself) no longer offers us clear guidance into the future: 'What we have lost is the sense of certainty about where the boundaries of punishment now lie, and the sense that we are following, long-term at least, an irreversible path of reform, amelioration and progress' (Pratt, 2000c: 141–2).

Further than Christie: beyond gulags western style

In a second paper Pratt offered a reconsideration of the hypothesis developed in Nils Christie's book *Crime Control as Industry*. For Christie (2000) growing prison populations around the world, especially in the USA, are not aberrations of modern societies but rather occur naturally within them. Christie applied Bauman's (1989) interpretation of the Holocaust to the penal realm: the forces of modernity (more specifically: the routinization of control and the production of moral indifference) not only made possible the genocide of the Jews during the second world war but also the recent increases in imprisonment in the western world.

In his paper Pratt acknowledged agreeing with many of the ideas that Christie expressed in his book but suggested that his analysis might have become outdated: 'he is writing about a stage of penal development that has indeed become characteristic of some modern societies, but one which those same societies may already be moving beyond' (Pratt, 2001a: 291). Indeed, in line with his argument as we outlined above, Pratt argued that Christie's gulag 'is no longer sufficient to absorb contemporary penal mentalities and sensitivities, thereby creating new possibilities for punishing' (Pratt, 2001a: 291). The build-up of the gulag, so Pratt argued, was possible by four processes that he elsewhere associated with modern 'civilized' punishment: disguise, removal, indifference, and bureaucratization. These are the building blocks that made possible the development of western gulags. Indeed, the conditions necessary for the civilizing of punishment *also* created the potential to move towards the western gulags. In other words, because the modern penal system could only come into existence because of bureaucratization and public indifference it *always* contained the possibility for unrelenting prison growth within it.

For Christie, therefore, this potentiality has come to fruition in recent times. Seen from his perspective there is 'a continuity of the same features of what we liked to think were the hallmarks of civilized penal arrangements—all that was needed was a little refinement of the machinery of punishment to cope with the increased demand' (Pratt, 2001a: 300). Yet, what Christie fails to capture, so Pratt argued, is that this is only part of the story and that, in fact, some of the building blocks of the western gulag have eroded ever since. Here Pratt referred to how public indifference gave way to involvement, and how the penal bureaucracy came under increasing attack. This has enabled the release of public sentiment and emotion which the modern penal system in earlier times firmly kept in check: the uncontrollable, unpredictable emotive forces which the 'managers of the gulag' wanted to contain have been unleashed and opened new possibilities for punishment such as notification laws for sex offenders, chain gangs, shame sanctions, the increased visibility of the prison, and so forth.

Updating Cohen: new visions of social control

As we saw earlier Pratt already took issue with Stanley Cohen's work in one of his last papers on controlling juvenile delinquency. In a 2002 chapter Pratt's critique of Cohen's (1985) *Visions of Social Control* was rather different in nature, that is, inspired and coloured by his own late 1990s/early 2000s attempts to come to terms with recent penal change. *Visions of Social Control* was a book about the extension, refinement and strengthening of the social control apparatus: contrary to the various intentions and multiple initiatives to move away from the formal control system in the 1960s and 1970s the 'nets' became wider, denser, and different. In addition, social control became more opaque and invisible: boundaries were blurring (inside/outside, guilty/innocent, imprisoned/released, and so forth) and gave way to a 'correctional continuum' while the public and formal apparatus of control were merging with the private and less formal.

According to Pratt, Cohen's work of the mid-1980s needed an update and revision. It was possible, he argued, 'to discern "visions of social control" which were not anticipated in his book—and some emerging patterns of control which seem to depart from the "master patterns" hitherto implicit in modern penal development' (Pratt, 2002b: 168). Cohen's work, therefore, dealt with 'a phase in modern penal development which has now passed—or is at least undergoing a process of significant reconfiguration' (Pratt, 2002b: 169). For Pratt the new penal developments that aim to shame and humiliate and that are expressive and ostentatious in nature, were no longer in need of sophisticated sociological deciphering. Seen from this perspective, Cohen's objective to expose the blurring and merging of social control arrangements, to unveil the benevolence of community programmes as different yet more control, no longer seems to be a challenging task for scholars doing research in this field. Indeed, as Pratt wrote on another occasion: 'We no longer need Stan Cohen's glossary of "social control talk" in front of us to help us understand what is going on. It has all become much clearer' (Pratt, 2000c: 133). Moreover, whereas a great deal of the social control literature of the 1980s was inspired by the Orwellian nightmare of totalitarian control, the state is no longer seen as oppressive or threatening. In line with the shifting axis of penal power and the growth of public involvement in penal affairs which we discussed earlier, Pratt suggested that we should now turn to a different novel which is better suited for our times: William Golding's *Lord of the Flies*. The central theme in Golding's book is not the shift towards a totalitarian state but instead the story of state power in retreat. For Pratt *Lord of the Flies* provided us with a disturbing vision of the future of social control, that is, it points at the inherent dangers in the current state of affairs engendered by the breakdown of 'civilized' punishment, increasing public participation and the rule of the mob.

Expanding and revising Bottoms: penal populism

In 1995 Bottoms coined the term 'populist punitiveness' which is 'intended to convey the notion of politicians tapping into, and using for their own purposes, what they believe to be the public's generally punitive stance' (Bottoms, 1995: 40). This term was soon picked up in the penological literature and has sparked a considerable amount of discussion ever since. Both words in Bottoms' term have obvious links with Pratt's interpretation of recent penal change: public involvement ('populist') and harsher punishment ('punitiveness') are, for Pratt, directly related to the changing axis of penal power. It should therefore not surprise us that Pratt would join the debate.

In a 2005 paper, co-authored with Marie Clark, Pratt explored penal populism in the context of New Zealand. According to Pratt and Clark New Zealand became 'an increasingly punitive society during the 1990s' (Pratt and Clark, 2005: 305)—at least for adult offenders. Whereas New Zealand is renowned around the world for the reform of its juvenile justice system by introducing family group conferencing in 1989, a model that has been welcomed by the global restorative justice movement and has been introduced in a number of other jurisdictions, the situation of adults looks very different. The rate of imprisonment in 2004 was 179 per 100,000 inhabitants. The daily average prison population increased from around 2,700 in 1985 to around 7,300 in 2004. Maori men are overrepresented in New Zealand penal institutions. Average length of imprisonment increased by 75 per cent between 1985 and 1999, and so forth (see Pratt and Clark, 2005: 304–307 for further details).

To understand this hardening of the penal climate Pratt and Clark explore the role of penal populism in policy-making in New Zealand. They identify four factors that help explain its origins and development: disenchantment with the existing democratic process; the dynamics of crime and insecurity in a time of deep social change; the growth and influence of 'victimization groups'; and the emergence of a new kind of penal expertise (that is, victims, activists, lobby groups, and so forth taking up the role of commentators on penal matters instead of academics or officials). Penal populism, then, impacted upon penal debate and practice in New Zealand but not simply as Bottoms would have it. While they acknowledge (in line with Bottoms) that political opportunism has been at play (that is, politicians playing the 'law and order' card to increase their popularity and to improve their chances of re-election), they also argue that the effects of penal populism have gone further than this and that politicians may easily lose control over the power of penal populism (Pratt and Clark, 2005: 304; Pratt, 2007: 3–4).

Reducing penal populism to political opportunism is to miss out, so Pratt argues, the crucial link between the rise of penal populism and the shift in the axis of penal power. In the previous chapter we encountered a similar line of reasoning about the role of politics: also Garland argued that recent penal developments cannot simply be explained by politicians exploiting the crime issue for electoral reasons and, related to that, they neither can freely 'choose' to punish differently. While Pratt and Garland disagree on the causes for this (the new axis of penal power versus the crime complex of late modernity) they agree upon the limits of politics as an explanatory factor and upon the ways in which the political space to act and think differently about punishment is constrained by factors beyond immediate political control.

Next to the expansion of the meaning and effects of penal populism Pratt also revised Bottoms' account in another way. Bottoms argued that 'populist punitiveness' co-existed and competed with three conceptual developments, that is: just deserts/human rights, managerialism, and invocations of community (Bottoms, 1995: 18). For Bottoms it seemed as if penal populism had the least promising future because it is, so he argued, closely tied to 'short-term political considerations' (Bottoms, 1995: 48). In Chapter 5 of *Penal Populism* Pratt reviewed the positioning of these other forces from the viewpoint of 2007. For Pratt 'a good part of the argument' set out in Bottoms' mid-1990s essay has since 'been overtaken by events' (Pratt, 2007: 126). He also added two new forces, which in the meantime, had come to the fore: incapacitatory and restorative penalties. For Pratt it was clear that, by 2007, penal populism had become one of the most significant forces at play: penal populism overrides the others which, in fact, are more likely to contribute to the growing influence of penal populism than compete with it.

Yet this does not imply that penal populism is inevitable. In a survey of three countries (Canada, Germany, and Finland) he argues that rather than expecting any tempering influence of those other forces one should rather explore those social and cultural arrangements that can act as barriers to penal populism. Canada, Germany, and Finland have, thus far at least (indeed, there are already 'cracks in the wall', see Pratt, 2007: 167–172) been able to erect such barriers because their civil service remained largely in control of penal events, their media was able to contribute to informed public debate and their welfare provisions provided solidity and stability (Pratt, 2007: 166).

Discussion

Thus far we have traced the intellectual trajectory of Pratt as a 'career criminologist', from the early 1980s until the present. Here we will further discuss some of the defining features of his particular way of making sense of penal change. In the next section we will highlight the value of the 'shock' approach that Pratt adopts in a number of his publications. Some of the problems in his thinking and writing, however, also follow from this eagerness to come to terms with 'new' penal developments. We will touch upon the empirical material he uses to develop his various interpretations of penal change; we will discuss the volatility in Pratt's use of theory and comparative analysis; and we will further explore one of the core concepts in his writing, that is, '(new) punitiveness'.

Throughout our discussion it will become clear that a number of problems only can come to light when we adopt a 'vertical' author-oriented approach. Situating intellectual products in the development of a scholarly career gives us the opportunity to perceive links with earlier or later work or, alternatively, to detect breaks, contradictory positions, theoretical shifts, and critical ambivalences. The discussion in this section and the remainder of this chapter, then, also demonstrates the merits of our methodological choice for coming to terms with the intellectual life-course of an author and its wider implications for scholarship in the field of the sociology of punishment.

Imagination and the value of the 'shock' approach

Pratt has a nose for new penal developments, and for new ways to make them intelligible. As we have seen throughout this chapter Pratt is especially concerned with exploring and patrolling the boundaries of punishment. His aim is to document where and how these are pushed, and to explain why this is happening. Despite numerous qualifications and temperings of the 'newness' in his publications it is those critical moments when such boundaries start to liquefy and take us into new directions, that move him to write on penal change. This also makes for eye-catching titles: *Towards the 'Decivilizing' of Punishment?* (Pratt, 1998b); *The Return of the Wheelbarrow Men* (Pratt, 2000c); *Emotive and Ostentatious Punishment: Its Decline and Resurgence in Modern Society* (Pratt, 2000d); *Beyond 'Gulags Western Style'?* (Pratt, 2001a); *The Decline and Renaissance of Shame in Modern Penal Systems* (Pratt, 2003b); *The New Punitiveness* (Pratt *et al,* 2005a); and so forth.

Over a period of almost three decades Pratt has been addressing the triple task of 'raising new questions, making new sightings and seeing connections between apparently unconnected phenomena' which, according to Garland and Sparks, is a pressing task for social theory in view of 'the remarkable pace of change that characterizes this field' (Garland and Sparks, 2000: 21). The imagination this calls for, is essential for a proper 'defamiliarization' of punishment. And, related to this, applying a 'shock' approach may be helpful to highlight 'the emerging new' rather than 'the old and the familiar'. This is one of the core tasks of the social sciences because, as Beck and Beck-Gernsheim argue, 'it is precisely the turbulences which annoy people and drive them forward to face issues' (Beck and Beck-Gernsheim. 1995: 10). Imagination, then, is highly important—not the least in relation to recent penal change which, as we argued in Chapter 1, has created an 'imaginative moment'.

However, in the case of *recent* penal change this is, as we suggested in Chapter 1, a hazardous business: there is no benefit from hindsight here which makes interpretive attempts more vulnerable to errors. In an evaluation of work undertaken in this area of research we need to take the dangers and inherent difficulties of the task at hand into account. This does not imply, however, that the elusive character of recent penal change is singularly responsible for potential mistakes being made by scholars in this field, nor that we automatically have to become 'milder' in our judgements about the texts we read. As Stones suggests elsewhere, there should be no 'disregard for the rigours of systematic thought, and for the attempt to forge standards of intellectual excellence in a particular sphere in order that the problems at hand can be addressed in the best of all available ways. Alongside *the imaginative moment* would be *the moment of discipline*' (Stones, 1996: 11). With these observations in the back of our mind, we will hereafter discuss some aspects of Pratt's work which turn out to be more problematic.

Limits to imagination: revisiting the empirical basis

Sometimes imagination can be pushed too far. Even the best scholars in this field at times 'float' at too high a distance from the murky all-too-real world. In a review of *Visions of Social Control* Peter Young referred to the book as 'a fine example of the sociological imagination at work' but wished that Cohen had 'tempered his imagination by a much closer empirical scrutiny of penal developments' (Young, 1986: 223). Also Pratt's interpretive work is, at times, built upon shaky empirical foundations. This may also explain the remarkably silent closure of the 'postmodern penality' debate.

Evidence versus anecdote on recent penal change

Pratt has an eye for the eccentric and the exotic. In part this follows from his willingness to explore how age-old boundaries of punishment come to be pushed into unfamiliar regions. However, sometimes he tends to give too much weight to the evidence he offers to substantiate his claims: the conclusions he draws are often built upon anecdote rather than clear-cut evidence.

In his work on dangerousness Pratt aims to identify and makes sense of an important recent trend in modern penality, that is, the punishment of persistent offenders, which is claimed to be present in 'English-based jurisdictions'. In order to illustrate the merits of his hypothesis he starts with the most extreme example, that is, a thief of a pizza slice who was sentenced to 25 years of imprisonment under California's harsh 'three strikes and you're out' law. For Australia, Pratt refers to four or seven strikes and in addition, is not dealing with fixed but indefinite detention. For Britain, he points at 'proposals' to introduce a two-strikes law whereas for New Zealand he argues that the introduction of a reviewable sentence 'has been considered'. Canada is not mentioned amongst these examples (Pratt, 1996a: 243–4; Pratt, 1999a: 133–4). On another occasion, Pratt again tries to make observations on the five English-based societies but draws almost exclusively from the USA. For the UK he mentions 'proposals' and he refers to a single newspaper article for New Zealand. Both Canada and Australia remain unmentioned (Pratt, 2000a: 136, note 1). Sometimes Pratt has to acknowledge that certain initiatives were abolished, such as the extended sentence in England and Wales in 1991 (Pratt, 1996b: 21) and a tough mandatory one-strike-law in Australia's Northern Territory (Pratt *et al*, 2005b: xiii), or that California's three-strikes-law stands out—even in the USA—in terms of its exceptional severity (Pratt and Dickson, 1997: 380). In fact, also his strongest example, the sentence of the infamous pizza slice thief was revisited (see Whitman, 2003: 57).

The strength of his empirical case, then, often decreases as he moves from (a particular state of) the USA to those other English-based jurisdictions: for the latter countries in the row he merely offers 'proposals' or 'considerations' and Canada, which forms an integral part of the five countries he makes statements on, hardly figures in the discussion. It raises questions as to what extent one can speak of 'important points of departure from penal trends of the last twenty years or so' (Pratt, 1996a: 244) that are observable and in need for interpretation in all five countries.

His later Elias-inspired work suffers from a similar parsimony of empirical detail. In a 1998 paper Pratt wrote about a 'new pattern of Western punishment' (Pratt, 1998b: 505) which was illustrated by four examples that were mostly derived from (parts of) the USA such as curfews, boot camps, chain gangs, and three-strikes laws, and similar initiatives. These examples did not apply to the USA as a whole but made him, nevertheless, generalize from local (and somewhat eccentric) penal developments to 'Western punishment' *en globo*. Somewhat further in the paper he acknowledges that these trends are 'concentrated' only in the USA (Pratt, 1998b: 506) yet, towards the end of the paper, it is nevertheless asserted that various aspects '*are* to be found in other societies' (Pratt, 1998b: 510). At other occasions he acknowledges that the 'renaissance of shame' does not seem to take place in England (Pratt, 2003: 192) and he presents Canada as a country where social and cultural arrangements were able to provide a *barrier* against penal populism (Pratt, 2007: 153–8). One of the most conspicuous examples in his Eliasian work was the Punitive Work Order which was introduced in 1996 in the Northern Territory (Australia). It offered him 'the clearest parallel' with the 'Wheelbarrow Men' of the Pennsylvanian chain gangs (Pratt, 2000c: 129) and it returned at numerous other places in his writings to support his case (see e.g. Pratt, 2000a: 145; Pratt, 2002b: 176). Yet, this initiative was quickly repealed afterwards. Nevertheless, while acknowledging this, it was *still* being used as an example in his latest book (Pratt, 2007: 31). As reader one wonders whether there is no other empirical material available. Indeed, the Punitive Work Order was not only fairly exotic (being restricted to a remote area in Australia), but apparently it was not strong enough to stand the test of time.

Pratt is not the only author working in this field whose empirical basis is, at times, rather thin when he broaches questions related to recent penal change: others have also been tempted to attach too much weight to developments that are often limited in time and space, or that are more symbolic than real (for critical discussions, see Daems, 2004: 142–3; Matthews, 2005a: 192–5). It might be that the time has come for a 'rehabilitation of the aberration', that is, to restore such exceptional penal developments to what they, in fact, are: locally determined initiatives that arise out of particular contextual circumstances but that often have no immediate wider relevance. To generalize from the eccentric and the exotic (or: to 'normalize' the 'aberration'), without compelling evidence from elsewhere, is more damaging than beneficial for the academic credentials of the sociology of punishment. The focus of research in such cases, instead, should be on the local circumstances which made these exceptional penal developments possible—as, for example, Zimring (1996) did in the case of the exceptionally tough 'three strikes and you're out' law in California.

In addition, Pratt is sometimes too fast in detecting and interpreting what are perceived to be significant penal developments. In one paper he writes: 'There is no longer the kind of bureaucratic resistance to these trends that we would have surely expected to find *just a few years ago*' (Pratt, 2001a: 306, [emphasis added]). In another paper he argues: 'It has only been *in the last few years* that the contours of this new arena of punishment have come into focus' (Pratt, 2002b: 177, [emphasis added]). Such 'real-time' interpretations run the risk of losing much of their appeal when time passes by and, as we have seen, so-called trend-setting examples disappear from the penal landscape. Moreover, in the particular case of Pratt, it is somewhat paradoxical to observe that an author who relies so heavily on the work of Elias, tends to be so quick to perceive discontinuities in long-term trends. Indeed, Elias and his followers in the field of punishment offer interpretations of (penal) change that extend over periods that cover centuries—not decades or years. In fact, Pratt's detailed historical work (dealing with two centuries of development and drawing upon extensive empirical detail (see Pratt, 2002a)) stands in sharp contrast to the way he tends to approach questions of *recent* penal change.

The silent closure of the 'postmodern penality' debate

Anno 2008 it might seem somewhat superfluous to devote a few pages to the 'postmodern penality' debate in the sociology of punishment. Indeed, scholars no longer tend to use the word 'postmodern': it seems as if it has been banned—silently—from academic communication and exorcised from collective memory. Those who, a few years ago, were persuaded by the argument and wrote confidently about significant 'breaks' that have led us into a new postmodern era, have shifted to other, less grand denominators for the current epoch—such as 'late modernity'—or have reverted to an unqualified 'modern society'.

However, the fact that a number of social scientists in general, and criminologists in particular, were persuaded by the postmodernist argument, says a great deal about how fast certain theoretical ideas can rise to prominence in current debate. And, related to this: how quickly they can evaporate—as if they had never existed. Earlier we saw how Pratt, *contra* Garland, joined the advocates of the 'postmodern penality' hypothesis. The author-oriented approach that we apply in this book allows us to trace how Pratt's position in this debate developed, shifted and even contradicted itself over a longer period of time.

Until well into the 1990s Pratt was convinced that penal modernism offered an adequate framework to think about penal developments. In his work on the history of punishment in New Zealand Pratt regularly affirmed that long-term modernizing trends were continuing into the present: 'Punishment "in the modern way"... *continues* its lengthy march away from corporeal sanctions and public involvement' (Pratt, 1992a: 249, [emphasis added]); 'any attempt to specify the identifying features of modern penality must take into account the *continuous* moves to have the punishment process hidden away' (Pratt, 1993: 392, [emphasis added]); 'Public sensibilities *still* dictate that criminals be hidden away in prisons rather than placed in the midst of local communities' (Pratt, 1994: 218, [emphasis added]).

Also in his work on dangerous offenders there were, in the first years at least, no indications that Pratt would soon deviate from this line of thinking. In 1995 he referred to the actuarial technology used to calculate risks of reoffending as firmly 'modern': 'this power and the knowledge it produces has a history that *goes back to the origins of modern society itself*' (Pratt, 1995: 24–5, [emphasis added]). In a paper that was published one year later Pratt even explicitly endorsed Garland's sceptical position on the merits of the 'postmodern penality' hypothesis and cited him approvingly (Pratt, 1996b: 22). We have to wait until 1998 to detect his first disagreement with Garland and to get a glimpse of his later 'postmodern penality' thesis: 'these new initiatives take us into territory *beyond the limits of modern penality* and stand in contrast to Garland's (1994: 30) claim that "if the apparatus of penality is changing, it is in its objectives and orientation, not its material forms"' (Pratt, 1998b: 506–7, [emphasis added]).

In the magical year 2000 something strange happens: while his paper *The Return of the Wheelbarrow Men* which we discussed earlier made, *contra* Garland, an explicit case for an 'emerging postmodern penality', there were two other papers where he rejected the idea that we entered an epoch of postmodern penality (Pratt, 2000b; Pratt, 2000d: 430–1). Moreover, in one of the latter papers Pratt defended the work of Elias explicitly *against* (post) modernist scholarship *tout court*, claiming that Elias' evolutionary approach could help us *transcend* the debate about modernity and postmodernity and, therefore, would make it futile (Pratt, 2000b: 191–2). After 2000 the 'post' prefix disappeared from his writings. In 2002 Pratt wrote about 'late modernity' (Pratt, 2002b: 173) and in his latest book *Penal Populism* the denominator is, again, 'modern society' (Pratt, 2007: 7, 36, 38, 66, 94,

121, 126 etc.). The circle is round: Pratt returned to his starting point of a decade ago.

This short history of an author's shifting and contradictory positions in a debate that has raged for almost a decade provokes two observations. First, the whole 'postmodern penality' discussion exemplifies how fast new and fashionable ideas sometimes tend to be picked up; how they start to fill up pages in scholarly journals and edited collections; how they create divisions between advocates and opponents; and how quickly they disappear—without a trace, so to speak. Indeed, nowadays nobody speaks any longer about postmodern penality. Also Simon, an early advocate of the 'postmodern penality' hypothesis (Simon, 1993; Simon, 1995; Simon, 1997) has shifted to 'late modernity' (Simon, 2001). This debate, for sure, has fulfilled an important function in sensitizing scholars in this field to potential discontinuities in penal development. Yet one wonders whether former advocates such as Pratt and Simon who nowadays tend to speak in other terms, have revised their earlier positions. Probably. Nevertheless, the remarkably silent (self-)closure of the whole debate stands in sharp contrast to its loud (and wrapped in eye-catching titles) kick-off. Individual scholars have, for obvious reasons, more to gain from opening debates than from closing them—especially if the latter implies acknowledging that earlier statements may have been premature or wrong. The question remains, however, whether this lack of self-critique and self-revision benefits the collective enterprise of making sense of penal change.

Second, these shifting positions in, and the closure of, the debate suggest that authors may, at times, change faster than the object under research. Whereas changes in punishment may prompt new ideas and perspectives, our discussion of the 'postmodern penality' debate makes clear that the relation also goes in the other direction: new ideas or perspectives may lead to other interpretations which tend to highlight certain aspects of the (unchanged?) object under research, while leaving other aspects out of the picture. The postmodern lens, then, invites an author to 'see' discontinuities at the expense of the continuities. All of this may sound pretty obvious yet it raises a crucial question: what has changed most, the object under research or the researching subject?

Volatile scholarship

The question formulated in the closing lines of the previous section is not meant to suggest that authors should abstain from adapting their theoretical frameworks. It is quite natural that an author, over an intellectual life span, and for good reasons, changes his theoretical position(s). In the previous chapter we saw, for example, how Garland in the mid-1980s moved from a Foucauldian/Marxist-inspired framework to a pluralist and pragmatic theoretical position which has directed his work ever since. Garland had his reasons for doing so: if he wanted to stay as close as possible to 'the integrity of the empirical object' (which was his declared intention) he needed to move to a multi-dimensional position. In the next section we explore how theory features in the work of Pratt. Despite a number of (superficial) similarities between Garland and Pratt (the influence of revisionist history writing and Foucault; the subsequent disenchantment with Foucault; the discovery of Elias; and so forth) there are some crucial differences in how both authors deal with theory. In the second section we have a closer look at how Pratt has dealt with the similarities/differences issue throughout his career.

Theoretical volatility

We have seen how the young Pratt of the 1980s was heavily influenced by Foucault, revisionist history writing, and the critical social control literature. Towards the end of the 1980s he started to revise Foucault and, for a moment, it seemed as if Pratt was, like Garland, moving towards a more pluralist theoretical framework. For *Punishment in a Perfect Society* he drew upon Foucault, Elias and colonialism to arrive at a more complex account of the history of modern penality in New Zealand. However, after the termination of this research project, there is no longer any indication that Pratt would join Garland's pluralism. His work on dangerousness was strongly inspired by Foucault-inspired governmentality studies. Thereafter, for *Punishment and Civilization* and his work on current trends towards the 'decivilizing' of punishment and the 'new punitiveness', he relies on Elias whose theoretical framework, as he recently argued, is able to capture recent penal change (Pratt, 2005a: 256–7).

As soon as Pratt had put his comfortable 1980s 'social control' clothes into the theoretical closet he seemed to have moved to a position which is both 'purist' and 'volatile' in nature. Whereas *within* the parameters of one research project one author or perspective seemed to provide him with all the answers (*the purist element in Pratt's use of theory*), he changed dramatically *in between* projects (*the volatile element in Pratt's use of theory*).

There is a crucial difference here with Garland's use of theory. Garland applies a multidimensional framework because of what he perceives to be the inherent failure of any singular 'purist' perspective to grasp punishment in all its complexity. Moreover, Garland's 'adaptive' stance towards theory, that is, that one's particular research question should guide one's selection of theoretical 'tools', also led him to avail himself of a number of theorists. But this should not be confused with Pratt's 'volatile' position: Pratt's volatility manifests itself *in between* research projects whereas Garland's adaptability exists *within* one project.

There are three observations we want to make about Pratt's volatility on the basis of our study of his intellectual life history.

First, at times the same developments are interpreted from different angles within subsequent projects and publications. His work on the history of punishment in New Zealand offers a clear example. In *Punishment in a Perfect Society* Pratt investigated in detail the origins of modern penality in New Zealand. As we have seen, Pratt emphasized thereby the unique history of the former British colony; drew attention to the obvious differences in penal development in Britain and New Zealand; and he worked within a Foucault/Elias/colonialism framework. For *Governing the Dangerous* Pratt looked at one particular aspect of penal history, that is, the governance of dangerous offenders, and treated New Zealand, Canada, Australia, the USA and the UK on the same terms. For *Punishment and Civilization* New Zealand, again, formed part of the English-speaking bloc but now the governmentality perspective made room for an Elias-inspired analysis. In his article *The Dark Side of Paradise* Pratt again focuses solely on New Zealand in order to explain its unique history of high imprisonment. Here he claims, relying on Durkheim, that its particularly strong social cohesion (which made it a 'paradise') has an exclusionary, 'dark side': New Zealand's 'famed qualities of friendliness and openness have been denied to those who were outside its narrow parameters of acceptability...the desire to defend paradise led to a marked intolerance of those who threatened the social cohesion' (Pratt, 2006a: 553).

Next to the volatility in stressing similarities versus differences, unique circumstances versus general tendencies, there is also a shift between theoretical perspectives. The connections between the various interpretations, however, remains largely unexplored: are New Zealand's high imprisonment rates to be explained by the 'decivilizing' of punishment, its recent neoliberal initiatives for dealing with dangerous offenders, or its Durkheimian close-knit community? If New Zealand's imprisonment rates have always been high (Pratt, 2006a: 542), if it has always had a strong populist tradition and scepticism of expert knowledge (Pratt, 2006a: 549) does this imply that the civilizing process was less pervasive in the former British colony than in the other four English-based societies? Depending on the theoretical perspective being applied, also the timing shifts: is the crucial moment for recent penal change in New Zealand to be situated in the early 1970s (Pratt, 2002a), the mid-1980s (Pratt and Clark, 2005; Pratt, 2006a), or in the early 1990s (Pratt, 1997a)? Such questions remain largely unexplored and unresolved—which brings us to our next observation.

Second, this volatility has not been matched by a degree of self-reflection and self-critique that seems to be indispensable for his use of theory, either to justify shifting positions, or to make connections between different interpretations. In his Elias-inspired work Pratt, again, starts criticizing Foucault but seems to forget his own year-long engagement in the mid- and late 1990s with Foucauldian ideas. Moreover, *at the same time as* he (again) started to write critically about Foucault in an attempt to demonstrate the superiority of Elias (Pratt, 1999b; Pratt, 2000b) papers were being published that were fully immersed in the Foucault-inspired governmentality tradition which neither mentioned Elias, nor contained any critical sections towards the Foucauldian approach (Pratt, 1999a; Pratt, 2000a; Pratt, 2000e; Pratt, 2001b; Brown and Pratt, 2000). While Pratt is often able to offer convincing theoretical discussions and interpretations in separate papers or clusters of papers, the persuasive power of these discussions tends to decrease when these are read jointly.

Third, in Chapter 2 we argued that Garland's choice for pluralism can help us explain why he was sceptical about the whole 'postmodern penality' debate and why the second 'Foucault-effect' left only a minor imprint upon his thinking and writing. Pluralism protected him, so to speak, from jumping too quickly onto the train of new theoretical developments. Pratt's volatile position, on the other hand, may have increased his susceptibility to take both theoretical innovations on board. His volatile theoretical position, so it seems, facilitated his engagement in both debates.

Geographical volatility

In Chapter 2 we saw how the similarities/differences discussion turned out to be one the most contentious issues being raised in the wake of the publication of Garland's *The Culture of Control*. In Pratt's work there is no clear choice for stressing similarities at the expense of the differences: his writings oscillate between discussions of particular developments in one jurisdiction on the one hand, and wide-ranging explorations touching upon the five English-based societies (or (post/late) modern society in general) on the other. Indeed, whereas his 1980s work, as we have seen, almost exclusively dealt with developments in Britain, he would thereafter start widening his geographical span in order to include Australia, Canada, New Zealand and the USA in his research (e.g. Pratt, 1997a; Pratt, 2002a) while, simultaneously, devoting a number of separate studies to New Zealand (e.g. Pratt, 1992a; Pratt and Clark, 2005; Pratt, 2006a). Two observations need to be made at this point.

First, Garland's methodological choice to treat the UK and the USA on the same terms has been strongly criticized. However, if one includes *also* Australia, Canada, and New Zealand into one's discussions, as Pratt does, the potential problems this brings in its wake may increase even further. Pratt is well aware that making general observations and offering global explanations is, in view of obvious differences between jurisdictions, a tricky business. At various places he softens his claims: the civilizing process takes effect on a very general level, but can also lead to differing, localized manifestations (Pratt, 2000d: 422); he stresses the importance of local contingencies (Pratt and Clark, 2005); he draws attention to the 'uneven scale of punitive development' (Pratt *et al*, 2005b: xvi); he emphasizes that the interconnection between civilizing and decivilizing is experienced differentially across societies (Pratt, 2005a: 267); and so forth. The difficulty of making generalized observations on a wide range of jurisdictions is nicely illustrated in the following passage taken from the introduction to the book *The New Punitiveness*. Here Pratt and his co-editors argued the following: 'What we have been charting here is a series of penal developments stretching over three decades affecting (and effecting) the shape and form of the penal terrain across the United States in particular, most of the other main English-speaking countries to a degree, and to a more limited extent in Europe' (Pratt *et al*, 2005b: xii).

There are a number of qualifications built into this phrase. If we read it carefully we can see how the strength of the case for the new punitiveness being a general phenomenon decreases progressively. It is stated that the changes affect the United States 'in particular' and, indeed, the examples Pratt and his co-writers offered (mass incarceration, three-strikes laws, sexual predator laws, chain gangs, death penalty, American 'supermax' prisons, and spartan prison regimes in Georgia (Pratt *et al*, 2005b: xii)) were *all* derived from (parts of) the USA. The generalization to other (unspecified) English-language jurisdictions is qualified in three ways: 'most' of the other 'main' English-speaking countries have 'to a degree' experienced similar penal developments. For Europe (which, again, remains unspecified) no examples were offered but nevertheless it is argued that the new punitiveness also manifests itself there 'to a more limited extent'.

The point we want to make is not that these other English-speaking jurisdictions or European countries are not experiencing penal developments that can be characterized as 'punitive'—there are a number of indications that this is indeed the case. Yet, by generalizing from a number of exotic and eccentric examples the case is not made persuasively. Countries such as Belgium, France, England, Spain, the Netherlands, and so forth have none of the (American) developments being summed up in the section that precedes the quoted phrase: mass imprisonment, three-strikes laws, sexual predator laws, chain gangs, death penalty, 'supermax' prisons, and the Georgian spartan prison regimes are *not* present in these various societies. On the other hand, they all have experienced increases in imprisonment rates, deteriorating prison conditions, and the move to more populist and politicized debates on penal issues. But the 'jump' from the anecdotal (American) evidence to those other societies does not offer enough weight to argue that the 'new punitiveness' is as general a phenomenon as it is claimed. It may well be that it is a proper description for (parts of) the USA, but more empirical detail is needed to generalize on other jurisdictions. The underlying assumption in using these American examples to illustrate the new punitiveness seems to be that 'what happens in the USA, also happens (to a lesser extent) elsewhere' (see e.g. Pratt, 2002c: 64–5). It remains unexplored, however, why the USA should be treated as paradigmatic for recent penal developments in western societies in general.

Second, in the previous section we argued that Pratt's theoretical volatility suffered from a lack of reflection on the relations between the different interpretations that he offered. The same applies to his geographical volatility: the connections between 'the particular' and 'the general' remain largely unexplored. Research in this field can be conducted at different levels, with differing degrees of abstraction and detail, yet it would be helpful if authors such as Pratt, who oscillate constantly between 'the general' and 'the particular', offered us more indications on how they perceive the connections between the two. Indeed, as we suggested in the previous section, at times it seems as if the 'local' studies on New Zealand contradict or put into doubt the 'global' claims being made about it in other publications.

Punitiveness: another hammering concept?

In recent years the concept of 'punitiveness' (and its little brothers and sisters) has experienced a remarkable rise in theoretical criminology. When scrolling through academic journals and book catalogues of publishers one regularly encounters notions such as: *punitiveness, populist punitiveness, new punitiveness, penal excess, punitive turn, penal populism, pénalisation, Punitivität, populisme pénal, populisme punitif, punitiviteit,* and so forth. The concept 'punitiveness' has acquired a prominent place in the vocabulary of the criminologist. In the first edition of the authoritative *The Sage Dictionary of Criminology*, which dates from 2001, there was no entry for 'punitiveness' (McLaughlin and Muncie, 2001). In its second edition, however, it was included—symbolizing and confirming the success of the concept in contemporary discussions on punishment and crime control (McLaughlin and Muncie, 2006).

However, the fact that 'punitiveness' has been able to expand the criminologist's vocabulary does not imply that there is a broad consensus on its value. In fact, Roger Matthews, who wrote the entry for the second edition of *The Sage Dictionary of Criminology*, was very sceptical: the definition remains vague; examples that are offered in the literature (such as shaming and new forms of managerialism) are often not punitive (that is, not intended to inflict pain and suffering on individuals); and the suggestion that increased punitiveness helps us explain current shifts in criminal justice policy is not convincing (Matthews, 2006a, see also

Matthews, 2005a, 2005b). Matthews is not alone: in recent years a number of writers have been critical about the sloppy ways in which the concept has entered academic writing and some have even expressed serious doubts about the usefulness of the concept (see e.g. Brown, 2005; Nelken, 2005; Nelken, 2006; Daems, 2007a).

Is history repeating itself? In fact, many of the critiques that are nowadays being levelled against the concept of 'punitiveness' sound remarkably similar as the questions that were raised two decades ago with respect to 'social control' (see e.g. Matthews, 1987; Chunn and Gavigan, 1988; Cohen, 1989). There is a danger here that 'punitiveness' becomes another 'hammering concept' (Cohen, 1989), that is, a concept that is copiously used to render different bits and pieces of penal reality manageable and comprehensible, but without much attention for the consequences.

A number of these conceptual critiques also apply to Pratt and his use of the notion of a 'new punitiveness'. Earlier in this chapter we already pointed at the problems of using eccentric and exotic anecdotes as evidence for significant penal change. But also the content of the concept remains unclear. In the introduction to *The New Punitiveness* Pratt *et al* argue that, next to the penal practices that we discussed earlier, there are a number of other indicators for the new punitiveness. These include: coercive and violent forms of policing communities, suicide and rape rates behind bars, the way a society addresses the problems of its poorest citizens, and the treatment of asylum seekers or refugees (Pratt *et al,* 2005b: xvii–xviii). The question to be asked, however, is the following: what is the criterion being used for including a diverse set of practices which range from chain gangs and the death penalty to the treatment of poverty and migration issues? It seems, at times, as if the 'new punitiveness' becomes an 'umbrella' term for various penal practices and social policies that Pratt *et al* are clearly worried about. The content of the concept, then, tends to be more determined by values and sentiments and less by a clear-cut criterion which allows us to distinguish what is 'in' from what is 'out'.

To use the new punitiveness as a broad denominator for the present state of affairs also misses out a great deal of what is currently going on—it throws a dark shadow over a penal terrain that is much more diverse and contradictory than the term seems to imply. With the shifting axis of penal power *also* restorative justice practices entered the penal terrain. However, it is difficult to see how these developments, where a punitive intent is most of the time absent, fit on the bigger picture (Daems, 2004). Electronic monitoring, one of the most recent innovations in punishment, offers another example. Beyens *et al* (2007: 37–38) recently interpreted this new sanction from an Eliasian perspective: for them there is a clear *continuation* of the 'civilizing' of punishment whereby offenders are expected to inhibit increasing demands of self-control, that is, the Eliasian movement from *Fremdzwang* to *Selbstzwang*. But also one of the most often used indicators for punitiveness—that is, increasing prison rates—are not as unproblematic as their copious use sometimes seems to suggest (see e.g. Kommer, 1994; Kommer, 2004; Daems, 2007a). If criminology wants to save the concept from the dustbin then more attention will need to be paid to its empirical content.[4]

Pratt as a Public Intellectual

In the opening lines of a recent chapter Pratt wrote that a colleague once introduced him to the participants of a seminar as 'an armchair academic': 'it was as if what I was doing was some sort of esoteric but largely irrelevant luxury' (Pratt, 2005b: 25). Pratt disagreed with the label of 'armchair academic' but he did not further explore why his work was not 'esoteric' or a 'largely irrelevant luxury'. In this section we will try to unveil the relevance of Pratt's work. This brings us towards the question of how an author combines 'thinking sociologically' with the possibility of 'thinking differently' about punishment. We will first trace Pratt's shifting critical positions, from the early 1980s until the present. We then have a closer look at how restorative justice, a movement that aims to develop a counter-force to many of the penal developments Pratt explores (and deplores), features in his

[4] There is no space here to enter into a lengthy conceptual discussion but at least two publications deserve special attention for those who are interested in a clearer delimitation and clarification of the concept. First, in *Harsh Justice* Whitman (2003) used ten different indicators to determine the comparative harshness of punishment in the USA on the one hand, and France and Germany on the other. On the basis of a point-by-point comparison he arrives at a composite picture of their relative harshness which forms the basis for his historical study. Second, a research group from the German Max Planck Institute has developed an 'onion'-model of punitiveness (das 'Zwiebelmodell' der Punitivität) which distinguishes between different layers at which empirical research can be undertaken (Kury *et al*, 2004).

work. To conclude this chapter we discuss the defensive strategy of Pratt.

Changes in Pratt's critical position: becoming a prophet

Pratt's critical position changed considerably over three decades of scholarship. In the early and mid-1980s there are explicit statements giving expression to his critical intent and, in addition, concrete proposals to guide practice towards more progressive ends. A 1981 paper on the influence of the 'New Right' in the UK was written out of the conviction that we need to identify what this political force exactly is if 'an alternative and coherent strategy is to be attempted' (Pratt, 1981: 371). His work on juvenile justice contained concrete proposals to engage with some of the 'social control' trends in dealing with youth delinquency. Pratt advised social workers to make an epistemological move from socio-psychological positivism to a phenomenology of the client: to let the youngsters speak for themselves so that the real problems, that is, the prospect of a life without employment upon leaving school, could rise to the surface. In one paper—with the telling title *Juvenile Justice, Social Work and Social Control: The Need for Positive Thinking*—Pratt directly addressed a social work audience to help them outline a proper and positive role for social work professionals involved in the juvenile justice system (Pratt, 1985c).

Next to his own concrete engagement he also exhorted his colleagues to become more directly involved in contemporary problems and challenges. In a review of a book containing a number of historical essays on social control, he called upon his colleagues to pay more attention to the pressing questions pertaining to the present: 'is there not a danger that the current emphasis, for sociologists working in this area, on understanding our present recourse to analysis of our past, becomes, instead, something of *a retreat from it?*' (Pratt, 1985b: 212, [emphasis added]). In his review of *Punishment and Welfare,* Pratt wished that Garland had paid more attention to 'prescriptions' for 'future change': 'a clearer theory of power and what this might entail for radical action and resistance would enable him to avoid some of the vague prescriptions he offers for future change' (Pratt, 1987c: 359).

However, Pratt was very well aware that the prospects for engaging successfully with the present and the acceptance of such proposals for change were, given the prevailing socio-political climate, grim indeed: 'in the British political context at least, pessimism is only too well justified' (Pratt, 1985a: 292–3). In a reflection on Mathiesen's (1974) *Politics of Abolition* he highlighted the impact this feeling of pessimism had on reformers themselves: 'Certainly, the expectations of liberals and reformers have declined since the heady days of the early 1970s, of which Mathiesen's work was a product' (Pratt, 1987a: 159). Pratt probably considered himself to be a member of that group with declined expectations. Indeed, over the years he would grow increasingly sceptical. In a 1990 paper on the future of the probation service in New Zealand he still argued that imprisonment levels could be reduced: 'Notwithstanding that prison numbers here are now at their highest ever level, *it is possible* to reduce these figures, a task which should surely be the main priority of the NZ Probation Service in the 1980s' (Pratt, 1990b: 115). But thereafter, we can hardly find any similar statements. Also the kind of concrete engagement with penal practice, such as the Matza-inspired proposals for youth workers, disappear from his writing.

As we have seen, in the 1990s Pratt would turn to historical questions. Yet, this was not meant to be an 'escape' strategy: Pratt aimed to find out what had happened in the past 'so that I could better understand " 'the present" ' (Pratt, 1992a: 9), to draw 'lessons from history' (Pratt, 1992b). Most characteristically, however, his papers started to contain warnings and aimed to bring into view the potential consequences of penal developments that, however reluctantly, are coming to the fore in contemporary penality (see e.g. Pratt, 2000c: 140–1; Pratt, 2001a: 306–7; Pratt, 2002a: 191; Pratt, 2003b: 192). If we are entering into a new era of punishment what, then, would or could be the implications for the future? If the boundaries of punishment come to be pushed and allow for new sanctions or the revival of previously unthinkable penal practices where, then, might this lead us? Pratt wants to confront his readers with the potential (dark) future in the hope that, so it seems, this would nullify the possibility of such a future being turned into an even more troubling present.

In this later phase of his career Pratt takes up the role of a prophet who predicts catastrophe in order to prevent it. As Bauman wrote, in a reflection on Dupuy's 'unavoidable catastrophe': 'prophesying the advent of that catastrophe as passionately and vociferously as we can manage is the sole chance of making the unavoidable avoidable—and perhaps even the inevitable impossible to happen' (Bauman, 2006: 176). Prophets, then, do not want their predictions to come true which, in fact, sounds highly *un*scientific in the strict sense of the word: scientists naturally want to come up with decent theories that have as much predictive power as possible. The prophet, however, wants to offer insight into what the future might bring and, thereby, prevent that future from becoming our present.

This may explain why Pratt pays so much attention to the 'dark sides' of social and penal arrangements: the totalitarian aspects of laws aimed at governing dangerous offenders (Pratt, 1997a); the destructive potential of releasing emotions from their modern 'straitjacket' (Pratt, 2000d); the uncivilized consequences of the 'civilized' prison (Pratt, 2002a); the exclusionary, 'outsider' producing flipside of the friendly close-knit New Zealand community (Pratt, 2006a); and so forth. It may help us understand why he devotes a disproportionately large share of his attention to the most shocking and eccentric penal developments. If our suggestion of Pratt being a modern prophet has some validity, then his empirical evidence is coloured dark, and deliberately so, in order to prevent the world from becoming even darker. Pratt, then, does violence to realistic and balanced descriptions of the (penal) world in the hope that that same (penal) world does not become more violent itself. There is, again, a crucial difference here with Garland: whereas Garland tries to remain as close as possible to 'the integrity of the empirical object' it seems as if Pratt's prophetic intentions nullify any such objective. For Garland description comes first; for Pratt description, at least in his multiple observations on *recent* penal change, seems to be subordinated to his prophetical intentions.

Pratt on restorative justice

In 1986 Pratt moved to New Zealand, a country that since 1989, with the introduction of family group conferencing in its youth justice system, attracted a great deal of attention from the global restorative justice movement. Moreover, in his work on the history of punishment in New Zealand Pratt described and analysed in detail how the indigenous Maori practices of conflict resolution came to be 'silenced' by the British colonizers. It was, therefore, to be expected that restorative justice would feature in his work. How does he explain the recent rise of restorative justice developments and how does he, as a critical thinker, orient himself towards a social movement that aims to provide a counter-force to what he describes as the new punitiveness?

For Pratt the rise of restorative justice as a more expressive form of justice and a more decentred modality of justice needs to be understood in terms of the changing axis of penal power which, as we have seen, allowed for more public involvement in the process of punishment. This implies, so he argues, that restorative justice shares the same 'penal DNA' as those other new penal developments such as chain gangs, stigmatizing shame sanctions, vigilantism, and so forth. Both the new punitive initiatives and restorative justice developments could only come to the fore because of these changes in the axis of penal power; together they benefit from the weakening of the penal bureaucracy to monopolize the punishment business: 'it owes its existence to *the decline* of the welfare state, and the decline of the particular arrangements of penal power characteristic of much of the modern period, which denied it, as well as the excesses of contemporary penality, an existence' (Pratt, 2006b: 62; see also Pratt, 2003b).

The fact that both developments can flourish on the ruins of modern penality also informs his stance towards restorative justice. As an 'evangelical' criminal justice reform movement it tends to blind its advocates to some undesirable, unintended consequences: 'it falls prey to a kind of evangelical criminology: the fervour with which it is pursued gives it a taken-for-granted status that can blind its followers to its implications' (Pratt, 2006b: 45). Pratt points here at other criminal justice movements (such as the late nineteenth century child savers in the USA, the borstal movement in Britain and the alternative to custody movement in England and the USA) with their history of failure, that is, the good intentions being turned into bad consequences.

The 'crusading zeal' (Pratt, 2006b: 49) also makes advocates turn a blind eye to the social conditions that made its emergence possible and which, as we have seen, *also* enabled the new punitiveness to rise to prominence. Pratt aims to bring into view the existential link between 'productive' shaming and 'stigmatizing' shaming (Pratt, 2003). Indeed, whereas a normative understanding of restorative justice sees it as an antidote ('the good') to current punitive developments ('the bad'), a sociological understanding teaches us that they share a common fertile soil on which to grow. The price to be paid for the success of restorative justice may well turn out to be a very high one. For Pratt it is more likely that the new punitiveness will profit the most from the current state of affairs: 'the empowerment of the public at a time when the sense of threat and insecurity are heightened as a result of law and order concerns seems likely to balance the scales in favour of the new punitive trends, in a penal realm that has lost its sense of stability, permanence and direction' (Pratt, 2006b: 63; see also Pratt, 2007: 139–43).

This does not imply that for Pratt restorative practices are inherently bad. In his historical work he already pointed out that the Maori traditions that were silenced by the colonists offered 'possible solutions to current penal problems': 'In effect... we can see, from these indigenous systems of justice, ways of giving better deals to victims; and preventing alienation from the process of law' (Pratt, 1991a: 123; see also Pratt, 1992a: 252). Indeed, as he wrote elsewhere: 'Ironically, a system of justice was silenced which could have made a significant contribution in solving many of the problems of today's justice system, not just in New Zealand, but in the West in general' (Pratt, 1991b: 316).

It is interesting to observe that this latter statement was made for an audience of sociologists (the paper being published in the *International Journal of the Sociology of Law*). When he wrote some years later for an audience of restorative justice advocates (in the book *Restorative Justice: International Perspectives*) his emphases were rather different: whereas his audience of sociologists was presented with a balanced picture of Maori sanctions, stressing its appealing aspects (Pratt, 1991b: 297–8, 316–17), he immediately, in the first pages, confronted his audience of restorative justice advocates with the dark side of Maori justice, that is, the destruction of a whole village and the right to pillage (Pratt, 1996c: 138). In the light of our discussion earlier in this chapter this should not surprise us: Pratt is keen on bringing into view the ambivalences of penal developments and, when writing for a restorative justice audience, this implies shaking the taken-for-granted notion of restorative justice being a straightforward and unproblematic solution to current problems. With this intention in the back of his mind, Pratt paints with black on the all-too-rosy-coloured picture as presented in some of the 'evangelical' writings of restorative justice advocates.

His various discussions of restorative justice, then, illustrate wonderfully his stance as a cautioner and a prophet. In addition, they illustrate how far he has moved from his earlier practical involvement: prophecies and warnings have taken the place of concrete suggestions for changing penal practice and the 'need for positive thinking'. For Pratt the rise of restorative justice is packed with ambivalence and this clearly worries him. Restorative justice is not 'waiting in the wings' and 'ready to step onto the vacated punishment stage': 'For me, there is a dark shadow stalking this phenomenon which it cannot dissociate itself from' (Pratt, 2001a: 306).

Ambivalence about bureaucracy: the defensive strategy

To conclude this chapter it is perhaps interesting to highlight the orientations towards the role of bureaucracy, expertise and elitist policy-making in Pratt's work because these have changed deeply as he moved through the different phases of his scholarly career. As a young scholar inspired by Foucault and the social control literature Pratt was critical of the 'bureaucratic-administrative type of law' that came to regulate truants and youth delinquents, that is, the burgeoning 'normalization' sector that managed young deviants by means of a growing number of interventions and the use of administrative discretion (Pratt, 1983b; Pratt, 1989b). In his papers on sexuality he problematized the proliferation of 'sex-experts' aimed at instructing and regulating our sexual habits (Pratt, 1982; Pratt, 1983e); and a similar scepticism or distrust towards criminal justice experts was present in his work on dangerous offenders (Pratt, 1997a) and in his writings which touched upon the 'helping professionals' (see e.g Pratt, 1990b: 108). In *Punishment in a Perfect Society* he openly criticized the inefficiencies of bureaucratic organizations which develop 'their own interests, shape policy to suit their own objectives' and which are 'never equipped to deal with the tasks they have been charged with' (Pratt, 1992a: 240). The meaning and significance of the 'history of failure' of criminal justice reform was better understood, so he added at the time, in Foucauldian terms: the 'failure of the prison and other penal sanctions serves a very important function: it reproduces criminality' and it 'reminds the public of the consequences of law-breaking and gives the impression that the offenders who are sent there...are at the heart of society's crime problems' (Pratt, 1992a: 240–1).

However, this view of the deeper functionality of inefficient bureaucracies and their experts being entangled in power/knowledge games, altered somehow when Pratt entered another stage in his intellectual development. In particular the shift to Elias in the late 1990s led him to reconsider the role of expertise and bureaucratic organization. As we have seen, Pratt was still critical about penal bureaucracies 'silencing' the stories of those being subjected to punishment, yet, from his Eliasian reading of penal history a much more positive appreciation came to the fore. Indeed, that very same bureaucracy and its expert-led policy making *also* played a decisive role in 'civilizing' penal systems: 'the very bureaucratization brought about by the civilizing process is in fact likely to have its own built-in defences against the impact of decivilizing forces' (Pratt, 2005b: 37). Here bureaucracies are no longer the impersonal people-processing machineries from his Foucault-years but they provide 'shields' against decivilization (Pratt, 2002a: 187).

And whereas he earlier criticized the powerful voice of the penal establishment that silenced other voices, we now see that part of his hope tends to be invested in that voice: 'when members of the criminal justice system *act in unison*, they can still present a formidable and sometimes insurmountable barrier for populism to climb' (Pratt, 2007: 147, [emphasis added]). In other words, the experts now *need* to speak and act with 'one voice' and the bureaucratic structures are *needed* to stop or slow down the rise of penal populism. In his recent work it is not so much the suppressed voices of truants, indigenous Maoris or prisoners that deserve a stronger echo but rather the voices of the criminal justice experts which, in view of a pervasive penal populism, have been 'silenced' by the direct link that has been forged between politicians and the public at large. With the shift from a Foucauldian to an Eliasian perspective his views on expertise and bureaucracy therefore began to change. At the same time he also, like Garland, became milder for, and even somewhat nostalgic towards, the post-war period, occasionally typifying it as 'a growing culture of tolerance and social solidarity' (Pratt, 2000a: 142) and deploring 'the shift away from a centralized, progressive penal policy' (Pratt, 2000c: 137). Against the background of the current 'new punitiveness' the older 'civilized' penal arrangements started to look much more attractive to the Pratt of the 2000s than to the Pratt of the 1980s.

This also implies that the strategy becomes much more defensive which, in the case of Pratt, can again be related to his prophetical ambitions, that is, his intention to warn us of what might come if we cross age-old boundaries and if we continue demolishing the institutional structures and forms of expertise that have shielded modern societies for so long from destructive emotional forces. However, here we also seem to be confronted with a difficulty in Pratt's position in public debate: How can the prophet communicate his message and hope to find a listening ear if his audience is, to a large extent, presumed to be unreceptive to the message and should be kept away from becoming involved in penal affairs?[5] Towards the end of *Penal Populism* Pratt suggests that we should make use of scandals to challenge penal populism (Pratt, 2007: 176). However, the crucial precondition for successful scandalization of punishment does not seem to be present in his account of recent penal change. Such interventions *presuppose* a public that is receptive to such forms of scandalization, that is, a public that is sensitive to the sufferings that might take place behind prison walls, in police cells, and so forth. However, as we have seen, according to Pratt's Eliasian story, people have come to tolerate the suffering of offenders and are less inclined to sympathize with their suffering. Scandalization, moreover, tends to further undermine the bureaucratic shield that he at other places seems to be willing to re-establish: scandals only can become visible, and can only enter public debate, if there is an open flow of information, not if secrecy is being reaffirmed. Lastly, scandalization not only tends to run counter to his own analysis, it also is, as he admits himself, '*ad hoc*, contingent and unpredictable' and it is 'subject to the whims of the media' (Pratt, 2007: 177). Indeed, in one of the endnotes of his book Pratt deplores that, despite multiple

[5] There is reason to believe that Pratt, over the years, grew increasingly sceptical about human nature and came to see the 'man and woman in the street' less as an ally and more as an obstacle on the road towards a humane penal system. In 1994 he wrote about 'the nonsense of the argument that I have heard put forward by one or two liberals that governments deliberately keep prisons secret places; if only the public know more about them, it would be much more supportive of decarceration strategies. In fact, the reverse is true' (Pratt, 1994: 218). In his discussion of Christie's work he argued, *contra* Christie's optimism concerning public involvement, that 'there is no essentialized goodness to human values and public sentiment: unleashing them may only add to the spiral of penal control' (Pratt, 2001a: 283). Indeed, as one reviewer of *Punishment and Civilization* argued: 'From Pratt's Eliasean perspective, there is no natural repository of sympathy and empathy within the public, and whatever there is may have already been expended on victims' (Vaughan, 2003: 245).

attempts, no journalist was willing to carry one of his own scandalizing stories (Pratt, 2007: 188: note 12).

Pratt's effort to safeguard a place for the academic voice in the public debate by promoting the use of scandals, is his latest attempt to combine 'thinking sociologically' with 'thinking differently'. However, upon closer examination, scandalization is utterly limited, it can only happen after damage has been done and, moreover, it seems to be inconsistent with his own analysis of penal change. In Chapter 2 we already suggested that authors such as Garland and Pratt, who started their scholarly careers almost three decades ago, have gradually started to think differently about 'thinking differently' itself. In the next two chapters we will see how Hans Boutellier and Loïc Wacquant have been able to safeguard a much more pronounced public voice in their work. Throughout their careers both authors have contributed more directly to public debate on penal issues but, as we will discuss at length in Chapters 4 and 5, this has come at a certain price.

4

Punishment and the Fragmentation of Morality

Introduction

The infliction of punishment not only takes place within certain boundaries; it also aims at patrolling certain boundaries, that is, at safeguarding a society's shared beliefs. According to Durkheim the sacred character of the *conscience collective* in simple societies with a mechanical solidarity, inspired harsh penal measures. The evolution towards more advanced societies with an organic solidarity changed the character of collective beliefs: the earlier religiously-inspired beliefs gave way to beliefs that were centred more on the value of the individual. Accordingly, the intensity of punishment tended to decrease and there was more space for restitutive law. Crime, then, came to be viewed differently: 'human criminality' in more advanced societies tended to provoke reactions that were less strong than those provoked by 'religious criminality' in simple societies.

In view of the social transformations of the past decades, in particular what is often referred to as processes of individualization, there is one theme that has given rise to heated discussions amongst social scientists and various other commentators: the emergence of a more pronounced and more pervasive moral individualism. Questions and answers about 'good' and 'evil' are no longer naturally transmitted by churches, traditions, communities, and so forth. As a result, the older moral codes which for a long time were more or less taken for granted, have been replaced with something different. We are no longer living in the times of Durkheim but the questions about morality, crime and punishment that fascinated the French sociologist about a century ago, have not lost any of their importance.

Hans Boutellier shares Durkheim's interest in morality and has been at the centre of this debate, trying to identify and explain the distinctiveness of what binds us in times of moral fragmentation, and what this implies for how we have come to understand crime and punishment. According to Boutellier our morality has been 'victimalized', that is, in a fragmented and individualized society the victim of crime has become the glue that holds the pieces together. It is to Boutellier's explorations of the morality of our times that we turn in this chapter. We will first discuss Boutellier's thesis of the victimalization of morality and how he came to think about the 'safety utopia'. We then explore the advantages and disadvantages of Boutellier's Durkheim-inspired analysis of our fragmented morality and its relation to punishment. We finish with an examination of Boutellier's particular way of being a public intellectual.

Punishment and the Victimalization of Morality[1]

Crime as a moral problem

In the late 1970s Boutellier undertook some research in a closed institution for young delinquents. Foucault's *Discipline and Punish* had only recently been published and this book, together with Goffman's work on total institutions, would offer the initial theoretical inspiration for his research. However, Foucault could hardly help him to make sense of the daily interactions between the youth workers and the youngsters. Despite their relatively young age these delinquents had already a great deal of life experience and demonstrated a remarkable self-confidence in their interactions with the supposedly more powerful staff of the institution. The behavioural patterns of the group leaders had nothing to do with disciplinary power: rather these testified to a 'survival strategy' in order to deal with the difficult and challenging behaviour of the youngsters (Boutellier and Van der Linden, 1980: 523). The youth workers were under a great deal of pressure which went unthematized: it was one of the 'institutional taboos'

[1] Throughout our discussion of Boutellier's work we rely in particular on our reading of the original publications in Dutch. His book *Solidariteit en slachtofferschap* (1993) appeared seven years later, in abridged format, as *Crime and Morality* (2000). His other book *De veiligheidsutopie* (2002) was translated as *The Safety Utopia* (2004). Both translations will be used when English-language quotes are infused in the text of this chapter. However, it is important to observe that the original publications were much richer (and longer) and that the English translations, at times, are too literal and, unfortunately, lose some of the liveliness of the original publications in Dutch.

(Boutellier and Van der Linden, 1980: 524). The whole (re)education philosophy, so he concluded, should not be understood from a Foucauldian perspective: instead of it being put to work in order to normalize the young deviants, it helped the youth workers to unload some of their daily tensions. In their interactions with the youngsters there was no (re)educative relationship at all. Yet, in the coffee room and during the many meetings they could, ideologically backed up by the (re)education philosophy, unload these various tensions.

A few years later Boutellier participated in a research project on youth work from the University of Leiden. Here he encountered similar and even more pressing problems: youth workers were powerless in giving moral guidance to the youngsters they were dealing with. They did not have any anchor points or language to confront them with their unacceptable behaviour. There was no moral discourse to separate right from wrong—youth workers did their difficult job in a 'moral vacuum' (see Boutellier, 1988a: 20–1; Boutellier, 1993a: 9–10; Boutellier, 2004c: 7–8). In 1985 Boutellier wrote a piercing critique which he announced as a personal reflection upon those feelings of powerlessness. The problem of youth work was first and foremost a moral problem: in the 1980s people working in the field had ended up in an 'ideologically and morally unprotected position'. They had difficulties in defining themselves as 'moral subjects', as sources of 'moral acting' (Boutellier, 1985a: 22; see also Boutellier, 1985b, 1988a, 1988b).

For Boutellier the questions to be addressed, then, were very different from the ones authors such as Garland and Pratt were devoting their research to in the 1980s. Instead of analysing discourse in terms of power/knowledge he probed for that *moral* discourse that seemed to be missing in the field. His point of departure, as he later explained in an interview, moved 'from politics to morality' (Van der Ven, 1998). Moral standards which used to be grounded in political or religious ideologies had vanished and there was a perceived need to clarify what exactly had taken their place. His academic and practical activities for the next two decades, therefore, were guided towards unveiling this new morality that came to characterize our times. However, as he wrote in the early 2000s, despite criminology being a discipline which at its core deals with normative issues, there was hardly any discussion on morality: 'Morality seemed to be an off-word, used by priests and theologians, but not by criminologists. A moral perspective was chosen only by the occasional right-wing criminologist such as James Q. Wilson' (Boutellier, 2002b: 20).

Boutellier's explicit aim was to shift the terms of debate on crime and punishment into a moral direction. In doing so he attacked two more established ways of thinking about crime in criminology. First, the structural approach which sees crime as following from socio-economic inequalities, as exemplified in the work of the Dutch criminologist Jongman and his research group at the University of Groningen. His Merton-inspired relative deprivation theory led Jongman to call into question the structure of Dutch society itself: the 'moral problem', then, was not crime but the type of society that tends to produce social inequalities and, in its wake, crime (Boutellier, 1991a: 228–30). However, if the problem of crime is turned into a political one it becomes impossible to interrogate the moral justification for crime itself: 'Jongman's socio-economic rationalization of criminal conduct makes it impossible to see the moral meaning of a criminal event as such' (Boutellier, 2000a: 35). The suffering or material damage that is caused, the trust that is violated, the community interest that is harmed: these all remain out of the picture—the question of morality, so Boutellier argued, should not be restricted to policy but needs to include the criminal act and the justifications the criminal offers for it.

Second, the various control criminologies, ranging from Hirschi to the newer rational choice theories. The assumption here is that each individual, when confronted with the same unique set of contextual factors, would act in the same way. The 'reasoning criminal', then, weighs costs and benefits and arrives logically at a decision either to break the law or to conform to it. This line of thinking, however, makes the criminal into a 'morally neutral actor' (Boutellier, 1993b: 316). Criminal behaviour, so Boutellier argues, is 'objectified' and reduced to a series of rational calculations. To the extent that morality is considered in these theories it is introduced as an independent variable in the equation, that is, as a factor that might increase or decrease the likelihood of rule-breaking (the dependent variable) to occur. Whereas the (relative) deprivation theories tend to turn crime into a *political* problem, the control criminologies reduce it to a *technical* problem that can be addressed by various forms of situational crime prevention (reducing opportunities, enhancing supervision, and the like). Both, however, fail to capture crime as a moral problem (Boutellier, 1993a: 14).

Boutellier's disagreements with these two strands of thinking help explain his difficult and ambivalent relationship towards criminology. Thinking about crime in moral terms, and assuming that all offenders are free to make moral choices *irrespective of* the context in which these decisions are made, poses serious problems for a criminology that aims to address the causes of crime. For Boutellier, then, it is not the 'explanation' but rather the 'justification' of criminal behaviour which is at stake (Boutellier, 1993b: 325). Seen from this perspective criminology is part of the problem because, so he argues, it tends to 'rationalize' the crime problem (Boutellier, 1993a: 13). Again, this critique towards criminology is very different from the one we encountered in Chapter 2. Whereas Garland approaches criminology as a 'practical ingredient' in past and current crime control strategies, for Boutellier criminology's 'never-ending debate on the causes of crime' (Boutellier, 1993a: 72) is the major obstacle to treat crime as a moral problem.

Revisiting Durkheim: the victimalization of morality

Since the mid-1980s Boutellier has been writing about contemporary morality and its relation to crime. In a series of essays he touched upon a broad range of topics such as prostitution (Boutellier, 1987; Boutellier, 1991c), child sex abuse (Boutellier, 1989), the relation between religion and crime (Boutellier, 1990) and crime prevention (Boutellier, 1991a). In *Solidariteit en slachtofferschap* (1993) which was later translated as *Crime and Morality* (2000) Boutellier glued his various explorations into crime and morality together within a Durkheimian framework. Indeed, unsurprisingly in the light of his deep interest in questions of morality, Boutellier did not turn to Elias, Foucault or Marx-inspired perspectives but found in Durkheim his core author. As we will see throughout this chapter, a Durkheimian interest in, and perspective on, questions of morality and solidarity have coloured his writings throughout his career.

In *Solidariteit en slachtofferschap* Boutellier argued that we are nowadays living with a fragmented morality. Processes of secularization (which have disconnected morality from its religious source, that is, God), depillarization (whereby the former (religious and ideological) pillars lost their grip on Dutch society) and individualization have led to a withering away of a once taken-for-granted collective morality—relativism and diversity are the code words in a postmodern society. Yet, this does not imply that we have entered a normless epoch—a situation of 'anything goes'. There is not so much a decrease or disappearance of morality but rather it has entered a new stage: 'Secularization has not led to a moral decline, but to a shift from moral claims by the community to moral claims by the victim' (Boutellier, 2000a: 46). His aim, then, is 'to confront the postmodern condition with its implicit morality' (Boutellier, 2000a: 10).

Boutellier's central claim is that the victim is the glue that holds a postmodern, fragmented, and individualized society together: the victim is the hard core around which the construction of morality takes place. The organic solidarity of Durkheim has been replaced by a 'victimalized morality' or a 'victim-oriented morality' (Boutellier, 1993a: 30). As he put it: 'Solidarity in present-day secularized and pluralistic society is no longer linked to either God or a collectivity of the kind Durkheim has in mind, but to the position of the victim. This is what I call the *victimalization of morality*' (Boutellier, 2000a: 15–16). We can disagree on anything and we all may have our own private views on what a 'good life' might be and how a 'good society' should look, yet at a certain specific point we draw a line: when confronted with the suffering of the victim we recognize ourselves as members of a moral community. The knowledge of our own vulnerability and the rejection of human suffering, pain, cruelty and humiliation bind us together. This implies that morality comes to be formulated in negative terms: We may no longer jointly strive towards the 'good', but we still feel connected in our common rejection of the 'bad'. Richard Rorty's (1989) question 'Are you suffering?' 'has become the dominant question in the normative discourse that emerged after the disappearance of the ideologically founded ethics of obligation' (Boutellier, 2000a: xii).

For Boutellier the recent attention to victims, then, has to be understood against the background of a fragmented morality. In somewhat functionalist terms he argues that a morally fragmented culture *needs* victims who are easy to recognize (Boutellier, 2000a: 65). Or, as he has put it elsewhere: 'Criminal justice policy needs the victim like, until recently, it needed the churches' (Boutellier, 1993b: 320, author's translation). Seen from this perspective, victimization seems to fulfil an important function of social integration and it helps to generate consensus in pluralist times. In the rejection of suffering and cruelty we seem to be able to speak on the same terms. The morally unified society of yore did not 'need' the victim—for the fragmented and pluralist society of nowadays, however, it becomes a central symbolic figure that helps us express our shared avowal of suffering, humiliation and cruelty.

These processes of secularization, depillarization and individualization have important implications for criminal law. Its commandments and prohibitions are no longer grounded in, and backed up by, a taken-for-granted morality that is woven together and supported by means of ideology and religion. Cut loose from a once clear-cut social order criminal law needs to legitimate itself in other ways (Boutellier, 2000a: 15). Here the victim appears as a kind of *Deus ex machina*: in the suffering of the victim the criminal justice system finds a new way for legitimating its actions. Crime and criminal justice no longer are peripheral in terms of enunciating and reinforcing moral values: they have moved into the centre of contemporary society and play a pivotal role in 'pronouncing moral truth' (Boutellier, 2000a: 11). Seen from this perspective, criminal law needs to play a more important role by bringing into view the limitations of the 'free play of moral powers': 'In a pluralistic society, criminal justice occupies an active moral position' (Boutellier, 2000a: 18).

This also implies that offenders come to be seen as bearers of morality: 'Instead of writing them off as immoral individuals, they should be called to account for the moral premises they are working from' (Boutellier, 2000a: 42–3). Boutellier refers to the offender as the 'postmodern criminal' who has taken the place of the 'deviant'. In a morally pluralist society (where there are hardly any clear-cut norms to deviate from) the notion 'deviance' has lost its meaning. Instead of the earlier 'deviant' who challenged the moral community we now encounter the 'postmodern criminal' who subordinates the other (that is, his victim) to his own liberal self-creation in a cruel, humiliating or harming way. Criminal behaviour, then, is not rejected because it is deviant with respect to the norms of the community, but rather because the offender places himself outside of communication and, in doing so, endangers his own right to speak (Boutellier, 1991b: 128–31; Boutellier, 1995: 29).

However, not all forms of suffering are granted the status of victimhood. Boutellier describes two processes of what he terms 'victimalization', that is 'a cultural process in which the suffering that is granted the status of victimhood is subject to change' (Boutellier, 2000a: 58). Indeed, for Boutellier victimhood is a dynamic moral criterion. His first case study was the victimalization of the sexually-abused child. Since the 1970s the moral meaning of child sex abuse has changed dramatically. Due to a number of developments (such as the understanding of incest in sexual rather than in reproductive terms; the role of feminism in bringing the sexually-abused child into view as a victim of male power; the individualization of children and the sentimentalization of the child-parent relationship; and changes in therapeutic practice) sexual child abuse became a hot topic throughout the 1980s leading to the victimalization of sexually-abused children.

In the case of prostitution the opposite happened. Here Boutellier identifies a process of 'de-victimalization'. The existence of prostitution in the Netherlands came to be generally accepted: the brothel prohibition was repealed and prostitution was legalized in order to improve and better regulate working conditions. The moral meaning of prostitution changed and the prostitute no longer came to be seen as a victim (Boutellier, 2000a: 115). According to Boutellier one can therefore speak of a 'subjectification of sexual morality' which forms part of 'a more general process in moral societal development'. This victimalized morality is 'far more concentrated on the issue of subjectivity in terms of suffering and humiliation' (Boutellier, 1991c: 209). And since the prostitute no longer is seen (or sees herself) as a victim of male sexuality a process of devictimalization could set in which, eventually, led to the repeal of the prohibition on brothelkeeping.

From diagnosis to intervention

As we saw earlier, Boutellier's interest in the morality of our times grew out of problems he encountered in the field. His 'diagnosis of western culture', as he put it in the foreword to the English translation of his book, was meant to provide 'points of departure for further normative reflection' (Boutellier, 2000a: xii). Boutellier's explicit aim was (and is) to make his diagnosis relevant for designing and redesigning crime policy. Indeed, in *Solidariteit en slachtofferschap* Boutellier indicated on numerous occasions that what he observes and analyses (what *is*) also points us to the way ahead (what *should* be). In the closing chapters of the book, and on various other occasions, he relied in particular on Richard Rorty (1989) to clarify and justify why a victimalized morality is also something we should embrace in times of a fragmented morality (see also Boutellier, 1991b; Boutellier, 1992). Rorty speaks of the 'liberal ironist': 'The ironist knows his most central convictions and desires are contingent. But as a liberal, he...is of the opinion that cruelty is the worst thing people can do to each other' (Boutellier, 2000a: 125–6). The condemnation of suffering and humiliation, which is already implicit in the liberal political philosophy but which came to be concealed behind 'the bureaucratic and politicized concepts of the welfare state' needs to be relived and emphasized and can lead us, so Boutellier tells us, out of the present 'moral crisis' without lapsing into 'nostalgic morality' or 'unrealistic radicalism' (Boutellier, 2000a: 142).

During his work on his PhD dissertation Boutellier was (since 1985) editor of *Justitiële Verkenningen,* a journal published by the WODC[2] which is tied to the Dutch Ministry of Justice. In the mid-1990s Boutellier changed position and became policy advisor for the Dutch Ministry of Justice. As general policy coordinator at the Prevention, Youth and Sanction Policy Directorate (*coördinator Algemeen Beleid bij de Directie Preventie, Jeugd en Sanctiebeleid*) he played an important role in developing community safety and community prevention projects. This policy function, so he wrote in the foreword to the English translation of his book, offered him the opportunity to initiate and support initiatives in line with the thesis of his book (Boutellier, 2000a: xii). Indeed, Boutellier argued that the government had become 'the bearer of our society's morality, and should make every effort to fulfill its task with care' (Boutellier, 2000a: 154). The state needs to relate in a credible way to the 'moral capital' of a culture (Boutellier, 1997b: 129). Occupying one of the many chairs of policy-maker himself, Boutellier also perceived it to be *his* responsibility to translate the normative message from his research into daily practice.

In his function as policy advisor Boutellier was in charge of the project 'Justice in the Neighbourhood' (*Justitie in de buurt*) which

[2] WODC stands for 'Wetenschappelijk Onderzoek-en Documentatie Centrum' ('Scientific Research and Documentation Centre').

started in 1997. In a number of urban areas offices were opened where the prosecutor and other judicial institutions could operate in a problem-oriented way, close to the public and other official bodies (see Boutellier, 1996a, 1997a, 1998a, 1999a, 1999b).[3] For our discussion in this book the details of these community safety programmes are not that important: the interesting thing to observe is, as we will elaborate further on in this chapter, how Boutellier's analyses of recent social and penal change—or what he (significantly) prefers to refer to as 'diagnoses'—have always been intertwined with a willingness to intervene. Boutellier is like a therapist who puts society 'on the couch' in order to come up with an appropriate remedy. His academic work has always been inspired by a deeply-ingrained and openly-expressed aspiration to make it useful for practical intervention. Indeed, initiatives such as 'Justice in the Neighbourhood' are, so he argues, 'a necessary and inevitable consequence of the new equilibration between law and morality' (Boutellier, 1996b: 17). In that sense, his approach towards his topic of research is remarkably different from Garland's and Pratt's which we have encountered in the previous chapters. There we saw how Garland's choice to remain as close as possible to 'the integrity of the empirical object' and Pratt's prophetical intentions have shaped their scholarship in specific directions. The particular (practical) choices Boutellier has made throughout his life-course have equally impacted upon his scholarship. We will return to these implications towards the end of the chapter. Now we turn to another important phase in his intellectual development.

Crime and Punishment in the Safety Utopia

After his work for *Solidariteit en slachtofferschap* and during his activities at the WODC and the Ministry of Justice Boutellier was connected to the Free University of Amsterdam. This link with the academic world kept, so he argued, the 'intellectual fire' burning (Boutellier, 2002a: viii). In numerous publications he

[3] For the same reason Boutellier also endorsed the idea of 'Communities that Care', that is, clearly steered multi-agency programmes designed to improve the situation at the level of problematic neighbourhoods. The concept was developed by two criminologists (David Hawkins and Richard Catalano) who, on the basis of a risk/strength analysis, plead for a form of criminologically-inspired community-building (see Boutellier, 1998b; Boutellier, 2000b).

gradually expanded and, in the light of new developments in the area of crime and unsafety, updated the thesis he had developed in the late 1980s and early 1990s. This would, eventually, lead to the publication of *De veiligheidsutopie* (2002) which was later translated as *The Safety Utopia* (2004).

From crime to unsafety: the safety utopia

In the preface to *The Safety Utopia* Boutellier referred to his second book as a sequel and formulated the connection with his earlier work in the following words: 'The victimalized culture has given birth to a safety utopia, that is the insight underlying this book' (Boutellier, 2004a: ix). The major change of the 1990s, so Boutellier argues, is the transformation of crime into a safety issue: the current culture can be described 'in terms of the desire for safety' (Boutellier, 2004a: 1). This desire does not come out of the blue. On the one hand safety has become 'one of the major social problems of the early twenty-first century': 'This is evident from population surveys where people list crime as their greatest concern, ranking above the environment, health and the economy. It is similarly evident from the attention in the media and the political arena. And it is clear from the attention focused on the criminal justice system' (Boutellier, 2004a: 31). On the other hand, the need for safety emerges in a context of 'vitality': a context of an 'unprecedented and uninhibited sense of freedom'. According to Boutellier people live nowadays in a world replete of opportunities for immediate gratification of needs and self-fulfilment. The 'need for safety' and the 'vital drive' are interrelated and emerge out of the same social conditions which Boutellier, following the German sociologist Ulrich Beck (1992), describes as the birth of a risk society. This situation gives rise to the safety utopia: a utopian desire for a convergence of maximum freedom and optimum protection.[4] This utopia needs to be distinguished from earlier modern utopias: 'contemporary utopian desire has assumed a different form than in the modern era. It is no longer a matter of equality, it is now

[4] The notion of the 'safety utopia' is nicely captured in Boutellier's image of the bungee-jumper (which also features on the cover of both the original book in Dutch and its English translation): bungee jumping is an act of expressive and hedonistic freedom (the vitality) but one is only prepared to take the risk on the assumption that the elastic rope will not break.

a matter of safety...In the risk society, the aim is not to achieve good, the aim is to prevent evil' (Boutellier, 2004a: 38; see also Boutellier, 1999c). In this (negative) formulation of the safety utopia resonates Boutellier's discussion of the victimalization of morality which we discussed earlier: not our striving to a common good, but our joint rejection of suffering, humiliation and cruelty binds us together: 'In a postmodern, vital culture that has lost the illusion of coherence, all the imagination can focus on, is what we reject. The utopian desire is the result of the reversal of this notion: *safety unites*' (Boutellier, 2004a: 8).

To illustrate this safety utopia Boutellier discusses at length two important features of current times: the attention given to sex offenders and the reactions to what is perceived to be 'senseless' violence. One crucial aspect of the vitality of contemporary culture is the libertarian sexual morality. Sexuality is all-present in public life: in video clips, advertisements, television commercials and, especially, on the Internet. There is an unprecedented openness to talk about sex; and multiple ways of experiencing lust—including pornography—have become acceptable and normal aspects of daily life. Following Giddens (1992) Boutellier makes the link with identity politics: choosing your own sexual lifestyle has become a defining feature of the vitality of contemporary society. Traditional mores and views no longer keep the sexual drive in check. However, at the same time there are much stricter rules for daily sexual interactions. And here the paradox of the safety utopia enters the picture and gives rise to an extremely complicated moral situation: 'erotic lust can be freely experienced within a situation that makes increasing demands on our self-control' (Boutellier, 2004a: 57). In the 1980s the focus was on sexual abuse in domestic settings. A decade later child pornography and child sex abuse were at the centre of attention. In the (what Boutellier terms) 'pornographic context' of sexual liberation the sex offender—and in particular the sexual child abuser—comes to personify the longing for safety.

The second example that Boutellier offers is the particular ways in which in recent years people have responded to 'senseless' violence, that is, forms of violence that seem to have a random character and that seem to happen without a clear-cut motivation. 'Senseless' violence is a side effect of the vital nature of the current risk culture. In view of the numbers (at one point Boutellier argues that there are about one million incidents every year in the

Netherlands) violence has become a normal aspect and needs to be understood against a vital background wherein wounded self-esteem leads to potentially violent escalations of inter-personal conflicts. Senseless violence forms part of this bigger problem of violent crime, so Boutellier argues. Such extreme manifestations of random violence, however, provoke strong emotional reactions. The silent marches and citizens' committees against violence are a clear manifestation of this. In the late 1990s (until July 2000) there were twenty-two silent marches in the Netherlands which generated enormous media attention and mobilized most of the time between a few hundred to a little more than a thousand participants. In addition, he identified sixteen committees against violence which grouped a few hundreds of people who were actively involved in civil action against violence.

In his discussion of this phenomenon Boutellier speaks again with a Durkheimian voice: 'Senseless violence makes people identify with the victims and their loved ones. Social cohesion is constructed to temporarily surround them' (Boutellier, 2004a: 11). Indeed, his Durkheimian lens makes him probe for cohesion and solidarity. Silent marches and citizens' initiatives provide opportunities for collective action, public mourning and the joint memorialization of victims. Participants in these initiatives identify with the victims and their loved ones and also politicians and public figures share in this collective rejection of violence. Against the vital background of violence, then, the desire for safety comes to be expressed in new ways.

Within the safety utopia the demand for criminal justice is greater than ever. According to Boutellier this demand derives in part from the fact that crime became a more conspicuous part of everyday life. He points to three factual observations: an increase in the crime problem (a ten-fold increase in police figures since 1960); an increase in the sensitivity to crime; and an increase in the political meaning of the crime problem for the state (that is, the legitimacy of the nation state comes under threat because, in holding the monopoly of violence, it promises safety to its citizens within its borders). These three developments have put extra pressure on the criminal justice system: 'the dominance of the safety issue has led to a shift in expectations as regards criminal justice. It is perceived as an urgent agency for establishing the social order.... the normative function of the criminal justice system is vast. Criminal justice has become people's business' (Boutellier,

2004a: 97). It has moved from the ideal-type position of an '*ultimum remedium*' institution to an 'urgent' one.

However, the increasing 'demand' is not being—and can never be—matched by a suitable 'supply'. Boutellier speaks of a 'criminal justice paradox' (see also Boutellier, 1996b): the meaning that criminal justice receives in current times cannot be lived up to. First, in a quantitative sense, the growth of the criminal justice system has not been able to satisfy the need. On the contrary: in view of the increasing crime problem relatively fewer crimes are being solved and dealt with by the system. Second, the supply is also restricted in a qualitative sense: the criminal justice system simply cannot do much because of some inherent features. The system often responds too late, it is extremely slow, and sanctions are generally not very effective. Third, the criminal justice system is limited because of dogmatic reasons. The idea of the '*ultimum remedium*' implies that it is designed as a 'last resort' that needs to be avoided as much as possible in order to restrict the exercise of state power to a minimum. It was never meant to be an institution to create order.

Punishment and the 'celebration of morality' in the safety utopia

In the *Safety Utopia* Boutellier, again, explicitly (and against critical, Foucauldian and Weberian perspectives in the sociology of punishment) embraced Durkheim as his theoretical guide. For Boutellier punishment is first and foremost a 'morally expressive enterprise' (Boutellier, 2004a: 109). Nevertheless the moral context in which the criminal justice system operates has deeply changed which resulted *inter alia* in the criminal justice paradox that we touched upon earlier. In this section we discuss the two responses—rationalization and moralization—that have been formulated to the criminal justice paradox. Unsurprisingly in the light of his Durkheimian background, Boutellier has devoted much more attention to the moralizing tendency, more in particular the place of 'new' moral practices that have in recent years developed in and around the criminal justice system. We then explore his Durkheim-inspired idea of the necessity of a criminal justice system and what Boutellier refers to as a civilized need to punish. We finish with a discussion of his model of 'governing security'.

Rationalization and moralization of criminal justice policy

The first response to the 'criminal justice paradox' is the rationalization of criminal justice. A business-like approach has pervaded the criminal justice system. Victims or potential victims are seen as 'customers' whereas the administration of sanctions against offenders are 'products': 'The criminal justice chain does not essentially differ in its approach from any other business process' (Boutellier, 2004a: 111). The second response is moralization and receives much more attention in Boutellier's writings. The criminal justice system has an important symbolic meaning as *pièce de résistance* in times of fragmented morality. But it fails to absorb the increasing demand. It is against this background, so Boutellier argues, that new moral practices can develop. Boutellier refers to 'the small morality' *(de kleine moraal)* that typifies these practices which exist in relation to the normative systems of police and judiciary (Boutellier, 2001c: 27). This 'small morality' encompasses interactive, emotional and intuitive reactions to crime. In recent years in and around the criminal justice system a number of such moral practices emerged, such as community service, compensation, victim assistance and support, neighbourhood crime prevention initiatives, neighbourhood mediation projects, victim-offender mediation.[5] Boutellier groups them together under the umbrella terms 'community justice' and 'restorative justice'. All of them are 'aimed at preventing escalation, at developing and confirming norms, at reparation of damage sustained by the victim or the community, and at reintegration of offenders' (Boutellier, 2001b: 76). For Boutellier these developments 'indicate a moralization of the safety problem. In and beyond criminal justice, practices are developing that formulate an answer closer to the normative nature of the criminal act, that take into account the motives of the offender, the suffering of the victim and the interests of the community' (Boutellier, 2001a: 79).

The recent interest in restorative justice developments, then, is not explained by the resurgence of shame and the release of emotions that used to be kept under control by the 'civilized' penal arrangements as Pratt suggests, but by the transformations of

[5] 'Beyond punishment: moral practices around the criminal law' ('De straf voorbij: morele praktijken rondom het strafrecht') was also the title of a conference that was organized on 15 March 2001. Boutellier was one of the editors of the conference proceedings (see Boutellier *et al*, 2001).

morality. For Boutellier restorative justice forms part of those new moral practices that could develop in the wake of the victimalization of morality and the criminal justice paradox: 'restorative justice is an attempt to add a morally inspired response to the scale of interventions which the criminal justice system so poorly delivers' (Boutellier, 2002b: 29). In restorative interventions the offender is addressed as a moral subject who has harmed his victim and he is held responsible and accountable for his act. Against the background of a victimalized morality restorative justice is able to re-invent the moral character of crime. Rorty's question 'Are you suffering?' is, so to speak, at the centre of a restorative setting and, with Durkheim, the norm is communicated and reaffirmed (see also Boutellier and Steketee, 2006: 24).

The ghost of anomie and the civilized need to punish

For Boutellier the term 'civilization' has a different meaning than for Pratt. In Chapter 3 we saw that Pratt uses the term in an Eliasian sense. For Boutellier, however, civilization refers to the freedoms and liberal achievements that we tend to cherish and that are endangered if we underestimate or fail to acknowledge the problem of crime (Boutellier, 2002a: viii). Society moves itself into a dangerous position if it does not address the crime and unsafety problem in a morally appropriate way. The Durkheimian ghost of an anomic state of normlessness seems to be ever-present in the safety utopia. For Boutellier we do not need a 'bureaucratic buffer' to keep dangerous emotions away and to create the institutional conditions for the 'civilization' of punishment but rather a 'civilization buffer' (*beschavingsbuffer*) that mediates between optimum self-fulfilment and a minimum of self-control (Boutellier, 2004a: 26).

In line with Durkheim, then, Boutellier argues that both crime and punishment are indispensable and functional features of a morally healthy society. 'In keeping with Durkheim, crime should...be viewed as a vital component of the morality of a society because it forces it to formulate and reformulate its moral principles' (Boutellier, 2000a: 146; see also Boutellier, 1991a: 131). And like Durkheim who argued that punishment reinforces the values of a society and plays a crucial role in establishing social cohesion, so Boutellier stresses the need for a criminal justice system as the normative hard-core of a vulnerable victimalized morality. The organic solidarity of Durkheim has been replaced by a victimalized morality but punishment continues to fulfil its role in the morality play of 'good' against 'evil'. Moreover, in the safety utopia the criminal justice system tends to become increasingly involved in this play: its (ideological and religious) back-up of yore has evaporated and, as a result, the criminial justice system has moved out of the periphery where it used to reside until a few decades ago. Here lies the key to understanding Boutellier's view on penal change. The 'call for more and harsher criminal justice' emerges out of 'the underlying need for a normative structure, within which our historically unprecedented freedom can be enjoyed in a safe manner' (Boutellier, 2001b: 76; see also Boutellier, 2000f). The strengthening of the criminal justice system, then, is one response to the criminal justice paradox and developments in morality (Boutellier, 2004c: 12). Indeed, given the sense of urgency the criminal justice system comes to play a much more central role in the normative construction of community. 'As society loses its communality, a stronger normative function is attributed to criminal justice' (Boutellier, 2004a: 102).

In recent times this 'need to punish' for the sake of morality has come to play a central role in what Boutellier refers to as a 'civilizing mission'. The hardening of the penal climate, then, does not have to be interpreted as a set-back in the civilization process. It does not so much follow from an irrational punitive need that has broken free but rather from the idea that leaving crime unpunished, eventually, will lead to the erosion of our modern-day civilization (Boutellier, 2004b: 40). The criminal justice system is being seen as the 'guardian of civilization' and fulfils a moral duty in punishing rule breakers (Boutellier, 2003: 228). If we want to prevent society from lapsing into a detrimental state of anomie, so Boutellier tells us, then we need to punish. This 'civilizing mission' has to be seen against the background of the changing meaning of crime: the moral rejection of rule-breaking in view of the victim's suffering tends to legitimate a tougher approach. The offender is no longer seen as the victim of factors beyond his control but as 'a person who makes the wrong choices' and this new identity, so Boutellier argues, leads to less understanding of his acts and makes us feel less compassionate for his situation (Boutellier, 2005d: 136–8). Confronted with the suffering of the emancipated victim, also the will to punish seems to have been emancipated.

What Pratt, then, from an Eliasian perspective, interprets as the decivilizing of punishment is, from Boutellier's moral approach, exactly the opposite: a 'civilizing mission' that wants law-breakers who cause victims suffering to be punished, is being identified as the moral driving force behind more punitive developments. Boutellier argues that such a mission runs against practical limitations: the criminal justice system can, in view of the criminal justice paradox, never fully satisfy the demands of this 'civilizing mission' (Boutellier, 2003: 229). Restorative justice can, to a certain extent (and only next to the criminal justice system), provide an answer to this problem, so he argues, but then it should offer a 'powerful alternative' (Boutellier, 2003: 229) which also satisfies this punitive sentiment. Nevertheless, despite the fact that the Dutch criminal justice system has been growing continuously over the past decades, a further expansion seems to be unavoidable and, in Boutellier's opinion, also desirable: 'The criminal justice system fulfils an important normative function and for this reason alone, it should be faithfully maintained. It is wise to somewhat expand its function as regards the size of the apparatus and the competence of the Police and Justice Departments so that it can continue to fulfil this normative function' (Boutellier, 2004a: 126).[6]

Governing security

Earlier in this chapter we saw how Boutellier, as policy-maker, was closely involved in community safety and prevention initiatives in the Netherlands. The projects 'Justice in the Neighbourhood' and 'Communities that Care' were, so he argued later, 'two examples of an increasing convergence of the social sector and the judicial

[6] Boutellier seems to have changed his opinion on the relationship between the victimalization of morality and increasing punitiveness. In a 1994 chapter for the book *Hoe punitief is Nederland?* ('How punitive is the Netherlands?') he tried to refute the hypothesis of Dutch authors such as Buruma (1994) that the victimalization process leads to a harsher treatment of offenders. Here he argued that the 'emancipated victim' is not all that revengeful and that it is far from certain that victimalization would lead to more punishment (Boutellier, 1994a). In recent years, however, he suggests that the increasing reliance on criminal law can be seen as a 'civilizing mission' in line with our new moral understanding of crime. And whereas in the mid-1990s he argued that victimalization can (and should) go hand in hand with a 'reserved criminal law' (*terughoudend strafrecht*) (Boutellier 1994a) or a 'minimal criminal justice system' (*strafrechtelijk ministelstel*) (Boutellier, 1995) he now, despite the considerable and continuing growth of the Dutch criminal justice system since he made these statements more than a decade ago, pleads for an even further expansion.

criminal law enforcement' (Boutellier, 2001a: 374). This idea that social and criminal policy are converging has been identified by Boutellier as one of the most important (and to be supported) developments in recent times which is, as he sees it, closely linked to his diagnosis of contemporary morality: 'On the "safety" theme a new moral consensus is maturing which among other things leads to a rearrangement of welfare and criminal justice institutions' (Boutellier, 2001a: 362–3). The social sector needs to assume more emphatically a normative position—their 'normative consciousness', as Boutellier puts it, needs to be stimulated (Boutellier, 2001a: 375): 'a normative élan is required whereby citizens, social organizations, the local authorities and the police and judicial authorities are held accountable for their responsibilities' (Boutellier, 2001a: 376; see also Boutellier, 2004a: 127–30). In his inaugural lecture 'More than Safe' (*Meer dan veilig*) for the Chair of Police and Safety Studies, delivered on 7 April 2005 at the University of Amsterdam (Boutellier, 2005a), and the third (expanded) edition of *De veiligheidsutopie* (Boutellier, 2005b)[7] he has further elaborated his ideas of a 'democratic safety policy'.

Boutellier (2005a: 22–4) introduces the image of the soccer team to picture his programme for society-wide governance of security. This team has 'to play a defensive game': 'In goal is the criminal justice system; this goalkeeper hears the balls flying around his ears. Being in this position he coaches the defensive line in order to position the defenders in a more effective way. This defensive line is made up of institutions that deal with risks—from private security companies to youth care for children at risk and from community policing to restorative justice approaches. This defensive line has to be supportive to the midfield that exists of organizations that play a general social role like schools, business corporations and social work agencies' (Boutellier, 2006a: 39). This depiction may lead to the impression that the criminal justice system comes at the end—the classical '*ultimum remedium*' idea. However, as Boutellier argues elsewhere, the criminal justice system is a normative reference-point—not an end-point—in the new safety

[7] This third edition of *De veiligheidsutopie* contains an 'Addendum' entitled 'On Governing a Fearful Society' ('Over het besturen van een bange samenleving') (Boutellier, 2005a: 233–55). In the second edition Boutellier already included an extra chapter 'The Coloured Safety Utopia' ('De gekleurde veiligheidsutopie') dealing with ethnicity, crime, and unsafety. (These chapters are not available in the English translation of the book.)

paradigm (Boutellier, 2005e: 40). Or, to put it in terms of his soccer metaphor: the goalkeeper can never be exchanged for a field player—to do so would jeopardize the game of the whole team.

The new moral practices, then, are forming an integral part of this programme—they are, so to speak, players in Boutellier's soccer team. In putting it like this, Boutellier seems to distance himself from restorative justice advocates who strive towards an independent model (the so-called maximalist position in the restorative justice literature). Instead of perceiving it as a countermovement in opposition to the criminal justice system he proposes to think of it as instrumental, that is, as another response (amongst many others) to the crime problem: 'An instrumental use of this opportunity seems to me to be a much more challenging perspective than sticking to the idea of having discovered another utopian world' (Boutellier, 2002b: 30). Indeed, as he argued more recently: 'Restorative justice is not so much an alternative as well as another strategy in security politics' (Boutellier, 2006a: 26).

Discussion

In his foreword to *The Safety Utopia* Sir Anthony Bottoms wrote that the book 'belongs on the bookshelf alongside other social-scientific analyses of our times such as Anthony Giddens's *The Consequences of Modernity* (1990), Richard Ericson and Kevin Haggerty's *Policing the Risk Society* (1997) and David Garland's *The Culture of Control* (2001)' (Bottoms, 2004: xi). As is to be expected from a foreword (which often is solicited by the author and, therefore, almost by definition praises a book) Bottoms subdued potential points for disagreement. However, the particular conventions that are at play in writing forewords are not the only reason for this nice compliment by one of Britain's most respected criminologists: on earlier occasions Bottoms had already welcomed *Crime and Morality* (2000), the English translation of *Solidariteit en slachtofferschap*. He was especially pleased by Boutellier's moral approach to crime (Bottoms, 2002) and the explanation he offered to account for the attractivity of restorative justice 'because it helps to provide an element of *normative clarification* in a morally changing society' (Bottoms, 2003: 103). With Bottoms we agree that Boutellier's moral approach and his reinvention of Durkheim for present times adds an original contribution to the debate on social and penal change.

However, on the basis of our study of Boutellier's intellectual life-course there are some crucial aspects of his thinking (and acting) that deserve some further comment. In addition, like Garland (but mostly for other reasons), also Boutellier's work has been received with a mixed response—especially in the Netherlands.[8] This may have gone unnoticed to English-language readers who neither have access to the major part of his publications nor to the various responses from Dutch-speaking criminologists and criminal lawyers. In particular for criminologists who cherish and value their discipline, reading Boutellier is not always a pleasant experience. Next to his recurring statements that aetiological criminology has done more damage than good (in terms of it being held responsible for obfuscating the moral meaning of crime) and is, in any case, of little use, Boutellier makes numerous other observations on criminology which tend to give a rather grim (mis)representation of the discipline, for example: (Dutch) critical criminology has slowed down theoretical development (Boutellier, 2004a: 122, note 6); unlike 'safety researchers' (*veiligheidsonderzoekers*) criminologists are not well-equipped to talk about safety because they have to restrict themselves to the study of crime (Boutellier, 2005a: 31, note 76); criminologists fail to acknowledge the 'reality of crime' (e.g. Boutellier, 2001a: 377–8); criminologists are not asking fundamental questions on crime and safety (Boutellier, 2004a: 139); criminology seems 'to have gotten completely bogged down in a technical, control-focused approach to the safety issue' (Boutellier, 2004a: 140); and so forth. Boutellier does not spare the 'criminological community' (a term that he, in one of those other polemical moments, found 'somewhat hilarious' (Boutellier, 2007c: 194)[9]) and, as we will see towards the end of this chapter, has proposed his own vision of what criminology should be, that is, a reflexive policy science.

[8] When he addressed his English-language audience Boutellier, somewhat myopically and self-indulgently, only highlighted the positive responses to *De veiligheidsutopie*, arguing that it was received with 'unexpected enthusiasm' which was 'almost too much to hope for' and that he, in view of the murder of Dutch politician Pim Fortuyn, had completed the book at 'the right moment' (Boutellier, 2004a: ix).

[9] This comment was directed at Willem de Haan who had used this term when he accused Boutellier of seriously misrepresenting Dutch criminology in *De veiligheidsutopie* (see De Haan, 2003).

Durkheim, solidarity, and the sociology of victimization

In putting the moral meaning of crime at the centre of his work Boutellier was somewhat ahead of his time. The mid-1980s were the heyday of a (often Foucault-inspired) social control tradition in criminology. Unlike Garland and (in particular) Pratt, Boutellier was never part of this research tradition. Inspired by his experiences with young delinquents he started to ask questions related to 'good' and 'evil', and aimed to address practical problems as to how to find and communicate a moral position in times of fragmentation. These issues were not that popular in the social control literature. Indeed, as he argued, when he started writing and thinking about morality in the 1980s this was rather an 'obscure theme' (Boutellier, 2004c: 8). At a time when the control of crime and deviance was at the forefront of the sociological agenda in criminology, it was not that obvious to plead for a moral perspective which approaches the offender not as a victim of the control apparatus but rather as a morally free individual.

In the meantime a lot has changed. After the publication of *Crime, Shame and Reintegration* Braithwaite (1989) was named a 'new Durkheim' (Scheff, 1990) because he drew attention to the moral, denunciatory component of social control. This book has had a deep impact on theoretical criminology and provided a significant stimulus for crime policy developments, in particular in the form of restorative justice initiatives. The upsurge of interest in the role of emotions in relation to crime and punishment also has led to a revival of interest in Durkheimian themes (see e.g. Karstedt, 2006). And the same holds true of the philosophy of punishment with influential work such as Antony Duff's (2001), centred around punishment as a mode of moral communication.

Durkheim seems to be back and it is one of the main contributions of Boutellier that he has been able (persistently) to bring him back into view.

Bureaucracy, science, and morality

Garland once proposed to investigate how modern administrative rationality and bureaucracy have impacted upon contemporary punishment, and how questions of value have come to be replaced by questions of technical efficacy (Garland, 1990b: 7). Also in his discussion of the 'criminologies of everyday life' Garland highlights the 'demoralizing' effect of situational crime prevention

(Garland, 1998a: 1146). Garland neither expands on these moral implications of current crime control developments nor does he give any normative evaluation of them. Also Pratt is well aware of the moral costs of certain crime control strategies. Processes of bureaucratization not only made the 'civilizing' of punishment possible but they also tended to push moral questions into the background. In line with Bauman and Christie, Pratt points to the moral indifference that came to be produced by closing off practices of punishment from the public. Involvement with penal matters declined and, in fact, formed one of the preconditions for humanizing the prison system. Because of this, as we have seen, Pratt seems to hold a somewhat ambivalent opinion about bureaucracy and expert-led crime policy: on the one hand, these seem to create a shield against revengeful attitudes towards offenders yet, on the other hand, they also lead towards a 'silencing' of other voices on punishment (in particular the voices of persons being punished themselves) and create, by making people morally indifferent to questions of punishment, the possibility that 'behind the closed doors' of the penal bureaucracy inhumane practices take place which tend to escape public debate.

Unlike Garland and Pratt, Boutellier puts morality at the centre of analysis and critique. *Contra* Garland's (reluctant) embracing of the new criminologies of everyday life in what we termed in Chapter 2 his 'personal adaptation strategy', Boutellier is much more critical of such criminologies and the practices they inform. The crime prevention initiatives in the late 1980s were indicted for their demoralizing consequences and his critique of rational choice theory was inspired by a similar set of concerns (Boutellier, 1993b). And *contra* Pratt's somewhat ambivalent position on the role of bureaucracy, Boutellier's critique is much more direct: bureaucracy and its framing of problems in a technical language, geared towards the twin (internal) goals of efficiency and efficacy, 'kills' morality and, thereby, strips society of adequate responses to that essential need for norm-confirmation, as evinced in Durkheim's theory—it turns criminal law into an instrument of social engineering and neglects the moral role it needs to play in a morally healthy society (see Boutellier, 1993b; Boutellier, 1994c). Whereas for Pratt the current increase in punishment is partly the result of the declining influence of bureaucracy, for Boutellier, the modern bureaucracy is partly responsible for the current crime problem and its morally inadequate penal responses. It has neglected the crucial moral role of the criminal law and needs to revive and rethink (that is, 'victimalize') that moral role if it is to come up with an answer that is suitable to the current problems.

For Boutellier, then, not only the 'morality of citizens' but also the 'ethics of the state' should be at the centre of public debate on crime (Boutellier, 1993b: 318). This is why he emphasizes the responsibility the government needs to face up to as the 'bearer of our society's morality'. If it wants to regain its legitimacy the state needs to rethink its normative position in a morally fragmented world. The strategies of 'radical rationalization' (turning government into a company) and a negative 'moralization of citizens' are bound to fail (Boutellier, 1994c). Seen from Boutellier's perspective also the idea of a 'bureaucratic buffer' is undesirable: instead of designing crime policy over the heads of citizens their moral involvement with issues of crime and punishment should be kept alive (Boutellier and Van Stokkom, 1995: 109). It is against this background that we need to understand his enthusiasm for projects such as 'Justice in the Neighbourhood', that is, decentralized and locally-embedded responses to problems of crime and unsafety (Boutellier, 1998a: 176–7; Boutellier, 1999a: 57), and his plea for conceptualizing governing security as a society-wide project: for the sake of a society's moral health questions related to crime and punishment are simply too important to leave them to the experts.

Morality, suffering, and victims of crime

For Pratt over the past decades a 'culture of intolerance' has come into existence: sensibilities to the suffering inflicted on offenders have hardened and we no longer seem to worry too much about what happens to them. However, in the same time period victims of crime also came into the picture. It is precisely this development that Boutellier highlights and that leads him to a totally different assessment of social and penal change. Whereas Boutellier does not use the term 'a culture of intolerance' one might infer from his account that from his position it would mean something rather different: Boutellier argues that we have become more intolerant towards human suffering—in particular the victim of crime's suffering—because of the victimalization of morality. For Pratt there is a declining sensitivity towards the suffering of offenders; for Boutellier there is an increasing sensitivity towards the suffering of victims (see also Boutellier, 1998c: 17). The main characters in their stories are totally different and lead them to divergent interpretations. According to Boutellier our increasing intolerance of crime leads us to call the postmodern criminal to account who, then, might get punished more harshly because, in causing suffering to the victim, he offends our stronger sensibility towards our fellow citizens who suffer from unjustified encroachments upon their private lives.

This also implies that the meaning of a general denominator as a 'culture of intolerance' is much more ambivalent than we learn from Pratt's linear 'decivilizing' story: if we read both authors together then it becomes much more difficult to speak in terms of (the lack of) a general sensibility to suffering—apparently our empathy with the hardship that others have to endure is conditional. As we will see further on, Boutellier's identification with the suffering of the victim and, in particular, the assumed cohesion-generating aspects of it, are problematic but for now it is important to note that Boutellier sensitizes us to a crucial aspect for understanding contemporary responses to crime: not only the suffering inflicted upon the bodies of the offender but also the suffering caused to the victim needs to be included in the picture—and this picture tends to become much more complicated and ambivalent than some recent accounts in the sociology of punishment present it to us.

The need to respond to crime, for the sake of morality

In line with Durkheim, Boutellier highlights the positive function that punishment fulfils: punishment clarifies and confirms a society's norms. In recent discussions on penal change this central insight of the sociology of punishment hardly receives any attention: confronted with the worldwide growth of penal systems, scholars working in this field have been inclined to focus on the sheer negativity of punishment, that is, its exclusionary and punitive aspects. Boutellier reminds us that a society needs to respond to crime if it wants to stay morally healthy and avoid lapsing into a state of anomie. He even, as we have seen, interprets this as a mark of 'civilization'. This sounds provocative, and later in this chapter we will touch upon Boutellier's silence on *how* this need has been satisfied in practice, but there is nevertheless a kernel of truth in it: a society that remains indifferent to transgressions of rules that are codified in criminal law might put its continuing existence in danger.

From this perspective Boutellier can also be much more positive about alternative sanctions and the new moral practices that he identifies: the standard critique of 'net-widening' needs to be qualified if these practices, as Boutellier suggests, fulfil a function of norm clarification and confirmation. Punitive responses are, in view of Boutellier's criminal justice paradox, always limited and the new penal practices that have entered the field have, from his perspective, not merely simply enlarged the 'fishing net' of the penal system but they also have provided new ways to communicate a society's normative boundaries. This is, indeed, why he welcomes restorative justice initiatives which tend to fulfil such a moral function *irrespective of* whether they have acted (or whether they are meant to act) as alternatives for classical criminal justice responses.

Limits to Boutellier's use of Durkheim

There are, however, limits to Boutellier's use of Durkheim. In this section we will first discuss how his moral reductionism obscures other important processes that are at work and, consequently, makes his hypothesis of the victimalization of morality less persuasive. We will then elaborate somewhat further the preconditions for creating cohesion around victimization and the role of struggles for recognition.

Moral reductionism

The impact of developments in morality upon our perceptions of crime and punishment and how we deal with them, are at the centre of Boutellier's research agenda. This does not mean that he is not aware of other interpretations. On the contrary: over the years Boutellier has continuously and explicitly defended his moral approach against other perspectives. Authors who refer to the 'moral panics' surrounding certain forms of victimization; who draw attention to the development of a 'victim culture'; who highlight the exclusionary aspects of current control arrangements; who point to the role of mass media and politics as an amplificatory factor in the current obsession with crime and unsafety; and so forth have encountered Boutellier on their road (see e.g. Boutellier, 1994a: 201; Boutellier, 1996b: 14–15; Boutellier, 2000a: 17, 61; Boutellier, 2000c: 9; Boutellier, 2000d: 442; Boutellier, 2000e: 317; Boutellier, 2001a: 379; Boutellier,

2002a: 4; Boutellier, 2004a: 41–4, 47, 75–80, 106–8, 124; Boutellier, 2005a: 200; Boutellier, 2005c: 69; Boutellier, 2007a: 37–8, 45; Boutellier, 2007b: 70; Boutellier and Van Stokkom, 1995). All of them fail, so he argues, to treat crime and punishment from a moral perspective. And, in doing so, they neglect the harsh and painful reality of crime and feelings of unsafety. His moral approach, then, is judged to be superior because it aims to take this 'cry for safety' as a starting point. Those who aim to relativize the reality of the problem are in his view 'cynical', 'unmasking' or 'rationalizing'. We will return to Boutellier's realism later in this chapter. Here we devote some thoughts to his thesis of the victimalization of morality. This thesis, so it will be argued, needs serious qualification. Moreover, our discussion aims to demonstrate that Boutellier's moral reductionism fails to capture some crucial mechanisms that are at work in the (selectivity or lack of) attention to victims. In other words, his unwillingness to engage with other perspectives seriously limits the persuasive power of his hypothesis.

According to Boutellier the victim has received an 'unprecedented status' (Boutellier, 1993b: 320) and there is a clear-cut '"victimological" turn in criminal law' (Boutellier, 1996b: 16). This is the empirical basis upon which his hypothesis is being built: the fragmentation of morality leads us to embrace the victim as a focal point for a 'morality without illusions' and this is reflected in an observable growth of attention to victims in formal responses to crime. However, there is reason to doubt that this victimological turn in criminal law actually took place in the 1980s and early 1990s—the period that Boutellier takes as his reference point in *Solidariteit en slachtofferschap*. It has often been argued that in this period victim compensation schemes remained under-funded; that victims were not being heard on their own terms; that despite all the victim-rhetoric they were hardly given any place in the criminal justice system; that initiatives were more symbolic than real; and so forth. Fattah argued that 'while many politicians may, for political gain, pay lip-service to the cause of crime victims, nothing significant is being done to alleviate their sufferings, to compensate their losses, or to redress the harm done to them' (Fattah, 1992: 44). Whereas Fattah (and others like Elias (1986; 1992; 1993)) made their observations in particular with respect to Anglo Saxon developments, similar observations were being made closer to home. In a critique of Boutellier, Kool

(1995) came to the same conclusion for the Dutch state of affairs: a close examination of victim policy in the Netherlands up to that time did not offer sufficient evidence to support Boutellier's claim of a victimological turn. The attention to victims of crime was mostly a 'paper reality'. Interestingly, Fattah, Elias, and Kool not only seemed to share the same conclusion on the poverty of actual victim policy but they also tended to highlight the *political* dimension of victimization: how victims come to be used for legitimating the state's power to punish.

After the publication of Boutellier's study in 1993 victim services expanded; victims' rights were being legislated for; reparative and restorative initiatives were further developed; the victim was being given a more prominent role in the criminal justice process (e.g. by means of victim impact statements); and so forth. A lot has been done and there clearly is at least a partial victimalization. But still the old critiques of 'more symbolic than real', 'more rhetoric than fact' make the idea of a wholesale victimalization of criminal justice not very plausible. Moreover, politicians and policy-makers continue to disregard sound victimological knowledge and turn the victim into a suitable figure for other agendas. For example, in 2002 the British government launched its *Justice for All* policy paper which aimed to 'rebalance the criminal justice system in favour of the victim'. At first sight this might seem like a confirmation of the British government's feelings of solidarity with the victim's suffering (and, indeed, it was in that sense that it came to be presented by government officials). However, on closer examination, the picture looks rather different. In the book *Reconcilable Rights? Analysing the tension between victims and defendants* (Cape, 2004a) academics and legal professionals (a number of whom deplored the fact that the British government did not solicit expert commentary upon its proposals on victim policy) shed other light on victim policy in England and Wales. The 'balancing' metaphor was skilfully deconstructed—most notably in the chapters by Cape (2004b) and Jackson (2004)—and appears as a highly problematic way of representing the stakes at issue, as if the two are entangled in a *zero sum* game and, moreover, as if they are encountering the same kind of problems and challenges when facing the power to punish. Contributors are highly critical of the ways in which victims are depicted in recent criminal justice policy. Victimhood has taken on a 'totemic' meaning with little connection to the real needs of victims and looks more like a 'political construct' that is used for purposes other than providing for victims, that is, catching and punishing more criminals by relaxing evidence rules and abolishing double jeopardy. In fact, these observations seem to suggest that the old critiques and worries about 1980s victim policy have not lost their validity. Moreover, as Garland and Pratt have taught us in the previous chapters, the growth of the mass media and the further politicization of the crime issue have made the victim even more into a suitable and welcome target to rally support for viewpoints and initiatives that often, in Fattah's powerful expression, 'pay lip-service to the cause of crime victims'.

Durkheim used law as an external index, a visible symbol for his invisible object of inquiry, that is, solidarity. However, if criminal law ('the external index') has not been fully victimalized, as we suggested above, then it may be that, if we would follow Durkheim's methodological prescription, that neither has solidarity been victimalized. Boutellier is well aware of the 'fragility' (Boutellier, 1994c), the 'temporariness', and the 'small basis' (Boutellier, 1993b) of the victimalized morality. He nevertheless attaches a great deal of 'moral weight' to the Dutch silent marches and citizen committees. As we saw earlier there were about four to six small marches each year which mobilized on average between a few hundred to a little more than a thousand participants. The committees against violence encompassed a few hundreds of people. In the light of the presumed scale of the problem (Boutellier himself claims that there are about 1 million acts of violence each year in the Netherlands) these numbers are fairly small to speak of a 'new social phenomenon' and to see them as a confirmation of 'the hypothesis that the victim plays a *solidarizing* role in the moral design of postmodern culture' (Boutellier, 2004a: 71). Moreover, in August 2006 the Dutch newspaper *NRC Handelsblad* devoted two articles to the decline of the silent marches and citizen groups against violence. Six years after Boutellier's research into the phenomenon and ten years after the murder of Joes Kloppenburg, there were hardly any silent marches anymore; the national day against senseless violence was abolished; many of the local action groups and the national organization for safety and respect had disappeared. Boutellier was interviewed by the journalist and had to acknowledge that his prediction that these initiatives were there to stay for a long time did not come true (see Bouma, 2006a; Bouma, 2006b).

Even though silent marches are remarkable phenomena that deserve special attention, the small numbers and the sharp decline suggest that we are in need of other tools to make sense of them. Boutellier's victimalized morality seems to be both *particular* and highly *volatile*. First, the issue of particularity. Boutellier has a tendency to speak in very general terms about a culture where everybody enjoys an unprecedented and unlimited freedom and where offending is an option within a freely-chosen life project. His description and analysis of the safety utopia seems to apply to everyone to the same degree, irrespective of obvious differences in education, social background, colour of skin, sex, class, income, or age. Indeed, as he argues in *The Safety Utopia*: 'Each culture has its own internal tensions as regards gender differences, class conflicts, or generation gaps. Although these contrasts have not disappeared in contemporary times, in the risk culture it is the friction between vitality and safety that occupies the central position' (Boutellier, 2004a: 8). However, as Buruma suggests, his diagnosis seems to apply in particular to 'those postmodern people with a high degree of existential security' (Buruma, 2003: 1168, author's translation). Van Swaaningen would probably agree with this: 'Those people to whom the question "Are you suffering?" is being addressed is a group which the contented class can identify with' (Van Swaaningen, 1995: 26, author's translation). Boutellier's assumption that postmodern society is a society of bungee-jumpers, a feast of unprecedented freedom and vitalism, sweeps obvious power differences and social inequalities under the carpet. The question whether the moral unity and consensus around victimization is the property of a particular social segment is not being asked—let alone addressed (see also Lea, 2002). In his discussion of the inadequacy of Durkheim's notion of the *conscience collective* Garland, inspired by similar observations, suggested that it would be more accurate to speak in terms of a 'ruling morality' or a 'dominant moral order' (Garland, 1990a: 52). Boutellier seems to make the same mistake as Durkheim. However, unlike Durkheim, he had the advantage that other perspectives were available which could have tempered his sweeping and generalizing statements. Unfortunately, his moral reductionism prevented him from seriously engaging with the actual make-up of postmodern women and men, and how they (horizontally) relate to each other and (vertically) to the state.

The same generalizing tendency is at play when he describes his two central characters as the 'postmodern criminal' and the 'emancipated victim'. There are for sure offenders who can be described as choosing crime as part of their life project, such as the classical 'professional thieves' and the newer expressive forms of deviance (such as joy-riding, 'happy slapping', and the like) that Boutellier takes as exemplary for the negative flip-side of vitalism. However, as almost every report on modern-day prison systems tells us, to a large extent penal institutions tend to be filled up with people of low education, often with major (mental) health problems and weak social skills, poor job prospects and fragmented social ties and family relationships. To argue that such people enjoy an unprecedented freedom to design their identities and choose their lifestyles as they feel, does violence to the empirical description of the characteristics of a large part of the offending population. The same holds true for the 'emancipated victim'. This victim, as Boutellier describes it, seems to harbour all potential feelings and attitudes a person might have when being victimized: sometimes he is revengeful, at other times not; sometimes he is conciliatory, at other times not; sometimes he is calculating, at other times not; and so forth. The 'postmodern criminal' and the 'emancipated victim' are constructions that tend to defy proper empirical description.

Second, the issue of volatility. There seems to be a strange paradox at work in Boutellier's victimalized morality. On the one hand, the victim is the hard-core in a morally fragmented society: he functions as the last point of convergence in a culture where everyone can hold diverging opinions about the good life. On the other hand, however, the content of the victim category is far from fixed. A large number of contingencies determine which forms of suffering are, in fact, being labelled 'victimhood'. It, then, becomes a 'contingent construction' or even an 'empty concept' open for any content (Groenhuijsen, 1994: 708; Hildebrandt, 1998: 44–5). As Verrijn Stuart (1994) suggested, everyone can answer Rorty's question 'Are you suffering?' with a simple 'yes'.

Boutellier was well aware of this. This is why he introduced the concepts of 'victimalization' to describe how certain forms of suffering become victimhood (in the case of child sex abuse), and 'devictimalization' for processes that go in the other direction (his case study of prostitution). In doing so, he realized that he came close to the labelling perspective in criminology, more specifically as it has been applied to victims by *inter alia* David Miers in a number of interesting essays (see Miers, 1980, 1989, 1990). However, from Boutellier's moral and realist perspective this would be like stepping on too shaky ground: if the victim is a mere construction then his whole theory would collapse like a house of cards. His answer to this puzzle was the following: 'What Miers presents as a general social psychology process should I feel be viewed as specifically characteristic of a fragmented morality' (Boutellier, 2000a: 63). However, this answer still leaves too much out of the picture: it still leaves open why certain forms of suffering go unnoticed; why other forms become 'victimalized'; and why formerly recognized victimhood becomes 'devictimalized'. The presumed specificity of the changing moral context does not offer us much guidance on which path will be followed. If victims (and silent marches) come and go; if we are at one moment preoccupied with victim A and at another (while forgetting about A) with B—what, then, are the mechanisms at play?

Preconditions for cohesion and struggles for recognition

Like crime, victimization is also a culturally relative concept: what is being termed 'victimization' in certain places and in certain time periods often is defined differently in other places and in other time periods. This sounds (or better: should sound) like a truism for criminologists but it often is not (Fattah, 1993). In the light of Boutellier's victimalization thesis this truism calls for closer attention to the preconditions that make people join in a common rejection of certain forms of suffering. Indeed, the cohesion and unity surrounding victims of crime that is at the centre of Boutellier's Durkheimian story, is far from self-evident and, in fact, it often is the result of, and goes hand in hand with, struggle and conflict.

In 1972 Quinney challenged victimologists to approach the victim as a 'social construction'. 'A victim cannot be taken for granted', so he opened his thought-provoking essay, and he continued: 'our conceptions of victims and victimization are optional, discretionary, and by no means innately given' (Quinney, 1972: 314). Quinney had a radical criminological objective in mind: he wanted to question conventional (ruling class) definitions of victims which enabled him, in a second step, to conceive of alternative victims—victims that according to his point of view received much less attention (he pointed to victims of police violence, war, the criminal justice system, state violence, and other forms of oppression). But at the same time he highlighted the processual character of how people 'become' victims. Whereas Becker,

Matza and others studied labelling processes in the sociology of deviance, so it is possible to explore how victim labels emerge and are being applied. Social scientists such as Miers (1980; 1989; 1990), Best (1997; 1999), and Rock (2002; 2004) have further explored these definitional issues.

When someone is named a 'victim', then an interpretive framework is being activated which entails a number of instructions on how we need to understand social relationships: victim descriptions tell us how we should interpret situations and how we should perceive or value the 'victimized' person. According to Holstein and Miller (1990: 108–13) victimization can be seen as a 'procedure' for deflecting responsibility; assigning causes to a complementary offender that is simultaneously being constructed; specifying responses and remedies (such as help or compensation), and accounting for failures without jeopardizing one's own identity. This also implies that being assigned the victim status may bring a number of advantages in its wake: sympathy, attention, innocence, financial compensation, and so forth (see Miers, 1990; Rock, 2002).

However, not everybody receives access to the victim category or is being identified as victim: membership needs to be earned. Potential candidates need to fulfil a number of conditions and they need to have certain characteristics. For example, the suffering should not be vague or ambiguous and should not be caused by the person itself. Variables such as age, dress code, sex, ethnicity and socio-economic status equally play an important role (Miers, 1990). The suffering needs to be represented in such a way that it fits with definitions of what justified victimizations and victims are. Sometimes these definitions may conflict: a person can be named a victim at the stage of prosecution but, at a later moment, when applying for compensation from a victim compensation fund, that same person can be denied the victim status because his behaviour does not square with the image of the innocent and needy victim (see e.g. Miers, 1980; Rock, 2004).

A selection takes place: some are included, others are excluded. And once being successfully admitted to the victim category there are expectations connected to the victim role: for example, sympathy can quickly evaporate when victims start selling their stories to tabloids or TV channels; when they do not undertake anything to prevent further victimization; when they give the impression of being ungrateful; and so forth. This may also imply that victims need to be represented, or represent themselves, as innocent or 'ideal' (Christie, 1986) in order to construct an unambivalent Boutellier-like consensus around them. As soon as more information becomes available, and the moment the exact context of the victimization becomes visible, the sympathy may wither away, and the victim status may become the object of contestation (Verrijn Stuart, 1994).

Because the victim status may also bring a number of advantages with it, there is often a struggle for recognition in the public sphere. The work of the Belgian historian Chaumont (1997) is exemplary in this respect: victims of genocide in general, and the Holocaust in particular, became entangled in a bitter conflict to be awarded the highest position in the hierarchy of suffering. For this reason, Ian Buruma (2002) was critical of a Holocaust Day: certain victims are put in the picture with competition and rivalry as a result. In the aftermath of tragedies the solidarity and unity amongst victims and others may quickly give way to conflict over money: who gets how much, and who gets it first? (Furedi, 1999: 34–5; Furedi, 2002: 95).

Seen from such a perspective, silent marches may produce solidarity as well as division. In May 2006, in the wake of a number of violent incidents, there was a wave of silent marches in Flanders. Whereas the media and politicians focused on the solidarity with the victims, and praised the joint rejection of violence by people participating in such events, other victims reacted in an embittered way. The marches created division by alienating the families of victims who received much less attention. They complained in the media that no march was being organized for their son or daughter; that there were no flowers from the King for their loved ones; that their relatives remained unmentioned in speeches of church leaders and politicians. The chairperson of the organization 'Parents of a Murdered Child' was embittered because their 'March of Hope', which was planned long before the wave of May 2006, hardly received any media coverage: 'We are no longer news, not spectacular enough. The newspapers wrote almost nothing about our March of Hope' (author's translation). She argued that this made the marches 'extra painful' for the members of her organization and described their march as 'the day of the forgotten victims' (Daems, 2006).

Paradoxically, then, these victims who are most directly affected by the aftermath of crime, did not feel part of the solidarity that is usually ascribed to such citizen initiatives. It is clear that Boutellier's Durkheimian understanding falls short on grasping these much less appealing aspects of the marches: whereas the media portrayed thousands of people walking side by side there were, a little further away from the cameras and microphones, others who felt that their suffering was not sufficiently recognized. There was clearly another mechanism at work. To interpret such marches solely as solidarizing events, then, is to miss out a great deal of what is actually going on. Because struggles for recognition always have a grand potential for conflict Bauman (2001), in another context, refers to them as 'recognition wars' and 'reconnaissance battles'. In perceiving solely solidarity, Boutellier fails to scratch the surface layer and does not get access to the much richer but, inevitably, much more ambivalent reality of our (selective) attention for victims of crime.

The problem, then, is that Boutellier's moral reductionism only makes him see cohesion, consensus, solidarity—that is, he focuses exclusively on what binds us together, not what tears us apart. Understanding the attention for certain victims and certain types of victimization from a labelling perspective or as a struggle for recognition seems to be better suited to explain the fragility, temporality and selectivity of that attention. In addition, Boutellier turns a blind eye to how victims can be used instrumentally. In a book on how victims have been used and abused in the American war on crime Markus Dubber argues that this war plays a 'communitarian function': the criminal serves as a convenient focus for uniting an otherwise disparate and divided community (Dubber, 2002: 23–6). In a long review essay of Dubber's book Robert Elias, a social scientist who has done extensive research on the political uses of victimization himself, explained how this leads to division: 'In practice this separation does not primarily divide real offenders from real victims but almost always divides instead along class and race lines, with the white middle class as the protected, innocent community and with the (especially black) lower class as the offenders' (Elias, 2004: 232–3). Sessar (1990) once coined the phrase 'tertiary victimization' to highlight how a presumed solidarity with victims hides other, less benign motives, such as a law and order agenda. Fattah for his part, significantly listed 'the danger that victim movements might turn into offender-bashing campaigns' first on his list of ten dangers of victim movements (Fattah, 1986: 2–3). To accuse such alternative perspectives on attention for victims as 'shortsightedness', as Boutellier (2000a: 61–2) does, is like putting a veil over crucial aspects of a reality that, unfortunately, is not all that rosy and genuinely impregnated by an interest in the victim's plight.

Hyperrealism: the other bad news story

In his critical discussion of recent work on punitiveness Matthews argued the following: 'In line with the media, many academics feel that only bad news is worth reporting' (Matthews, 2005a: 181). As we saw in the previous chapter, Pratt tends to fall prey to this tendency in focusing disproportionately on the worst features of the current penal landscape—in particular in his discussion of the 'new punitiveness'. In the case of Boutellier we hear a different 'bad news' story: not punishment but crime and unsafety are described in a way that, despite his numerous criticisms directed at criminologists who, in his opinion, are not acknowledging the 'reality' of the problem, does violence to that very same reality that he wants to take as a starting point for his explorations of contemporary social and penal developments.

Earlier in this chapter we saw how Boutellier subordinates alternative explanations for the growing attention to victimization to his moral perspective by arguing that these fail to take the problem of crime and unsafety seriously or, even worse, tend to explain it away. Boutellier is right that certain criminologists in the past have shied away from addressing increasing crime rates and have, at times, made it somewhat easy for themselves by referring to problems of measurement, changes in rates of detecting, reporting and registering crime, the growth of police forces, and so forth. And there is also a kernel of truth in the following statement: 'Intellectuals are often more interested in the structural violence of the authorities or in processes of exclusion than in the problems that generate them' (Boutellier, 2006a: 34).[10]

[10] This sentence also captures wonderfully Boutellier's 'bottom-up' approach: 'structural violence' and 'exclusion' *follow from* the harsh reality of the crime problem. The sequence goes uni-directionally from crime to punishment. This is a constant in his Durkheimian understanding of crime and punishment: the criminal justice system, in its function as guardian of the victimalized morality, plays a *reactive* role in order to avoid a state of anomie or normlessness and to reaffirm the vulnerable morality of our times. In the next chapter we will see how Loïc Wacquant (in terms that resonate with the classical work of Rusche and Kirchheimer) argues exactly the opposite: for him punishment plays a *proactive*

However, in his eagerness to confront criminology with, and liberate it from, this 'state of denial' he tends to exaggerate the problem at hand. One number that appears again and again in his publications is the ten-fold increase in crimes registered with the Dutch police. For example: 'The registrated crime rate is about ten times what it was in 1960, which forces us to examine how "we" relate to each other' (Boutellier, 2000a: 21; see also Boutellier, 1991a: 224). The more obvious and first thing to examine, however, is this number itself. Boutellier does not mention the simple demographic fact that also the population in the Netherlands had grown considerably since 1960. No serious attempt is being made to discuss basic methodological issues such as changing reporting and registration rates. Between 1980 and 2004 reported crime in the Netherlands almost doubled (from 700,000 to 1,300.000). However, as Wittebrood and Nieuwbeerta (2006) recently demonstrated in a careful analysis of police figures, almost three-quarters of this increase is explained by the fact that crimes were more often registered by the police, a quarter because victims reported them more often and only one per cent because of a real increase in crime (see also Wittebrood, 2007: 107–26). To put the numbers into (a methodologically sound) perspective is not the same as 'denying' the problem: it is part of criminological 'responsible speech' to give a fair and (to put it in somewhat awkward terms) really realistic description of what has happened in terms of crime developments.

In *The Safety Utopia* Boutellier estimates that there are about 1 million acts of violence in the Netherlands.[11] The Dutch Fund for compensating victims of crime, however, argues that about 20,000 to 30,000 victims are eligible for compensation each year (see Buruma, 2003). These measures are, of course, very different

role in disciplining and punishing those groups that have become 'superfluous' for current neoliberal societies.

[11] 'Once we realize the figures that are involved, the relevance of the discussion will be clear. An estimated million violent offences a year means eight violent offences for every 100 people above the age of sixteen. If they are evenly distributed over the entire population, it means that in a matter of ten years, almost everyone will have had this experience' (Boutellier, 2004a: 63–4). Boutellier acknowledges that 'this reasoning is demagoguery' (Boutellier, 2004a: 64) but nevertheless does not seem to be willing to deviate from his alarmistic statements: 'It is no exaggeration though to state that among the Dutch, violence has become a rather commonplace phenomenon because of our own experiences, those of our friends and relatives, and the media attention focused on it' (Boutellier, 2004a: 64).

in nature and the Fund receives applications in respect of more serious forms of violence yet, in view of the grand difference in proportion—1 crime for the Fund against 33 to 50 in Boutellier's estimate—one would expect at least some reservation instead of taking the highest and most alarming number available on the market of crime figures to arrive at a 'criminological diagnosis' of the current problem of violence. In a reflection on a research that estimates that there are about 20,000 to 25,000 registered cases of 'physical violence primarily directed against individuals and committed on the street' Boutellier, without any methodological explanation or reservation, multiplies the number by ten in order to bridge the gap between police figures and victim surveys and concludes that, therefore, there are more than 200,000 incidents of public violence in the Netherlands every year (Boutellier, 2004a: 62, note 1). At another place he argues that victim surveys reveal that about 5 million victimizations take place each year—a number that he, again without any methodological justification, multiplies by two in order to include victimless crimes (such as drug offences, corporate crime, organized crime, soccer violence, and so forth) in the overall picture. This number of 10 million, then, becomes the starting point for a 'sober approach of the current safety problem' which is presented in 'the right proportions' (Boutellier, 2004d: 116–17, 121). Again, in his willingness to confront his readers (and those criminologists who he thinks are still in denial) his figures tend to be selected in such a way that the crime problem is presented as more urgent and pressing than one might expect from his 'diagnostic' ambitions.[12]

At numerous occasions Boutellier argues that safety has become a 'number one issue'. In *The Safety Utopia* he offers the following evidence to convince his readers of the urgency of the safety problem: 'This is evident from population surveys where people list crime as their greatest concern, ranking above the environment, health and the economy. It is similarly evident from the attention

[12] A reviewer of Boutellier's first book argued that reading Boutellier is like 'listening to a demagogic speaker': 'either you like what he says and you allow him to continue for hours or, to the contrary, you are quickly satisfied and want to leave the room even before the break' (Ruimschotel, 1993: 409, author's translation). Also Willem de Haan was critical of the fact that there was no inclination at all in *Solidariteit en slachtofferschap* to relativize the crime problem (De Haan, 1994: 372). The alarmistic overtones in Boutellier's work have only increased with the years.

in the media and the political arena. And it is clear from the attention focused on the criminal justice system' (Boutellier, 2004a: 31). There is, however, no discussion of the survey methodology that was being used or results of surveys that might identify other worries.[13] Moreover, to take attention being paid to safety in the media and politics as evidence is all too easy. The role of the media and politics is much more complicated and many researchers argue that they have played an active agenda-setting and public opinion-forming role rather than passively 'reflecting' what lives in the underbelly of society (see e.g. Beckett, 1997; Zimring *et al*, 2001: 231–2; Altheide, 2002; Cavender, 2004). In sum, to draw attention to methodological issues, or to identify other relevant factors such as disproportionate media attention or political opportunism, is not the same as denying that there is a problem—rather it is a matter of responsible criminological scholarship.[14]

The egg came before the chicken: 'democracy at work'

Which came first: the chicken or the egg? This well-known dilemma entertained (and irritated) even the ancient Greek philosophers: the egg is laid by the chicken but the chicken emerges from the egg. The combined force of an uncompromising moral perspective (that is, Boutellier's moral reductionism) and an equally uncompromising realism moves Boutellier to put the egg

[13] Zygmunt Bauman, an author who often appears in Boutellier's recent publications, reads another 'number-one-issue' (job insecurity) in surveys: 'Little wonder that according to the surveys of concerns, worries and fears of contemporary Europeans, joblessness...occupies the uncontested topmost position' (Bauman, 2005: 70).

[14] In a recent review essay on the work of Theodore Dalrymple Boutellier argues that crime rates have been decreasing drastically. In an endnote he expresses his astonishment about the fact that this has hardly received any attention in the Netherlands (see Boutellier, 2007b: 71, 73, note 3). For a reader of Boutellier's work this remark sounds somewhat surprising: as we have seen, Boutellier has been at the forefront to (over-)emphasize the problem of crime, and hammering down the harsh reality of crime and victimization in the Netherlands without much feeling for qualification or close study of the figures himself. His book *The Safety Utopia* was explicitly intended to contribute to public debate on safety in the Netherlands. In particular with this objective in mind it would attest of more 'responsible speech' (Bauman, 1990) if Boutellier presented a much more balanced and nuanced picture in his book instead of adding a 'criminological diagnosis' to the public debate that only tends to confirm the alarmist voices in the media and political arena.

first: there *are* real exponential increases in crime rates, feelings of unsafety, and worries about both ('the egg') and, therefore, governments respond to this accordingly ('the chicken'). We *first* have the 'need for safety' and only *then* politics is obliged to step in (see e.g. Boutellier, 1996b: 18; Boutellier, 2004a: 31–2, 47). In line with Durkheim, Boutellier analyses penal change from the bottom up. Developments in the moral make-up of a society stimulate a need and demand for safety which, in turn, is directed at those who are politically in charge. 'The people demand…the disciplining of the other' (Boutellier, 2004d: 118, author's translation) is a statement that often reappears in his publications. This demand, then, seems to move from the 'underbelly' of a fearful citizenry to a political and judicial system that feels called upon to react.[15] In putting the egg before the chicken Boutellier seems to subscribe to the 'democracy-at-work' thesis (see Cullen *et al*, 1985: 19).

However, Aristotle already came to the conclusion that both the chicken and the egg had always coexisted. Slightly adapted to our theme one might argue that this position is quite well captured in the following statement: 'Public attitudes are both a cause and an effect of the politics of criminal justice' (Zimring *et al*, 2001: 161). Boutellier is only willing to see the first part, that is the cause ('bottom-up'), and pays no attention to the effect ('top-down'). It seems as if the demand for 'safe freedom' is directly whispered in the listening ear of the politician who has no voice himself. In the previous chapters, however, we have seen how authors such as Garland and Pratt highlighted a tendency towards penal populism whereby politicians actively tap into fears for political gain. Boutellier is well aware that a system confronted with a 'criminal justice paradox' feels a pressing need for legitimating the state's monopoly of the power to punish. This observation, however, would make political systems rather more than less vulnerable for top-down attempts to reconquer some of that lost legitimacy.

At this point it is perhaps interesting to observe that Boutellier does not pay much attention to detailed descriptions of *how* the penal climate in the Netherlands has changed over the past two

[15] Even though this may, at first instance, sound remarkably similar to what Melossi (1989) called the 'legal syllogism', it is important to realize that for Boutellier it is not so much crime *as such* that drives punishment but rather the changing moral context wherein feelings of unsafety and experiences of victimization take a new moral meaning that is the (moral) driving force for societal responses to crime and unsafety.

decades. As we saw earlier in this chapter, punishment plays an important role in Boutellier's story and he regularly emphasizes the important communicative function it fulfils. However, there is hardly any discussion of the remarkable growth of imprisonment in the Netherlands. In the mid-1980s criminologists such as Rutherford (1984) and Downes (1988) devoted studies to the Dutch reductionist prison policy. Until that time the Netherlands was renowned amongst prison experts around the globe for its liberal penal system. It is surprising that Boutellier, apart from briefly mentioning that the 'supply' of the Dutch criminal justice system always and inevitably lags behind in satisfying the 'demand', does not pay more attention to how much this 'supply' in fact has increased over the past twenty years (see e.g. Boone and Moerings, 2007; Downes, 2007; Downes and Van Swaaningen, 2007).

To focus more closely on how the 'need' for punishment has been satisfied in practice would probably reveal that, as we suggested above, there are hardly any 'postmodern criminals' in prison. And it would also suggest, then, that other perspectives that bring the *power* to punish more directly into view might be needed to see how that unspecified need for punishment comes to be translated into certain penal outcomes. Indeed, as Boone and Moerings argue, after discussing the explosive growth of the Dutch prison capacity: 'The conclusion then has to be that the Netherlands, from a country that was famous for its tolerance towards deviant behaviour, has become a country that solves its problems with minority groups and problem groups by locking them up' (Boone and Moerings, 2007: 28, author's translation). In Chapter 5 we will see how Loïc Wacquant deals with such questions.

Boutellier's use of theory

Unlike Pratt's use of theory which, as we saw in the previous chapter, has become volatile since the early 1990s, Boutellier's use of theory has been remarkably consistent. His framework has been—and still is—Durkheimian. Boutellier is well aware of other theoretical developments but he has always kept them at a safe distance. At times other authors are being used—such as Rorty and Shklar in the late 1980s and early 1990s, and Bauman from the late 1990s onwards—but only to the extent that they fit into his moral framework which is, as we have seen throughout this chapter, strongly inspired by Durkheim.

In addition, his use of theory is pragmatic. However, it is important to emphasize the difference with Garland's pragmatic stance towards theory. For Garland, one's theoretical framework needs to be adapted to the particular question that one aims to address. Theories are like tools which are selected and used to solve a specific problem. For Boutellier, however, the pragmatic use of theory has less to do with the problem he aims to address, and much more with his explicit and ever-present willingness to intervene. The use of theory, then, becomes pragmatic in the sense that one's choice of a theory tends to be guided by the openings the theory might provide for action. To put it in a more concrete way: Boutellier's choice of Durkheim, and his remarkable faithfulness during more than a quarter of a century to a moral approach to crime, needs to be understood against the background of Boutellier's simultaneous interest and involvement in policy-making. We will discuss this at length in the concluding section of this chapter.

Boutellier as a Public Intellectual

One cannot understand Boutellier's intellectual life-course if one does not take into account the public role he has, since the early 1980s, designed for himself. Unlike Garland and Pratt, Boutellier has always been closely involved with policy-related questions. His research on the morality of our time, and its relation to problems of crime and punishment, has always been undertaken against the background of a particular way of being publicly involved. It is not a coincidence that his career moves between universities, policy-oriented research institutions and the Dutch Ministry of Justice. Boutellier always has been close to policy-making—and deliberately so—and this has coloured his writing and thinking. His Durkheimian perspective to make sense of the world; his multiple calls to take problems of crime and unsafety seriously; his explicit addressing of normative questions; and so forth: they all become intelligible if one realizes that for Boutellier the 'diagnosis' of society always needs to be steered towards 'remedying' its pathological features. Like a therapist Boutellier puts society 'on the couch' in the hope that, after a number of sessions, the patient's 'Super-ego' is able to regain control over the recalcitrant 'Id'.

The moral crusade of Hans Boutellier

Boutellier has a mission. He likes to quote Durkheim who once argued that only eras that are morally divided could be inventive in the field of morals (see e.g. Boutellier, 1991b: 115; Boutellier, 1993a: 8; Boutellier, 2001b: 79; Boutellier, 2004c: 11; Boutellier, 2007a: 46). Contemplating morality, so he argued recently, only becomes interesting if it can contribute to new formulations for social reality (Boutellier, 2007b: 73). Boutellier wrote this in reaction to the upsurge of conservative thought in the Netherlands in general, and the remarkable (and related) success of Theodore Dalrymple's work in particular. For Boutellier there is no harking back to a lost civilization. The 'old days' are forever gone: a return to the rule-guided morality that was embedded in, and supported by, the religious and ideological pillars of Dutch society is neither possible nor desirable. However, if society changes, and if it starts to think differently about questions of 'good' and 'evil', then it becomes important to rethink its moral parameters. Ever since his early experiences as a psychology student in a closed institution for young delinquents this became the central problem to which he would devote his whole professional career.

Boutellier realized that, even though the criminal law might be the hard-core of a victimalized morality, he could not invest all his hope in it. Like Durkheim who had a special interest in education, also Boutellier devoted in *Solidariteit en slachtofferschap* close attention to 'normative upbringing' (Boutellier, 2000a: 155). The new generations needed to be acquainted with the *do's* and *don'ts* of the victimalized morality. Such calls directed at families, schools, communities and the like were made during Boutellier's life-course. Most recently, for example, he has pleaded to reinvent the normative function of schools in the light of rising school violence. The vitalist life-style of pupils needs to be 'channeled': the school system is not only there to award degrees but also, so he argues, for 'good conduct'. His advice for teachers to emphasize their position and strengthen their authority became thereby highly detailed: 'His or her authority is based upon clothes, form of address, greeting, acting properly and giving compliments for norm-conforming behaviour' (Boutellier, 2004e, author's translation). This interest in the question what a 'good education' for the new generations in our liberal times can and should be (and on which terms it can be judged properly) also made him participate in the debate on the role of youth protection and youth care. In that sense he argued that: 'Care for children starts with strengthening and supporting the family situation' (Boutellier, 2002c: 37, author's translation) and has pleaded for light forms of 'forced' educational support (such as courses and training) (Boutellier, 2002c: 37–8).

Whereas Boutellier's objective of moral renewal remained more or less the same over the years, the scope of that morality tended to expand. In the early 1990s he still believed that a victimalized morality which revolves around a joint rejection of suffering was potentially enough for the regulation of human interaction. In a reaction to the critique that such a morality is too limited he wrote: 'I am...of the opinion that the sensibility vis-à-vis the victim has greater relevance than would seem to be the case in the first instance. Environmental issues can affect future generations, problems in the cities can harm the marginalized segments of society and cause mass insecurity, and in the social sector there are victims of poor working conditions and structural unemployment' (Boutellier, 2000a: 154). Environmental pollution, urban unrest and wild market economy: they all have their 'victims' and, therefore, were potentially within the reach of the victimalized morality. However, over the years Boutellier more and more realized that a negative victimalized morality is, in the end, insufficient. With Evelien Tonkens he explains why this is the case: (1) a victimalized morality is too thin to regulate relationships between citizens; and (2) it offers a basis that is too small for communality, (3) for questions related to the 'good life', and (4) for positive values such as equality and self-development (see Boutellier and Tonkens, 2006: 181–2). For Boutellier the increasingly 'vitalist' culture has produced *en masse* crime and unsafety as one of its pathological excesses. In view of the scale of the problem the small and negative morality fell short on drawing boundaries and setting behavioural norms for day-to-day human interactions.

It is interesting to observe, then, that the clearly identifiable suffering of the victim of crime that he placed at the centre of his victimalized morality in the late 1980s and early 1990s has been expanded to much less visible (or even, as yet, not caused) forms of suffering on the one hand, and supplemented with suggestions for basic norms to regulate social interaction that do not seem to have any direct connection to the notion of a victim on the other. Boutellier's 'civilizing' mission penetrates deeper and deeper and moves from the public realm of the criminal law to the most private aspects of people's lives: he starts with proposals to remoralize the hard-core of criminal law and ends up knocking at the doors of family households to tell them how to raise their children and giving advice on the dress code of teachers. It is here that his mission (or what he terms a 'civilizing offensive' (Boutellier, 2000a: 157; Boutellier, 2006d) or 'the road of moral disciplining' (Boutellier, 2004d: 119)) tends to become a moral crusade: the perceived urgency of the crime and unsafety problem brings him to remoralize the whole of society. All of us, both individually and in our various capacities as teachers, parents, youth workers, mediators, police officers, judges, criminologists, and even artists,[16] are called upon to join Boutellier's soccer team and to play a defensive game against crime and unsafety as the excesses of a vitalist culture.

Unlike Pratt who, like a modern-day prophet, wants to offer insight into what the future might bring in the hope that it helps prevent that future becoming our present, Boutellier is firmly oriented in the here and now: his scholarship and policy-oriented activities are meant to make a difference to a society that has become all too vital and that, in his opinion, is in need of boundaries and moral renewal. Boutellier, then, is not a prophet but rather a proselytizer who, backed up by a set of ideas of how the world functions, tries to convert people to accept his diagnosis and act accordingly. And whereas Pratt's disproportionate attention to new punitive developments can be partly explained by his prophetic intentions (*People, be aware of the devastating consequences of the penal choices you make!*) so Boutellier's exaggerations of the crime and unsafety problem become partly understandable by his proselytizing ambitions (*People, be aware of the disintegrating*

[16] In an interview in the Dutch newspaper *NRC Handelsblad* which appeared in June 2002, Boutellier told the journalist that he had recently visited an exhibition which had shocked him because of its extreme form of vitalism: 'I was recently in the Centre Pompidou in Paris and saw there an abhorring exhibition: whole videowalls with mutilation-art' (Oostveen, 2002, author's translation). In an opinion article published in December 2002 in the same newspaper Boutellier (2002d) argued that also artists and the cultural sector should strive towards a 'new moral radicalism'. Artists and the cultural sector had for too long solely focused on 'vitalism', for example, in normalizing violence and sexuality. However, like all other players in Boutellier's soccer team also they had to play a role in the remoralization of society. In a reaction, published one week later, Vloet (2002) was highly critical of this instrumentalization of art 'in service of the state' which had, so she illustrated, been applied in recent years in the USA and which had a long tradition in Russia.

and anomic implications of failing to acknowledge and respond to the problems of crime and unsafety!). Not armchair scholarship but a proselytizing mission has driven Boutellier towards a moral crusade against the pathologies of contemporary culture.

Criminology and policy: relevance on top

This moral crusade has had deep implications for his scholarship. As we have seen earlier, Boutellier sets a number of alternative frameworks aside as 'cynical', 'sceptical', 'unmasking', 'rationalizing', and so forth. One of his central critiques was that they fail to take the problem of crime and unsafety seriously. As a diagnostician with an eye for prescribing appropriate remedies his scholarship has been infused with a large dose of pragmatism. Boutellier is more interested in 'construction, going with the flow' (*constructie, het meebewegen*) than in 'deconstruction, the act of unmasking' (*deconstructie, de ontmaskering*) (Boutellier, 2005c: 70). He starts not so much from the question 'What *should* we do?' but rather from 'What *can* we do?' (see e.g. Boutellier, 2004c: 11). For him a 'politics of the achievable' (*politiek van de haalbaarheid*) is to be chosen over a 'politics of illusions' *(politiek van illusies*) (Boutellier, 2004d: 121). This also explains why he prefers to speak of 'diagnosis' instead of 'analysis': 'In the diagnosis resonate the feasability and effectiveness of the solution' (Boutellier, 2005a: 32, author's translation).

In the (Dutch) foreword to *The Safety Utopia* Boutellier acknowledged that at the time of writing he was closely involved in policy issues due to his function at the Ministry of Justice. However, so he argued, the book had been written out of a 'need for reflection' whereby he deliberately wanted to keep a distance from the 'heat of politics' (Boutellier, 2002a: vii). Nonetheless, a close examination of his intellectual life-course demonstrates that there is (what one might term) a 'policy bias' at work in his writing. His uncompromising Durkheimian framework and hyper-realism; his optimism; his view of criminology: all of them become intelligible if we keep his policy intentions in the back of our minds.

First, as we have seen, Boutellier has demonstrated a remarkable consistency in his use of theory: Durkheim has always been his guide and there was never a moment of doubt about the superiority of his moral approach to crime and punishment.

Despite the fact that Boutellier demonstrates a deep awareness of other sociological perspectives[17], he has never compromised on his framework to make sense of social and penal change. This moral perspective, however, is also the most attractive theoretical option for a policy-maker. To see offenders as morally free actors who have abused their vital freedom is, for policy-makers, much more interesting and manageable than other forms of analysis. If crime is first and foremost a moral problem (and not a political one, as Jongman suggested, see above) then potential remedies are immediately within the reach of policy-makers: the diagnosis, then, does not call into question the deeper structures of society but enables the policy-maker to focus on the vital lifestyles of (potential) offenders; on developing new moral practices; on providing services for victims, and so forth.

Such a theoretical option also becomes interesting for another reason: the exclusive focus on a society-wide consensus about the urgency of the crime problem ('safety unites', so Boutellier tells us) and the presumed cohesion that surrounds various forms of suffering make it possible to present the demands that come from the underbelly of society in a unified way ('the cry for safety') to which policy-makers can more easily respond. From Boutellier's perspective, those in charge simply answer a real and justified need for safety and thereby fulfil their democratic duties. Earlier we referred to this as the 'democracy-at-work' thesis. In sum, by eliminating conflict and dissension from his framework of analysis, Boutellier is able to paint a streamlined picture of postmodern criminals, emancipated victims, fearful and worried citizens, and responsive policy-makers. It should be clear that any diagnosis which has these four characters as its protagonists, is highly appealing to politicians. However, from an analytic point of view a number of important questions and problems remain unaddressed and suggest that Boutellier's diagnosis has been too much affected by the 'policy bias'.

[17] Because Boutellier has read (and quoted) Garland's *Punishment and Modern Society* we can also assume that he is aware of the limits of Durkheim's work which Garland outlined in detail in Chapter 3 of his book. At no point does Boutellier address any of the fundamental questions that Garland raises about Durkheim, nor does he take Garland's answers to these questions into account. According to Willem de Haan *The Safety Utopia* suffers from a lack of self-reflexivity upon the possibilities and limits of Boutellier's theoretical affiliations and his closeness to Dutch safety policy (De Haan, 2003).

Second, from a policy perspective Boutellier cannot afford to suggest, as Garland did, that there is an inevitable lack of clear-cut 'exit-scenarios'. To do so, would make him *persona non grata* in the eyes of policy-makers who are eager to be presented with immediate solutions to what are perceived to be pressing problems. His 'policy bias', then, also helps us explain why he is much more optimistic. In a reply to Garland's dark-coloured culture of control, he wrote the following: 'The fact that this utopian desire is dominated by the safety issue does not necessarily mean it is unattractive. The safety utopia does not have to assume the form of a culture of control where a strong state promotes the interests of the well-to-do in the name of safety. It implies a definite call for moral reflection, for a renewed formation of local communities, a strengthening of the capacity for empathy, and a reconsideration of impassive market thinking' (Boutellier, 2004a: 132). This optimism also flows from his diagnosis as we have outlined it above: if the noses of citizens, police officers, judges, prosecutors, and politicians all point in the same direction, then there is, indeed, every reason to believe that they will take up their respective positions in Boutellier's soccer team. However, if the diagnosis is flawed in this respect, then there is reason to suggest that not every player will be devoted to the cause of the team.

Third, as we have seen throughout this chapter, Boutellier has not spared the 'criminological community'. In particular aetiological criminology has been blamed for neglecting the moral meaning of crime. But also critical and interactionist perspectives in criminology have been accused of all the sins of the world. If Boutellier makes a diagnosis, then one might expect a remedy—this is no different in this respect. The solution, so he argued, is that criminologists should address crime and unsafety as political strategic questions: 'As a discipline concerned with political strategy, criminology can contribute much more to the public debate on crime and safety than is now the case' (Boutellier, 2004a: 140). Criminology needs to be a 'reflexive policy science' (Boutellier, 2004a: 143). Perceived as such, criminologists should be less sceptical and more pragmatic, that is, oriented towards decision-making and with a clear view of the strategic implications of their research (Boutellier, 1994b; Boutellier, 2006b; Boutellier, 2006c; see also Nieuwenhuijsen, 2006).

This outline of a criminology *à la* Boutellier, again, demonstrates how close he is situated to the world of policy-making, and how much he desires that others would join him. However, without entering a discussion on the many criminologies that have been designed over the past century, there are a number of issues that, in the light of discussions on penal policy and punishment, could be briefly mentioned to demonstrate why a criminology as 'reflexive policy science' is limited and not as desirable as Boutellier presents it to us.

Next to the obvious question of how theory-development and policy-critique should be possible if the parameters of criminological research are being set by the various employers of such criminologists, there are the crucial issues of what we might term the 'unheard voices' and the 'irrelevant questions'. First, as Pratt indicated in *Punishment and Civilization* policy-makers at times, deliberately or otherwise, silence the voices of those being punished: the penal bureaucracy was highly successful in presenting *its* truth as *the* truth of the modern prison. In recent history criminologists have played, and continue to play, an important role in preventing that such voices remain unheard. And, interestingly, this has not been restricted to the voices of deviants or prisoners but also includes the victims of crime. In fact, feminist criminologists who have played a major role in bringing male violence into the daylight, would probably not have been able to do this to the same extent if their agendas were being set by a (then) male-dominated political establishment. This same holds true for the voices of victims that hardly receive any social attention or media coverage. In a recent study Condry (2007), for example, reconstructs the stories of the relatives of serious offenders and describes at length the difficulties they face and the shame they feel. For policy-makers who are interested in strategic questions about how to tackle crime and how to reduce feelings of unsafety, Condry's study probably is deemed to be irrelevant (and maybe even annoying) but, nevertheless, it confronts them and the public at large with some less appealing and largely invisible consequences of penal policy.

Second, the study of Condry leads us to the 'irrelevant questions'. There are many questions being asked in contemporary criminology that have no direct policy-relevance but that are, nevertheless, important for our understanding of crime and punishment. Luckily there are still PhD dissertations and research reports being written about prison life, about desistance of crime, or about gross violations of human rights and transitional justice. It is an achievement of criminology that it has become a more independent discipline—even though this independence is being challenged everyday (see e.g. Walters, 2003; Fijnaut, 2004; Fijnaut, 2005; De Haan, 2006). This does not imply that policy-oriented research should not be undertaken—far from it. In fact the major part of research in criminology is policy-oriented and often for good reasons and at times with positive implications, both for policy development and public debate. But the idea of turning criminology into a 'reflexive policy science' is too limited to grasp the complexities of crime and punishment and closes too many doors to 'unheard voices' and 'irrelevant questions'. Transgressing boundaries, as Durkheim tells us, is at times indispensable for innovation. This truism not only applies to morality but also to criminology.

5

Punishment and the Rise of the Penal State

Introduction

The revisionists of the 1970s and early 1980s were particularly concerned with demonstrating how, throughout history, the state's power to punish came to serve, deliberately or otherwise, certain interests and groups. In view of the expansion of penal systems in recent times the various uses and abuses of law's violence again came under close scrutiny. It begged the question whether recent penal change could be related to changing distributions of power; the transformation of capitalism; the emergence of new post-Fordist relations of production; the build-up of a distinct consumer society, and so forth. The work of our last author, Loïc Wacquant, is directly concerned with such questions. In his writings he complements his research on urban marginality and the spread of neoliberalism with the study of the growing reliance on law-enforcement instruments. For Wacquant, penal change needs to be understood against the backdrop of the role punishment has come to play in terms of social stratification and symbolic division.

We will first touch upon three important moments or passages in Wacquant's life-course that help us better understand his scholarship on punishment. We then discuss his work on urban marginality, the American ghettos and the French *banlieues* and we clarify how this research has been complemented by his writings on the mass incarceration of blacks in the USA and his work on the rise of the penal state. Next we offer a critical discussion of Wacquant's scholarship on punishment. We conclude the chapter with an exploration of Wacquant's role as a public intellectual.

Via Bourdieu, New Caledonia, Ghetto, and Boxing Ring into the Prison

Unlike Garland, Pratt, and Boutellier, Wacquant's thinking about crime and punishment is from a more recent date, the first publications dealing directly with penal issues being published in the mid-1990s. However, this does not mean that his earlier writings are of a lesser interest for our study. In fact, the origins of his interest in questions of punishment, and the particular angle from which he would broach such questions, only become fully understandable if the reader is aware of some defining moments or passages (or what he once referred to as 'culture shocks' (see Wacquant, 2005e)) in his life-course. It will then become clear that his publications on punishment spring from, and continue, a line of research that came to full fruition in the decade before he turned to aspects of penal change. Three of these moments or passages are of particular interest here: his meeting with Pierre Bourdieu in 1980 and the ensuing friendship and collaboration with the renowned French sociologist; his fieldwork in the late 1980s and early 1990s in Chicago and, simultaneously, his signing up at a boxing gym in a black neighbourhood; and, related to the second element, the growing awareness of the impact of the criminal justice system on the lives of people residing in the ghetto.

Wacquant met Bourdieu for the first time in November 1980. At that time he was enrolled as a first-year student in industrial economics at the École des Hautes Études Commerciales, one of France's *grandes écoles*. Wacquant was disappointed and bored with his studies and, after attending a lecture by Bourdieu, followed by a nightly *tête-à-tête* in a nearby cafeteria with the sociologist and some other students discussing the upcoming elections in France, he decided to take up sociology at the University of Paris. From a teacher Bourdieu gradually turned into a friend and close collaborator. After his studies Wacquant spent two years as an apprentice researcher on the South Pacific island of New Caledonia, in order to avoid doing military service, and kept in close contact with Bourdieu (see Wacquant, 2002e: 180–1; Wacquant, 2005e).[1] For his PhD research he moved in 1985 to Chicago to undertake research under the supervision of William

[1] Wacquant was a member of the sociology laboratory of Nouméa's ORSTOM Center (Office de la Recherche Scientific et Technique Outre-Mer) in the period 1983–85. Here he did research on inequality in the education system of New Caledonia which presented 'a mirror image of the colonial society, with its segmented, hierarchical pattern of crosscutting relations of ethnic and class domination' (Wacquant, 1989: 212; see also Wacquant, 1986; Wacquant, 1987; Wacquant, 1988).

Julius Wilson. At the University of Chicago Wacquant and a number of other graduate students organized in Winter 1987 a workshop on Bourdieu's sociology which, eventually, resulted in the publication of the influential book *An Invitation to Reflexive Sociology* (Bourdieu and Wacquant, 1992). In the next years Wacquant would contribute to the Bourdieu-directed collective work *La misère du monde* (Bourdieu, 1993); his first book-length study on punishment *Les prisons de la misère* (1999) was published in the Bourdieu-launched *Raisons d'agir* series which was set up to provide an outlet for bringing accessible texts by progressive social scientists on contemporary civic issues to a broader public; he co-authored a number of essays with the French sociologist and published papers in the interdisciplinary journal *Actes de la recherche en sciences sociales* which was founded in 1975 by Bourdieu; he wrote numerous essays on Bourdieu's sociology for an English-speaking audience; after Bourdieu's death in January 2002, Wacquant wrote a number of obituaries and essays on his former mentor (e.g. Wacquant, 2002f; Wacquant, 2003c); and, most recently, he edited a book on *Pierre Bourdieu and Democratic Politics* (Wacquant, 2005a).

Bourdieu deeply inspired Wacquant's way of practising sociology and, perhaps mostly, as he put it in an essay co-authored with Craig Calhoun devoted to the memory of Bourdieu, the idea of 'social science with conscience', that is Bourdieu's commitment to 'the principle that research must matter for the lives of others' (Calhoun and Wacquant, 2002: 3). For our understanding of Wacquant's writings on punishment it is in particular Bourdieu's critique of neoliberal globalization, a theme to which he devoted the last years of his life (see e.g. Bourdieu, 1998; Bourdieu, 2001), that left an imprint on Wacquant's work on penal change, that is, 'a worldwide trend toward commodification, state deregulation, and competitive individualism agressively exemplified and promoted by the dominant class of the fin-de-siècle United States' (Calhoun and Wacquant, 2002: 10).

Second, originally Wacquant was planning to write a doctoral thesis on colonialism in New Caledonia, a place where he had spent two years prior to coming to Chicago. However, due to a conflict with a superior in New Caledonia who systematically stole his work he changed theme (see Morvandiau *et al*, 2001). Wacquant's appartment in Chicago was on East 61st Street, two blocks into Woodlawn, a desolate and poor black neighbourhood with no high school, movie theatre, library or job centre (see Eakin, 2003). He became interested in the ghetto, that 'city in the city' so close to his prestigious new academic home and decided to turn it into the subject for his PhD research. This interest in the plight of America's black population in general, and the ghetto in particular, has stayed with him ever since. Later in this chapter we will discuss this at greater length by demonstrating how his late 1980s/early 1990s work on the black ghetto formed the immediate background for, and the first step to, his study of how prison and ghetto meet and mesh.

In August 1988 Wacquant enrolled in a local boxing gym in order to gain access to the young black men from the neighbourhood. He hoped that it would offer him a valuable observation point to study the daily reality of the black ghetto (Wacquant, 2004b: ix). However, soon the boxing virus would infect him: he attended the gym for the next three-and-a-half years; trained regularly alongside the local boxers; earned his very own ring name *Busy Louie*; and considered aborting his academic career to 'turn pro' (Wacquant, 2004b: 4). What started as an interesting (though functional) entrance point to the world of the black ghetto turned into a passion and became a second object of study, parallel to his investigations of social life in the ghetto (Wacquant, 2004b; see also Keucheyan, 2003). Over the years Wacquant would write numerous papers on what he terms a 'carnal sociology' and, eventually, the book *Corps et âme* (2001) which appeared a few years later as *Body and Soul* (2004).

Third, even though it went largely unthematized during his work on the ghetto and the art of boxing in the late 1980s and early 1990s, there were, dispersed over these publications, indications of Wacquant becoming aware of the deep impact of the criminal justice system on the private lives of people living in the ghetto in general, and his fellow-boxers in the gym in particular. Violence, drugs, prostitution and occasionally murder, were normal aspects of living in the black ghetto. His friends in the gym carried mace with them for self-protection. Many had done time and considered the prison as a normal part of their lives. He would later recall on different occasions how his interest in the criminal justice system grew out of these first-hand experiences in the ghetto and the boxing gym (see e.g. Blum and Neitzke, 2001; Eakin, 2003; Hilhorst, 2005). And, interestingly, Wacquant would occasionally infuse small illustrations of his time in Chicago in his later writings on punishment, thereby indicating how much his scholarship on urban marginality is connected to his work on punishment. For example, to illustrate how the classical 'convict code' was replaced by the 'code of the street' he referred to the experience of Ashante, one of his former boxing friends at the gym (Wacquant, 2001a: 111); when he discussed how part of the costs of incarceration are being transferred onto prisoners and their families he mentioned how the phone calls he received from his best friend and informant from the South Side of Chicago were billed seventeen times the rate he ususally paid (Wacquant, 2002c: 29 (note 11)); or when he discussed how blackness and criminality are being conflated, he added between brackets how his boxing coach DeeDee instructed him 'to keep a brisk speed for fear that the police would stop us on grounds that a young white man and an old black man riding together in a beat-up Plymouth Valiant in that area must be up to legal mischief' (Wacquant, 2005c: 129).

In the previous chapter we have seen how Boutellier's experiences in a closed institution for young delinquents sparked his life-long interest in the morality of our times. Also in the case of Wacquant a particular experience seems to have sensitized him to certain aspects of punishment, and directed his subsequent research on penal change accordingly. There are, however, two crucial differences that help us explain the deep differences between the scholarship of both authors. First, for Wacquant the eye-opening 'space' was not a closed institution for delinquent youths, but the 'island of order and virtue' (Wacquant, 2004b: 17–31) that the boxing gym offered in a desolate and crime-ridden black ghetto. Second, whereas Boutellier, dissatisfied with a (Foucault-inspired) control perspective, made the move 'from politics to morality' (Van der Ven, 1998), Wacquant saw the importance of politics and power being reaffirmed in how black people were being treated by the penal system. For Wacquant punishment did not become an object of study in order to sharpen its communicative function in a morally fragmented world, but to demonstrate the structuring and divisive function it plays in contemporary society.

If Wacquant wanted to come to a proper understanding of the plight of blacks in modern-day America, he could not shy away from addressing penal change more directly. In the next section we will see how his work on urban marginality in general, and on the American ghetto in particular, brought him to consider questions related to punishment. In addition, we will discuss how, according to Wacquant, the upsurge and global-wide spread of neoliberalism has been complemented by a 'neoliberal penality' and the rise of the penal state.

Urban Marginality, Ghetto, and Banlieues[2]

The American Black Belt: from 'communal' ghetto to 'hyperghetto'

The term 'ghetto' has a long history which goes back to the Jewish diaspora, whereby Jews were consigned to special districts in medieval European cities. Wacquant detects four constituent elements: stigma, constraint, spatial confinement, and institutional encasement. Economic exploitation and social ostracization are its two central purposes: 'to maximize the material profits extracted out of a group deemed defiled and defiling and to minimize intimate contact with its members so as to avert the threat of symbolic corrosion and contagion they carry' (Wacquant, 2004d; see also Wacquant, 2005h).

The dual rationale of economic exploitation and social ostracization not only governed the old Jewish ghettos but also the African-American ghettos in the Fordist twentieth-century metropolis. Between 1916 and 1930 a grand migration took place from the south of the United States to the industrial cities of the north: 1.5 million people moved to New York, Philadelphia, Chicago and Detroit in an attempt to escape racial oppression and in the hope to build a new life in the 'promised land' with its pressing need for manual labour. In the 1940s and 1950s there was a second wave of almost 3 million black people. This population influx in the industrial cities of the north would feed the formation of the urban ghettos (see Wacquant 1993b: 43–46).

Their unskilled labour, then, was indispensable for the industries in the north (that is, the element of 'economic exploitation')

[2] It is important to note that the year of publication of his book *Parias urbains* (2006) may give the reader the false impression that the empirical material it draws upon, is from a more recent date. However, as Wacquant indicates in the afterword to his book, it draws upon his original work in the late 1980s and subsequent publications in scientific journals and edited books, covering the period between 1987 and 1997 (Wacquant, 2006a: 289–90).

but, at the same time, they were not allowed to mix freely with the white population. Over the years white hostility would increase and patterns of discrimination and segregation hardened in housing, schooling, public accommodation, and the like (that is, the element of 'social ostracization'). As such, millions of African-Americans were forced to seek refuge in ghetto-like spaces which came to be referred to as the 'Black Belt' where they developed their own 'black city within the white' with its very own network of separate institutions parallel to the 'white city'. Wacquant speaks of the 'communal' ghetto of the Fordist era (Wacquant, 1998a: 143).

At the time of Wacquant's research in the late 1980s and early 1990s there was not much left over of this 'communal' ghetto. Towards the end of the twentieth century it was being turned into a 'hyperghetto' (Wacquant, 1994: 233–4). A major part of his research was devoted to the description of this newly-formed hyperghetto and the analysis of the causal factors that made the transformation possible. The hyperghetto that Wacquant witnessed in Chicago, was characterized by physical decay and had turned into a highly dangerous place with soaring crime rates, a pervasive drug trade and a high number of homicides. Moreover, the ghetto suffered from serious depopulation as better-off families were moving to other areas in the city; from rising joblessness and soaring and endemic poverty; and from organizational decline due to the erosion of the older organizational infrastructure of the 'communal' ghetto. In such a context the informal economy and illegal trade thrives well (see also Wacquant and Wilson, 1989). In terms of explanation, Wacquant argued that this transformation to the hyperghetto had been largely decided from outside—'external factors' have been responsible for the implosion of the post-war 'communal' ghetto (Wacquant, 1994: 250). Most important, however, were not the impersonal workings of broad macroeconomic and demographic forces but the willful decision of the 'urban elites' to abandon the ghetto to such forces (Wacquant, 2006a: 88; see also Wacquant, 1998c). As a result, the ghetto has lost its erstwhile economic function because in the new economy there is no longer a need for its reservoir of cheap, unskilled, industrial labour and, related to this, the ghetto also lost its organizational capacity: daily life is no longer structured by the institutions of the 'city within the city' (Wacquant, 2006a: 110).

The French Red Belt: les banlieues

Throughout his work on urban marginality Wacquant tried to keep an eye on comparative issues. In *Parias urbains* he aimed to unveil the similarities and, in particular, the differences between the American Black Belt and the French Red Belt, that is, the traditional industrial 'workers' cities' in France (Wacquant, 1993a: 367). When Wacquant was doing his research on the American ghetto the French *banlieues* were a hot topic in public debate: a moral panic, instigated by urban unrest, swept the country, and moved the *banlieues* to the centre of attention. This scenario was more recently repeated with the riots of November 2005 (see Traag, 2006). The media, politicians, and some academics drew alarming parallels with the American situation and were quick to term the degraded working-class neighbourhoods 'immigrant ghettos'. But, so Wacquant stressed, the French *banlieues* were not ghettos and he warned against an all too quick transatlantic diffusion of concepts and theories (Wacquant, 2006a: 147). European poverty was not being 'Americanized'.

For the French part of his comparative analysis Wacquant focused on the Red Belt city of La Courneuve and its public housing concentration called 'Quatre Mille'. At the surface there were some similarities between La Courneuve and the South Side ghetto of Chicago which he summarized as follows: 'both locales were found to have a declining population with a skewed age and class structure characterized by a predominance of youths, manual workers and deskilled service personnel, and to harbour large concentrations of "minorities" (North African immigrants on the one side, blacks on the other) that exhibit unusually high levels of unemployment caused by de-industrialization and labour market changes' (Wacquant, 1996a: 236–7). But to infer from these similarities that the French *banlieues* were becoming like American ghettos, was a bridge too far and to miss a crucial point. Both constituted two different socio-spatial formations: 'To simplify greatly: exclusion operates on the basis of colour reinforced by class and state in the Black Belt, but mainly on the basis of class and mitigated by the state in the Red Belt' (Wacquant, 1993a: 368). The apparent similarities, then, tend to mask deep differences in scale, structure and function between the American ghetto and the French *banlieue* (Wacquant, 1992a; Wacquant, 1992b; Wacquant, 1995; Wacquant, 2006a: 155–69). To take poverty, unemployment, insecurity and the like as indicators for ghettoization is like sweeping the defining aspect of the ghetto under the carpet, that is, it being the product and instrument of group power (Wacquant, 2004d).

After his comparison of the Black Belt and the Red Belt and, in particular, after having identified the crucial differences between the two and having explained why there are no ghettos in France, Wacquant turns to a discussion of a number of characteristics they both (and also other urban areas) increasingly tend to share. He refers to this as a new 'regime of urban marginality'. Here the contrast is not so much comparative (between the ghetto and the *banlieue*) but rather historical (between post-war (until the mid-1970s) and currently emerging features of dealing with urban poverty). His discussion, therefore, is no longer restricted to the two urban areas he dissected earlier but extends to 'First World cities' more generally.

According to Wacquant First World cities are confronted with 'advanced marginality' which is, ideally and typically, characterized by six distinctive features: (1) wage labour no longer offers a solution to urban marginality and social destitution but becomes instead, because of it being a source of fragmentation and precariousness, part of the problem; (2) advanced marginality is increasingly disconnected from short-term upward fluctuations in the economy, that is, economic growth hardly translates into extra jobs whereas social conditions and life chances do worsen during economic recessions; (3) advanced marginality is not diffused throughout working class areas but tends to concentrate in well-identified, bounded and increasingly isolated territories which get associated with disorder, dereliction and danger and, therefore, become increasingly stigmatized; (4) advanced marginality is characterized by territorial alienation, that is, marginalized urban populations can no longer identify with, and feel secure in, the places they inhabit; (5) for people living in these areas there is no longer a viable hinterland, that is, individuals who are durably excluded from paid employment can no longer rely on collective informal support; (6) advanced marginality develops in the context of class decomposition, rather than class formation or consolidation, under pressure of *de*proletarianization rather than proletarianization. The fragmented new urban poor no longer has a common idiom (unlike in the heyday of the trade unions) to forge a sense of common purpose and condition (see

Wacquant, 1996b: 123–28; Wacquant, 1999c: 1640; Wacquant, 2006a: 241–55).

Four structural logics are being held responsible for jointly producing this 'new regime of urban marginality'. First, the macrosocial dynamic, that is, rising social inequality in a context of overall economic advancement and prosperity. Second, the economic dynamic, that is, the elimination of numerous low-skilled jobs in the western cities due to automation and foreign labour competition, on the one hand, and the degradation and dispersion of basic conditions of employment, renumeration and social insurance, on the other. Third, the political dynamic, that is, the retrenchment and disarticulation of the welfare state resulting in state institutions playing both a more generative and less remedial role with respect to advanced marginality. Fourth, the spatial dynamic, that is the increasing concentration of the new marginality in specific urban areas which, therefore, become susceptible to processes of stigmatization (see Wacquant, 1999c: 1641–44; Wacquant, 2000b: 110–15; Wacquant, 2006a: 270–79). According to Wacquant there are three ways to respond to this advanced marginality: patching up the existing programmes of the welfare state; the criminalization of poverty via punitive containment of the poor in isolated neighbourhoods and prisons; and a fundamental reconstruction of the welfare state, for example, by instituting a universal citizen's wage that severs subsistence from work. Unsurprisingly, for Wacquant only the last option offers a viable response to the current predicament.

Earlier we argued that a discussion of Wacquant's work on urban marginality in general, and the American ghetto in particular, is indispensable for a proper understanding of how he makes sense of penal change and what place punishment is being given in his overall account. Indeed, his writings on punishment *continue* and hook on to his earlier research on the ghetto and urban marginality. In the next section we will see how, in his opinion, the ghetto and the prison have fused together, heralding yet another phase in America's long history of ethno-racial domination. Somewhat further in this chapter we will discuss how his research on the penal state, and its global spread, builds upon his work on urban marginality and the neoliberal revolution that is held responsible for both, the decline of the social state and the rise of the penal state. In both cases, the study of racial domination in the United States on the one hand, and the global spread of neoliberalism on the other hand, punishment came, in Wacquant's opinion, to play too important a role to leave it out of the composite picture. In doing so, Wacquant acknowledges that addressing questions related to punishment and penal change, at times, and perhaps increasingly so, becomes indispensable to answer sociology's central question: how is social order possible? And because of this, he has over the years on numerous occasions urged his fellow sociologists to bring punishment to the centre of their research agendas (see e.g. Wacquant, 2001a: 96; Wacquant, 2002a: 15; Wacquant, 2002d: 389; Wacquant, 2006a: 11, 41–2).

Prisons becoming ghettos, and vice versa[3]

Over the past decades the prison population in the United States increasingly became coloured black. In 1989, for the first time in American history, black people were in the majority in terms of entering state prisons. The incarceration rate for African-Americans doubled in ten years: from 3,544 inmates per 100,000 in 1985 to 6,926 per 100,000 in 1995, nearly eight times the figure for the white population (919 per 100,000). Young black men in the ghettos especially seem to end up in high numbers into the American prisons. For them the prison became like a 'normal' institution to which they had easier access than to higher education, health care, or unemployment benefits (Wacquant, 2005d: 32). Indeed, jail is 'perceived as continous with the ghetto, representing merely an extension of life in the Black Belt' (Wacquant, 1996a: 250).

If US prisons were coloured black, however, then this was not for reasons to do with crime. Throughout the twentieth century blacks have always been over-represented in the carceral system because they commit proportionately more crimes than whites owing to differences in class composition and socioeconomic stability, and black segregation in the ghettos. However, this does

[3] Also here a footnote needs to be added to avoid any confusion. An Italian (shorter) version of *Deadly Symbiosis: Race and the Rise of Neoliberal Penality* appeared in 2002 as *Symbiose mortale: Neoliberalismo e politica penale.* At the time of writing the (longer) English-language version was scheduled to be published by Polity Press. We have used the Italian version of the book and the table of contents of the English-language edition (to be found at: http://cas.uchicago.edu/workshops/scg/PENALMILITARIZATION-ChiWorkshop.doc, accessed: 23 July 2007) to reconstruct the storyline. The Italian book and a number of published articles and book chapters provide the backbone for our discussion.

not explain the recent deepening of the gap between black-white incarceration. Their share in serious crime, for example, decreased from 51 per cent in 1973 to 43 per cent in 1996 (Wacquant, 2005b: 19–21). Moreover, whereas the difference between arrest rates for whites and blacks has been stable between 1976 and 1992, the white-black incarceration gap grew from 1 in 5 to 1 in 8 (Wacquant, 2002b: 43). Wacquant suggests that it is the enforcement of laws that are most likely to lead to the incarceration of poor African-Americans (more specifically, the concentration of the war on drugs on the dark ghetto) that is responsible for the current racial disproportionality in imprisonment. And this leads him to his central hypothesis, that is, 'a new relationship has been established between imprisonment and the caste division that underlies the structure of US society since the uprisings that shook the ghetto' (Wacquant, 2005b: 20). In other words, the penal system increasingly came to play a crucial role in America's continuing history of racial domination.

The roots of this history go back almost four centuries. Wacquant identifies four 'peculiar institutions' that have, throughout American history, 'defined, confined and controlled' African-Americans. First, from the early beginnings of the colony, slavery (1619–1865) played a major role in satisfying the need for labour on the plantations. Eventually this created an enduring racial caste line separating black slaves from white freemen. Second, the Jim Crow system (1865–1965), that is, a whole ensemble of legal and social codes that prescribed complete separation of the races and held sway in the agrarian south. This system ensured legally enforced discrimination and segregation to compensate for the fact that slaves, after the Civil War, had become free labourers. Third, the ghetto (1915–1968)—or more precisely: the 'communal' ghetto that we encountered earlier—which came to be formed after the Great Migration of millions of black people to the industrial metropolitan centres in the North.

According to Wacquant the crisis of the ghetto gave rise to a fourth 'peculiar institution', that is, the institutional complex that came to be formed by the remnants of the ghetto (that is, the creation of the hyperghetto) and the prison system. Here lies the key to explaining the recent blackening of the American prison population: 'slavery and mass imprisonment are genealogically linked…one cannot understand the latter—its timing, composition, and smooth onset as well as the quiet ignorance or acceptance of its deleterious effects on those it affects—without returning to the former as a historic starting point and functional analogue' (Wacquant, 2002b: 41–2). The prison came to fulfil an 'extra-penological' function by filling up the gap of the eroding caste cleavage. Wacquant points at the remarkable similarities between the ghetto as an 'ethno-racial prison' and the prison as a 'judicial ghetto'. Indeed, as he argued, the prison 'is...formed of the same four fundamental constituents, stigma, coercion, physical enclosure and organizational parallelism and insulation, that make up a ghetto, and for similar purposes' (Wacquant, 2000a: 383; Wacquant, 2001a: 115).

The reshaping of the Black Belt into a hyperghetto resulted in the ghetto becoming more like a prison. First, the racial segregation of the communal ghetto came to be overlaid with class segregation: only those situated at the bottom of the social hierarchy stayed within its borders. In that sense the social characteristics of its residents came to resemble those of the inmates inside the prison. Second, the ghetto lost its positive economic function and became, like the prison, to play a mere negative function of storage of a surplus population. Third, whereas the black ghetto used to be replete of communal institutions, it is now state institutions of social control that are predominant. These institutions are no longer at the service of the community but play the role of custodian of the black residents on behalf of the white society. Fourth, as a little black city within the white city, the communal ghetto protected its residents from external forces. This 'buffering function' has been lost and everyday life became increasingly conflict-ridden and violent. Public housing 'prisonized' and public schools function as 'institutions of confinement'.

At the same time the prison became more like the ghetto. First, the axis of stratification has shifted from the vertical cleavage between prisoners and guards to the horizontal cleavages among prisoners. Here racial affiliation became the 'master status trait'. Second, the old 'convict code' that regulated life behind bars has been overwhelmed by the 'code of the street', that is, 'the predatory culture of the street, centered on hypermasculinist notions of honour, toughness, and coolness has entered into and transfigured the social structure and culture of jails and prisons' (Wacquant, 2001a: 110). Third, the prison has lost any of its positive purposes and solely neutralizes offenders both materially (by removing them from the free world) and symbolically (by drawing a sharp line between criminals and law-abiding citizens). Fourth, the judicial stigma of penal conviction has increasingly turned into life-long negative symbolic capital 'like the stain of "race" construed as a dishonouring form of denegated ethnicity' (Wacquant, 2001a: 114). Fifth, and most obvious, the prison resembles the ghetto because a great majority of the inmates are coming from the ghettos and will return there upon release. Moreover, like in the ghetto, black inmates are under direct supervision of whites.

Wacquant emphasizes that America's 'peculiar institutions' are 'race-making' institutions: they do not merely process but rather produce ethno-racial divisions (Wacquant, 2001a: 116–17). Also the prison, then, has become such a 'race-making' institution, in particular in reviving and solidifying the centuries-old association of blackness with criminality. In addition, the penalization of the race question has led to its depoliticization: the problems created by America's enduring ethno-racial division are being reframed as problems of law and order and this reframing, in turn, delegitimates any attempt to call into question and subvert America's unequal racial order. According to Wacquant the prison system in the United States, then, has become 'a major engine of symbolic production in its own right' (Wacquant, 2001a: 119). Next to it being the major institution for signifying and enforcing blackness it also induces civic death by pushing inmates out of the social compact. This happens in three ways: prisoners are denied access to valued cultural capital (that is, by expelling them from higher education); they are excluded from social redistribution and public aid; and they are banned from political participation.

The Rise and Export of the Penal State

Earlier we saw how Wacquant's first-hand experiences in, and his research on, the ghetto had directed his sociological gaze to the 'darkening' of the American prison population. His writings on urban marginality, however, remained not restricted to Chicago's South Side: on the one hand the French *banlieues* came under close scrutiny and, on the other hand, he made, under the banner of a 'new regime of urban marginality', more general observations on the plight of people living in the disreputable city zones of the 'First World'. Also this work on 'advanced marginality' was perceived to be incomplete as long as questions related to punishment and penal change remained untouched. It is at this point that we need to situate Wacquant's work on the penal state: it continues his work on the changing face of marginality in post-Fordist societies.

This also implies that his (localized) work on the punishment of blacks residing in the American ghettos needs to be related to his (more globalized) work on the rise of the penal state and the spread of neoliberal penality. It is to this 'fuller analysis' (Wacquant, 2001a: 97) that we will now turn. Our discussion will rely on his books *Les prisons de la misère* (1999) and *Punir les pauvres* (2004), and a number of articles and book chapters published in English and French.[4]

America's neoliberal experiment

Wacquant has a deep interest in the USA. A major part of the research he conducted over the past two decades, is devoted to the dissection of various aspects of American society: from its ghettos and its prisons, to its sociology and its anthropology. This magnet-like attraction can in part be explained by the details of his personal biography: since the mid-1980s Wacquant has studied, lived and worked in various places in the USA and is, at this moment, a sociology professor at the prestigious University of Berkeley in California. However, there is more to this special relationship with the US than mere biographical coincidence: since its formation, America has an image of itself as a country of democratic, technological and socio-economic innovation. According to some it should therefore serve as a role model for the rest of the world. Others, however, may discard such claims as arrogant, parochialist or ethnocentric, and attribute it to a misplaced and dangerous sense of superiority (America's routine disregard of international rules and its long history of unilateralism, for example, is heavily criticized by human rights lawyers all over the globe).

As a Frenchman in America Wacquant is one of those outsiders who strongly disagrees with the idea that America should serve

[4] His book *Les prisons de la misère* has thus far been translated in 14 languages. At the time of writing, the English-language edition (to be published by the University of Minnesota Press) had not appeared yet. There is also an English edition scheduled of *Punir les pauvres* entitled *Punishing the Poor: The New Government of Social Insecurity* (to be published with Duke University Press) but also this translation had not been published yet. We will occasionally rely on the Dutch translation of the book (*Straf de armen*) which appeared in 2006.

as a role model. The USA, so he argued recently, is 'the epicentre of the neoliberal revolution that is now sweeping the globe, and, as such, it offers an extraordinary laboratory for scrutinizing the major social transformations of our age' (Wacquant, 2005e: 14). To a large extent his sociological interest in America finds here its origins. Indeed, as we will see, it is this 'neoliberal revolution' that is being held responsible for deep changes in social and penal policy. The idea of America being a 'laboratory' returns at different points throughout his work (see e.g. Wacquant, 1996d; Wacquant, 2004a). In this section we will discuss how America, according to Wacquant, has experimented with social and penal innovations, and the detrimental side effects this experimentation brought in its wake. To typify America as a 'laboratory' has another advantage for a better understanding of Wacquant's overall story: experiments in laboratory settings are usually meant to be replicated elsewhere, or to find their way into various practical and transferable applications.

Decline of the (semi-)social state, rise of the penal state

Over the past decades a major social experiment took place within American borders. Under the heading 'misery of the social state' (*Misère de l'État social*) Wacquant describes in *Punir les pauvres* how since the mid-1970s the social state in the USA has been in steady decline—with as an acceleration point the year 1996 when President Clinton reformed the welfare system. The American social state was never as developed nor as generous as the ones on the European continent. This is why Wacquant prefers to speak of a *semi*-social state. However, there is also a qualitative difference between the (American) *État charitable* and the (continental European) *État-providence*. In the former poverty is approached from a moralistic and moralizing perspective whereby compassion and not solidarity functions as the guiding principle. The goal, then, is not to reaffirm social relationships, and even less to reduce inequalities, but rather to alleviate the most obvious and appalling forms of misery and to demonstrate society's moral sympathy with those who are in a less fortunate position (Wacquant, 2004a: 61–2). This *État charitable* has two different and sharply separated parts: the *social insurance* system which is reserved for those who are employed, and the *welfare* system which deals exclusively with assistance for dependent or needy persons. Those who (want to) benefit from the latter need to fulfil a number of requirements and are subjected to specific conditions. This bifurcation of social assistance springs from the prime objective of the *État charitable*: to strengthen the mechanisms of the free market and to stimulate or force those who are (temporarily) out of work to (re)turn to the labour market (Wacquant, 2004a: 65–7).

Wacquant documents in detail how, from the 1970s onwards, this *État charitable* has been in a process of continuous retreat. The 1960s 'War on Poverty' of President Lyndon B Johnson was gradually substituted by a 'war against the poor'. Indeed, as Wacquant demonstrates, it was the *welfare* programmes that suffered the most from successive reforms. This happened in three ways: (1) by means of budgetary cuts (allowances under the 'Aid to Families with Dependent Children (AFDC)' scheme, for example, reduced by more than a half between 1970 and 1995); (2) by means of administrative measures (that is, by erecting a high number of bureaucratic obstacles to discourage people from applying for state aid); and (3) by simply abolishing large parts of the state aid programmes. To a lesser but still considerable extent, also those benefiting from the *social insurance* system were subject to similar reforms. The consequences were devastating. By the end of 1994 there were 40 million Americans living in poverty, that is 15 per cent of the total population. One white family in ten, and one African-American in three was living below the poverty line (Wacquant, 2004a: 68–78).

The real death-blow to America's *welfare* system, however, was given in 1996 by President Bill Clinton with the 'Personal Responsibility and Work Opportunity Reconciliation Act' which ended, in the President's words, 'welfare as we know it'. According to Wacquant the use of the word 'reform' was a euphemism that put a gloss on the abolition of support for poor children and substituted it for an obligation to work in unqualified and underpaid jobs for their parents—the so-called move from *welfare* to *workfare*. This 'reform', then, was targeted at poor families and needy persons and left the programmes that benefited the middle classes, that is, *social insurance* as opposed to *welfare*, untouched. The objective was not to reduce poverty but rather to fight the alleged 'culture of dependence' (Wacquant, 1996d; Wacquant, 1997c: 23–5).

The results of three decades of experimentation with social policy are high levels of (child) poverty, large groups with no or poor health insurance, a thriving informal economy, and so forth. This all happened at a time when social inequalities and economic insecurities were rising: whereas those at the top of American society saw their pay cheques increasing and were living the American Dream, those at the bottom were locked in poverty and low- or underpaid jobs, and suffered from the ramifications of deindustrialization, large-scale 'downsizing' operations, the degradation of working conditions, and increasing competition and suspicion in the workplace (see Wacquant, 1996c). This is the socio-economic side of the American experiment. However, whereas the state withdrew from the economy and continuously reduced its social role, it enlargened the scope and intensity of its penal intervention. At this point the penal state enters the story of Wacquant.

Over the same time as America embarked on its socio-economic experiment there was the start of a remarkable and unprecedented growth of the American penal system. Wacquant identifies five dimensions. First, a vertical expansion, that is, the remarkable growth of the US prison population which now counts more than 2 million inmates. Second, a horizontal expansion, that is, the additional enlargement of the penal net through an increasing use of probation and parole which implies that nowadays about 6.5 million Americans are under criminal justice supervision. Third, the advent of penal 'Big government', that is, the disproportionate growth of criminal justice budgets which makes the correctional sector one of America's largest employers. Fourth, the resurgence and development of a private industry of imprisonment, that is, the increasing presence of the market in the punishment business and the rise of privatized, company-controlled prisons. Fifth, a policy of carceral 'affirmative action' whereby African-Americans have a greater chance of coming under penal supervision (Wacquant, 1999a: 71–94; Wacquant, 2002c: 19–21; for more details, see Wacquant, 1998d; Wacquant, 1998f; Wacquant, 1998g; Wacquant, 2004a: 119–221; Wacquant, 2005b). The build-up of this gigantic apparatus comes at a high cost. Four strategies have been implemented to deal with the financial burden: various services have been abolished or reduced, and living standards have been lowered; technology is increasingly being used to lock more people up with fewer staff and to reduce the cost of service delivery; part of the costs of incarceration are transferred onto prisoners and their families; and deskilled labour is being reintroduced in penal institutions (Wacquant, 2002c: 21–28).

According to Wacquant this penal state has two 'privileged targets' (*cibles privilégiées*): black people coming from deprived city areas on the one hand, and sex offenders on the other hand (Wacquant, 2004a: 225–65). We saw earlier how the hyperghetto and the prison meet and mesh and take control over a large group of young urban blacks. For the second group, sex offenders, Wacquant illustrates how especially since the mid-1990s a number of states in the USA have enacted notification and registration laws for sex offenders—in particular in the wake of the so-called Megan's Law, named after Megan Kanka, a small girl from New Jersey who was raped and murdered by a paedophile released on parole. According to such laws the names and details of sex offenders are registered in large databases that are accessible to the public ('registration') and either the local authorities, or the offenders themselves, need to inform local communities that a sex offender is in their presence ('notification'). These laws have not been without adverse consequences: numerous incidents, humiliations, hostilities, threats and the like make the reintegration of such offenders almost impossible. Their reputation is damaged; employers fire them; their families live in shame; they often are forced to move elsewhere; and occasionally they commit suicide. According to Wacquant, the penal state has turned itself against such offenders who are no longer perceived to be in need of medical treatment but are rather seen as threats that need to be 'contained' in order to strengthen public security and the protection of victims (see Wacquant, 1999e; Wacquant, 2001c).

The commercial carceral-assistential complex

According to Wacquant the rise of the penal state cannot be explained in terms of it being a simple response to rising crime rates: he rejects the 'legal syllogism' and argues that the continuous expansion of the penal system in the USA happened during a prolonged period of stagnation which was followed by a period of decrease in crime rates in the 1990s (see Wacquant, 2001e: 60; Wacquant, 2004a: 134–5; Wacquant, 2005b: 11–13). The real explanation, so he argues, needs to be found in the new link that has been forged between the (declining) social state and the (growing) penal state (Wacquant, 2001e: 59).

The reduced and redesigned social state is increasingly geared towards disciplining those at the bottom of the social hierarchy, that is, by transforming social services into instruments of surveillance and control (e.g. by making *welfare* conditional upon fulfilling requirements with respect to work (*workfare*); sexual behaviour; school results of children; single mothers having to live with their parents; and so forth (Wacquant, 2004a: 79–80)). The penal state, for its part, responds to the social dislocations provoked by the retreat of the *État charitable* (Wacquant, 2004a: 85). The result is a 'commercial carceral-assistential complex' (*un complexe commercial carcéro-assistantiel*), which functions according to a gendered division of labour: the carceral component handles mainly men and the assistential component keeps an eye on women and children (Wacquant, 1997c: 31; Wacquant, 1999a: 93–4; Wacquant, 2004a: 115).

This reconstruction of the American *État charitable* leads to a new type of state which is different from both the welfare state and the liberal minimal state. Inspired by the Greek figure of the centaur (that is, creatures composed of part human and part horse) Wacquant speaks of an *État-centaure*: a state with a liberal head and an authoritarian body (Wacquant, 2004a: 63). The new way of governing social insecurity is perceived to be closely linked to the rise of neoliberalism as an 'ideological project' and as a 'governmental practice', which aims to subordinate all aspects of human existence to the free market and celebrates individual responsibility. Penal change, then, is intricately bound up with the neoliberal revolution (Wacquant, 2004a: 21).

From America to Europe and beyond

Earlier we saw that Wacquant prefers to typify America as a laboratory. Since it is the birthplace and centre of the neoliberal revolution it provides social scientists with a unique case to study the transformations that have been following in its wake. Analysing American developments, then, is not only an interesting but also a pressing task to undertake: indeed, if, as Wacquant suggests, this revolution has been sweeping the globe, then this implies that, sooner or later, the same kind of transformations might take place in other parts of the world. Seen from this perspective, the recent American history offers insight in what the foreseeable future might bring for other nations. It is against this background that we need to understand Wacquant's interest in the USA: for him it is the 'living laboratory of the neoliberal future' (Wacquant, 2004a: 11–19; Wacquant, 2007). According to Wacquant experimentation in this neoliberal laboratory has sparked a number of ready-made products which have been exported to different corners of the globe.

How neoliberal 'penal commonsense' spreads over the globe

America's experiment has resulted in the partial replacement of the social state by a penal state which has no equivalent in the world. However, so Wacquant argues, to understand the specificities of the American experience, does not imply that America should be given the 'status of particularity' (*status de particularité*) (Wacquant, 1998e: 3). In European countries imprisonment rates have also been increasing; immigrants and foreigners are overrepresented in penal institutions which often suffer from serious overcrowding; penal policies have hardened; public debate focuses on crime, urban unrest and incivilities; and so forth. For Wacquant there are enough indications to argue that also in Europe a tendency towards the 'expansion of the penal treatment of misery' can be observed (Wacquant, 1998e: 5). We will return in more detail to what Wacquant has to say about the European path to the penal state in the next section. For the moment it is sufficient to note that America should not be treated as an 'outsider' or 'anomaly' on the global scene.

For Wacquant there is a clear link between the rise and global spread of neoliberalism and the worldwide diffusion of US-style police strategies and penal policies. In *Les prisons de la misère* he observes how politicians, criminologists and journalists tend to speak in a remarkably similar language; how alike their problem formulations are; and how the same solutions echo all over the globe. Wacquant gives the example of zero tolerance: this policing strategy was pioneered in New York City in the 1990s but quickly found its way into various other parts of the world. From France to Brazil people started to speak about 'tolérance zéro', 'tolerância zero', 'Null Toleranz', 'tolleranza zero', 'nultolerantie', and so forth. For Wacquant this is not a mere coincidence: rather it testifies to the internationalization of the 'new punitive *doxa*' ('la nouvelle *doxa* punitive' (Wacquant, 1999a: 13)). This 'new punitive *doxa*' forms the penal component of the 'Washington consensus' (Wacquant, 1999a: 62). Here, again, it becomes clear why Wacquant needed to turn to questions of penal change in order to 'complete' his work on advanced marginality and neoliberalism: we are dealing with an integrated whole, a complete US-made yet globalizing neoliberal package, with crime control 'talk' and 'action' as an essential component in order to tackle increasing social insecurity and marginality. Neoliberal socio-economic policies go hand in hand with a distinctive neoliberal penality. And just as the USA has been exporting and imposing its socio-economic policies by means of organizations such as the World Bank, the WTO and the like, so it has spread its home-made 'penal common sense' all over the globe.

Interestingly, Wacquant does not stop at discussing these developments *in abstracto* but describes in detail how parts of the world come to speak and think alike—in compliance with the new *pensée unique*. The transatlantic diffusion of US-made *doxa* on security happens in three stages. First, the gestation, implementation and showcasting in American cities. Wacquant illustrates how 'zero tolerance' policing was implemented in New York and came to be sold to the world as an example of the way ahead for policing the metropolis. This happened with the help of neoconservative think tanks such as the Manhattan Institute which, like they did earlier when launching an ideological attack against the welfare state, promoted such crime control strategies (and their concomitant theories such as the 'broken windows theory') during high-profile lunch seminars, conferences, book publications, and so forth. Second, the import/export of this new penal commonsense. Here England serves as 'acclimation chamber' and 'Trojan horse' with a view to conquering the European continent. Over the years American neoconservative thinkers such as Charles Murray and Lawrence Mead, and former New York City police commissioner William Bratton, were invited to London to give well-advertised lectures, attended by influential journalists and policy-makers, on how England should adopt the presumably successful American-made social and penal policies. But also study visits are being undertaken across the Atlantic to learn from the American experiences. Third, the 'scholarly whitewash' or 'academicization', that is, how these policies are given a (pseudo) scientific gloss by local intellectuals. Or, as he put it in an interview, it is about 'selling a conservative pig in a criminological poke' (Wacquant, 2001d: 83). For example, in France, so Wacquant argues, the IHESI (Institut des hautes études de la sécurité intérieure) and 'Institut de criminologie', based in Paris, have taken up the role of repackaging and reselling the American security ideologies (see Wacquant, 1999a: 22–63; Wacquant, 1999d; Wacquant, 2003a; Wacquant, 2004a: 50–58).

Wacquant's interest in this travelling of neoliberal penality led him to widen his gaze to South America, in particular Brazil. This is not a coincidence because Latin-American countries have been incited to adopt US-made economic policies and, therefore, so Wacquant argues, they also became vulnerable to take over its police strategies and penal policies. The consequences, however, are much more dramatic here because such countries suffer from high levels of poverty and crime, their social welfare programmes are underdeveloped, and police and judicial agencies are corrupt and participate in large-scale state violence. In such a fragile context the adoption of the neoliberal crime control remedies tends to install a 'dictatorship over the poor' (see Wacquant, 2003b; Wacquant, 2005i).

The European road to the penal state: social panopticism

Despite the strength of the neoliberal *doxa* and its imperialistic diffusion by powerful institutions Europe is not slavishly copying the American model and there is no wholesale criminalization of poverty. Rather, so he suggests, there seems to be a European road to the penal state in the making which has two characteristics. First, an accentuation of both the social and penal regulation of social insecurity. In France, for example, social intervention has been increasing by various initiatives such as creating and sponsoring (youth) jobs; raising the level of public aid packages; extending the reach of the guaranteed minimum income; instituting universal health coverage; and so forth. However, at the same time penal intervention was also strengthened by stationing riot police squads and special surveillance units in sensitive neighbourhoods; by enforcing anti-begging ordinances; by increasing penalties for recidivism; by restricting release on parole; and so forth. Second, in Europe there is less reliance on the prison: the penalization of poverty is mainly effected by means of the police and the courts. The logic, then, is more panoptic than retributive or segregative. This implies that social service bureaucracies are actively taking part in the European way of governing social insecurity. Wacquant therefore launches the notion 'social panopticism' (see Wacquant, 1999a: 114–22; Wacquant, 2001b: 406–8; Wacquant, 2001d: 83–4).

At first sight this European road to the penal state may seem more benign than the American one but it nevertheless points in the same direction and leads to a similar destiny. The only way out, so Wacquant argues, lies in the construction of a truly European social state, that is, a state committed to the expansion and strengthening of social and economic rights (Wacquant, 2001b). Indeed, as long as the USA and Europe remain faithful to the pervasive neoliberal ideology and the policies it informs, they are destined to walk into the same direction which is, inevitably, one that leads towards more penal intervention. There are, then, differences in the means that are being used on both sides of the Atlantic, and the same holds true for the sheer scale of punishment but, at a deeper level, the similarities prevail (Wacquant, 1999a: 100).

Moreover, so Wacquant adds, foreigners residing within European borders do not seem to have access to the European road of social panopticism. Their over-representation in penal institutions suggests that they, like black people in the US prison system, are most directly affected by the new way of governing social insecurity: 'throughout Europe, it is foreigners... who are massively over-represented within the imprisoned population, and this is to a degree comparable, nay in some places superior, to the "racial disproportionality" that afflicts blacks in the United States' (Wacquant, 1999b: 216). The upcoming penal state in Europe, then, like its bigger brother on the other side of the Atlantic, directs its resources primarily at these 'suitable enemies'. For Wacquant these 'transatlantic parallels' provide extra reason to remain sceptical about the idea that the USA is exceptional (Wacquant, 2005d: 32; Wacquant, 2006c: 84). Moreover, in both cases, so Wacquant suggests, locking up these groups *en masse* serves a 'depoliticizing' function, that is, it obscures society's responsibility in creating their plight (Wacquant, 2005d: 43).

The role of punishment in a divided society

Before entering a more in-depth discussion of Wacquant's work on punishment, here we briefly summarize the different functions punishment fulfils in his overall account. There are at least two aspects in his work which result in punishment being attributed an important role in a (socially and racially) divided society. First, whereas Boutellier acknowledges that each society has its own 'internal tensions as regards gender differences, class conflicts or generation gaps' (Boutellier, 2004a: 8) he nevertheless is of the opinion that these have receded into the background: 'in the risk culture it is the friction between vitality and safety that occupies the central role'. In a morally fragmented society, then, punishment solely plays a crucial norm-clarifying role. Wacquant could hardly be further removed from Boutellier's account: for Wacquant society is not morally fragmented but socially and racially divided. Instead of the 'internal tensions' having become less important they have only increased further with the advent of post-Fordism, the rise of advanced marginality and (in the USA) the crisis of the ghetto as an instrument in racial control. In Wacquant's account the *power* to punish re-enters the picture: penal change has to be understood against the background of preserving, and even deepening, the social and racial cleavages in a society that over the past three decades has become more rather than less divisive.

Second, and related to this, whereas Garland interprets punitive developments in a culture of control as a strategy of denial, that is, as a somewhat helpless and inherently ineffective response of a state apparatus that experiences difficulties in acknowledging that, faced with the predicament of high crime rates, it can no longer live up to the high expectations that follow from its monopoly on crime control, there Wacquant holds another opinion and opposes his interpretation to Garland's (see Wacquant, 1998e: 5; Wacquant, 1999a: 138). For Wacquant there not only is no predicament (cf. in his opinion the crime problem has not worsened) but, in addition and more fundamentally, the idea of powerless politicians and criminal justice agencies 'denying' such a predicament, fails to capture the crucial political responsibility in the build-up of the penal state. Just as the implosion of the communal ghetto and its subsequent 'hyperghettoization' was intepreted as a 'political creation of the state', so the strengthening of its penal arm needs to be seen against a long series of deliberate and conscious decisions aimed at slimming down the social state and expanding the penal sector. The state apparatus is not only a highly powerful one which uses its penal resources 'to bolster the social, racial and economic order' (Wacquant, 2005b: 15) but it is also manned and steered by political actors that have much more freedom to act (differently) than Garland suggests.

Against the background of an analytic framework which stresses both power and political agency one can identify at least five different functions that punishment fulfils in Wacquant's account. First, a disciplinary function. Punishment disciplines those fractions of the working class that buck at the new precarious service jobs. With the penal sword of Damocles swinging above their heads, they think twice before revolting against the low-paid and insecure jobs and deciding to opt for a life in illegality. This disciplinary power is also being activated for those who, after having done time, re-enter the free world. In a recent interview Wacquant illustrated this with another first-hand experience from the ghetto: his old friend Ashante from the boxing school having two convictions thus far, now takes any unattractive low-paid job that is available for him to avoid being sentenced to life imprisonment under the three-strikes-and-you're-out-rule (see Hilhorst, 2005). Second, a function of neutralization. The penal system neutralizes and warehouses the most disruptive elements in society and those who are considered superfluous in view of the transformations in the demand for labour in the new economic situation. Punishment plays the function of a 'social vacuum cleaner' (*aspirateur social*) (Wacquant, 2004a: 298) that cleanses the streets of the human waste (that is, the unemployed, drug addicts, the mentally ill, the needy, small thieves, the *sans papiers*, and so forth) that is produced *en masse* in the wake of the economic transformations. Third, it reaffirms state authority in the limited domain (law and order) that it still holds for itself after its retreat from social provision and economic regulation (on these three functions, see Wacquant, 2001b: 405; Wacquant, 2001d: 82; Wacquant, 2004a: 28). Fourth, a function (specific to the USA) of ethno-racial control. In response to the crisis of the ghetto, the American penal system has become, together with the newly-emerged hyperghetto, the fourth 'peculiar institution' in America's long history of racial division. Fifth, a symbolic function. Boundaries are not only drawn and reaffirmed by disciplining and neutralizing certain groups deemed undesirable or superfluous but also by creating symbolic divisions that reinforce the material ones (and vice versa), for example, by conflating crime with blackness (in the USA) or with migration (in Europe), by reinforcing and dramatizing the demarcations between the presumably law-abiding community and criminals, by pointing out where we need to look for the 'suitable enemies' which are made visible in police operations and penal practices, and so forth (see e.g. Wacquant, 1999b: 219–20; Wacquant, 2004a: 36; Wacquant, 2006a: 14–16).

Discussion

Even though Wacquant started to address questions related to penal change fairly recently he acclimatized at a remarkable speed to the small international penological milieu: in 1998 he edited a special issue of *Actes de la recherche en sciences sociales* devoted to the theme 'From the Social State to the Penal State' (*De l'État social à l'État pénal*) which contained papers by *inter alia* Christie, Garland, Melossi, Western, Beckett and Harding; in February 2000 he was invited by Garland to speak in New York at the conference 'The Causes and Consequences of Mass Imprisonment in the USA'; his first book on punishment *Les prisons de la misère* (1999) received laudable reviews in two major English-language journals *Punishment and Society* (Deflem, 2001) and *Theoretical Criminology* (Harcourt, 2001) that usually are rather sparse in discussing work published in French; his papers were published in major criminological journals[5] and numerous scholars with an interest in the sociology of punishment have included chapters by Wacquant in their edited volumes (see Garland, 2001b; Gilligan and Pratt, 2003; Pratt *et al,* 2005a; Armstrong and McAra, 2006); in May 2006 he organized (with Bruce Western) a conference entitled 'Probing the Penal State' at the University of Berkeley, with the participation of eminent punishment scholars such as Garland, Simon, Spierenburg and Zimring[6]; and, next to these more 'formal' indications of his quick immersion in the little world of international penology, there are numerous notes of thanks to Richard Sparks (e.g. Wacquant, 1999a: 164 (note 49); Wacquant, 2002d: 389; Wacquant, 2003a: 178 (note 12); Wacquant, 2006c: 83), David Garland (Wacquant, 2001a: 121; Wacquant, 2006c: 83) and others which suggest that over the

[5] Thus far three of his papers have been published in *Punishment and Society*, one found its way into *Theoretical Criminology* and another in the *European Journal of Criminal Policy and Research*. An interesting detail: Wacquant is probably record-holder of having published the longest paper ever in the history of *Punishment and Society*. Whereas prospective authors for scholarly journals usually have to adhere to strict editorial rules in terms of the number of words being allowed (in the case of *Punishment and Society* authors who want to submit their work for review need to limit their papers to 8,000 words which, in printed form, would count for an estimated 16 to 18 pages in the journal) he managed to have a paper of 40 pages included in a 2001 issue.

[6] See: http://igov.berkeley.edu/conferences/Penal%20State%20Schedule.doc (Accessed: 26 July 2007).

years also informal contacts and back-room discussion on work-in-progress have flourished. Clearly, there must be something in his scholarship that enabled him to become, in a relative short period of time, a central nod in the relatively small network of researchers touching upon questions related to penal change.

However, it would be a mistake to infer from this successful socialization process that his work has been received without much critical comment. Whereas his penological writings found their way relatively quietly into the usual publication circuits[7], he made (and provoked) much more noise in other corners of the academic world. Indeed, Wacquant is also the *enfant terrible* of (American) sociology and anthropology. In 2002 the editorial board of the prestigious *American Journal of Sociology* offered him no less than 65 pages to criticize three ethnographic studies and to formulate a piercing judgement on the state of American sociology: 'US sociology is now tied and party to the ongoing construction of the *neoliberal* state and its "carceral-assistential complex" for the punitive management of the poor, on and off the street' (Wacquant, 2002g: 1471). Predictably, the responses of the three attacked authors were not mild either. They carried the following telling titles: 'The Ideologically Driven Critique' (Anderson, 2002), 'What Kind of Combat Sport Is Sociology?' (Duneier, 2002) and 'No Shame: The View from the Left Bank' (Newman, 2002). On the occasion of the publication of *Body and Soul* (Wacquant, 2004b) the editors of *Symbolic Interaction* decided to reverse the process: now it was Wacquant (2005f) who was placed in a defensive position and who received punches from a number of attackers.

[7] Wacquant's rapid and deep immersion in the safe life-world of (mostly Anglo Saxon) scholars working on themes that fall within the ambit of the sociology of punishment may also have protected him against their (potential) critique. With the notable exceptions of Matthews who wrote about the 'myopic nature' of Wacquant's work (Matthews, 2006b: 93; see also Matthews, 2005a), and Nelken who argued that Wacquant falls prey to the 'evil causes evil' fallacy (Nelken, 2006: 264), there has been, as far as I know, little critical (printed) discussion of his work on punishment in the major criminological journals. In France Ocqueteau, who was personally accused by Wacquant of uncritically promoting American import products such as zero tolerance on French soil (Wacquant, 2004a: 52; see also Wacquant, 2004f: 130 (note 28)), responded with a biting review of *Punir les pauvres*. In his review with the telling title 'Punir les pauvres, le degré zéro de la pensée gauchiste!' Ocqueteau ridiculed the hypothesis Wacquant advances in his book and accused him in turn of misreading and misrepresenting his own work (Ocqueteau, 2004).

For outsiders, situated at a safe distance from the battlefield, these polemical attacks and counter-punches are not only enjoyable but also highly instructive. Moreover, in the case of Wacquant, they also tell us a great deal about the author behind the text. Wacquant is a fighter: not only literally, as an ex-boxer from the slums, but also as a *provocateur* in the academic world and a combative opponent of the neoliberal globalization in his academic writings. In 2001 the French film-maker Pierre Carles made a documentary about Bourdieu with the title '*La sociologie est un sport de combat*' *(Sociology is a Martial Art)* which, arguably, is also the *Leitmotiv* of Wacquant (see Cyran, 2001).

Moving beyond Rusche and Kirchheimer

The Italian criminologist Alessandro De Giorgi recently concluded his review of the classical political economy of punishment—starting with Rusche and Kirchheimer's pioneering study *Punishment and Social Structure*, followed (with some time lag) by a wave of neo-Marxist studies on the relationships between punishment and labour market, and ending with Melossi's 'grounded labelling theory'—by stating that it had limited capacity 'to take into consideration the social and economic transformations which are taking place in western societies since the 1970s' (De Giorgi, 2006: 39). The reason, so he argued, was that this political economy of punishment was referring to a specific socio-economic paradigm, that is, Fordist capitalism and the welfare state. When De Giorgi observed that 'materialist criminologists' had failed to consider the impact of such transformations, he added a footnote which directs the reader to a paper by Wacquant (De Giorgi, 2006: 40 (note 111)). For De Giorgi Wacquant was 'an exception' to this unfortunate blind spot in contemporary thinking about the consequences of socio-economic transformations upon punishment (see also De Giorgi, 2007: 252, 256–7).

Wacquant's work, indeed, bears the imprint of a tradition of research that in recent years has somewhat receded into the background. To a certain extent this also seems to be the case in general sociology in the wake of the 'cultural turn' in the social sciences (see Smart, 2003: 174). Wacquant needs to be credited for having contributed to rethinking an old penological tradition for current times. In Chapter 1 we argued that the unpredictability of recent penal change called for a reworking of the classical perspectives in the sociology of punishment. Just like the authors in the three previous chapters who aimed to rethink and reinvent some of the classical perspectives in the sociology of punishment to make them useful for the present, so Wacquant brings some older critical perspectives on punishment back to life and reworks them for our post-Fordist epoch. In this respect he is well aware that the questions he asks, and the answers he provides, bear resemblances with the classical work by Rusche and Kirchheimer. Indeed, and predictably in view of Wacquant's analytic framework, their book *Punishment and Social Structure* returns regularly in his publications (see e.g. Wacquant, 1999a: 100; Wacquant, 2000a: 387 (note 8); Wacquant, 2001a: 121 (note 3); Wacquant, 2002b: 52 (note 20); Wacquant, 2004a: 17). However, at the same time he does not intend to fall prey to a form of crude economism (see e.g. Wacquant, 2001a: 121–2 (note 3); Wacquant, 2004a: 17). In fact, it is possible to arrive at (what one might term) four 'rules of thumb' that guide Wacquant's thinking on punishment: (1) there is an indirect link between economic forces and penal policy, with political actors playing a crucial role in determining how impersonal economic transformations will affect the balance between social and penal policies; (2) economic forces do not restrict their sphere of influence to the labour market but extend (in view of neoliberalism being a complete ideological package of assumptions about how human beings and society function) to aspects of crime-causation ('rational-choice' theory), models of law enforcement ('zero-tolerance' policing), theories of punishment (deterrence and incapacitation), and the like; (3) the prison controls groups that, for various reasons (including reasons of an economic and racial nature), are deemed to be undesirable or superfluous; (4) the penal system plays an important symbolic function by drawing, dramatizing and enforcing group boundaries.

Such an expanded framework, arguably, opens possibilities for a much richer account than the older quantitative studies on the labour market hypothesis which Howe (1994: 32) once (somewhat disrespectfully) called 'numbingly dull'. This also applies to his emphasis of the symbolic dimension of the penal system, that is, the penal system plays a role both in terms of 'social stratification' and 'symbolic division' (see Wacquant, 2002a: 15). In the remainder of this section we briefly touch upon three issues that Wacquant's particular way of making sense of penal change brings into view and that remain somewhat in the background in other accounts.

First, the crucial role of race in American (penal) history. One of the recurrent critiques levelled at Garland's *The Culture of Control* (e.g. Western, 2004) and Whitman's *Harsh Justice* (e.g. Steiker, 2003; Kaplan, 2006) is that both authors hardly touch upon the question of race in the USA. A major contribution of Wacquant is that he moved race to the centre of his research and is able to offer an original explanation for the 'blackening' of the US prison population. Moreover, his account of how prison and ghetto meet and mesh entails a more wide-ranging lesson for the sociology of punishment. Whereas in aetiological criminology we have been familiar for many years with 'crime hot spots', that is areas that for a variety of reasons are more vulnerable to be affected by crime, there has been much less discussion of (what one might term) 'penal hot spots'. Wacquant's research suggests that certain neighbourhoods or areas might be more prone to punishment than others—just as some neighbourhoods and areas are more prone to crime. Such 'penal hot spots' usually get lost in discussions on punishment and penal change that predominantly refer to national imprisonment rates, nationwide developments in crime, changes in state budgets, alternative measures, and the like. There is, therefore, a highly interesting suggestion for future research buried in Wacquant's work on the ghetto and prisons, that is, to break down aggregate numbers to lower levels and to study local patterns of punishment.

Second, Wacquant brings into sharp view one of the darkest secrets of contemporary societies, that is, that certain groups of people increasingly become 'superfluous' and no longer seem to be able to fulfil a useful function for society (see e.g. Wacquant, 2006a: 32, 78, 106, 110, 158, 178, 273). One of the key features of post-Fordist economic systems is that they manage to produce more with fewer people, that economic growth is possible without creating extra jobs. Mass production no longer needs mass mobilization of labour. In recent years eminent sociologists such as Bauman (2004) and Sennett (2006) have, like Wacquant, drawn attention to how contemporary societies produce large quantities of 'useless' people, or what Bauman refers to as 'human waste'. Inevitably, this also poses problems for the 'human waste disposal industry' (the term is, again, Bauman's), not the least if the older welfare-inspired mechanisms of dealing with the poor, the unemployed, the homeless, and the like come under increasing attack. Like Wacquant Bauman also suggests that penal systems play a growing role in absorbing those people that are no longer able to participate in such a highly competitive society of consumers.

Third, to a certain extent Wacquant continues the approach adopted by Garland in *Punishment and Welfare*. As we saw in Chapter 2 for Garland the origins of the penal-welfare complex at the end of the nineteenth century could not be understood without taking into account the crisis of social and penal regulation in Victorian times. Garland's analysis combined Foucault- and (to a lesser extent) Marx-inspired theoretical insights to make sense of penal change. However, whereas Garland in *The Culture of Control* finished the storyline of his 1985 study by moving it into the present, he *discontinued* his 1985 approach. Indeed, as we discussed earlier, Garland gradually switched to a pluralist position which made any one-dimensional perspective—including his own in *Punishment and Welfare*—unattractive.

Wacquant's discussion of the relationship between the 'social state' and the 'penal state'; the formation of a 'commercial carceral-assistential' complex; the emergence of a new type of state, that is, the *État-centaure* which takes over from the welfare state and which is liberal-paternalist in nature; and his close attention to the regulatory function of punishment: to a certain extent[8] they resemble the emphases that Garland had put in *Punishment and Welfare* and, moreover, continue (more than Garland himself) the approach that the young Garland adopted (see also Wacquant, 1999a: 150, 189 (note 171)).

This brings us to a highly interesting point for further discussion. In Chapter 2 we have seen that Garland had good reasons to revise the approach he adopted in *Punishment and Welfare*. The book formed part of a stream in revisionist history-writing

[8] We deliberately write 'to a certain extent' because there are at least two crucial differences. First, in *Punishment and Welfare* Garland devoted a great deal of attention to the role of criminological knowledge in the formation of the penal-welfare complex and his study, therefore, was much more inspired by Foucault than by the political economy of punishment. Even though Wacquant touches upon the disciplinary function of punishment he is much more wedded to a reworked political economy of punishment. Criminological knowledge only enters his story in the case of criminologists using their academic credentials to import and 'academicize' the neoliberal crime control strategies. Second, even in 1985, at a time when Garland's work was still much more directly oriented towards a critique of the penal system, his book was much more 'detached' than Wacquant's which takes as its starting- and endpoint a critique of the neoliberal revolution.

which, throughout the 1980s, came under increasing attack *inter alia* with the help of Garland himself who started to discover Elias and Geertz, to reread Durkheim, and to criticize Foucault. What Garland won from his shift to a pluralist position was a more complex description of how punishment actually functions, a position that enabled him to pay more fully respect to 'the integrity of the empirical object'. The price he needed to pay for this, however, was the loss of the possibility of putting analysis directly to use for critique. If Wacquant adopts a much more straightforward perspective which approaches penal change from a specific angle, that is, a position that is much closer to the one of the young Garland than the multidimensional one of the middle-aged Garland, then the gains and losses reverse: what Wacquant wins in terms of possibilities for critique he loses in terms of arriving at a proper description of punishment in all its complexity. We will return to this topic in Chapter 6.

America and the rest of the world

As we have seen throughout this chapter, America plays an important role in Wacquant's scholarship. This makes it highly interesting to investigate where he can be positioned in the 'American exceptionalism' debate that we touched upon earlier in Chapter 2. That will be the theme of the next section. We then pay more attention to the travelling of policies in Wacquant's work.

American exceptionalism, or not?

There is a tension at work in Wacquant's treatment of the USA which remains largely unresolved. On the one hand, in his discussion of the unique history of racial segregation in the USA, Wacquant suggests that the American conception of 'race' as national 'principle of social vision and division' is 'virtually matchless in the world for its rigidity and consequentiality' and that the USA stands alone as a 'slaveholding republic' (Wacquant, 2005c: 127). The USA is an 'exceptional society' in terms of its rigorous use of its system of racial classification (Wacquant, 2006a: 190). The crucial role of race makes him speak about America's 'racial exceptionalism' (Wacquant, 2001a: 122 (note 4)). And, with Bourdieu, he seemed to endorse the 'American exceptionalist' argument as we discussed it in Chapter 2: 'If the USA is truly exceptional, in accordance with the old Tocquevillian theme untiringly renewed and periodically updated, it is above all for the *rigid dualism* of its racial division' (Bourdieu and Wacquant, 1999: 51).

Because of this unique history of racial segregation Wacquant insisted that French *banlieues* were not (becoming) ghettos; that there was no transatlantic convergence that leads to the emergence of ghettos in European cities; and that there was no 'Americanization' of urban poverty in European cities (see e.g. Wacquant, 2006a: 9, 289–90; Wacquant, 2006e: 8–11). In his work on the over-representation of blacks behind American bars he continued using 'exceptionalist' statements in two different respects. First, to highlight the sheer unique scale of the American prison population, that is, the penal state in the USA is 'truly exceptional' (Wacquant, 2000b: 117) and America's mass imprisonment is being set apart as 'carceral exceptionalism' (Wacquant, 2002d: 388). Second, such an exceptionalism not only seems to follow from ethno-racial domination as a unique cause, but also because of the unique consequences of mass incarceration in terms of 'race making' (Wacquant, 2005c: 128).

However, as soon as Wacquant starts developing his theory of neoliberal penality, and as soon as he launches his hypothesis of the 'new penal common sense' travelling around the globe to turn every society into American satellites, he seems (and needs) to soften his exceptionalist statements. Indeed, here he warns that America should not be given the 'status of particularity' (*status de particularité*) (Wacquant, 1998e: 3) and he does his utmost best to argue *against* the idea of America being exceptional (see Wacquant, 1999a: 95; Wacquant, 1999b: 216; Wacquant, 2001f; Wacquant, 2002g: 1522–3; Waquant, 2005d: 32; Wacquant, 2006c: 84; see also Heijne, 2006).

> This leads one to think that, *extreme* though it may be, the carceral trajectory of blacks in the United States could be less idiosyncratic than the catch-all theory of 'American exceptionalism' would have one believe. One can even hypothesize that, the same causes producing the same effects, there is every chance that the societies of Western Europe will generate *analogous*, albeit less pronounced, situations to the extent that they, too, embark on the path of the penal management of poverty and inequality, and ask their prison system not only to curb crime but also to regulate the lower segments of the labor market and to hold at bay populations judged to be disreputable, derelict, and unwanted (Wacquant, 1999b: 216).

When read carefully, it is striking to note that the word 'race' does not appear in this lengthy quote. Wacquant hypothesizes that, *the same causes producing the same effects*, western European countries might generate 'analogous' situations as in the USA. However, in order to make such 'transatlantic parallels' possible he needs to 'delete' *the* major cause that he discusses elsewhere at length, that is, the meeting and meshing of the American prison and the hyperghetto which form America's fourth 'peculiar institution'. If Wacquant does not want to abandon his 'prison-meets-hyperghetto' hypothesis how, then, can it ever be possible to have 'the same causes producing the same effects' in Europe? Indeed, as he repeatedly argued, the history of racial segregation in the USA is unique and there are no ghettos in Europe but how, then, can the 'same causes' ever be present in Europe and lead towards the 'same effects' as for imprisonment of blacks in American prisons?

It seems as if America's exceptional imprisonment record is being polished to fit the 'neoliberal penality' theory. Indeed, Wacquant now refers to the 'penal management of poverty and inequality' and to the prison being used 'to regulate the lower segments of the labour market', that is, those aspects that fit his *other* hypothesis, that is, the global spread of the penal state which finds its origins in the USA. Wacquant also *needs* to do this: his theory of 'neoliberal penality' is built upon the idea that *if* other countries import America's neoliberal socio-economic policies *then* they also will import its penal state. There is no place for the (unique) 'race' explanation in this (general) theory and, therefore, it needs to be 'deleted' to prevent jeopardizing the whole theory.

Wacquant also adopts a second strategy in an attempt to save his 'neoliberal penality' theory from the American exceptionalist argument. In a more recent paper he compares foreigners, migrants and second-generation immigrants being confined in prisons in the European Union with blacks being locked up in the USA. In both cases there is a clear disproportionality: foreigners are over-represented in the prison systems of EU countries and the same holds for blacks in the US prison system. This leads him, again, to see 'transatlantic parallels' between Europe and the USA (Wacquant, 2005d: 34). And in both cases these disproportionalities are interpreted as following from a shift to neoliberal penality (Wacquant, 2005d: 44).

In this second strategy, then, he does not 'delete' race but rather, in view of the 'transatlantic parallels' that he observes, aims to incorporate it in his general theory of neoliberal penality. And, indeed, at first sight it seems to work: just as the USA has a disproportionately high number of blacks in prison, so Europe has a disproportionately high number of postcolonial immigrants in its penal institutions, and both regulate them in the same 'neoliberal' way, that is, both use penalization to 'depoliticize' tricky questions related to their racial and colonial pasts.

However, also in this case Wacquant seems to be too quick to identify the 'transatlantic parallels' that he needs to uphold his general theory of neoliberal penality. First, as evidence for the 'transatlantic parallels' Wacquant calculates the ratio between the proportion of foreign inmates in the prison population and the proportion of foreigners in the total population. According to this measure the USA is only ranked tenth in his table: its number is 3.9 (that is, there are 3.9 times more Blacks in prison compared to their share in the general population) which is well below EU countries such as Spain (11.2), Italy (10.5), Greece (8.3), the Netherlands (7.4) etc. This leads him to the conclusion that the situation in Europe might be even worse than in the USA: 'in nine of fourteen members of the European Union, the disproportionate incarceration of foreigners is superior to the demographic over-representation of blacks in American jails and prisons' (Wacquant, 2005d: 35). However, Wacquant's focus on these ratios leaves, of course, the grand differences in *absolute* numbers out of the picture. Even if we add up all the absolute numbers of the 15 EU countries which he includes in his table we arrive at 77,419 foreigners[9] which is more than 10 times less than the situation in the USA with 816,600 blacks. In using ratios Wacquant obfuscates the enormous differences in scale: in his eagerness to see 'transatlantic parallels' it seems as if he tends to forget what he at other times refers to as America's 'carceral exceptionalism' (Wacquant, 2002d: 388).

Second, for the very same reason that Wacquant argues elsewhere that *banlieues* are not ghettos, that is, because they are not homogeneous but highly heterogeneous, so foreign inmates in EU prisons are not a homogeneous group. In 2003, for example,

[9] 7,700 (Spain) + 10,900 (Italy) + 2,200 (Greece) + 3,700 (Netherlands) + 1,600 (Portugal) + 14,200 (France) + 3,200 (Belgium) + 1,100 (Sweden) + 339 (Norway) + 25,000 (Germany) + 1,900 (Austria) + 450 (Denmark) + 127 (Finland) + 203 (Ireland) + 4,800 (England) = 77,419 foreigners in 15 EU countries in 1997 as opposed to 816,600 blacks in the USA (for the numbers, see Wacquant, 2005d: 34 (Table 1)).

there were 108 different nationalities in Belgian prisons. The largest group came from North Africa (34 per cent), followed by eastern Europe (23 per cent), southern Europe (17 per cent) and neighbouring states (10 per cent) (see Snacken *et al,* 2004: 21). Many, then, do not come from former European colonies—this is especially the case for eastern Europeans. In any case, it should be clear that drawing 'transatlantic parallels' between the mass incarceration of one group in the USA which has suffered from almost four centuries of racial segregation on the one hand, and the incarceration of a heterogeneous group of foreigners in Europe where there has been no history of slavery or ethno-racial division on the other hand, seems to be too far-fetched.

In sum, there remains a deep and unresolved tension in Wacquant's work between his America-*specific* explanation for the mass incarceration of blacks (the 'prison-meets-ghetto' hypothesis) on the one hand, and his *general* explanation derived from the (America-born) 'neoliberal revolution' that is sweeping the globe on the other hand. If, as he argues, 'slavery and mass imprisonment are genealogically linked' and if 'one cannot understand the latter...without returning to the former' (Wacquant, 2002b: 41–2) then we are dealing with an 'exceptionalist' argument which does not apply to other states (which, then, also do not need to worry too much about becoming 'Americanized'). On the other hand, if penal developments in the USA have to be understood as resulting from its neoliberal experiment, then 'exceptionalism' moves out of the picture: the socio-economic neoliberal policies, as well as the penal ones, are, in the end, transferable to other states (which, then, have good reasons to worry about 'Americanization'). While both hypotheses might seem plausible *on their own*, the fact that they are simultaneously endorsed by one author is much more problematic. We discussed this tension here at length because it has serious consequences for his scholarship, in particular, as we will see further on, for the alleged functional link between the decline of the social state and the rise of the penal state.

Travelling of 'penal commonsense': a one-way ticket

In Chapter 2 we briefly argued that some European criminologists and criminal justice specialists are worried about an 'Americanization' of European criminal justice systems. For them the American experiment has failed and they are not inclined to have it replicated in their backyard. However, at the same time, there are also other Europeans who welcome American ideas or developments on crime control and who, just like Tocqueville and Beaumont who travelled in the nineteenth century to America to study its prisons, cross (in person or otherwise) the Atlantic to learn from the American experiences. In the framework of his 'neoliberal penality' theory Wacquant illustrates how such mechanisms of 'import/export' of criminal justice policies work out in practice. According to Wacquant's scheme of thinking America is the centre, the 'living laboratory' of the neoliberal revolution and, consequently, ideas and policies tend to move *from* America *to* abroad (Wacquant, 2001f: 87).

Wacquant's work on neoliberal penality needs to be situated within a broader analysis and critique of the neoliberal revolution and the 'new planetary vulgate' that originated in the USA and, from there, spreads all over the globe (see Bourdieu and Wacquant, 1999; Bourdieu and Wacquant, 2000). For Wacquant the 'law-and-order vulgate' or the 'new security doxa' (Wacquant, 2006d: 96) forms an indispensable component of neoliberalism: this is why he focuses on the role of American and British 'think tanks' and the processes of transfer from the USA to the UK and, from there, to continental Europe and South America. In part Wacquant's hypothesis on the travelling of the 'new penal commonsense' derives its strength from its partaking in such a more wide-ranging neoliberal programme. It all seems to 'fit': the socio-economic neoliberal policies inevitably need a penal complement and, therefore, if the larger hypothesis of the 'new planetary vulgate' travelling the world holds true, then this should also be the case with the smaller hypothesis of the 'law-and-order vulgate'. However, there are at least three comments that we want to make that tend to decrease the strength of this hypothesis.

First, Wacquant uses 'zero tolerance' policing as his prime example of how this new 'law-and-order vulgate' is conquering the world. In view of his framework this choice is perfectly understandable: it is a highly-visible police practice that was popularized in New York City, one of America's most important cities, and that seemed to have travelled at a remarkable speed, as he illustrated at length in *Les prisons de la misère*. However, when one looks somewhat closer at these developments and probes beyond the rhetoric, then 'zero tolerance' hardly seems to have had any impact on policing strategies around the world. In the

UK, the country singled out by Wacquant as the 'acclimation chamber' for Europe, the impact of zero tolerance remained, with the exception of some small experiments, limited to the level of rhetoric (Newburn, 2002: 167–8; Jones and Newburn, 2002: 185–9, 193–5; Newburn and Jones, 2007). Also on the European continent it was hardly successful. For example, Wacquant names Belgium as one of the countries being affected by the 'globalization of zero tolerance' (see Wacquant, 1999a: 46, 55). However, even Philippe Mary, a strong advocate of the 'penalization of the social' (*pénalisation du social*) hypothesis which has some resonances with the move from the 'social state' to the 'penal state' of Wacquant, and who, like Wacquant, points at the rise of neoliberalism as a central motor behind social and penal change, admits that in Belgium zero tolerance hardly had any impact. With the local exception of the city of Lokeren in July 1998 it did not enter Belgian soil, except, again, at the level of discourse (Mary, 2003: 47–52). Moreover, even *within* the USA zero tolerance remained largely limited to New York City. Indeed, when Wacquant tried to unmask the myth that zero tolerance is responsible for New York's crime drop he referred to other major *American* cities such as Boston, Chicago and San Diego which, with different policing strategies, also managed to have pronounced drops in crime (Wacquant, 1999a: 19–22). And, to conclude, even in New York City, straight in the heart of the 'neoliberal Mecca', as Wacquant already illustrated at length in *Les prisons de la misère*, zero tolerance came under attack, following incidents of excessive police violence and the pressures it created upon police and judicial resources (Wacquant, 1999a: 28–34). More recently, Wacquant himself gave his major illustration a fatal stab when he added that zero tolerance 'is scarcely used any longer as a law-enforcement strategy' (Wacquant, 2006d: 104). The conclusion one can draw from these observations, then, is that the impact of zero tolerance has been meagre indeed. Its fate reminds us of the fate of some other examples that we have encountered throughout this book. Like Pratt's exotic illustrations that did not stand the test of time, and Boutellier's interpretation of silent marches as a lasting moral movement that turned out to be flawed, so Wacquant's prototypical example of how neoliberal security doxa has been travelling the world has quickly lost its persuasive power.

Second, the idea of a 'new penal commonsense' travelling from the USA to the rest of the world has as its advantage that it enables

Wacquant to locate clearly the 'sources of evil'. However, it fails to capture the fact that policies tend to travel in many directions, that influence is not unidirectional and that a great deal of such excursions lead to other places than the USA. In Europe, for example, there is a great deal of 'knowledge transfer' and travelling of human rights standards, both through the work of NGO's and in the midst of the inter- and supranational organizations. The Council of Europe plays a key role in this respect, in particular through its Committee for the Prevention of Torture and Inhuman or Degrading Treatment or Punishment (CPT) which has helped in improving living conditions in European penal institutions and in setting new standards regarding humane treatment of prisoners. In recent years, moreover, it has explicitly challenged pre-trial detention and sentencing policies of member states, inspired by the idea that reducing prison populations is the best way to prevent ill-treatment (see Murdoch, 2006). In a reflection upon the decline of imprisonment rates in eastern Europe Van Zyl Smit noted the following: 'One may speculate that there is a relationship between the increased concern for human rights in eastern Europe as the countries of the region have been drawn into complying with pan-European standards and the decline in absolute prison numbers' (Van Zyl Smit, 2006: 108). The diffusion and export of human rights standards arguably has had an important impact upon penal developments at a European level. Sometimes this influence goes quite far, like when the Council of Europe was only willing to admit Russia as a member if it would abolish the death penalty (which it did in 1996, see Cavadino and Dignan, 2006b: 439), or the European Union which diffuses and exports human rights standards by formulating conditions for states who want to become members of the Union.

The restorative justice movement provides another example. One of the most recent innovations in Belgian juvenile law, for example, was directly inspired by the experiences in New Zealand with family group conferencing. Like a modern-day Tocqueville a Belgian criminology professor travelled in 1990 to New Zealand and returned full of enthusiasm (see Walgrave, 2002: ix). Over the years there have been numerous such study-visits, with at times equally enthusiastic responses and resulting in similar practical initiatives, to various projects in countries all over the world. These visits do not appear on the front pages of newspapers and they are not heavily sponsored by influential think-tanks or rich private security companies but, nevertheless, they often have a more lasting impact (as in the above cited example) than the 'zero tolerance' example of Wacquant.

Third, the idea of a 'new penal commonsense' does not take into account that much of this 'penal commonsense' is far from new and, moreover, that it does not always come from outside. For ages people have had (and still have) their very own commonsense ideas about crime and punishment. The opinions that people hold about crime and punishment often sound remarkably similar to what Wacquant perceives to be the neoliberal 'new penal commonsense': for many people prison 'works' because they think it deters potential criminals and incapacitates those already convicted; more security guards are thought to be the best solution to keep pickpockets away from shopping malls; video surveillance is seen as a panacea for curbing street violence and reducing anti-social behaviour; and so forth. Such opinions have not necessarily been whispered in the ears of people by the neoliberal gurus of our time—indeed, they do not necessarily spring from a well-elaborated ideological system but often originate from folk-wisdom ('Once a thief, always a thief') or because 'it just feels right'. Wacquant is right in arguing that in recent years such commonsense has been repackaged in (semi)scientific theoretical models (such as the 'broken windows' theory) and has found ideological support in neoliberal assumptions about how the world functions. However, it is a bridge too far to assume that everyone (including politicians) who make commonsense statements about crime and punishment have fallen prey to the neoliberal revolution. Moreover, this also implies that commonsense cannot be simply kept 'at the borders': down-to-earth commonsense is part of any society and, therefore, stopping neoliberalism at the gates will not suffice to eradicate it.

Indispensable and functional links between social and penal state?

Everything seems to 'fit' in Wacquant's story: the USA is the producer of both neoliberal social and economic policies and their necessary 'law and order' component; the social state and the penal state are inversely related to each other; zero tolerance is the indispensable complement of mass incarceration; where the penal state has not experienced an upsurge yet, there the social state is still strong (and vice versa); and so forth. Moreover, Wacquant identifies a great number of 'indispensable' complements, 'direct' and 'necessary' connections, 'complementary' developments, and 'functional' links (see e.g. Wacquant, 1998f: 7; Wacquant, 1999a: 71, 89, 136, 140; Wacquant, 2001e: 61; Wacquant, 2003a: 169; Wacquant, 2004a: 27). This makes the story that he brings utterly 'tight': everything seems to be closely, functionally and necessarily related to each other. There are, however, a number of reasons why the indispensable and functional link between the (rise of) the penal state and the (decline of) the social state is not as indispensable and functional as Wacquant suggests.

First, Wacquant's 'prison-meets-ghetto' theory is not only difficult to reconcile with his 'neoliberal penality' theory but it also tends to weaken the alleged *indispensable* link between the rise of the penal state and the decline of the social state. If we need to understand the mass incarceration of black people in the USA as resulting from the withdrawal of the American semi-welfare state *together with* a history of racial segregation then this implies that the latter is being *added* to the former (or vice versa, because Wacquant does not discuss which one should have causal priority). It nevertheless calls into question the necessary causal link between the decline of the social state and the rise of the penal state: a *unique* factor is being infused in a *general* explanation whereby it is far from clear which one has been more important. Or to put it differently: seen from his dual theory it may well have been the case that the rise of the penal state, as exemplified in the mass incarceration of black people, has been more caused by the crisis of the ghetto than by the retreat from the social state.

Second, in his discussion of the United States *in general* (that is, when he does not focus in particular on the ghettos) Wacquant argues that the rise of the penal state cannot be seen as an answer to rising crime rates. Contrary to the ghettos where crime and violence are ever-present and have risen sharply (see e.g. Wacquant, 1996a: 248–51; Wacquant, 1997a: 341–3; Wacquant, 1998b: 6–7), there has, on an aggregate national level, not been a rise in crime over the past decades. In this period, as he explains, there rather was a stagnation, followed by a decrease in crime rates (see Wacquant, 2001e: 60; Wacquant, 2004a: 134–5 ; Wacquant, 2005b: 11–13). However, if the decline of the social state in the United States did not cause additional problems of crime and if, therefore, the expanding penal state is without an additional object to which it can direct its 'penal fist', then one can wonder why there is a necessary *functional* link between the decline of the social state and the rise of the penal state. If the withdrawal of the social state did not cause extra problems of crime why, then, is there a *need* for such an expansion of the penal state?[10] Moreover, if neoliberalism has been the driving force of social and penal change in the USA why, then, did it expand its costly penal state exponentially? For a neoliberal society, which embraces market efficiency and which is deeply aversive towards 'Big Government', spending billions of dollars on an over-sized criminal justice system that it does not really need, seems to be like a bad investment. If crime is not the problem, why, then, can the USA not have a small social state *and* a small penal state?

Third, what does this all imply for Europe? If in the American case *both* the decline of the social state *and* the crisis of the ghetto are needed to explain the rise of the penal state then this has two implications for Europe. On the one hand, it implies that there can never be a wholesale 'Americanization' of European penal policy. Indeed, as he repeatedly argued, there are no ghettos in Europe and the race history in the USA is unique. On the other hand, if in the United States 'race' has played such a big role, then it may also be that European countries have their unique elements which determine penal policy. In that sense, the prediction that 'a "downward" convergence of Europe on the social front... will *ineluctably* result in an "upward" convergence on the penal front' (Wacquant, 2000b: 117, [emphasis added]) seems to be too easy and forges too direct a link between the two.

Fourth, for Wacquant the social and the penal state are intricately connected to each other which implies that if the one is 'downsized' then the other is 'upsized'. However, a rise of the penal state does not necessarily have to be an indication of a weakening of the social state, nor can a shrinking of the penal state simply be linked to a strengthening of the social state. For example, for many years Belgium has kept its imprisonment rate under control by releasing prisoners solely for reasons of prison-overcrowding

[10] At times Wacquant also contradicts himself. At a certain point in *Punir les pauvres* he describes the penal state not as a powerful instrument and functional element in the government of advanced marginality but rather as 'incomplete', 'incoherent' and 'often incompetent'. Moreover, the penal state seems to be highly *dysfunctional*: it cannot answer the irrealistic expectations that have engendered it, nor the social functions it needs to fulfil (Wacquant, 2004a: 62).

(that is, a managerial logic kept the penal state under control, not a social one). On the other hand, in 2007 new courts were being created in Belgium which will oversee the execution of prison sentences and which will decide on different aspects related to early release. This development has been welcomed by criminologists and criminal lawyers because many share the basic philosophy behind the reform, that is, that the judiciary should oversee the post-sentencing phase and have its say in it. However, it is also predicted that this reform will lead to increases in the prison population (that is, a human rights logic might lead to an expansion of the penal state, not a social one) (Daems, 2008). In sum, there are many factors at play in the growth or shrinkage of the penal state which suggest that to perceive an indispensable link with the fate of the social state is a deeply flawed depiction.

Fifth, and more fundamentally, one can ask whether the denominator 'the American penal state' is of much analytical value. It has repeatedly been clarified that the 50 different states in the USA have diverging punitive patterns (see Zimring and Hawkins, 1991; Frost, 2006).[11] Wacquant makes the same mistake as Pratt in taking exotic and eye-catching examples from a limited number of states, that are then offered as evidence or illustration for the rise of *the* American penal state. For example, when Wacquant illustrates the five tendencies in America's patterns of punishment in *Les prison de la misère* (Wacquant, 1999a: 71–94) the major part of the examples come from one single state, that is California (Wacquant, 1999a: 73–4, 77–8, 80–3). When he illustrates the practice of putting convict files online he argues that this happens in a dozen states, in particular Illinois, Florida,

[11] It is highly implausible that Wacquant is not aware of the great variety *within* the United States. There are at least four reasons why we can assume that ignorance cannot explain his lack of attention for the undeniable variation within the USA: (1) his close contact with eminent and experienced criminologists such as David Garland and Richard Sparks; (2) the elaborated reference lists in his publications which testify of a deep awareness of the relevant penological literature; (3) the fact that he already cited Zimring and Hawkins' 1991 study *The Scale of Imprisonment* which includes a chapter 'Fifty-one different countries' in two articles of 1998 (Wacquant, 1998f: 8 (footnote 3); Wacquant, 1998g: 124 (note 1)); (4) and his demonstrated sensitivity towards comparative complexities and differences as exemplified in detail in his work on the American ghetto and the French *banlieues*. Towards the end of this chapter we will explain this self-induced amnesia by relating his academic work to his role as a public intellectual struggling against neoliberal doxa.

and Texas (Wacquant, 1999a: 76). When he writes about the sky-rocketing budgets it is New York, Texas, Florida and, again, California that deserve special mentioning (Wacquant, 1999a: 78). When he discusses the privatization of the prison system he counts about twenty states and names Texas, Florida, Colorado, Oklahoma, Tennessee and, again, California as the forerunners (Wacquant, 1999a: 83). The greatest number of states, however, remain 'anonymous': as a reader one can wonder why 38 states are not putting files online, why budgets are not increasing everywhere that rapidly, or why about thirty states are not having privatized prisons. From Wacquant's illustrations we learn that some states are, indeed, undoubtedly penal states (in plural). However, if one continuously refers to the same (groups of) state(s) (and California in particular)[12] then the reader might get suspicious: maybe *the* American penal state does not exist? Maybe the 'irresistible advent of the American penal state' (Wacquant, 1999a: 89, author's translation) is not that irresistible after all?

To conclude, Wacquant's hypothesis of the indispensable and functional link between the (rise of the) penal state and the (decline of the) social state leaves too much out of the picture and, in fact, turns out to be shaky when it is being read together with his 'prison-meets-ghetto' theory. If the latter is able to explain (a large part of) the rise of the penal state, as Wacquant insists, then this implies that the decline of the social state has not been the sole reason for the rise of punishment in the USA. In addition, this suggests that also Europe has, next to its (decreasing) commitment to welfare, its particular factors that can explain penal developments. A correlation between social provision and state activity to deal with social problems on the one hand, and the use of punishment on the other hand, has often been identified in penological research (see e.g. Cavadino and Dignan, 2006a; Cavadino and Dignan, 2006b; Downes and Hansen, 2006) but to reformulate such a correlation in the Wacquantian formula of 'downsizing A leads to upsizing B' is to suggest too direct a relationship between the two and misses too much of the mediating

[12] A similar excavation of the examples Wacquant offers in Chapter 4 ('*Le "grand enfermement" de la fin de siècle*') and Chapter 5 ('*L'avènement du "Big Government" carcéral*') of *Punir les pauvres* would also reveal that the majority of the illustrations are derived from a small number of states. And also here he disproportionately mines the state of California and its biggest city Los Angeles for examples to paint a grim overall picture of *the* American penal state.

factors that are in need of further clarification. Indeed, as Downes and Hansen emphasize in the conclusion of a chapter on the relationship between the commitment to welfare and the scale of imprisonment: 'The nature of the relationship between the two is, nevertheless, still in need of elucidation by further research, and is likely to be highly mediated rather than simple or direct, calling for the use of different methods to explore its complexities' (Downes and Hansen, 2006: 154).[13]

The 'evil causes evil causes evil' fallacy

Wacquant focuses exclusively on the darkest of penal developments: mass imprisonment; registration and notification laws for sex offenders; boot camps, curfews, and chain-gangs; the inexorable growth of parole and probation, and the like. In a rare moment of putting the dark brush aside (significantly buried in a footnote) Wacquant acknowledges that penal policies are not 'monolithical', that in their evolution one can detect 'diverging tendencies' or even 'contradictory' ones, and he refers to reconciliation, mediation, depenalization and individualization of penalties (see Wacquant, 1998e: 4 (note 4)). However, these diverging and contradictory developments are not of interest to him and deserve no further attention. In the light of his 'neoliberal penality' theory this also becomes understandable: these dark-coloured penal developments have evil roots, that is, the neoliberal revolution

[13] Towards the end of *Les prisons de la misère* Wacquant at one point seems to acknowledge that his 'strong' theory of neoliberal penality is not that strong after all. First, whereas he throughout the book (and elsewhere) is keen on emphasizing the necessary and indispensable functional link between the social and the penal state he here uses less strong words such as 'more likely' (*plus probable*) and 'more pronounced' (*prononcé*) (Wacquant, 1999a: 139). It is remarkable to notice that a trained sociologist as Wacquant formulates this as a hypothesis at the end of his book whereas, throughout the whole manuscript, he already aimed to demonstrate that, for him, this is no longer a hypothesis (that is, a statement that is still open to both confirmation and rejection) but a raw reality. Second, he demonstrates how countries such as Austria, Finland and Germany decreased their prison populations between 1985 and 1995 with respectively 29, 25 and 6 per cent. Here he points at the role of penal policy in terms of generalizing the fine, enlarging conditional release and sensibilizing judges (Wacquant, 1999a: 149). However, in pointing to the role of penal policy (and, therefore, indirectly, to other factors than those captured in his theory of the penalization of poverty), he implicitly indicates that, again, the link between the decline of the social state and the upsurge of the penal state, is not all that tight.

that sweeps the globe. All of the above-mentioned developments are, in Wacquant's opinion, to be related to the advent of neoliberalism in the USA and, when it is exported, this also becomes the case in other parts of the world.

There is, then, also a clearly identifiable and localizable source of all this evil: the USA. In one of his papers on urban marginality, Wacquant argued that his work should not be mistaken for 'a polemic against the United States stamped in the coin of anti-Americanism' (Wacquant, 2004e: 96; Wacquant, 1997b: 321; see also Bourdieu and Wacquant, 1999: 52 (note 1)). However, for readers of his texts it is probably difficult to suppress the impression that there is, in fact, at least some anti-Americanism or 'America bashing' present in his work: America as a nation, and 'Americanization' as a process (Wacquant, 2001e: 51–4), are continuously associated with features that are, in Wacquant's viewpoint, deeply negative. America is, as he termed it in Bourdieu's *La misère du monde*, a 'negative utopia' (Wacquant, 1993c: 278). And this also explains why Blairism was seen to represent 'a danger for Europe' because it threatened to 'Americanize' the continent (Wacquant, 2001e: 55) and, similarly, why Great Britain's 'unprecedented hyperinflation' is explained by it being a '*promue comptoir et pilote de l' "américanisation" du pénal en Europe*' (Wacquant, 2004a: 134).

Because in Wacquant's scheme of thinking 'bad' (neoliberalism) causes 'bad' (the penal state), Nelken, (2006: 264) recently suggested that he falls prey to the 'evil causes evil' fallacy. One might even argue that this description should be extended with one more 'evil' because, in fact, for Wacquant it is 'bad' (America) causes 'bad' (neoliberalism) causes 'bad' (the penal state). This is why we prefer to speak of the 'evil causes evil causes evil' fallacy. There are at least three problems in Wacquant's scholarship that become visible if we approach it from this angle.

First, from Wacquant's perspective it becomes impossible to identify, let alone to make sense of, positive developments—especially within American borders. In such a story there is neither place for penal innovations such as restorative justice nor for alternative sanctions that aim to provide a constructive response to crime. Also the unintended consequences of penal reform initiatives that flow from 'good intentions' (such as 'net-widening', 'thinning the mesh' and the like) cannot be thematized: in Wacquant's 'black or white' story there is no place for shades of grey.

Second, it remains largely unclear what the link is between the penal developments that are summed up at the beginning of this section, and how exactly they flow from 'neoliberal penality'. What do such diverse practices and developments as mass imprisonment, zero tolerance, chain gangs, and notification laws for sex offenders have in common? The criterion for being included in Wacquant's list, so it seems, is primarily because they are judged to be 'bad'–not because they have something in common that justifies their being grouped together (see also Chapter 3 where we identified a similar problem in our discussion of the 'new punitiveness'). It is also unclear how the neoliberal revolution in the USA has been able to stimulate such a variety of penal developments.

Third, Wacquant's perspective nullifies the possibility that, as Nelken rightly suggests, 'bad' can come from 'good', and 'good' can come from 'bad' (Nelken, 2006: 264). Indeed, one of the major strengths of Whitman's (2003) study *Harsh Justice* is that he demonstrated how America's (good) egalitarian tradition and Europe's (bad) aristocratic tradition have—via the opposing processes of *levelling down* and *levelling up*—resulted in highly different legal cultures at both sides of the Atlantic which can explain, in part, why the USA treats its offenders much more harshly than continental Europe. The 'evil causes evil causes evil' fallacy closes the door for grasping such ambivalent historical processes.

Wacquant as a Public Intellectual

Pierre Bourdieu, so Wacquant wrote recently, 'engaged with issues of power, public policy, and social justice in a manner that breached the accepted separation of science and life, the conceptual and the personal, and continually crossed that "sacred border between culture and politics, pure thought and the triviality of the agora" that he saw as one major obstacle to a genuine democracy' (Wacquant, 2005g: 1). This apt description of his former mentor and collaborator could have been a self-description. Already in his first publications on the educational system in New Caladonia, and well before his PhD research on the black ghetto, Wacquant demonstrated a deep interest in various aspects of social and ethnic inequality (Wacquant, 1989). Such a deep interest in, and an openly expressed revulsion at, how certain groups in society, because of their place in the social hierarchy or the colour of their skin, see their opportunities of living a decent life being crumbled or reduced to almost zero, has remained with him ever since.

In the previous chapter we argued that we could not understand Boutellier's intellectual life-course if we did not take into account the public role he had designed for himself. The same applies to Wacquant. Just as Boutellier's scholarship is deeply influenced by his closeness to the world of policy-making, so Wacquant's academic writings have been sharply shaped by the way he intends to relate to the wider world: for Wacquant sociology is a martial art and his first opponent is neoliberal *doxa*.

Breaking the wall: an ex-boxer's struggle against neoliberal doxa

Critical thought is most fruitful, so Wacquant argued recently, if it questions: 'in a continuous, active, and radical manner, both established forms of thought and established forms of collective life—"commonsense" or *doxa* (including the *doxa* of the critical tradition) along with the social and political relations that obtain at a particular moment in a particular society' (Wacquant, 2004c: 97). One of the major obstacles to such a critical thought, however, is what Wacquant termed the '*symbolic Great Wall* formed by neoliberal discourse and its manifold by-products, which have invaded all spheres of cultural and social life' (Wacquant, 2004c: 99). And this symbolic Great Wall has been erected by America with its unseen 'power to universalize particularisms' and which is 'now tacitly constituted as model for every other and as yardstick for all things' (Bourdieu and Wacquant, 1999: 41–2). The USA has succeeded in becoming 'the symbolic Mecca of the World' (*cette Mecque symbolique de la Terre*) from which a new planet-wide language springs and is being disseminated and universalized (Bourdieu and Wacquant, 2000).

As we have seen throughout this chapter, Wacquant holds the neoliberal revolution responsible for the deplorable fate of those situated at the bottom of society. Wherever it arrives, the neoliberal revolution brings a stream of social destruction and human debris in its wake (Wacquant, 1998d: 21). It is obvious that there is more than a healthy dose of academic curiosity at work here. For Wacquant it is clear that the neoliberal experiment yields high costs. Like the rats and the rabbits in the laboratories of the pharmaceutical and cosmetic industries, so the guinea pigs of the neoliberal experiment suffer, day-in day-out, from numerous adverse and, at times, life-threatening side effects. Moreover, none of them has been asked to participate in the experiment—let alone that they consented. This implies that millions of guinea pigs are continuously locked in a laboratory that is neither of their own making nor of their own choosing. Blacks in ghettos; poors in marginalized city zones; drug users, mentally ill and homeless people in prisons; (other) blacks and immigrants locked up *en masse* behind bars—they can only be set free when the experiment is terminated, the laboratory is dismantled, and the 'Doctor Evils' of this world are removed from their powerful positions.

Seen from this perspective it should not come as a surprise that Wacquant, like his former mentor Bourdieu, joined a global struggle against the neoliberal revolution. Two years after the impressive collective work on the misery in French society in which 22 researchers, including Wacquant, participated and that led to the publication of *La misère du monde* (Bourdieu 1993) the collective *Raisons d'agir* was established to further this cause. This collective aims at the political mobilization of intellectuals and strives towards the construction of a 'collective, autonomous and international intellectual' (*intellectuel collectif autonome international*) which is perceived to be needed to counteract the global rise of neoliberalism (Lebaron and Mauger, 2003). Indeed, the main obstacle to critical thought, so Wacquant argued, is the formation of a true *neoliberal international* 'anchored by a network of think-tanks centered on the east coast of the United States and relayed by the great international institutions, the World Bank, the European Commission, the OECD, the WTO, etc., which diffuse the products of false science at an exponential speed in order to better legitimate the socially reactionary policies implemented everywhere in the era of the triumphant market' (Wacquant, 2004c: 100; see also Wacquant, 2001f). The best way to counteract this 'neoliberal international', so he and other participants in *Raisons d'agir* believe, is to join intellectual forces and enter the ring to fight the ruthless opponent.

Raisons d'agir publishes small, accessible and low-priced books on topics of public relevance that are meant to inform public debate. In addition it participates in organizations that are critical about neoliberal globalization. In doing so the collective hopes that a space will gradually be opened for 'an alternative to the neoliberal barbarism' (*Raisons d'agir*, 2003: 2). And, interestingly, in the light of this objective we encounter yet another content for the word 'civilization': not Pratt's Elias-inspired reading of recent history in terms of 'civilization/decivilization', nor Boutellier's 'civilizing offensive' against a vital culture that seems to be out of control, but Bourdieu's emphatic call to oppose the destruction of civilization. In December 1995, at a time of major social unrest in France, Bourdieu delivered a speech in Lyon ('*Contre la destruction d'une civilisation*') in which he expressed his solidarity with the strikers (Bourdieu, 1998: 30). And, in fact, after outlining the 'historical choice' Europe has between following the American example of imprisoning the poor and the creation of citizens' rights (such as a basic income), lifelong education and formation, general access to housing and health service, Wacquant writes, in the very last sentence of *Les prisons de la misère*, that this choice bears down to choosing for the type of civilization Europe wants to offer to its citizens (Wacquant, 1999a: 151).

Wacquant's goal, then, is not to establish a 'bureaucratic buffer' (like Pratt) or a 'civilization buffer' (like Boutellier) but an 'ideological buffer' (or what he terms, 'a breakwater of resistance' (Wacquant, 2004c: 100)) which furthers the struggle against American-made economic, social and penal concepts in order to prevent Europe (and the rest of the globe) from becoming like the USA. This calls for a perennial battle against the imperialism of neoliberal *doxa* and its concomitant *nouvelle doxa punitive* (Wacquant, 1999a: 13). It is here that his interest in the spread of 'neoliberal penality', conceived as a logical and necessary component of neoliberal social and economic policies, finds its origins. And it therefore becomes understandable why Wacquant's focus became narrowed down to its most abhorring, exclusionary, and divisive aspects: punishment, for Wacquant, is one more battle ground to reconquer terrain from the powerful neoliberal opponent.

Escaping the penal state?

For Wacquant this battle against the neoliberal penal state needs to be threefold: first, on the level of words and discourses; second, on the front of judicial policies and practices (that is, to thwart the multiplication of measures that tend to widen the penal net and to propose a social, health, or educational alternative whenever feasible); third, on a European level (that is, forging links between activists and researchers, in line with what *Raisons d'agir* intends to do) (see Wacquant, 2001b: 410; Wacquant, 2001d: 85–6; Wacquant, 2004f: 131–3; Blum and Neitzke, 2001: 73–4). It is interesting to observe the combative, even belligerent, language he uses in this respect: for Wacquant there is much to be gained from 'forging links between activists and researchers who work on the *penal front* and those who *battle* on the *social front*... to optimize the intellectual and practical resources to be invested in this *struggle*' (Wacquant, 2001d: 86, [emphasis added]). Clearly, for Wacquant, we are in the midst of a war and forces need to be joined to escape the stranglehold of the neoliberal opponent. But, in the end, as he also suggests by referring to the 'social front', the struggle needs to go one step further: the problem of crime and punishment needs to be repoliticized (Wacquant, 2004f: 129). The real solution for stopping the advent of the penal state is no different from the solution for stopping the progress of 'advanced marginality': there is a need for a 'revolution in public policy' which, in the end, boils down to instituting a guaranteed minimum income or 'basic income' plan, 'that is, by granting unconditionally to all members of society on an individual basis, without means test or work requirement, adequate means of subsistence and social participation' (Wacquant, 1996b: 131; see also Wacquant, 2006a: 10–11, 261–3, 287, 293). If traditional wage labour is no longer available to everyone and, moreover, if it is in itself a source of precarization, then, 'public policies designed to counter advanced marginality must work to facilitate and smooth out the severance of subsistence from work, income from paid labour, and social participation from wage-earning' (Wacquant, 1996b: 130). The real alternative to the penalization of poverty, then, is a truly European social state (Wacquant, 2001b: 410; Wacquant, 2004f: 133).

Where Boutellier and Wacquant come together

Wacquant and Boutellier seem to disagree on almost every point imaginable. Now that we have discussed Wacquant's position in the wider world it is easier to understand why this is the case. It is interesting to observe that Wacquant, like Boutellier, often uses the term 'diagnosis' to typify his writings (see e.g. Wacquant, 1996c: 66; Wacquant, 1999c: 1640; Wacquant, 2000b: 108; Wacquant, 2006a: 155, 170). However, it is obvious that their respective 'diagnoses' are utterly different—and so are the proposed 'remedies'. Boutellier wants us to join in his moral crusade against the excesses of an all too vital culture. Wacquant tries to convince us to step in the ring to fight a round against the heavy-weight neoliberal opponent. However, despite their many differences of opinion, both authors share common ground on one thing: the 'proselytizing' ambitions of Boutellier and the 'boxing' aspirations of Wacquant leave a deep imprint upon their scholarship which, in the process, comes to be deeply coloured by the public roles they have designed for themselves. In both cases 'analysis' is subordinated to 'diagnosis', and making the 'diagnosis' is directed at those parts of the social body that they, for diverging reasons, judge to be in need for urgent treatment. Whereas Garland chooses to remain as close as possible to the 'integrity of the empirical object', there Boutellier and Wacquant have opted for the other answer to Garland and Young's puzzle: both have deliberately adopted a one-dimensional perspective which enables them to arrive at clear-cut 'remedies' (a moral crusade versus a plea for reinventing the (European) social state) to what they perceive to be the proper 'diagnosis' (a vitalist culture that is running out of hand versus the global spread of the neoliberal revolution).

In the previous chapter we argued that Boutellier's 'proselytizing' ambitions have had a number of unfortunate consequences for his scholarship: a 'policy bias' has directed his scholarly attention at certain aspects of the object under research while blinding him to those aspects that were less appealing to him or that would jeopardize his policy-oriented ambitions. Also in Wacquant's work there is a clear bias at work which is very different from Boutellier's but which, nonetheless, produces a similar set of unfortunate consequences. Wacquant's 'critical bias' does not derive from his closeness to the world of policy-making, as in the case of Boutellier, but from the fact that his scholarship has as its start- and endpoint a relentless critique of the neoliberal revolution. We will here highlight three implications of this bias for his scholarship: Wacquant's production of a streamlined picture of penal change that fits his critical project; a somewhat unsociological understanding of political agency; and the impossibility of justifying punishment.

First, whereas Boutellier presents us with a streamlined picture of postmodern criminals, emancipated victims, fearful and worried citizens, and responsive policy-makers, there Wacquant paints an equally streamlined picture with a different set of characters, that is, criminals engaging in protopolitical action against 'violence from above', poor families and crime-ridden neighbourhoods, and policy-makers who forsake their political responsibility in protecting the weak against the Darwinian struggle of a survival of the fittest ignited by the neoliberal revolution. Wacquant's 'critical bias' directs his attention at the most appalling penal developments which best serve the function of exemplifying the dark side of the neoliberal experiment. As a result his account of penal change, as we argued earlier in this chapter, leaves too much out of the picture. Whereas Boutellier, as the right hand of the policy-maker, only sees cohesion, a cry for safety, and the end of society's 'inner tensions', there Wacquant, as the self-declared spokesman of the poor, the unemployed, ethnic minorities, and so forth, only sees division and domination. The unfortunate result of Wacquant's streamlining operation is that his objective to unmask the reigning *pensée unique* in thinking about crime and punishment (see e.g. Wacquant, 2001d: 84; Wacquant, 2004a: 24), leads him to create his very own *pensée unique*.

Second, his 'critical bias' leads Wacquant to adopt a somewhat unsociological understanding of political agency. Wacquant regretted that the Left in France (and Jospin in particular) did not 'launch a bold policy of decriminalization and decarceration, that it would increase the perimeter and prerogatives of the social state, and diminish those of the penal state' (Wacquant, 2001b: 408–9). Unlike Garland who is at pains to highlight how political decisions are always structured by social and cultural conditions and that, therefore, we have to look further than the 'usual suspects' (such as politics and media) (Garland, 2004a), and unlike Pratt (2007: 3–4) who stresses that politicians cannot simply turn off penal populism at will but that they are, to an important extent, also a plaything of the broader context that made its rise to prominence possible, Wacquant seems to take off his sociological glasses and perceives them through an activist lens as freely-choosing and somewhat omnipotent actors. Whereas those at the bottom of the social hierarchy are depicted as the hapless victims of 'violence from above' and are forced to live their lives in illegality, there those at the top, and politicians in particular, seem to be not socially constrained at all. To think about political agency in this way may be an attractive (and necessary) option for the activist who aims to stir the consciousness of policy-makers and incite them to act accordingly, yet it is difficult to see how this can be an option for a sociologist who aims to map and explain the social constraints and determinants of human (including politician's) behaviour. In the previous chapter we argued that Boutellier's scholarship suffered from his closeness to the world of policy-making, that is, Boutellier writes too much with policy objectives in the back of his mind. In the case of Wacquant it is the writer as activist who often takes over from the writer as sociologist.

Third, one might wonder if, from Wacquant's perspective, penal interventions can ever be justified. At one point Wacquant insisted that we should not deny the reality of crime nor the necessity to respond to it—including with penal responses when they are appropriate (see Wacquant, 2004f: 129). However, from his conception of crime as either a protopolitical act against 'violence from above' or a natural outgrowth of living in poverty and being locked in low-paid jobs how, then, can a *penal* response ever be justified, that is, a response not meant to remedy a social or health deficit but a moral transgression codified in criminal law? His view of the world precludes the possibility that a penal response can ever be 'appropriate': in his deeply unjust society which falls continuously apart into two hemispheres, there can never be justified penal responses. The only conclusion one can draw from Wacquant's perspective and his concept of crime, is that punishment becomes unjustifiable. The only logical position that can follow from his analysis, then, is the abolitionist position. Indeed, there seems to be an (unexpressed) promise in his work that, if we would live in a social(ist) paradise where there is no longer a need to fight against the by then eradicated 'violence from above' and where poverty is extinguished, crime will disappear, prisons will empty and the need to punish will evaporate.[14]

[14] That this is wishful thinking was already acknowledged in the mid-1980s by some of the 'new criminologists' (Taylor *et al*, 1973) who then turned to a 'left realist' position. Wacquant seems to return to this old-school Marxist-inspired tradition which, however, has already long since lost its appeal and viability in contemporary criminology and developed into new forms of critical thought. Unfortunately Wacquant nowhere discusses these developments in theoretical criminology.

6

Persuasive Criminology

Introduction

In a short piece published in 1930 in the French literary journal *Europe* René Maublanc shared with his readers some personal memories about Émile Durkheim. One of them is particularly interesting in the light of the theme of this book. The first time Maublanc met Durkheim in private the French sociologist told him: 'If you want to mature your intellect, devote yourself to the scrupulous study of a grand master, disassemble a system in its most secret components. That is what I have done, and my teacher was Renouvier' (Maublanc, 1930: 299, author's translation). The irony is, of course, that over the past century book shelves in libraries across the globe have been filled up with studies devoted to Durkheim's life and work, confirming and contributing to his own status as grand master in classical sociology.

Following Durkheim's advice is common practice in philosophy and sociology where studies about singular authors, ranging from the founding fathers to the younger gods, are regularly undertaken. In these disciplines devoting time and energy to the study of one leading scholar is widely perceived to be one of the most rewarding activities a researcher can undertake for his or her personal intellectual growth. This stands in sharp contrast to criminology: there are hardly, if any, book-length treatments of the life-courses of the brightest minds in criminology's intellectual history. For sure, we have textbook treatments of key figures such as Beccaria, Lombroso or Sutherland; and occasionally we have biographies (e.g. Radzinowicz, 1999) and introductory notes to *Festschrifts* honouring the careers of respected colleagues (e.g. Downes *et al,* 2007) but these do not even come close to what Durkheim had in mind when he gave his instructions to Maublanc. Criminology has a rich history of studying 'career criminals' but a rather poor record when it comes to studying 'career criminologists'.

This is unfortunate and we hope that this book will inspire others to embark on longitudinal author-oriented studies in criminology. In this last chapter we will argue, moreover, that such studies have a much wider relevance than fulfilling some personal needs of the individual criminologist. Indeed, they can offer us insight in the procedures that have been applied, and the decisions that have been made, throughout an intellectual life-course. They disclose the processes, the *making* sense of penal change, which most of the time remain invisible when one exclusively looks at intellectual end-products. More in particular, they help us better assess the persuasiveness of particular accounts and offer us the opportunity to discuss criminology's public persuasiveness more closely, a timely topic in view of recent calls directed at criminologists and other social scientists to participate more directly in public debate and to engage more passionately with penal policy.

The central theme throughout this final chapter, then, is the problem of persuasion: how and towards which ends do our four authors aim to persuade their audiences? When we write about a persuasive criminology in this chapter we neither use Garland's Foucault-inspired definition of criminology, nor Boutellier's definition of criminology as a reflexive policy science. We rather agree with Sutherland that the scope of criminology includes the study of the processes of making laws, of breaking laws, and of reacting to the breaking of laws (see Cressey, 1955). Questions related to punishment and penal change are at the centre of such a criminology.

The Art of Persuasion: Scientists, Prophets, Proselytizers, and Boxers

In Chapter 2 we have seen how the young Garland of the early 1980s conducted his study on the history of the penal-welfare strategy from a Foucault/Marx-inspired framework. In those early years of his career his work was explicitly concerned with engagement. For Garland it was crucial to construct 'alternative strategies of control' which would draw upon 'ideologies of collective and social responsibility, popular participation, democratic regulation and the accountability of expertise'. With Peter Young, in their important book with the telling title *The Power to Punish*, he argued that the production of knowledge about the social world is always steered at changing it. Alternative forms of penality needed to be constructed which were 'more socialist, more popular, more democratic'. However, soon after the publication of *Punishment and Welfare* Garland started to move to a pluralist theoretical position. His earlier theoretical framework became one framework amongst several others, notably those derived from Durkheimian and Eliasian social thought. From his pluralist position, there was no *a priori* superiority of the one above the other. Respect for the 'integrity of the empirical object' moved to the centre of Garland's agenda when studying punishment and penal change.

This eagerness to understand punishment in all its complexity had implications for how he could and would relate to his object of research. To move away from the early Foucault/Marx-inspired framework implied that punishment was no longer merely about discipline and regulation: it was also about irrational emotions and passions, and it always operated within certain morally and culturally defined boundaries. Such a pluralist theoretical position seemed to be irreconcilable with advocating the 'alternative strategies of control' of the early 1980s: even if it were possible to construct such strategies, their viability and efficacy would be limited by the tragic quality of punishment, that is, the fact that punishment is always beset by 'irresolvable tensions' and inescapably marked by 'moral contradiction' and 'unwanted irony'. A multidimensional sociology of punishment, then, is not only burdensome for the researcher because of the higher degrees of analytic complexity that it requires, but also because of the implications for one's relation to the object of research: revealing multiple causes, effects and meanings makes it much more difficult to launch a straightforward critique and single out that one panacea that would liberate the penal world of all evil. Garland was well aware that this was the price he needed to pay for his theoretical choice. But for him the gains of arriving at a more truthful description of punishment outweighed the losses. In *The Culture of Control* and, more recently, in his work on capital punishment and on the place of culture in the sociology of punishment, he reaffirmed the value of the multidimensional approach. Nowadays Garland relates to his object of research as a 'dispassionate observer' who aims to investigate issues with which one is 'passionately involved' but with 'a detachment that permits one to grasp complexities and to minimize the projection of one's own wishes and fears onto the phenomenon'.

The mixture of descriptive, explanatory, critical and normative elements has, over the course of Garland's intellectual trajectory, become more skewed to description and explanation. This is also the case for how he relates to his readers. We label his position, for matter of convenience, the position of the 'scientist'. This is not to argue that the three other authors are not scientists because, for sure, they are closely involved in scholarly work and hold important positions at prestigious universities. The crucial difference, however, relates to how they aim to persuade their readers: whereas Garland aims to increase the persuasive power of his accounts by means of description and analysis, that is, elements that we usually associate with science, the three other authors aim to achieve persuasion to an important extent by other means. Pratt as 'prophet', Boutellier as 'proselytizer', and Wacquant as 'boxer' use other—so to speak, 'extra-scientific'—rhetorical means to convince their readers of the strength of the accounts they offer. In particular in the cases of Boutellier and Wacquant these 'extra-scientific' elements enable them to come up with a much sharper critique and to arrive at a much more pronounced normative position.

In Chapter 3 we discussed at length how Pratt, throughout the 1980s, was strongly inspired by the work of Foucault, revisionist history writing, and the critical social control literature. Towards the late 1980s, and in particular in the run up to his study *Punishment in a Perfect Society*, he started to reconsider his theoretical framework: Pratt gradually moved away from the Foucauldian position and became convinced of the value of the Eliasian perspective to understand the history of modern penality in New Zealand. For a moment it seemed as if Pratt, like Garland, would adopt a pluralist theoretical framework. However, our discussion of his subsequent research demonstrated that his position was both 'purist' and 'volatile' in nature. In the mid-1990s he would return to Foucault for his study *Governing the Dangerous* which was, as we have seen, strongly inspired by the Foucault-inspired governmentality literature. In his next research project, which culminated in the publication of *Punishment and Civilization*, Elias was his main author. Some years later Pratt explicitly reaffirmed that, in his opinion, Elias was the sole classical author who could provide us with a framework that was able to grasp recent penal change. Pratt's account of the changing axis of penal power (with its concomitant rise of penal populism) and the decivilization of punishment were, therefore, inspired by the German sociologist.

Throughout his intellectual life-course Pratt would also relate in different ways to his object of research. Like the young Garland, the young Pratt was in the early years of his academic career closely engaged with the themes he was researching. In the early 1980s his work on the New Right in the UK was driven by the need to find 'an alternative and coherent strategy'. His research on juvenile delinquency and social work inspired attempts at initiating an ideological challenge and altering working practices of social workers in order to stop pathologizing young truants and lessen the regulation they were subjected to. With the years, however, Pratt grew increasingly sceptical about the prospects of progressive change. From the 1990s onwards there are no longer the practical suggestions oriented towards improving day-to-day practice in his published work. Pratt's turn to historical questions in this period, however, was not meant to be an escape strategy. Exploring the past, so he argued, could help him to understand better the present and would assist him in drawing lessons from history.

The most important change in his relationship towards his object of research happened towards the end of the 1990s. From then onwards it is possible to see him adopting a position that we earlier referred to as 'prophetic'. Pratt's work became increasingly infused with warnings and outlines of possible futures: according to Pratt the boundaries of punishment came to be pushed, and we were entering into a new era of punishment which had, if the emerging tendencies would consolidate and intensify, deep implications for our futures. We termed his position 'prophetic' because it seemed as if Pratt aimed to confront his readers with the potential (dark) future in the hope that this would nullify the possibility of such a future being turned into an even more troubling present. Like a prophet Pratt predicts catastrophe in order to prevent it. Perceiving his relationship to his object of research as a shift to such a prophetical position helps explain his disproportionate attention for the dark sides of social and penal arrangements; it could explain why he focused so much on chain gangs, 'three strikes and you're out' laws, austere prison regimes, punitive work orders, boot camps, mass imprisonment, and so forth; it also helps understand his interest in the 'postmodern penality' hypothesis with its suggestion that we have entered a new epoch.

This prophetical position has implications for how Pratt aims to achieve persuasion: as we suggested in Chapter 3, Pratt's empirical evidence is coloured dark, and deliberately so, in order to prevent the world from becoming even darker. His readers are being presented with a selection of the available evidence to warn them of the dark future that lies ahead of them, and that is already in the process of becoming their present. Whereas Garland as 'scientist' aims to persuade his audience in particular by means of description and analysis, there Pratt as 'prophet' does violence to 'realistic' and 'balanced' descriptions of the (penal) world in the hope that it would not become more violent itself.

In Chapter 4 we discussed how Boutellier, after his experiences in a closed institution for young delinquents, became interested in the morality of our times. In the early 1980s this topic was somewhat unfashionable. Sociological criminology was particularly interested in the control machinery and moral questions related to 'good' and 'evil' were hardly touched upon. Boutellier identified more with the youth workers than with the youngsters: their problems of giving moral guidance to the young delinquents who demonstrated a remarkable self-confidence, started to interest him. Indeed, for Boutellier such youth workers had ended up in an 'ideologically and morally unprotected position'. In order to address crime as a moral problem Foucault, one of the most popular authors of the 1980s, was perceived to be not very helpful. Boutellier turned to Durkheim and launched his hypothesis of the victimalization of morality in his first book *Solidariteit en slachtofferschap*. With his follow-up study *De veiligheidsutopie* Boutellier would expand his gaze and reflected more widely on the meaning of safety in a vitalist culture.

Throughout his career we observed a remarkable consistency in his use of theory. From the early beginnings until now his framework is Durkheimian. Boutellier was well aware of other theoretical developments but he always kept them at a safe distance. Authors such as Rorty or Bauman were being used but only to the extent that they fit into his moral framework. Boutellier's career-long choice for Durkheim becomes better understandable if we consider more closely the role in public life that he has designed for himself. Boutellier's academic work on the morality of our times was always driven by a deep-ingrained aspiration to make it useful for practical intervention. His 'diagnosis' of society was always steered toward 'remedying' its pathological features. Earlier we argued that his position can be labelled the position of the 'proselytizer': Boutellier's mission to identify what binds people together in a morally fragmented society has driven him towards a moral crusade against the pathologies of contemporary culture. Unlike Pratt who, like a modern-day prophet, presents his readers with images of what the future might bring, Boutellier is firmly oriented towards the present: his scholarship and policy-oriented activities are meant for the instant treatment of a society that is in need of boundaries and moral renewal.

Boutellier's proselytizing ambitions have implications for how he aims to persuade his audience. In order to convince the reader of the need and viability of his moral crusade Boutellier paints a streamlined picture of postmodern criminals, emancipated victims, fearful and worried citizens, and responsive policy-makers. Instead of highlighting the darkest of penal developments (as the prophet does) Boutellier aims to strengthen his case by insisting on the harsh reality of crime and unsafety. It is also here that his uncompromising reliance on Durkheim needs to be understood: the bottom-up approach of Durkheim with its consensual view on society, is most useful for his larger mission and his intention to remain a loyal ally for the policy-maker.

Chapter 5 was devoted to the work of Wacquant. Wacquant's interest in crime and punishment was, like Boutellier, sparked by a personal first-hand experience: his fieldwork in a black ghetto in general, and his enrolment in a local boxing gym in particular, sensitized him to the deep impact of the criminal justice system on the lives of the residents in the ghetto and the functions this system fulfils in post-Fordist America. For Wacquant the study of punishment became a necessary complement to his work on marginality. This happened in two ways. First, his study of the transformation of the American ghetto brought him to study how, in a time of the decline of the 'communal' ghetto of yore and the mass imprisonment of blacks, the contemporary 'hyperghetto' and the prison meet and mesh. Second, his more wide-ranging observations on the rise of advanced marginality in First World cities led him to consider more closely the increasing reliance on the penal system. The upsurge of the penal state was in particular related to the rise of neoliberalism: a neoliberal penality had seen the light in the United States and was being exported to other countries around the globe.

Wacquant's analysis of penal change bears clear resemblances with the line of research initiated by Rusche and Kirchheimer, that is, the political economy of punishment which investigates relationships between economic systems and forms of punishment. However, as he himself indicated, his approach is different in a number of respects. Wacquant emphasized in particular the importance of political agency; he insisted on treating neoliberalism as a complete ideological package about how human beings and society function; he drew attention to the multiple groups that are being disciplined and controlled by the penal system; and he highlighted the symbolic function of penal systems which draw, dramatize and enforce group boundaries. His deep critique of the spread of neoliberal penality needs to be understood against the background of how he relates to his research object. For Wacquant there is an indispensable link between the neoliberal revolution and the rise of the penal state. Neoliberalism is held responsible for rising inequalities in the USA and those other places where it settles in. Sociology as 'martial art' needs to be mobilized in a struggle against neoliberal *doxa*. Like his former mentor Bourdieu and other participants in the collective *Raisons d'agir* Wacquant joined in a global-wide struggle against the neoliberal revolution. Wacquant's position, then, is the position of the 'boxer' who uses his sociological gloves to fight a round against the ruthless opponent.

In terms of persuasion, Wacquant presents the reader with a streamlined picture that squares well with the public 'boxing' role that he has designed for himself. The characters of his account are criminals engaging in protopolitical action against 'violence from above', poor families residing in crime-ridden and deprived neighbourhoods, and policy-makers who fail to take political responsibility in protecting the weak against the detrimental side-effects of the neoliberal revolution. In order to convince the reader of the need to join the ring against the neoliberal enemy, Wacquant directs the attention of his audience to the most appalling penal developments (such as mass imprisonment, registration and notification laws for sex offenders, boot camps, and so forth); he sees crime control policies travelling in one direction (from the USA to elsewhere); and he identifies transatlantic parallels which enable him to highlight how similar causes lead to similar effects. As we argued earlier, in Wacquant's account 'evil' (America) breeds 'evil' (neoliberalism) breeds 'evil' (the penal state) and to demonstrate this, penal change is approached from its darkest, that is, its most exclusionary and divisive, side.

The reader of this book may have noticed that, as we progressed, the chapters contained more biographical detail. This is not a coincidence. As we moved closer towards the end of our study, it became increasingly important to include 'extra-scientific' information because, in fact, the authors became more engaged in 'extra-scientific' activity and relied more on 'extra-scientific' rhetorical means to persuade their readers. The building blocks of Chapter 2 were mainly academic texts and commentary by other researchers in this field, which enabled us to detail Garland's scholarly development. Also in Chapter 3 we were rather sparse in providing detail that went beyond the academic world. Pratt's move to New Zealand in the mid-1980s was important to understand how his attention shifted towards developments in his new academic home. However, his scholarly texts seemed to suffice to understand both his scholarly trajectory and his shift to a prophetical position.

From Chapter 4 this changed. The ideas which Boutellier expressed in his writings and the scholarly choices he made, only became intelligible if we read his work against the background of, and in relation to, his closeness to the world of policy-making and his role in public life in the Netherlands. In Chapter 5 there was a similar need to situate Wacquant's work in a wider project of public involvement: his academic work was intended to inform the struggle against the neoliberal revolution. It should not surprise us, then, that Boutellier and Wacquant continuously commute between their roles as scholars in an academic world and as intellectuals in the public domain, the activities developed in the first informing the second, and vice versa. Indeed, for both authors we needed to supplement academic writings with short publications for newspapers and non-specialist journals, interviews, and so forth. Both authors use such popularized pieces and communication channels to transfer their various messages to a wider audience. In Chapters 4 and 5 we argued that their public roles had a deep impact upon their academic writing. On the one hand it enabled them to arrive at a clear-cut 'diagnosis' (a vitalist culture that is running out of hand versus the global spread of the neoliberal revolution) which informed an equally clear-cut 'remedy' (a moral crusade versus a plea for reinventing the (European) social state). On the other hand, however, it had a number of unfortunate consequences for their scholarship due to a 'policy bias' (in the case of Boutellier) and a 'critical bias' (in the case of Wacquant). In Chapter 5 this tension was brought into clear daylight: the Wacquant of 2007 resembled to a certain extent the Garland of 1985. However, what Wacquant won in terms of critique by adopting a one-dimensional perspective, he lost in terms of arriving at a proper description of punishment. For Garland, on the other hand, the gains and losses reversed: his major preoccupation since the mid-1980s had been to move to a multidimensional sociology of punishment which would enable him to pay respect to the integrity of the empirical object.

The Means and Ends of Persuasion

The problem of evaluation (for readers) is preceded in time by the problem of persuasion (for writers): if writers produce a text and they want their audiences to accept it—which is usually the case—then they need to persuade them. The question to be addressed, then, becomes: How do authors aim to persuade their readers, and towards what ends? And inevitably following from this, the question: Why should we, as readers, be persuaded by an author's account? Persuasion in the social sciences is a highly complex matter. Academic texts are rhetorical objects, means to persuade, ways of convincing fellow-researchers, and (as it is often the case in discussions on punishment) a larger audience of particular interpretations of the world out there (Gross, 1990). Social scientific research can be perceived as 'a form of rhetoric with particular means and rules of engagement' (Bauer *et al*, 2000: 11). In rhetorical analysis a distinction is usually being made between *logos*, *pathos*, and *ethos*. Every text, including texts dealing with issues of punishment and penal change, has a mixture of these three elements: 'Logos refers to the logic of pure argument, and the kinds of arguments used. Pathos refers to the kinds of appeal and concession made to the audience, taking into account the social psychology of emotions. Ethos involves the implicit and explicit references made to the status of the speaker, which establish his or her legitimacy and credibility for saying what is being said' (Bauer *et al*, 2000: 11).

To perceive criminology as a rhetorical enterprise, as we will be doing here, is not to argue that criminological speech is indistinguishable from the speech of the lawyer, the judge, the politician, the journalist, and so forth. Rather it implies acknowledging the basic fact that 'the scientific ideal of a rhetoric of pure argumentative rationality, without pathos or ethos, is an illusion' (Bauer *et al*, 2000: 11). This also raises the question where the voice of the criminologist on penal issues differs (or should differ) from those other voices on the matter. Indeed, as the Dutch criminologist Elisabeth Lissenberg told her students at the occasion of her inaugural lecture for the Chair of Criminology at the University of Amsterdam: 'everyone who has not studied the subject will be able to tell you more about crime than yourself' (Lissenberg, 1989: 22, author's translation). And yet, as criminologists, we are convinced (or, to put it differently, we persuade ourselves) that what we say and write adds something extra *because we have studied it*. In the mid-1990s Nelken drew our attention to the need for rhetorical reflexivity. On that occasion he offered the following questions for criminologists to reflect upon, thereby inviting them to think more deeply about their own rhetorics:

> How does, and how should, criminological argument relate to the techniques of description and persuasion used by those (police, prosecutors, judges, journalists, offenders, other criminologists etc.) whose communications they analyse and often criticise? What, if anything, makes it superior? Are some forms of writing more reflexive than others? Is there a limit to the extent to which it is practical or desirable to reveal the props of production which make accounts convincing? (Nelken, 1994: 18).

The problem of persuasion, which is at the centre of Nelken's thought-provoking questions, has become more pressing in recent times. It has regularly been observed that, paradoxically, the remarkable success of criminology (in terms of enrollment of students, professional associations, academic journals and publication outlets, attendance at conferences, and so forth) has been matched by a decreasing influence on policy development and public debate (Garland and Sparks, 2000). Public discussions on crime and punishment, as Pratt argued elsewhere in this book, are dominated by the voices of politicians, victim groups, journalists, and so forth. Criminology seems to suffer from a persuasion deficit: in times as ours when 'crime talk' flourishes, the criminologist's voice seems—somehow, somewhere—to get lost.

In a recent issue of the journal *Theoretical Criminology* this observation has animated a debate on the need for a 'public criminology'. In their introduction the editors Chancer and McLaughlin pointed out that the thematic issue had two purposes: first, to outline a range of views on criminology's public status and its relationship to public policy formation and intellectual practice; second, to highlight the need for a diversity of 'public criminologies' that could help move policies in more progressive directions. Indeed, as they added, in their opinion 'much more could be done than at present, particularly since there would seem to be broad criminological consensus about many policy issues facing us including punitive policies around the globe as well as the detrimental consequences of a range of harms and risks' (Chancer and McLaughlin, 2007: 156). It is not a coincidence that they mention 'punitive policies around the globe' as one of the 'many policy issues' facing criminologists because, indeed, a larger number of criminologists have in recent years expressed worries about, and directed their research towards, such issues. Garland and, in particular, Pratt and Wacquant have been central figures in this debate.

Such a 'public criminology', then, also needs to be a 'persuasive criminology' because, obviously, it wants its message to travel successfully from sender to receiver. And, in view of those other voices that tend to monopolize the debate on crime and punishment, its voice needs to sound more persuasive: there is a need, as Currie argues in the same thematic issue, for a 'vocal and influential criminology', 'an assertively "public" criminology' (Currie, 2007: 176). Towards the end of his paper Currie raises the following important question: 'Does that mean we abandon our longstanding standards for the proper conduct of research?' He quickly and confidently answers: 'Of course not' (Currie, 2007: 189). The question is important because it makes a brief reference to what sets the 'criminological voice' apart from those other voices, that is, criminology's scientific credentials make the voice of the criminologist distinctive from (which does not necessarily mean superior to) the voices of others. In this respect Bauman once coined the phrase 'responsible speech'. What he writes about sociology also applies to criminology:

> sociology (unlike common sense) makes an effort to subordinate itself to the rigorous rules of responsible speech, which is assumed to be an attribute of science (as distinct from other, reputedly more relaxed and less vigilantly self-controlled, forms of knowledge). This means that the sociologists are expected to take great care to distinguish—in a fashion clear and visible to anybody—between the statements corroborated by available evidence and such propositions as can only claim the status of a

provisional, untested guess. Sociologists would refrain from misrepresenting ideas that are grounded solely in their beliefs (even the most ardent and emotionally intense beliefs) as tested findings carrying the widely respected authority of science. The rules of responsible speech demand that one's 'workshop'—the whole procedure that has led to the final conclusions and is claimed to guarantee their credibility—be wide open to an unlimited public scrutiny; a standing invitation ought to be extended to everyone to reproduce the test and, be this the case, prove the findings wrong. Responsible speech must also relate to other statements made on its topic; it cannot simply dismiss or pass by in silence other views that have been voiced, however sharply they are opposed to it and hence inconvenient' (Bauman, 1990: 12)

Currie's answer ('Of course not') to his self-imposed question may have been too quick and too confident. One of the major advantages of our 'vertical' author-oriented study is that it puts the writer at the centre of attention and that we were able, towards the end of each chapter, to probe more deeply into how each of our authors develops their own public identity, that is, how they perceive, and give flesh to, the relationship between their scholarly activities and public debate and policy formation. This also enabled us to arrive at a more detailed picture of how they aim to persuade their readers, and which ends they pursue. In our brief recapitulation earlier in this chapter we have, at several points, deliberately used the word 'extra-scientific' in order to indicate that, in an attempt to increase the persuasive power of their accounts, some have deliberately used means that might testify of 'irresponsible speech'. Let us illustrate this.

One major problem that we highlighted in Pratt's account is his reliance on a small number of eccentric and exotic examples that are often solely derived from parts of the USA but that, nevertheless, form his empirical basis to make statements about the five English-based jurisdictions or 'western punishment' in general. The same applies to the concept 'new punitiveness'. Upon closer examination also here the presented empirical detail was sparse and mostly derived from some states in the USA. The concept itself, moreover, lacked a sound criterion that would help us decide which practices exactly can be categorized under its umbrella. In Chapter 3 we suggested that the content of the term is more determined by values and sentiments, that is, it tends to group practices and policies that Pratt is worried about, and less by a clear-cut social scientific criterion.

Pratt is probably aware of these limits. We cannot only assume this from his long experience as an informed writer on punishment but also because, on earlier occasions, he has made the same comments on empirical detail and conceptual clarity that we now make about his work. For example, in a paper where he argued against the idea that intermediate treatment provides evidence of a Foucauldian disciplinary type of punishment he highlighted that the few examples that would support such a hypothesis seemed to be 'very atypical', particularly 'when one considers the diversity that is to be found in the full range of intermediate treatment projects'. In addition, training programmes were 'comparatively minor developments within the general system of punishment' (Pratt, 1990a: 228). On another occasion he argued that 'we should be careful not to use "social control" as a catch-phrase concept, thereby neglecting the complexities implicit in it', and he warned against 'the dangers of talking too generally of "social control"' (Pratt, 1985b: 211–12). In order to increase the persuasiveness of his account of recent penal change Pratt seems to have put such comments aside: the end of persuasion (that is, to convince the reader of his 'prophecies' about the dark penal future that lies ahead of us) have led him to adopt means of persuasion that, from the requirements of 'responsible speech', seem to be questionable.

In the case of Boutellier the 'extra-scientific' means of persuasion are even more clearly present. In Chapter 4 we pointed to how his treatment of crime and unsafety figures was devoid of any attempt to put the figures in context and steered towards demonstrating (and, at times, exaggerating) the seriousness of the problem at hand. Boutellier also never deviated from his Durkheimian moral perspective: no attempt was being made to seriously consider other perspectives and, in a time period covering more than two decades, there has never been any engagement with the criticisms levelled at the Durkheimian perspective. In his case, the end of persuasion (that is, to convince his readers of the seriousness of the crime problem and of the need to remoralize the whole of society) prevented him from examining basic issues and alternative perspectives which, again, are questionable in the light of 'responsible speech'.

Also in the case of Wacquant we raised questions of how he aims to persuade his audience. The empirical examples he offers for detailing the American penal state were mostly derived from a small number of American states, and California in particular. The indispensable and functional links between the penal and the social state were, upon closer examination, far from indispensable and functional. The impact of his major illustration of how 'neoliberal penal commonsense' travels, that is, 'zero tolerance', was minor. There are a number of indications which suggest that also Wacquant was well aware of these limits: in a 1998 paper he acknowledged that penal policies are not 'monolithical', that one can detect 'diverging' and even 'contradictory' tendencies, and he referred to practices of mediation, reconciliation, depenalization and individualization of penalties; in *Les prisons de la misère* he already indicated that 'zero tolerance' was on the decline in New York City; and, as a trained sociologist, he regularly has severely criticized the work of colleagues that do not live up to the high standards of sociological research. Wacquant's end of persuasion (that is, to convince the reader of the evils of the American-born neoliberal ideology with its concomitant neoliberal penality), then, has steered his sociological gaze to the most appalling American penal developments that would help him convince his readers about the location of the source of all evil and make them join in his battle against the neoliberal revolution.

The question remains, however, whether Pratt and, in particular, Boutellier and Wacquant, would be bothered about our questioning of the means they deploy to increase the persuasive power of their accounts. Their 'prophetic', 'proselytizing' and 'boxing' aspirations may have led them to persuade their audience by using 'irresponsible speech' but, in the end, it certainly paid off. Pratt's papers are being published in the major international criminological journals which, in turn, add to his status as a leading writer on punishment. In the introduction to the English-language edition of *De veiligheidsutopie* Boutellier was happy to tell his English-language audience that the book was received with 'unexpected enthusiasm' which 'was almost too much to hope for' in his home country. Boutellier did not bother to mention that readers with a training in criminology (such as Willem de Haan or René van Swaaningen) were much more sceptical. Indeed, in view of his 'proselytizing' aspirations he may never have intended them to be part of his audience and, therefore, he did not feel the need to persuade them. Also Wacquant seems to have been successful in persuading his audience: he is a regularly-invited speaker in all corners of the globe; his papers on punishment seem to find their way easily into the important criminological and sociological journals; his books are being translated into numerous languages; major periodicals (from *The New York Times* in the USA to *De Morgen* in Belgium) give him the floor to voice his concerns; and, in activist circles, he is being conferred the status of a principled opponent of America-made neoliberalism.

Writing on Punishment: Towards a Persuasive Criminology

Maybe they are not bothered, but do we as readers (in our capacities of citizen *and* criminologist) have to be bothered? As we wrote earlier, texts produced by academics on punishment and penal change, inevitably exhibit a mixture of *logos*, *ethos,* and *pathos*. To argue straightforwardly that *ethos* and *pathos* need to be reduced as much as possible so that *logos* can reign, would testify to an unrealistic assessment of how making sense of penal change actually happens in practice. It would also invite the comment that claiming scientific neutrality is, in itself, a value statement. What we can do, however, is to argue that individual researchers might endanger the *ethos* of criminology (that is, its status as a scientific discipline) if they do not play by the rules. For the sake of the scientific status of criminology, and in order to preserve the distinctiveness of the voice of the criminologist in the wider world, there are limits to the kinds of persuasion that we, as criminologists, can resort to. A persuasive 'public criminology' is, first and foremost, a persuasive criminology, that is, its means of persuasion need to be informed by 'responsible speech'. In the remainder of this chapter we elaborate this further.

Self-persuasion as point of departure

Creating knowledge starts with self-persuasion: authors need to convince themselves that what they write, makes sense and is worthwhile of being presented to, and examined by, a broader audience. Throughout the process of writing this book we have wondered sometimes to what extent the demands to arrive at self-persuasion have somehow been softened: Pratt's selective use of exotic and eccentric examples to substantiate the thesis of the 'decivilization of punishment' and the 'new punitiveness' is at odds with his own critical comments on the lack of empirical detail and conceptual unclarity; Boutellier's decade-long uncompromising and uncritical use of Durkheim is difficult to reconcile with the fact that he is aware of the limits of Durkheim and a series of alternative perspectives which he routinely accuses of not taking crime and unsafety seriously; Wacquant's declared awareness of 'diverging' and 'contradictory' penal developments, and his demonstrated sensitivity for comparative issues, is difficult to reconcile with the highly streamlined pictures he presents to elaborate his general theory of neoliberal penality.

Self-persuasion then, is not restricted to playing by the rules of the game but includes bending back on one's own accumulated body of research and intellectual trajectory, that is, it calls for a kind of biographical reflexivity. We raised this issue most explicitly in Chapter 3. There we argued that Pratt's volatile scholarship was not matched by a degree of self-reflection and self-critique that seems to be indispensable for his use of theory. This lack of biographical reflexivity has sometimes unfortunate consequences. For example, a reviewer of *Punishment and Civilization* argued that the book remains 'too loyal to Elias' framework' and suggested the following: 'Had Pratt infused his theory with the logic that Foucault develops in *Discipline and Punish*...he could have reached greater depths of explanation' (Austin, 2004: 104). This remark by Andrew Austin, who is probably unfamiliar with Pratt's Foucault-inspired work, makes perfect sense in his evaluation of the book as a stand-alone piece of research. However, in view of our exploration of Pratt's intellectual life-course it sounds somewhat awkward. Pratt could have avoided such remarks by infusing his texts with more self-reflective passages—demonstrating where, how, and why he departs from his earlier scholarship when travelling between different theoretical perspectives and research projects. Unfortunately, this is hardly the case. In a 2005 paper Pratt presented Elias as offering us (*contra* Foucault, neo-Marxism, and Durkheim) a theoretical framework to understand the new punitiveness and wrote the following about governmentality: 'these emotive and expressive sanctions which deliberately provoke human sensibilities rather than suppress them, seem to run counter to the kernel of "rationality" that is epistemologically embedded in Foucault's later work on governmentality (see Foucault, 1991)' (Pratt, 2005a: 256). While we can fully agree with that comment it would have been more honest if Pratt referred to his own extensive writings inspired by governmentality which were much more elaborated and focused on penal developments than Foucault's sketchy and unfinished papers. This would also have offered his readers an indication of how Pratt revised his own earlier work in the light of later research. By presenting the critique towards governmentality as a critique to Foucault instead of as a self-critique, he chose not to disclose an important part of his own intellectual past and gives his readers the (false) impression that he, unlike Foucault, did not fall into the rationality trap.

In this book we disclosed a number of contradictions and shifts in thinking: Pratt's shifting understanding and evaluation of penal bureaucracies (impersonal people-processing machineries or indispensable shields against decivilization?); Wacquant's different ways of understanding punishment in the USA (exceptionalism or not?); Boutellier's shift from endorsing a 'reserved criminal law' or a 'minimal criminal justice system' in the mid-1990s to his plea for a further expansion of the Dutch criminal justice system at the start of the twenty-first century. Due to time pressure researchers usually read the texts of colleagues in a functional way: we look for what we can use for our own purposes. Most of us do not have the luxury to skim through hundreds or thousands of pages of academic production by one single author. It may therefore be useful to stimulate longitudinal studies of career criminologists as a separate topic for inquiry. Building a tradition of these kind of studies in criminology may, like in philosophy or sociology, have a fruitful impact on the discipline at large and sensitize the new generations to questions related to intellectual development and biographical reflexivity. Moreover, if the study of authors' intellectual life-courses reveals questions that they themselves leave untouched or unresolved throughout their careers, then these may pose particularly challenging puzzles for future research: what is, for example, the proper role of bureaucracy and expertise in the domain of punishment? What exactly is distinctive about American punishment, and what is not? Does a society 'need' punishment to remain morally healthy and, if so, how much and what form should it take?

Choosing to know

Accounts on recent penal change will always be partial and limited. Indeed, 'ways of seeing' are always 'ways of non-seeing'. Authors need to make numerous choices related to what facts to investigate; how to investigate those facts; and how to make sense of them. They can never illuminate 'the whole stage'. The task of stories is 'to create a picture one can absorb, comprehend and retain out of the anarchy of blots and stains one can neither take in nor make sense of' (Bauman, 2004: 17). 'Eliminating', so Bauman tells us, 'is not a negative movement, but a positive effort to organize the environment' (Bauman, 2004: 18). Seen from such a perspective, partiality is not only inevitable but it even turns into a virtue: it helps an author to bring into view those 'parts of the stage' that deserve special attention and it assists the reader in absorbing the story that the author brings. Garland, Pratt, and Wacquant explicitly acknowledge, at various places in their oeuvre, that their accounts are, out of necessity, generalizations which leave some parts of the stage in darkness. To an important extent this argument is valid and it reminds us that a written text can only contain a limited number of words.

However, our interrogation should not stop here. As we suggested earlier in this chapter, processes of generalization (or what we termed 'streamlining' in the case of Boutellier and Wacquant) can also be inspired by other, 'extra-scientific' motives and, therefore, should not seduce the reader to adopt a position of 'anything goes' or 'let a thousand flowers bloom'. The problem with such a position is that it fails to examine the procedures that authors routinely apply. It suggests accepting the 'product' without further examining the 'production process', that is, the rhetorical strategies that social scientists deploy. This holds in particular for the writings of criminologists. As Ericson recently remarked: 'They are intended to move their audiences to more principled courses of actions in dealing with crime and security' (Ericson, 2003: 64). Throughout this book we have seen how selectivity, dramatization, and distortion were routinely used to increase the persuasive power of particular accounts and to move various audiences into certain directions.

In Chapter 4 we quoted Matthews who likened discussions on punitiveness to media reporting: 'In line with the media, many academics feel that only bad news is worth reporting' (Matthews, 2005a: 181). Such a comparison with journalism is illuminating because news gathering and editing involve 'procedures not to know' (Fishman, 1978). Fishman borrowed that phrase from Dorothy Smith who once made a distinction between ideology and social science. The crucial difference between ideology and knowledge is situated in the use of procedures as a 'means not to know' (Smith, 1974: 40). Choosing not to know may be an option for newspapers or TV channels that scrutinize the world out there for eye-catching, sensational and, therefore, newsworthy items but as a procedure it does not belong in the tool-kit of a persuasive criminology that aims to adhere to the rules of 'responsible speech'.

It is our contention that analytic pluralism may help in avoiding or, at a minimum, acknowledging various distortions which flow from the use of procedures as 'means not to know'. Throughout our study we became increasingly persuaded by this important aspect of Garland's work which sets him apart from the three other authors. As we discussed at length in Chapter 2, Garland's move to a multidimensional sociology of punishment was inspired by the need to pay fuller respect to the 'integrity of the empirical object': a one-dimensional framework was felt to be too constraining and ultimately counterproductive. This became also clear for some of the authors discussed in this book. Whereas the exclusive choice of Durkheim or a variant of the political economy of punishment, made for a coherent story and paved the way for a clear critique and normative position, there were simply too many aspects that were missing in the accounts of Boutellier and Wacquant. The choice of a multidimensional framework which takes the inherent complexity of punishment and penal change as its point of departure may, indeed, be the most fruitful starting point for a proper understanding of punishment and penal change. From such a perspective, also the work of the other authors can be used as resources that are in need for further expansion and revision in future research. Boutellier's hypothesis on the victimalization of morality, for example, is an interesting one but it is, as we argued in Chapter 4, in need of further research because it only focuses on the generation of consensus around victimization and fails to capture a number of divisive aspects related to struggles for recognition and access to victim definitions. Wacquant's work on how criminal justice policy travels from the USA to other parts of the globe is, again, important but fails to capture other ways of policy travelling and is in need of closer attention for the practical impact of such travelling.

The moment of discipline

In Chapter 1 we argued that recent penal developments created a 'hot spot' or an 'imaginative moment' for intellectual activity and innovative scholarship. This is somewhat similar to what happened a century ago. Indeed, as Susanne Karstedt recently observed: 'Recent developments in the sociology of punishment again demonstrate the prolific partnership with theoretical sociology that we observe for the nineteenth and beginning of the twentieth centuries. Now and again, penal sensibilities and the actual organization of punishment function as expressions and illuminations of wider cultural shifts and profound social change' (Karstedt, 2007: 59). In such circumstances imagination is highly important. This is even more so in view of the 'failure of the classics': a prerequisite to solve some of the newer problems that great thinkers such as Durkheim, Foucault, Rusche and Kirchheimer, and Elias could not foresee is that criminology plays the role of a welcoming host to creative scholarship.

However, as we wrote in Chapter 3, the 'imaginative moment' needs to go hand in hand with the 'moment of discipline' because, unlike novelists who enjoy an almost unlimited freedom to write, there are obvious restrictions to the speech of criminologists. In return, however, this brings a number of benefits in its wake. Academic writers on punishment, deliberately or otherwise, can use their *ethos*, and that of the discipline they belong to, to enhance the persuasiveness of their stories when they bring them to the wider world. Their voices have a certain authority because of their professional training; their publications in important academic journals or with respected publishers; their reputation of holding prestigious research positions or professorial chairs; their membership of the editorial boards of leading journals; and so forth. In sum, their belonging to 'a network of authority relationships' (Gross, 1990: 13) gives their voice a special quality.

The authors in this book are well aware of such benefits. For example, Boutellier argued that *De veiligheidsutopie* was written out of a 'need for reflection' and told his readers that he deliberately wanted to keep a distance from the 'heat of politics'. In presenting the book like this, Boutellier suggests to his audience that his book is the product of independent scientific inquiry and that its contents are not tainted by his professional ties to the

Dutch Ministry of Justice. Pratt somehow disliked being labeled an 'armchair academic' when he was introduced to the participants of a seminar that he attended. Nevertheless, the use of such a description conveys a message about how he was perceived by his audience, that is, as a detached scholar who is situated at a safe distance from the dirty world of crime and punishment. Wacquant's Bourdieu-inspired vision of sociology as 'martial art' communicates the message that social scientists committed to such a scientific practice dispose of a distinctive set of skills which are indispensable to see things that others cannot see. It makes it possible 'to take apart the false commonplaces, reveal the subterfuges, unmask the lies, and point out the logical and practical contradictions of the discourse of King Market and triumphant capitalism' (Wacquant, 2004b: 101), and allow for unmasking various 'scholarly myths' such as the existence of 'French-style' ghettos (Wacquant, 1992a; Wacquant, 1992b), the 'underclass' (Wacquant, 1996e), 'zero tolerance' (Wacquant, 1999a), the 'law and order' *doxa* (Wacquant, 2006d). The same applies to Garland who refers to himself as a 'dispassionate observer', that is, someone who is committed to a scientific position that is marked by a certain degree of detachment that permits him to grasp complexities that others, again, are not able to grasp.

Such (self-)descriptions fulfil an important explicit and implicit function. On the one hand they spread the message to various audiences that their voices are somehow distinctive, that they have a cultural capital that others lack. On the other hand, they implicitly acknowledge that science matters. Now that the postmodernist debunking has somehow receded into the background, time has come to reclaim part of the public sphere. Science matters, then, not so much in absolute philosophical terms of 'epistemological superiority' but in more down-to-earth sociological ones. Indeed, as Harbers once argued, we are not dealing here with vertical differentiation in terms of truth and objectivity as the Olympus-model suggests but with horizontal differentiation in terms of the division of labour within the Agora (Harbers, 1992: 49). It is the craftman-like, controlled and controllable approach, that differentiates the criminologist's voice from other voices on the topic and this is also the key argument in favour of the superiority of the knowledge he or she offers. As Roger Hood suggests: 'the voices of criminologists will be heard only if they can speak in their "wider-ranging role" from a firm base of empirical research, and research that can make claims to be scientifically rigorous, in the sense that it is repeatable, reliable and valid. This is what distinguishes criminology from other types of discourse about crime. Unless legitimacy can be claimed for this view, the "criminologist" will be treated as just another person with an "opinion" on the subject' (Hood, 2002: 159).

The anti-political position

We would argue that such a claim to legitimacy also implies adopting, safeguarding, and defending a certain intellectual position in the public debate which we, following George Konrád, term anti-political: 'Anti-politics is the political activity of those who don't want to be politicians and who refuse to share in power' (Konrád, 1984: 230). Konrád pictured the relationship between politics and anti-politics as follows: 'The relationship between politics and anti-politics is like the relationship between two mountains: neither one tries to usurp the other's place; neither one can eliminate or replace the other' (Konrád, 1984: 231). A criminology that aims to be anti-political welcomes the division of labour between intellectuals and politicians, and accepts and cherishes the different rhetorical mixtures of *logos, pathos,* and *ethos*. An anti-political criminology does not have the ambition nor the pretension to take the place of politicians. It recognizes that science has a peculiar rationality different from politics: 'organizing ideas' cannot be the same as 'organizing men and things' (Pels, 1992; 1995). It therefore also accepts that public debate on crime and punishment happens at a number of distinctive levels—moral, religious, commonsense, political, practical, scientific—and that its legitimate place is at the level of knowledge. Such an anti-political criminology patrols closely the borders of the discipline in order to safeguard its *ethos* and to build up a collective identity of a scientific community that has a crucial role to play in the public debate. Following the rules of responsible speech, then, is indispensable for the public accountability of such a criminology and for maintaining a form of scientific persuasion.

An anti-political criminology does not have to have a set of ready-made answers to pressing policy issues. Towards the end of Chapter 4 we opposed Boutellier's conception of criminology as a reflexive policy science which is oriented towards political decision-making and is strongly preoccupied with the strategic implications of its research. Criminology should do much more because it knows much more and can enrich the public debate in many different ways. As Zedner recently argued: 'There is no absolute reason why the ability of criminology to inform or influence policy-making should be taken as a measure of success; any more than one would judge Durkheim by his influence on suicide levels' (Zedner, 2003: 202). Moreover, as she added, 'the common assumption that criminological theory, with its tendency to radical critique and unverifiable abstraction, is incapable of influence is to misunderstand the subtle, indirect ways in which knowledge can generate social understanding and inform the policy agenda' (Zedner, 2003: 227). Entering the debate on crime and punishment is much more than playing society's diagnostician and offering recipes for the perceived illnesses. It is also about 'revealing complexities', 'questioning certitudes' and 'puncturing the false hope of simple solutions' (Zedner, 2003: 234). This is, arguably, an important and valuable contribution to any public discussion on crime and punishment that only criminologists, as the professional gate-keepers of an accumulated body of criminological knowledge, can offer.

There are many forces at work that aim to push criminology's role in the public sphere either into a political or an apolitical direction. The danger of making it political is that criminology comes to be subsumed under an ethico-political vision and only admits certain areas of research as worthy of attention. Mathieu Deflem was one of the rare voices to highlight this problematic aspect in the public sociology debate in the USA. Public sociology was revealed as a thinly veiled disguise of a particularistic version of Marxist sociology, promoted by the 2003–04 President of the American Sociological Association, Michael Burawoy (2005). There was the danger that sociology would turn into a form of political activism thereby, paradoxically, jeopardizing the role of sociology in the wider world and damaging its scientific credentials.[1] The recent call of three Scandinavian criminologists, published in the newsletter of the European Society of Criminology, that criminologists should dissociate themselves from the Stockholm

[1] Mathieu Deflem, an Associate Professor in Sociology at the University of South Carolina, launched a campaign 'Save Sociology' and maintained a website which was regularly updated between the summer of 2004 and the autumn of 2006 (<http://www.savesociology.org>).

Prize in Criminology can be understood as a plea against an apolitical criminology. Balvig, Christie, and Tham claim that the type of criminology being promoted by the prestigious Prize, that is, an applied criminology at the service of the state, and the procedure for awarding it, lead to the creation of a 'tame criminology' (Balvig *et al*, 2008). An anti-political criminology needs to be constantly on its guard for challenges coming from both sides—the political and the apolitical—in order to preserve a legitimate and productive place in the public debate. This implies acknowledging that the ordering of ideas is not the same, and can never be the same, as the ordering of men and things.

Bibliography

Adams, J. (2001) 'Book review: David Garland, The Culture of Control', *Times Higher Education Supplement*, 7 September 2001.

Albrecht, H.-J. (2001) 'Post-adjudication Dispositions in Comparative Perspective' in M. Tonry and R.S. Frase (eds) *Sentencing and Sanctions in Western Countries*, New York: Oxford University Press.

Altheide, D.L. (2002) *Creating Fear. News and the Construction of Crisis*, New York: Aldine de Gruyter.

Anderson, E. (2002) 'The Ideologically Driven Critique', *American Journal of Sociology*, 107(6): 1533–50.

Aranda Ocaña, M., G. Chaves Castillo, M, Moreno Aldea, J.D. Posada Segura, C. Rivas Trullols and I. Rivera Beiras (2005) *El populismo punitivo. Análisis de las reformas y contra-reformas del Sistema Penal en España (1995–2005)*, Barcelona: Universidad de Barcelona.

Armstrong, S. and L. McAra (eds) (2006) *Perspectives on Punishment: The Contours of Control*, Oxford: Oxford University Press.

Austin, A. (2004) 'Book Review, J. Pratt, Punishment and Civilization', *Journal of Intercultural Studies*, 25(1): 101–04.

Balvig, F., N. Christie and H. Tham (2008) 'Whither the Stockholm Prize?', *Newsletter of the European Society of Criminology*, 7(1): 1, 8–9.

Bauer, M.W., G. Gaskell and N.C. Allum (2000) 'Quality, Quantity and Knowledge Interests: Avoiding Confusions' in M.W. Bauer and G. Gaskell (eds) *Qualitative Researching with Text, Image and Sound*, London: Sage.

Bauman, Z. (1989) *Modernity and the Holocaust*, Cambridge: Polity Press.

—— (1990)*Thinking Sociologically*, Oxford: Basil Blackwell.

—— (2001) *Community. Seeking Safety in an Insecure World*, Cambridge: Polity Press.

—— (2004) *Wasted Lives. Modernity and its Outcasts*, Cambridge: Polity Press.

—— (2005) *Work, Consumerism and the New Poor (Second Edition)*, Maidenhead: Open University Press.

—— (2006) *Liquid Fear*, Cambridge: Polity Press.

—— (2007) 'Morele uitdagingen van het vloeibaar moderne leven' in T. Daems and L. Robert (eds) *Zygmunt Bauman. De schaduwzijde van de vloeibare moderniteit*, The Hague: Boom Juridische Uitgevers.

Beck, U. (1992) *Risk Society. Towards a New Modernity,* London: Sage.
—— (1994) 'The Reinvention of Politics: Towards a Theory of Reflexive Modernization' in U. Beck, A. Giddens and S. Lash (eds) *Reflexive Modernization. Politics, Tradition and Aesthetics in the Modern Social Order,* Cambridge: Polity Press.
—— and E. Beck-Gernsheim (1995) *The Normal Chaos of Love,* Cambridge: Polity Press.
Beckett, K. (1997) *Making Crime Pay: Law and Order in Contemporary American Politics,* New York: Oxford University Press.
—— (2001) 'Crime and Control in the Culture of Late Modernity', *Law and Society Review*, 35(4): 899–929.
Best, J. (1997) 'Victimization and the Victim Industry', *Society,* May/June: 9–17.
—— (1999) *Random Violence. How we Talk about New Crimes and New Victims,* Berkeley: University of California Press.
Beyens, K., R. Bas and D. Kaminski (2007) 'Elektronisch toezicht in België. Een schijnbaar penitentiair ontstoppingsmiddel', *Panopticon*, 28(3): 21–40.
Blum, E. and P. Neitzke (2001) 'Armut als Delikt. Ein Gespräch mit Loïc Wacquant', *Mittelweg*, 36(6): 65–74.
Blumstein, A. and J. Cohen (1973) 'A theory of the stability of punishment', *Journal of Criminal Law and Criminology,* 64(2): 198–207.
Boone, M. and M. Moerings (2007) 'De cellenexplosie. Voorlopig gehechten, veroordeelden, vreemdelingen, jeugdigen en tbs', *Justitiële Verkenningen*, 33(4): 9–30.
Bottoms, A. (1977) 'Reflections on the Renaissance of Dangerousness', *Howard Journal of Criminal Justice*, 16(2): 70–96.
—— (1995) 'The philosophy and politics of punishment and sentencing' in C. Clarkson and R. Morgan (eds) *The Politics of Sentencing Reform*, Oxford: Clarendon Press.
—— (2002) 'Morality, crime, compliance and public policy' in A. Bottoms and M. Tonry (eds) *Ideology, Crime and Criminal Justice,* Cullompton: Willan Publishing.
—— (2003) 'Some Sociological Reflections on Restorative Justice' in A. Von Hirsch, J. Roberts, A.E. Bottoms, K. Roach and M. Schiff (eds) *Restorative Justice and Criminal Justice: Competing or Reconcilable Paradigms?,* Oxford: Hart Publishing.
—— (2004) 'Foreword' in H. Boutellier, *The Safety Utopia,* Dordrecht: Kluwer Academic Publishers.
Bouma, J.-D. (2006a) 'Een rugzak die niet af kan. De strijd tegen zinloos geweld, tien jaar na de dood van Joes Kloppenburg', *NRC Handelsblad*, 12 August 2006.
—— (2006b) 'Animo voor stille tocht tegen geweld is gesleten', *NRC Handelsblad*, 17 August 2006.

Bourdieu, P. (ed) (1993) *La misère du monde,* Paris: Éditions du Seuil.
—— (1998) *Contre-feux. Propos pour servir à la résistance contre l'invasion néo-libérale*, Paris: Raisons d'Agir.
—— (2001) *Contre-feux 2. Pour un mouvement social européen*, Paris: Raisons d'agir.
—— and L. Wacquant (1992) *An Invitation to Reflexive Sociology*, Cambridge: Polity Press.
—— and L. Wacquant (1999) 'On the Cunning of Imperialist Reason', *Theory, Culture and Society*, 16(1): 41–58.
—— and L. Wacquant (2000) 'La nouvelle vulgate planétaire', *Le Monde diplomatique*, May: 6–7.
Boutellier, H. (1985a) 'Met alleen nog de persoon als inzet. Het jongerenwerk en de moraal', *Welzijnsmaandblad,* 39(3): 19–23.
—— (1985b) 'Jongerenwerk en moraal. Een interview met jongerenwerker Har van de Berg', *Psychologie en Maatschappij*, 9(3): 386–90.
—— (1987) 'Prostitutie en moraal', *Justitiële Verkenningen*, 13(1): 7–35.
—— (1988a) 'Jongerenwerk tussen norm en werkelijkheid', *Justitiële Verkenningen*, 14(5): 9–32.
—— (1988b) 'Jeugdcultuur en de moraal. Een gesprek met Paradiso-directeur Huib Schreurs', *Justitiële Verkenningen*, 14(5): 33–39.
—— (1989) 'Seksueel misbruik van kinderen. Van pijnlijk geheim tot spektakelstuk', *Justitiële Verkenningen,* 15(6): 8–33.
—— (1990) 'De secularisering van moraal. Een beschouwing over de relatie tussen godsdienst en criminaliteit', *Justitiële Verkenningen,* 16(6): 10–43.
—— (1991a) 'Criminaliteit als moreel vraagstuk: vijf jaar justitieel preventiebeleid' in P.B. Cliteur, P.A. Van Gennip and L. Laeyendecker (eds) *Burgerschap, levensbeschouwing en criminaliteit. Humanistische, katholieke en protestantse visies op de kwaliteit van de huidige samenleving*, Amersfoort: De Horstink.
—— (1991b) 'Ironie als deugd. Een beschouwing over filosofie en criminaliteit', *Psychologie en Maatschappij*, 15(2): 115–33.
—— (1991c) 'Prostitution, criminal law and morality in the Netherlands', *Crime, Law and Social Change*, 15(3): 201–11.
—— (1992) 'Richard Rorty en de sociaal-democratie', *Socialisme en Democratie*, 49(4): 169–71.
—— (1993a) *Solidariteit en slachtofferschap. De morele betekenis van criminaliteit in een postmoderne cultuur*, Nijmegen: SUN.
—— (1993b) 'Over de morele keuze voor criminaliteit', *Tijdschrift voor Criminologie*, 35(4): 314–26.
—— (1994a) 'Het geëmancipeerde slachtoffer. Een nadere beschouwing over solidariteit en slachtofferschap' in M. Moerings (ed) *Hoe punitief is Nederland?*, Arnhem: Gouda Quint.

Boutellier, H. (1994b) 'Criminologie van de toekomst. Een literatuurverkenning' in M.M.J. Aalberts, J.C.J. Boutellier and H.G. van de Bunt (eds) *Rechtsverzorging en wetenschap. Een plaatsbepaling van het WODC bij het afscheid van J. Junger-Tas*, Arnhem: Gouda Quint/WODC.

—— (1994c) 'De zorgzame staat. Over het morele motief in overheidsbeleid', *Justitiële Verkenningen*, 20(6): 85–101.

—— (1995) 'De moraal van de kwetsbaarheid', *Filosofie Magazine*, 4(5): 27–29.

—— (1996a) 'Recht op de buurt. Experimenten met huizen van Justitie', *Tijdschrift voor de Sociale Sector*, 12: 4–8.

—— (1996b) 'Beyond the criminal justice paradox. Alternatives between law and morality', *European Journal on Criminal Policy and Research*, 4(4): 7–20.

—— (1997a) 'Right to the community. Neighbourhood justice in the Netherlands', *European Journal on Criminal Policy and Research*, 5(4): 43–52.

—— (1997b) 'Kwetsbaarheid en zorgethiek. Over de morele motieven van een postmoderne staat', in M. Verkerk (ed) *Denken over zorg. Concepten en praktijken*, Utrecht: Tijdstroom.

—— (1998a) 'De stille revolutie van Justitie', *Proces*, 77(11/12): 175–77.

—— (1998b) 'Justitie en opvoeding: overwegingen bij het nieuwe beleid', *Perspectief*, 5: 8–10.

—— (1998c) 'De vrolijke wereld volgens Kunneman', *Tijdschrift voor de Sociale Sector*, 11: 16–17.

—— (1999a) 'A Letter from the Netherlands: Recent Initiatives in Community Justice', *Crime Prevention and Community Safety*, 1(4): 57–62.

—— (1999b) 'De toekomst van Justitie in de buurt. Van wild idee tot structureel beleid', *Tijdschrift voor de Sociale Sector*, 7/8: 10–13.

—— (1999c) 'De veiligheidsutopie. Contouren van strafrechtelijk beleid', *Recht der Werkelijkheid*, 20(3): 23–40.

—— (2000a) *Crime and Morality. The Significance of Criminal Justice in Post-Modern Culture*, Dordrecht: Kluwer.

—— (2000b) 'Redactioneel. Communities that Care', *Tijdschrift voor Criminologie*, 42(4): 301.

—— (2000c) 'De pornografische context van zedendelicten. Een beschouwing over de huidige seksuele moraal', *Justitiële Verkenningen*, 26(6): 9–24.

—— (2000d) 'The pornographic context of sexual offences. Reflections on the contemporary sexual mentality', *European Journal on Criminal Policy and Research*, 8: 441–57.

—— (2000e) 'Het geluid van stille marsen. De maatschappelijke betekenis van burgerinitiatieven tegen geweld', *Tijdschrift voor Criminologie*, 42(4): 317–32.

—— (2000f) 'De postmoderne zondeval. Een beschouwing over veiligheid, strafrecht en humanisme', *Tijdschrift voor Humanistiek*, 1(1): 4–14.
—— (2001a) 'The Convergence of Social Policy and Criminal Justice', *European Journal on Criminal Policy and Research*, 9: 361–80.
—— (2001b) 'A Letter from the Netherlands: The Postmodern Fall of Man—An Essay on Safety, Criminal Law and Humanism', *Crime Prevention and Community Safety,* 3(2): 71–79.
—— (2001c) 'Nieuwe tijden, kleine moraal. De actualiteit van moraliteit en veiligheid' in H. Boutellier, H. Kunneman and J. Leest (eds) *De straf voorbij. Morele praktijken rondom het strafrecht,* Amsterdam: Uitgeverij SWP.
—— (2002a) *De veiligheidsutopie. Hedendaags onbehagen en verlangen rond misdaad en straf*, The Hague: Boom Juridische Uitgevers.
—— (2002b) 'Victimalization and restorative justice: moral backgrounds and political consequences' in L. Walgrave (ed) *Restorative Justice and the Law*, Cullompton: Willan Publishing.
—— (2002c) 'Jeugdbescherming als speerpunt van jeugdzorg', *Justitiële Verkenningen*, 28(9): 29–39.
—— (2002d) 'Kunst moet een nieuw moreel radicalisme uitdragen', *NRC Handelsblad*, 7 December 2002.
—— (2003) 'Over irrationaliteit en beschaving', *Proces*, 82(5): 223–30.
—— (2004a) *The Safety Utopia. Contemporary Discontent and Desire as to Crime and Punishment*, Dordrecht: Kluwer Academic Publishers.
—— (2004b) 'Beschavingspretenties van straf en herstel' in B.A.M. Van Stokkom (ed) *Straf en herstel. Ethische reflecties over sanctiedoeleinden,* The Hague: Boom Juridische Uitgevers.
—— (2004c) 'Op zoek naar waarden, normen en wat dies meer zij' in H. Boutellier, P. De Beer and C. Van Praag (eds) *Bindingsloos of bandeloos. Normen, waarden en individualisering,* The Hague: Sociaal en Cultureel Planbureau.
—— (2004d) 'Discussie over het veiligheidsbeleid' in E. Brugmans and M. Buijsen (eds) *Krakend recht en verharde moraal. Maatschappelijke ontwikkelingen en hun invloed op recht en moraal,* Nijmegen: Valkhof Pers.
—— (2004e) 'Scholen moeten gedragsnormen bijbrengen', *De Volkskrant*, 26 January 2004.
—— (2005a) *Meer dan veilig. Over bestuur, bescherming en burgerschap,* The Hague: Boom Juridische Uitgevers.
—— (2005b) *De veiligheidsutopie. Hedendaags onbehagen en verlangen rond misdaad en straf (derde druk, met twee extra hoofdstukken)*, The Hague: Boom Juridische Uitgevers.
—— (2005c) 'Tussen voorzorgcultuur en veiligheidsutopie. Reactie op Roel Pieterman', *Recht der Werkelijkheid*, 26(1): 67–70.

Boutellier, H. (2005d) 'Veiligheid. De burger als slachtoffer en verantwoordelijke' in M. Hurenkamp and M. Kremer (eds) *Vrijheid verplicht. Over tevredenheid en de grenzen van keuzevrijheid (Jaarboek TSS, Tijdschrift voor Sociale Vraagstukken),* Amsterdam: Van Gennep.

—— (2005e) 'Een nieuwe ordening: een verkenning van de relatie tussen veiligheid, recht en vertrouwen' in R. Pieterman, P. Dekker and H. Elffers (eds) *Veiligheid, vertrouwen en good governance*, The Hague: Elsevier Juridisch.

—— (2006a) 'The vital context of restorative justice' in I. Aertsen, T. Daems and L. Robert (eds) *Institutionalizing Restorative Justice*, Cullompton: Willan Publishing.

—— (2006b) 'Tussen waarheid en werkelijkheid: de nuances van beleidsonderzoek', *In de Marge*, 15(1): 29–36.

—— (2006c) 'Valkuilen voor sociologen. Kanttekeningen vanuit beleidsonderzoek' in G. Engbersen and J. De Haan (eds) *Balans en toekomst van de sociologie,* Amsterdam: Pallas Publications.

—— (2006d) 'Tussen porno en participatie. Over de nieuwe rol voor de sociale sector', *Tijdschrift voor de Sociale Sector,* May: 10–13.

—— (2007a) 'Kristallen in vloeistof. Veiligheid in het werk van Zygmunt Bauman' in T. Daems and L. Robert (eds) *Zygmunt Bauman. De schaduwzijde van de vloeibare moderniteit*, The Hague: Boom Juridische Uitgevers.

—— (2007b) 'Het gemakkelijke gelijk van Theodore Dalrymple: Boekessay', *Socialisme en Democratie,* 64(1/2): 68–73.

—— (2007c) 'Het onbekende slachtoffer. Bespreking: J.J.M. van Dijk, The Mark of Abel', *Tijdschrift voor Criminologie,* 49(2): 194–99.

—— and L. Van der Linden (1980) 'Kriminaliteit en heropvoeding. Een strijd om de verbeelding', *Psychologie en Maatschappij*, 13: 514–27.

—— and B. Van Stokkom (1995) 'Consumptie van veiligheid. Van verzorgingsstaat tot veiligheidsstaat', *Justitiële Verkenningen*, 21(5): 96–111.

—— H. Kunneman and J. Leest (eds) (2001) *De straf voorbij. Morele praktijken rondom het strafrecht,* Amsterdam: Uitgeverij SWP.

—— and M. Steketee (2006) 'Herstelbemiddeling voor jeugdigen in Nederland', *Tijdschrift voor Herstelrecht,* 6(3): 9–25.

—— and E. Tonkens (2006) 'Conclusies. De aarzelende opkomst van een praktische publieke moraal' in E. Tonkens, J. Uitermark and M. Ham (eds) *Handboek moraliseren. Burgerschap en ongedeelde moraal*, Amsterdam: Van Gennep.

Braithwaite, J. (1989) *Crime, Shame and Reintegration,* Cambridge: Cambridge University Press.

—— (2003) 'What's Wrong with the Sociology of Punishment?', *Theoretical Criminology*, 7(1): 5–28.

Brown, D. (2005) 'Continuity, rupture, or just more of the "volatile and contradictory'"? Glimpes of New South Wales' penal practice behind and through the discursive' in J. Pratt, D. Brown, M. Brown, S. Hallsworth and W. Morrison (eds) *The New Punitiveness. Trends, Theories, Perspectives*, Cullompton: Willan Publishing.

Brown, E.K. (2006) 'The dog that did not bark: punitive social views and the "professional middle classes"', *Punishment and Society*, 8(3): 287–312.

Brown, M. and J. Pratt (2000) 'Introduction' in M. Brown and J. Pratt (eds) *Dangerous Offenders: Punishment and Social Order,* London: Routledge.

Bruner, J.S. (2003) 'Do Not Pass Go. Review of the Culture of Control. By David Garland', *The New York Review of Books*, 25 September 2003.

Burawoy, M. (2005) '2004 ASA Presidential Address. For Public Sociology', *American Sociological Review*, 70(1): 4–28.

Burchell, G., C. Gordon and P. Miller (eds) (1991) *The Foucault Effect. Studies in Governmentality,* London: Harvester Wheatsheaf.

Buruma, I. (2002) 'Competing for victimhood', *The Guardian*, 29 January 2002.

Buruma, Y. (1994) 'Victimalisering van het strafrecht' in M. Moerings (ed) *Hoe punitief is Nederland?,* Arnhem: Gouda Quint.

—— (2003) 'Opstand der slachtoffers. De cultuursociologische en strafrechtelijke invalshoeken', *Nederlands Juristenblad*, 23: 1166–74.

Calhoun, C. and L. Wacquant (2002) '"Social Science with Conscience": Remembering Pierre Bourdieu', *Thesis Eleven*, 70: 1–14.

Cape, E. (ed) (2004a) *Reconcilable Rights? Analysing the tension between victims and defendants*, London: LAG Education and Service Trust Limited.

—— (2004b) 'Overview: Is reconciliation possible?' in E. Cape (ed) *Reconcilable Rights? Analysing the tension between victims and defendants,* London: LAG Education and Service Trust Limited.

Castel, R. (2003) *L' insécurité sociale. Qu'est-ce qu'être protégé?*, Paris: Éditions du Seuil.

Cavadino, M. and J. Dignan (2006a) *Penal Systems. A Comparative Approach,* London: Sage.

—— —— (2006b) 'Penal policy and political economy', *Criminology and Criminal Justice*, 6(4): 435–56.

Cavender, G. (2004) 'Media and Crime Policy. A Reconsideration of David Garland's *The Culture of Control*', *Punishment and Society*, 6(3): 335–48.

Ceretti, A. (ed) (2005a) *Pena, controllo sociale e modernità nel pensiero di David Garland. Atti del convegno in onore di David Garland Università di Milano-Bicocca 1° marzo 2004*, Milan: Giuffrè Editore.

Ceretti, A. (2005b) 'Presentazione' in A. Ceretti (ed) *Pena, controllo sociale e modernità nel pensiero di David Garland. Atti del convegno in onore di David Garland Università di Milano-Bicocca 1° marzo 2004*, Milan: Giuffrè Editore.

Chancer, L. and E. McLaughlin (2007) 'Public criminologies. Diverse perspectives on academia and policy', *Theoretical Criminology*, 11(2): 155–73.

Chaumont, J.-M. (1997) *La concurrence des victimes. Génocide, identité, reconnaissance*, Paris: La Découverte.

Christie, N. (1986) 'The Ideal Victim' in E.A. Fattah (ed) *From Crime Policy to Victim Policy,* Houndsmills: MacMillan.

—— (2000) *Crime Control as Industry. Towards GULAGS, Western Style (Third Edition)*, London: Routledge.

Chun, D.E. and S.A.M. Gavigan (1988) 'Social Control: Analytical Tool or Analytical Quagmire?', *Contemporary Crises*, 12: 107–24.

Cohen, S. (1985) *Visions of Social Control,* Cambridge: Polity Press.

—— (1986) 'Review of Punishment and Welfare: A History of Penal Strategies. By David Garland', *British Journal of Criminology*, 26(4): 409–11.

—— (1989) 'The Critical Discourse on "Social Control": Notes on the Concept as a Hammer', *International Journal of the Sociology of Law*, 17: 347–57.

Condry, R. (2007) *Families Shamed. The Consequences of Crime for Relatives of Serious Offenders*, Cullompton: Willan Publishing.

Conrad, J.P. (1969) 'Introduction (The Future of Corrections)', *Annals of the American Academy of Political and Social Science*, 381: xi–xiii.

Crawford, A. (1997) *The Local Governance of Crime: Appeals to Community and Partnerships*, Oxford: Oxford University Press.

Cressey, D.R. (1955) 'Hypotheses in the Sociology of Punishment', *Sociology and Social Research*, 39: 394–400.

Cullen, F.T., G.A. Clark and J.F. Wozniak (1985) 'Explaining the Get Tough Movement: Can the Public be Blamed?', *Federal Probation*, 49(2): 16–24.

Currie, E. (1997) 'Market, Crime and Community', *Theoretical Criminology*, 1(2): 147–72.

—— (2007) 'Against marginality. Arguments for a public criminology', *Theoretical Criminology*, 11(2): 175–90.

Cyran, O. (2001) La sociologie est un sport de combat, 15 February 2001, Available at <http://www.homme-moderne.org/images/films/pcarles/socio/cyran.html>.

Daems, T. (2004) 'Is it all right for you to talk? Restorative justice and the social analysis of penal developments', *European Journal of Crime, Criminal Law and Criminal Justice*, 12(2): 132–49.

—— (2005) 'Repeat victimisation and the study of social control', *International Journal of the Sociology of Law*, 33(2): 85–100.

—— (2006) 'Marsen die tweedracht zaaien', *De Standaard*, 26 May 2006.

—— (2007a) 'Deconstructing punitiveness. Book review: N. Frost, The Punitive Turn', *Crime, Law and Social Change*, 47(2): 129–33.

—— (2007b) 'Kritiek en normativiteit in bestraffingssociologie', *R&R: Rechtsfilosofie en Rechtstheorie*, 36(1): 77–92.

—— (2008) 'Compatible victims? Prison overcrowding and penal reform in Belgium', *International Journal of Law, Crime and Justice*, 36 (3): 153–67.

Daly, K. (2004) 'Pile it on. More texts on RJ', *Theoretical Criminology*, 8(4): 499–507.

De Giorgi, A. (2006) *Re-Thinking the Political Economy of Punishment. Perspectives on Post-Fordism and Penal Politics*, Aldershot: Ashgate.

—— (2007) 'Toward a political economy of post-Fordist punishment', *Critical Criminology*, 15(3): 243–65.

De Haan, W. (1994) 'Boekbespreking: H. Boutellier, Solidariteit en slachtofferschap. De morele betekenis van criminaliteit in een postmoderne cultuur', *Recht en Kritiek*, 20(4): 369–76.

—— (1995) 'The Netherlands: A Classic Case of Recarceration?' in D. Melossi (ed) *Social Control, Political Power, and the Penal Question: For a Sociology of Criminal Law and Punishment*, Oñati: The Oñati International Institute for the Sociology of Law.

—— (2003) 'In een kwaad daglicht. De toestand in de Nederlandse criminologie besproken door dr. J.C.J. Boutellier', *Tijdschrift voor Criminologie*, 45(1): 71–78.

—— (2006) 'Criminologie dreigt slachtoffer te worden van haar succes', *Delikt en Delinkwent*, 36(6): 609–21.

—— (2007) 'Migration and the Changing Culture of Control in The Netherlands. From Multicultural Drama to Cultural Trauma' in H. Hess, L. Ostermeier and B. Paul (eds) *Kontrollkulturen. Texte zur Kriminalpolitik im Anschluss an David Garland (Kriminologisches Journal 9. Beiheft)*, Weinheim: Juventa.

De Tocqueville, A. (1988) *Democracy in America*, Birmingham, Alabama: The Legal Classics Library.

Dean, M. (1999) *Governmentality. Power and Rule in Modern Society*, London: Sage.

Deflem, M. (2001) 'Book review: L. Wacquant, Les prisons de la misère', *Punishment and Society*, 3(2): 307–08.

Downes, D. (1988) *Contrasts in Tolerance. Post-war Penal Policy in The Netherlands and England and Wales*, Oxford: Clarendon Press.

—— (2007) 'Visions of Penal Control in the Netherlands', *Crime and Justice: A Review of Research*, 36: 93–125.

—— and K. Hansen (2006) 'Welfare and Punishment in Comparative Perspective' in S. Armstrong and L. McAra (eds) *Perspectives on Punishment: The Contours of Control*, Oxford: Oxford University Press.

Downes, D. and R. Van Swaaningen (2007) 'The Road to Dystopia? Changes in the Penal Climate of The Netherlands' in M. Tonry and C. Bijleveld (eds) *Crime and Justice in the Netherlands*, Chicago: University of Chicago Press.

—— P. Rock, C. Chinkin and C. Gearty (2007) 'Introduction' in D. Downes, P. Rock, C. Chinkin and C. Gearty (eds) *Crime, Social Control and Human Rights. From moral panics to states of denial. Essays in honour of Stanley Cohen*, Cullompton: Willan Publishing.

Dubber, M.D. (2002) *Victims in the War on Crime. The Use and Abuse of Victims' Rights*, New York: New York University Press.

Duff, A. (2001) *Punishment, Communication, and Community*, Oxford: Oxford University Press.

Duneier, M. (2002) 'What Kind of Combat Sport Is Sociology?', *American Journal of Sociology*, 107(6): 1551–76.

Durkheim, É. (1969) 'Deux lois de l'évolution pénale' in É. Durkheim, *Journal sociologique*, Paris: Presses Universitaires de France.

—— (1996) *Sociologie et philosophie*, Paris: Quadrige.

Dwyer, C.D. (2004) 'The "Complex"ity of Imprisonment—The Northern Ireland Experience', *The Cambrian Law Review*, 35: 97–114.

Eakin, E. (2003) 'A Professor Who Refuses to Pull His Punches', *The New York Times*, 8 November 2003.

Eick, V. (2007) '"Going glocal in Los Angeles". Nonprofits zwischen Workfare und lokaler Kriminalpolitik' in H. Hess, L. Ostermeier and B. Paul (eds) *Kontrollkulturen. Texte zur Kriminalpolitik im Anschluss an David Garland (Kriminologisches Journal 9. Beiheft)*, Weinheim: Juventa.

Elias, R. (1986) *The Politics of Victimization: Victims, Victimology, and Human Rights*, New York: Oxford University Press.

—— (1992) 'Which Victim Movement? The Politics of Victim Policy' in E.A. Fattah (ed) *Towards a Critical Victimology*, New York: St. Martin's Press.

—— (1993) *Victims Still. The Political Manipulation of Crime Victims*, London: Sage.

—— (2004) 'The Law of Personhood: A Review of Markus Dirk Dubber's Victims in the War on Crime: The Use and Abuse of Victims' Rights', *Buffalo Law Review*, 52: 225–56.

Ericson, R.V. (2003) 'The Culture and Power of Criminological Research' in L. Zedner and A. Ashworth (eds) *The Criminological Foundations of Penal Policy: Essays in Honour of Roger Hood*, Oxford: Oxford University Press.

Fattah, E.A. (1986) 'Prologue: On Some Visible and Hidden Dangers of Victim Movements' in E.A. Fattah (ed) *From Crime Policy to Victim Policy. Reorienting the Justice System*, London: MacMillan.

—— (1992) 'Victims and Victimology: The Facts and the Rhetoric' in E.A. Fattah (ed) *Towards a Critical Victimology*, New York: St. Martin's Press.

—— (1993) 'La relativité culturelle de la victimisation. Quelques réflexions sur les problèmes et le potentiel de la victimologie comparée', *Criminologie*, 26(2): 121–36.

Feeley, M.M. (2003) 'Crime, Social Order and the Rise of Neo-Conservative Politics. Review Essay: David Garland, The Culture of Control', *Theoretical Criminology*, 7(1): 111–30.

—— and J. Simon (1992) 'The New Penology: Notes on the Emerging Strategy of Corrections and its Implications', *Criminology*, 30(4): 449–74.

Fijnaut, C. (2004) 'De criminologie in Nederland. Een grensoverschrijdende bespiegeling', *Tijdschrift voor Criminologie (Jubileumuitgave 'Een Vlaamse spiegel')*, 5–8.

—— (2005) *Onwetendheid en wetenschap in de criminologie. WODC-lezing 2005*, The Hague: Wetenschappelijk Onderzoek-en Documentatiecentrum.

Fishman, M. (1978) 'Crime waves as ideology', *Social Problems*, 25(5): 531–43.

Foucault, M. (1977) *Discipline and Punish. The Birth of the Prison*, New York: Pantheon Books.

—— (1980) 'Prison Talk' in C. Gordon (ed) *Power/Knowledge. Selected Interviews and other Writings, 1972–1977*. Brighton: Harvester.

—— (1986) *The Care of the Self. The History of Sexuality, Volume 3*, New York: Pantheon Books.

—— (2002) 'Questions of Method' in J.D. Faubion (ed) *Power. Essential works of Foucault 1954–1984. Volume 3*, London: Penguin Books.

Franke, H. (1990a) *Twee eeuwen gevangen. Misdaad en straf in Nederland*, Utrecht: Het Spectrum.

—— (1990b) 'De mythe van het achterstallig onderhoud. Het huidige detentiebeleid in historisch-sociologisch perspectief', *Tijdschrift voor Criminologie*, 32(4): 323–33.

Frase, R.S. (2004) 'Historical and Comparative Perspectives on the Exceptional Severity of Sentencing in the United States', *George Washington International Law Review*, 36: 227–37.

Frost, N.A. (2006) *The Punitive State. Crime, Punishment, and Imprisonment across the United States*, New York: LFB Scholarly Publishing LLC.

Furedi, F. (1999) *Courting Mistrust. The Hidden Growth of a Culture of Litigation in Britain*, London: Centre for Policy Studies.

—— (2002) *Culture of Fear. Risk-taking and the Morality of Low Expectation. Revised Edition*, London: Continuum.

Garapon, A. and D. Salas (1996) *La République pénalisée*, Paris: Hachette.

Garland, D. (1980) 'Book review: M. Cain and A. Hun, Marx and Engels on Law; C. Sumner, Reading Ideologies; P. Hirst, On Law and Ideology', *Sociology*, 15(1): 127–30.

—— (1981) 'The Birth of the Welfare Sanction', *British Journal of Law and Society*, 8(1): 29–45.

—— (1982) 'Book review: P. Carlen and M. Collison (eds), Radical Issues in Criminology', *The Howard Journal*, 21: 184–85.

—— (1983) 'Durkheim's Theory of Punishment: A Critique' in D. Garland and P. Young (eds) *The Power to Punish*, London: Heinemann.

—— (1985a) *Punishment and Welfare. A History of Penal Strategies*, Aldershot: Gower.

—— (1985b) 'The Criminal and His Science: A Critical Account of the Formation of Criminology at the End of the Nineteenth Century', *British Journal of Criminology*, 25(2): 109–37.

—— (1985c) 'Politics and Policy in Criminological Discourse: A Study of Tendentious Reasoning and Rhetoric', *International Journal of the Sociology of Law*, 13: 1–33.

—— (1986a) 'Foucault's "Discipline and Punish": An Exposition and Critique', *American Bar Foundation Research Journal*, 11(4): 847–80.

—— (1986b) 'The punitive mentality: Its socio-historic development and decline', *Contemporary Crises*, 10: 305–20.

—— (1990a) *Punishment and Modern Society: A Study in Social Theory*, Oxford: Oxford University Press.

—— (1990b) 'Frameworks of Inquiry in the Sociology of Punishment', *British Journal of Sociology*, 41(1): 1–15.

—— (1992) 'Criminological Knowledge and its Relation to Power: Foucault's Genealogy and Criminology Today', *British Journal of Criminology*, 32(4): 403–22.

—— (1994a) 'Of Crimes and Criminals: The Development of Criminology in Britain' in M. Maguire, R. Morgan, and R. Reiner (eds) *The Oxford Handbook of Criminology*, Oxford: Oxford University Press.

—— (1994b) 'Book review: P. Spierenburg, The Prison Experience: Disciplinary Institutions and Their Inmates in Early Modern Europe', *Journal of Modern History*, 66(1): 117–20.

—— (1995a) 'Penal Modernism and Postmodernism' in T.G. Blomberg and S. Cohen (eds) *Punishment and Social Control*, New York: Aldine de Gruyter.

—— (1995b) 'Surveillance and Society', *Criminal Justice Matters*, 20: 3–4.

—— (1996) 'The Limits of the Sovereign State: Strategies of Crime Control in Contemporary Society', *British Journal of Criminology*, 36(4): 445–71.

—— (1997a) 'Governmentality and the Problem of Crime: Foucault, Criminology, Sociology', *Theoretical Criminology*, 1(2): 173–214.
—— (1997b) 'The Punitive Society: Penology, Criminology and the History of the Present', *Edinburgh Law Review*, 1: 180–99.
—— (1998a) 'Criminology, Crime Control, and "The American Difference"', *University of Colorado Law Review*, 69: 1137–62.
—— (1998b) 'Book review: R. Bergalli and C. Sumner (eds), Social Control and Political Order', *British Journal of Criminology*, 38(2): 321–24.
—— (1998c) 'Book review: A. Crawford, The Local Governance of Crime', *British Journal of Criminology*, 38(3): 516–19.
—— (1999a) 'Punishment and Society Today', *Punishment and Society*, 1(1): 5–10.
—— (1999b) 'The commonplace and the catastrophic: Interpretations of crime in late modernity', *Theoretical Criminology*, 3(3): 353–64.
—— (2000a) 'The New Criminologies of Everyday Life: Routine Activity Theory in Historical and Social Context' in D. Garland, A. Von Hirsch and A. Wakefield (eds) *Ethical and Social Perspectives on Situational Crime Prevention,* Oxford: Hart Publishing.
—— (2000b) 'Ideas, Institutions and Situational Crime Prevention' in D. Garland, A. Von Hirsch and A. Wakefield (eds) *Ethical and Social Perspectives on Situational Crime Prevention,* Oxford: Hart Publishing.
—— (2000c) 'The Culture of High Crime Societies: Some preconditions of recent "law and order" policies', *British Journal of Criminology*, 40(3): 347–75.
—— (2001a) *The Culture of Control: Crime and Social Order in Contemporary Society*, Oxford: Oxford University Press.
—— (ed) (2001b) *Mass Imprisonment. Social Causes and Consequences*, London: Sage.
—— (2001c) 'Introduction: The meaning of mass imprisonment', *Punishment and Society*, 3(1): 5–7.
—— (2002) 'The cultural uses of capital punishment', *Punishment and Society*, 4(4): 459–87.
—— (2004a) 'Beyond the Culture of Control', *Critical Review of International Social and Political Philosophy*, 7(2): 160–89.
—— (2004b) 'The Work of Theory', *Perspectives (ASA Theory Section Newsletter)*, April: 5, 19–21.
—— (2005a) 'Prefacio a la edición en español' in D. Garland, *La cultura del control. Crimen y orden social en la sociedad contemporánea*, Barcelona: Gedisa.
—— (2005b) 'Capital Punishment and American Culture', *Punishment and Society*, 7(4): 347–76.
—— (2005c) 'Book review: Brian Jarvis, Cruel and Unusual: Punishment and US Culture', *Social and Legal Studies*, 14(2): 299–302.

Garland, D. (2006a) 'Concepts of Culture in the Sociology of Punishment', *Theoretical Criminology*, 10(4): 419–47.

—— (2006b) The *American Death Penalty: A theoretical Problem for Sociological Analysis,* Institute of Governmental Studies, University of California, Berkeley: Center on Institutions and Governance Working Paper No. 50. Available at </http://igov.berkeley.edu/workingpapers/index.html>.

—— (2006c) 'Postcards from the Edge: Photographs of Torture in Abu Ghraib and the American South' in R. Behr, H. Cremer-Schäfer and S. Scheerer (eds) *Kriminalitäts-Geschichten. Ein Lesebuch über Geschäftigkeiten am Rande der Gesellschaft,* Hamburg: LIT Verlag.

—— (2007a) 'Rethinking the symbolic-instrumental distinction. Meanings and motives in American capital punishment' in A. Brannigan and G. Pavlich (eds) *Governance and Regulation in Social Life: Essays in Honour of W.G. Carson,* London: Routledge-Cavendish.

—— (2007b) 'The Peculiar Forms of American Capital Punishment', *Social Research*, 74(2): 435–64.

—— (2007c) 'High Crime Societies and Cultures of Control' in H. Hess, L. Ostermeier and B. Paul (eds) *Kontrollkulturen. Texte zur Kriminalpolitik im Anschluss an David Garland (Kriminologisches Journal 9. Beiheft),* Weinheim: Juventa.

—— (2007d) 'Death, denial, discourse: on the forms and functions of American capital punishment' in D. Downes, P. Rock, C. Chinkin and C. Gearty (eds) *Crime, Social Control and Human Rights. From Moral Panics to States of Denial. Essays in Honour of Stanley Cohen,* Cullompton: Willan Publishing.

—— and P. Young, (eds) (1983a) *The Power to Punish,* London: Heinemann.

—— and P. Young. (1983b) 'Towards a Social Analysis of Penality' in D. Garland and P. Young (eds) *The Power to Punish*, London: Heinemann.

—— and R. Sparks (2000) 'Criminology, Social Theory, and the Challenge of Our Times' in D. Garland and R. Sparks (eds) *Criminology and Social Theory,* Oxford: Oxford University Press.

Giddens, A. (1992) *The Transformation of Intimacy. Sexuality, Love, and Eroticism in Modern Societies,* Cambridge: Polity Press.

Gilligan, G. and J. Pratt (eds) (2003) *Crime, Truth and Justice. Official Inquiry, Discourse, Knowledge,* Cullompton: Willan Publishing.

Grimshaw, R. and J. Pratt (1985) 'Responses to Truancy Among the Juvenile Panel of a Magistrates' Court', *British Journal of Criminology,* 25(4): 321–43.

Groenhuijsen, M.S. (1994) 'Boekbespreking: H. Boutellier, Solidariteit en slachtofferschap. De morele betekenis van criminaliteit in een postmoderne cultuur', *Delikt en Delinkwent*, 24(7): 704–08.

Gross, A.G. (1990) *The Rhetoric of Science*, Cambridge, Massachusetts: Harvard University Press.
Hagan, J. (2004) 'Twin Towers, Iron Cages and the Culture of Control', *Critical Review of International Social and Political Philosophy*, 7(2): 42–48.
Harbers, H. (1992) 'Gevraagd: een sociologie van intellectuelen' in L. Nauta and G. de Vries (eds) *De rol van de intellectueel. Een discussie over distantie en betrokkenheid*, Amsterdam: Van Gennep.
Harcourt, B.E. (2001) 'Book review: L. Wacquant, Les prisons de la misère', *Theoretical Criminology*, 5(4): 487–92.
Hassemer, W. (2000) 'Die neue Lust auf Strafe', *Frankfurter Rundschau*, 20 December 2000.
Heijne, B. (2006) '"Globalisering is geen natuurkracht", Interview met Loïc Wacquant'. *NRC Handelsblad Magazine*, 2 April 2006.
Hess, H., L. Ostermeier and B. Paul (eds) (2007) *Kontrollkulturen. Texte zur Kriminalpolitik im Anschluss an David Garland (Kriminologisches Journal 9. Beiheft)*, Weinheim: Juventa.
Hildebrandt, M. (1998) 'Slachtofferschap en de legitimatie van het strafrecht', *R&R: Nederlands Tijdschrift voor Rechtsfilosofie en Rechtstheorie*, 27(1): 39–54.
Hilhorst, P. (2005) 'Anti-universiteit van Amerika', *De Volkskrant*, 4 June 2005.
Holstein, J.A. and G. Miller (1990) 'Rethinking victimization: An interactional approach to victimology', *Symbolic Interaction*, 13(1): 103–22.
Hood, R. (2002) 'Criminology and Penal Policy: The Vital Role of Empirical Research' in A. Bottoms and M. Tonry (eds) *Ideology, Crime and Criminal Justice*, Cullompton: Willan Publishing.
Howe, A. (1994) *Punish and Critique. Towards a Feminist Analysis of Penality*, London: Routledge.
Hudson, B. (2003) *Justice in the Risk Society. Challenging and Re-affirming Justice in Late Modernity*, London: Sage.
Hughes, G. (2004a) 'Besturen via misdaad en geweld? Publiek-private samenwerking bij de aanpak van criminaliteit en geweld in Engeland en Wales', *Justitiële Verkenningen*, 30(7): 24–40.
—— (2004b) 'Straddling Adaptation and Denial: Crime and Disorder Reduction Partnerships in England and Wales', *The Cambrian Law Review*, 35: 1–22.
Hutchinson, S. (2006) 'Countering catastrophic criminology. Reform, punishment and the modern liberal compromise', *Punishment and Society*, 8(4): 443–67.
Hutton, W. and A. Giddens (2001) 'Preface' in W. Hutton and A. Giddens (eds) *On the Edge. Living with Global Capitalism*, London: Vintage.
Ignatieff, M. (1978) *A Just Measure of Pain. The Penitentiary in the Industrial Revolution, 1750–1850*, New York: Pantheon Books.

Jackson, J. (2004) 'Putting victims at the heart of criminal justice: the gap between rhetoric and reality' in E. Cape (ed) *Reconcilable Rights? Analysing the tension between victims and defendants,* London: LAG Education and Service Trust Limited.

Jones, T. and T. Newburn (2002) 'Policy convergence and crime control in the USA and the UK: Streams of influence and levels of impact', *Criminal Justice*, 2(2): 173–203.

Kaiser, G. (2003) 'Buchbesprechung: David Garland, The Culture of Control', *Monatschrift für Kriminologie und Strafrechtsreform*, 86(3): 234–40.

Kaplan, P.J. (2006) 'American Exceptionalism and Racialized Inequality in American Capital Punishment', *Law and Social Inquiry*, 31(1): 149–75.

Karstedt, S. (2006) 'Emotions, Crime and Justice: Exploring Durkheimian Themes' in M. Deflem (ed) *Sociological Theory and Criminological Research: Views from Europe and the United States,* Amsterdam: Elsevier.

—— (2007) 'Explorations into the sociology of criminal justice and punishment: leaving the modernist project behind', *History of the Human Sciences*, 20(2): 51–70.

Kelk, C. (2006) 'Het gevangeniswezen in zwaar weer', *Delikt en Delinkwent,* 36(2): 101–10.

Keucheyan, R. (2003) 'Une expérience de sociologie charnelle. Entretien avec Loïc Wacquant', *Solidarités*, 29: 18–20.

Kilcommins, S. and B. Vaughan (eds) (2004a) The Crime Complex and the Reorientation of Justice (Thematic issue), *The Cambrian Law Review*, 35.

—— and B. Vaughan (2004b) 'A Perpetual State of Emergency: Subverting the Rule of Law in Ireland', *The Cambrian Law Review*, 35: 55–80.

Köllisch, T. (2007) 'Risikomanagement und selektive Punitivität als "Kriminalpolitik von unten"', *Kriminologisches Journal*, 39(4): 243–59.

Kommer, M. (1994) 'Punitiveness in Europe—A comparison', *European Journal on Criminal Policy and Research*, 2(1): 29–43.

—— (2004) 'Punitiveness in Europe revisited', *Newsletter of the European Society of Criminology*, 3(1): 1, 8–12.

Konrád, G. (1984) *Antipolitics,* London: Quartet Books.

Kool, R. (1995) 'Beleidswaarde van slachtofferschap', *Nemesis*, 2: 36–43.

Kreissl, R. and L. Ostermeier (2007) 'Globale Trends und lokale Differenzen—Kulturen der Kontrolle und politische Steuerung in Hamburg und München' in H. Hess, L. Ostermeier and B. Paul (eds) *Kontrollkulturen. Texte zur Kriminalpolitik im Anschluss an David Garland (Kriminologisches Journal 9. Beiheft),* Weinheim: Juventa.

Kuhn, A. (1996) 'Incarceration rates: Europe versus USA', *European Journal of Criminal Policy and Research*, 4(3): 46–73.

Kury, H., H. Kania and J. Obergfell-Fuchs (2004) 'Worüber sprechen wir, wenn wir über Punitivität sprechen? Versuch einer konzeptionellen und empirischen Begriffsbestimmung' in R. Lautmann, D. Klimke and F. Sack (eds) *Punitivität (Kriminologisches Journal 8. Beiheft)*, Weinheim: Juventa.

Kurzman, C. and L. Owens (2002) 'The Sociology of Intellectuals', *Annual Review of Sociology*, 28: 63–90.

Lagrange, H. (2003) *Demandes de sécurité. France, Europe, États-Unis*, Paris: Éditions du Seuil.

Lautmann, R., D. Klimke and F. Sack (2004) 'Vorwort' in R. Lautmann, D. Klimke and F. Sack (eds) *Punitivität (Kriminologisches Journal 8. Beiheft)*, Weinheim: Juventa.

Lea, J. (2002) 'Book review: H. Boutellier. Crime and morality: the significance of criminal justice in post-modern culture', *International Criminal Justice Review*, 12: 149–50.

Lebaron, F. and G. Mauger (2003) 'Éléments pour une histoire', *Les cahiers de l'association Raisons d'agir*, 1 (June): 3–6.

Lehne, W. and C. Schlepper (2007) 'Die "präventive Wende" in Deutschland: Auf dem Weg zum rationalen Sicherheitsmanagement?' in H. Hess, L. Ostermeier and B. Paul (eds) *Kontrollkulturen. Texte zur Kriminalpolitik im Anschluss an David Garland (Kriminologisches Journal 9. Beiheft)*, Weinheim: Juventa.

Lipset, S.M. (1996) *American Exceptionalism: A Double-Edged Sword*, New York: W.W. Norton and Co.

Lissenberg, E. (1989) *Verlagen en verheffen. Rede uitgesproken bij de openbare aanvaarding van het ambt van hoogleraar in de criminologie aan de Universiteit van Amsterdam op dinsdag 16 mei 1989*, Alphen aan den Rijn: Samsom H.D. Tjeenk Willink.

Loader, I. and R. Sparks (2004) 'For an Historical Sociology of Crime Policy in England and Wales since 1968', *Critical Review of International Social and Political Philosophy*, 7(2): 5–32.

Lowman, J.R., J. Menzies and T.S. Palys (1987) 'Introduction: Transcarceration and the Modern State of Penality' in J.R. Lowman, J. Menzies and T.S. Palys (eds) *Transcarceration: Essays in the Sociology of Social Control*, Aldershot: Gower.

Lynch, M. (2002) 'Book review: David Garland, The Culture of Control', *PoLAR: Political and Legal Anthropology Review*, 25(2): 109–12.

Mannheim, H. (1939) *The Dilemma of Penal Reform*, London: George Allen and Unwin.

Mary, P. (2003) *Insécurité et pénalisation du social*, Brussels: Éditions Labor.

Mathiesen, T. (1974) *The Politics of Abolition* Oslo: Universitetsforlaget.

Matravers, A. and S. Maruna (2004) 'Contemporary Penality and Psychoanalysis', *Critical Review of International Social and Political Philosophy*, 7(2): 118–44.

Matravers, M. (ed) (2004) 'Managing Modernity. Special issue', *Critical Review of International Social and Political Philosophy*, 7(2).

Matthews, R. (1987) 'Decarceration and Social Control: Fantasies and Realities' in J. Lowman, R.J. Menzies and T.S. Palys (eds) *Transcarceration: Essays in the Sociology of Social Control,* Aldershot: Gower.

—— (2002) 'Crime and Control in Late Modernity. Review Essay: David Garland, The Culture of Control', *Theoretical Criminology*, 6(2): 217–26.

—— (2005a) 'The myth of punitiveness', *Theoretical Criminology,* 9(2): 175–201.

—— (2005b) 'Punitive Myths', *Criminal Justice Matters,* 60: 8–9, 40.

—— (2006a) 'Punitiveness' in E. McLaughlin and J. Municie (eds) *The Sage Dictionary of Criminology, Second Edition*. London: Sage.

—— (2006b) 'Book review: J. Pratt, D. Brown, M. Brown, S. Hallsworth and W. Morrison (eds), The New Punitiveness', *The Howard Journal*, 46(1): 93–94.

Matza, D. (1969) *Becoming Deviant,* Englewood Cliffs: Prentice Hall.

Maublanc, R. (1930) 'Durkheim. Professeur de philosophie', *Europe*, 296–303.

McAra, L. (1999) 'The Politics of Penality: An Overview of the Development of Penal Policy in Scotland' in P. Duff and N. Hutton (eds) *Criminal Justice in Scotland,* Aldershot: Ashgate.

—— (2004) 'The Cultural and Institutional Dynamics of Transformation: Youth Justice in Scotland, England and Wales', *The Cambrian Law Review*, 35: 23–54.

—— (2005) 'Modelling penal transformation', *Punishment and Society*, 7(3): 277–302.

McLaughlin, E. and J. Muncie (eds) (2001) *The Sage Dictionary of Criminology,* London: Sage.

—— —— (2006) *The Sage Dictionary of Criminology, Second Edition,* London: Sage.

Melossi, D. (1989) 'An introduction: Fifty years later, *Punishment and Social Structure* in comparative analysis', *Contemporary Crises*, 13(4): 311–26.

—— and M. Pavarini (1981) *The Prison and the Factory. Origins of the Penitentiary System*, Basingstoke: MacMillan.

Miers, D. (1980) 'Victim Compensation as a Labelling Process', *Victimology*, 5(1): 3–16.

—— (1989) 'Positivist victimology: a critique', *International Review of Victimology*, 1(1): 3–22.

—— (1990) 'Critical victimology', *International Review of Victimology*, 1(3): 219–30.

Monkkonen, E. (2006) 'Homicide: Explaining America's Exceptionalism', *American Historical Review*, 111(1): 76–94.

Morgan, R. (1991) 'Book review: David Garland, Punishment and Modern Society', *British Journal of Criminology*, 31(4): 431–33.
Morvandiau, S. Lefèvre and S. Rétif (2001) 'Loïc Wacquant: "La sociologie en technicolor"', *L' Oeil électrique*, 20.
Murdoch, J. (2006) 'Tackling Ill-Treatment in Places of Detention: The Work of the Council of Europe's "Torture Committee"', *European Journal on Criminal Policy and Research*, 12(2): 121–42.
Nelken, D. (1994) 'Reflexive Criminology?' in D. Nelken (ed) *The Futures of Criminology*, London: Sage.
—— (2005) 'When is a society non-punitive? The Italian case' in J. Pratt, D. Brown, M. Brown, S. Hallsworth and W. Morrison (eds) *The New Punitiveness. Trends, Theories, Perspectives*, Cullompton: Willan Publishing.
—— (2006) 'Patterns of Punitiveness', *The Modern Law Review*, 69(2): 262–77.
Newburn, T. (2002) 'Atlantic Crossings. "Policy Transfer" and Crime Control in the USA and Britain', *Punishment and Society*, 4(2): 165–94.
—— and T. Jones (2007) 'Symbolizing crime control: Reflections on Zero Tolerance', *Theoretical Criminology*, 11(2): 221–43.
Newman, K. (2002) 'No Shame: The View from the Left Bank', *American Journal of Sociology*, 107(6): 1577–99.
Nieuwenhuijsen, P. (2006) 'Beleid vs. onderzoek. Hans Boutellier: "De afstand is gigantisch"', *City Journal. Wetenschappelijk Tijdschrift voor de Steden*, 2: 6–7.
O'Donnell, I. (2004) 'Interpreting Penal Change: A Research Note', *Criminal Justice*, 4(2): 199–206.
O'Malley, P. (1992) 'Risk, Power and Crime Prevention', *Economy and Society*, 21: 252–75.
—— (1999) 'Volatile and contradictory punishment', *Theoretical Criminology*, 3(2): 175–96.
—— (2002) 'Review symposium. David Garland, The Culture of Control', *Punishment and Society*, 4(2): 259–61.
O'Sullivan, E. and I. O'Donnell (2007) 'Coercive confinement in the Republic of Ireland. The waning of a culture of control', *Punishment and Society*, 9(1): 27–48.
Ocqueteau, F. (2004) 'Punir les pauvres, le degré zéro de la pensée gauchiste!' *Champ pénal*, October 2004.
Oostveen, M. (2002) 'De cultuur van de bungeejumper. Sociaal-psycholoog Hans Boutellier over Nederlandse onbehagen', *NRC Handelsblad*, 29 June 2002.
Pastor, D.R. (2006) 'La deriva neopunitivista de organismos y activistas como causa del desprestigio actual de los derechos humanos', *Jura Gentium. Revista de filosofía del derecho internacional y de la política global*, 2(1).

Pels, D. (1992) 'Kennispolitiek en anti-politiek. Notities over intellectuele autonomie' in L. Nauta and G. De Vries (eds) *De rol van de intellectueel. Een discussie over distantie en betrokkenheid*, Amsterdam: Van Gennep.

—— (1995) 'Knowledge Politics and Anti-Politics. Towards a Critical Appraisal of Bourdieu's Concept of Intellectual Autonomy', *Theory and Society*, 24(1): 79–104.

Poveda, T.G. (2000) 'American Exceptionalism and the Death Penalty', *Social Justice*, 27(2): 252–67.

Pratt, J. (1981) 'Sexuality and the popular appeal of the new right', *Contemporary Crises*, 5(4): 369–81.

—— (1982) 'The Sexual Landscape—Repression or Freedom?', *Theory, Culture and Society*, 1(1): 65–84.

—— (1983a) 'Reflections on the Approach of 1984: Recent Developments in Social Control in the UK', *International Journal of the Sociology of Law*, 11: 339–60.

—— (1983b) 'Law and Social Control: A Study of Truancy and School Deviance', *Journal of Law and Society*, 10(2): 223–40.

—— (1983c) 'Folk-lore and Fact in Truancy Research. Some Critical Comments on Recent Developments', *British Journal of Criminology*, 23(4): 336–53.

—— (1983d) 'Intermediate treatment and the normalization crisis', *Howard Journal of Penology and Crime Prevention*, 22: 19–37.

—— (1983e) 'Recent Contributions to the Sociology of Sex', *Theory, Culture and Society*, 1(3): 150–56.

—— (1985a) 'The Legacy of Foucault. Review Article', *International Journal of the Sociology of Law*, 13: 289–93.

—— (1985b) 'Review: S. Cohen and A. Scull (eds), Social Control and the State', *International Journal of the Sociology of Law*, 13: 210–12.

—— (1985c) 'Juvenile Justice, Social Work and Social Control. The Need for Positive Thinking', *British Journal of Social Work*, 15: 1–24.

—— (1985d) 'Delinquency as a Scarce Resource', *The Howard Journal*, 24(2): 93–107.

—— (1986a) 'Diversion from the Juvenile Court: A Critique of Progress and a History of Inflation', *British Journal of Criminology*, 26(3): 212–33.

—— (1986b) 'Pornography and Everyday Life', *Theory, Culture and Society*, 3(1): 65–78.

—— (1987a) 'Dilemmas of the Alternative to Custody Concept: Implications for New Zealand Penal Policy in the Light of International Evidence and Experience', *Australian and New Zealand Journal of Criminology*, 20: 148–62.

—— (1987b) 'A Revisionist History of Intermediate Treatment', *British Journal of Social Work*, 17: 417–35.

—— (1987c) 'Review: D. Garland, Punishment and Welfare', *International Journal of the Sociology of Law*, 15: 357–59.
—— (1988) 'Law and Order Politics in New Zealand 1986: A Comparison With the United Kingdom 1974–9', *International Journal of the Sociology of Law*, 21: 103–26.
—— (1989) 'Corporatism: The Third Model of Juvenile Justice', *British Journal of Criminology*, 29(3): 236–54.
—— (1990a) 'Crime, time, youth and punishment', *Contemporary Crises*, 14: 219–42.
—— (1990b) 'The Future of the Probation Service in New Zealand', *Australian and New Zealand Journal of Criminology*, 23: 105–16.
—— (1990c) 'From Habitual Criminals to Reformative Detention: The Origins of the Modern Punishment System of New Zealand', *Criminal Justice History: An International Annual*, 11: 55–87.
—— (1991a) 'Punishment, History and Empire', *Australian and New Zealand Journal of Criminology*, 24: 118–38.
—— (1991b) 'Citizenship, Colonisation and Criminal Justice', *International Journal of the Sociology of Law*, 19: 293–319.
—— (1992a) *Punishment in a Perfect Society. The New Zealand Penal System: 1840–1939*, Wellington: Victoria University Press.
—— (1992b) 'Punishment and the Lessons from History', *Australian and New Zealand Journal of Criminology*, 25: 97–114.
—— (1993) '"This is not a Prison": Foucault, the Panopticon and Pentonville', *Social and Legal Studies*, 2: 373–96.
—— (1994) 'Review Essay. Understanding Punishment: Beyond "Aims and Objectives..."' *Australian and New Zealand Journal of Criminology*, 27: 213–21.
—— (1995) 'Dangerousness, Risk and Technologies of Power', *Australian and New Zealand Journal of Criminology*, 28: 3–31.
—— (1996a) 'Reflections on recent trends towards the punishment of persistence', *Crime, Law and Social Change*, 25: 243–64.
—— (1996b) 'Governing the Dangerous: An Historical Overview of Dangerous Offender Legislation', *Social and Legal Studies*, 5: 21–36.
—— (1996c) 'Colonization, Power and Silence: A History of Indigenous Justice in New Zealand Society' in B. Galaway and J. Hudson (eds) *Restorative Justice: International Perspectives*, Amsterdam: Kugler.
—— (1997a) *Governing the Dangerous. Dangerousness, Law and Social Change*, Annandale: The Federation Press.
—— (1998a) 'The rise and fall of homophobia and sexual psychopath laws in postwar society', *Psychology, Public Policy and Law*, 4: 25–49.
—— (1998b) 'Towards the "Decivilizing" of Punishment?', *Social and Legal Studies*, 7(4): 487–515.

Pratt, J. (1999a) 'Governmentality, Dangerousness and Neoliberalism' in R. Smandych (ed) *Governable Places. Readings on Governmentality and Crime Control*, Aldershot: Dartmouth.

—— (1999b) 'Norbert Elias and the Civilized Prison', *British Journal of Sociology*, 50(2): 271–96.

—— (2000a) 'Sex Crimes and the New Punitiveness', *Behavioral Sciences and the Law*, 18: 135–51.

—— (2000b) 'Civilization and Punishment', *Australian and New Zealand Journal of Criminology*, 33(2): 183–201.

—— (2000c) 'The Return of the Wheelbarrow Men; Or, the Arrival of Postmodern Penality?', *British Journal of Criminology*, 40: 127–45.

—— (2000d) 'Emotive and Ostentatious Punishment. Its Decline and Resurgence in Modern Society', *Punishment and Society*, 2(4): 417–39.

—— (2000e) 'Dangerousness and Modern Society' in M. Brown and J. Pratt (eds) *Dangerous Offenders: Punishment and Social Order*, London: Routledge.

—— (2001a) 'Beyond "Gulags Western Style"? A Reconsideration of Nils Christie's Crime Control as Industry', *Theoretical Criminology*, 5(3): 283–314.

—— (2001b) 'Dangerosité, risque et technologies du pouvoir', *Criminologie*, 34(1): 103–21.

—— (2002a) *Punishment and Civilization. Penal Tolerance and Intolerance in Modern Society*, London: Sage.

—— (2002b) 'Critical Criminology and the Punitive Society: Some New "Visions of Social Control"', in K. Carrington and H. Russell (eds) *Critical Criminology. Issues, Debates, Challenges*, Cullompton: Willan Publishing.

—— (2002c) 'The Globalization of Punishment', *Corrections Today*, February: 64–66.

—— (2003) 'The Decline and Renaissance of Shame in Modern Penal Systems' in B.S. Godfrey, C. Emsley and G. Dunstall (eds) *Comparative Histories of Crime*, Cullompton: Willan Publishing.

—— (2005a) 'Elias, punishment, and decivilization' in J. Pratt, D. Brown, M. Brown, S. Hallsworth and W. Morrison (eds) *The New Punitiveness. Trends, Theories, Perspectives*, Cullompton: Willan Publishing.

—— (2005b) 'Explaining the history of punishment' in B.S. Godfrey and G. Dunstall (eds) *Crime and Empire 1840–1940. Criminal justice in local and global context*, Cullompton: Willan Publishing.

—— (2006a) 'The Dark Side of Paradise. Explaining New Zealand's History of High Imprisonment', *British Journal of Criminology*, 46(4): 541–60.

—— (2006b) 'Beyond evangelical criminology: the meaning and significance of restorative justice' in I. Aertsen, T. Daems and

L. Robert (eds) *Institutionalizing Restorative Justice,* Cullompton: Willan Publishing.

—— (2007) *Penal Populism,* London: Routledge.

—— and R. Sparks (1987) 'New voices from the ship of fools. A critical commentary on the renaissance of "permissiveness" as a political issue', *Contemporary Crises,* 11: 3–23.

—— and P. Treacher (1988) 'Law and order and the 1987 New Zealand election', *Australian and New Zealand Journal of Criminology,* 21: 253–68.

—— and M. Dickson (1997) 'Dangerous, Inadequate, Invisible, Out: Episodes in the criminological career of habitual criminals', *Theoretical Criminology,* 1(3): 363–84.

—— and M. Clark (2005) 'Penal populism in New Zealand', *Punishment and Society,* 7(3): 303–22.

—— D. Brown, M. Brown, S. Hallsworth, and W. Morrison (eds) (2005a) *The New Punitiveness. Trends, Theories, Perspectives,* Cullompton: Willan Publishing.

—— D. Brown, M. Brown, S. Hallsworth and W. Morrison (2005b) 'Introduction' in J. Pratt, D. Brown, M. Brown, S. Hallsworth and W. Morrison (eds) *The New Punitiveness. Trends, Theories, Perspectives,* Cullompton: Willan Publishing.

Quensel, S. (2007) 'Lösen staatliche Akteure ein High-Crime-Problem? Einige methodische Fragen zu Garlands "Culture of Control"' in H. Hess, L. Ostermeier and B. Paul (eds) *Kontrollkulturen. Texte zur Kriminalpolitik im Anschluss an David Garland (Kriminologisches Journal 9. Beiheft),* Weinheim: Juventa.

Quinney, R. (1972) 'Who is the victim?', *Criminology,* 10(3): 314–23.

Radzinowicz, L. (1991) 'Penal regressions', *Cambridge Law Journal,* 50(3): 422–44.

—— (1999) *Adventures in Criminology,* London: Routledge.

Raisons d'agir (2003) 'Raisons d'agir', *Les cahiers de l'association Raison d'agir,* 1 (June): 2.

Reiner, R. (2002) 'Prisoners in the Cage. The Fear of Crime and the End of Social Optimism', *Times Literary Supplement,* 25 January: 3–4.

Reuband, K.-H. (2007) 'Steigende Kriminalitätsbedrohung, Medienberichterstattung und Kriminalitätsfurcht der Bürger' in H. Hess, L. Ostermeier and B. Paul (eds) *Kontrollkulturen. Texte zur Kriminalpolitik im Anschluss an David Garland (Kriminologisches Journal 9. Beiheft),* Weinheim: Juventa.

Rock, P. (2002) 'On becoming a Victim' in C. Hoyle and R. Young (eds) *New Visions of Crime Victims,* Oxford: Hart Publishing.

—— (2004) *Constructing Victims' Rights: The Home Office, New Labour, and Victims,* Oxford: Oxford University Press.

Rode, I., H. Kammeier and M. Leipert (eds) (2005) *Neue Lust auf Strafen*, Münster: LIT Verlag.

Rorty, R. (1989) *Contingency, Irony and Solidarity*, Cambridge: Cambridge University Press.

Rose, N. and P. Miller (1992) 'Political Power Beyond the State: Problematics of Government', *Economy and Society*, 21: 173–205.

—— (1999) *Powers of Freedom. Reframing Political Thought*, Cambridge: Cambridge University Press.

Rothman, D.J. (1971) *The Discovery of the Asylum. Social Order and Disorder in the New Republic*, Boston: Little, Brown and Company.

—— (1980) *Conscience and Convenience. The Asylum and its Alternatives in Progressive America*, Boston: Little, Brown and Company.

Ruimschotel, D. (1993) 'Besprekingsartikel: Het mondige slachtoffer als bron van morele legitimatie van het strafrecht', *Tijdschrift voor Criminologie*, 35(4): 400–16.

Rumgay, J. (2003) 'Book review: David Garland, The Culture of Control', *Journal of Forensic Psychiatry and Psychology*, 14(2): 439–44.

Rusche, G. and O. Kirchheimer (1968) *Punishment and Social Structure*, New York: Russell and Russell.

Rutherford, A. (1984) *Prisons and the Process of Justice. The Reductionist Challenge*, London: Heinemann.

—— (1986) *Prisons and the Process of Justice (Paperback Edition)*, Oxford: Oxford University Press.

Sack, F. (2004) 'Wie die Kriminalpolitik dem Staat aufhilft. *Governing through Crime* als neue politische Strategie' in R. Lautmann, D. Klimke and F. Sack (eds) *Punitivität (Kriminologisches Journal 8. Beiheft)*, Weinheim: Juventa.

Salas, D. (2005) *La volonté de punir. Essai sur le populisme pénal*, Paris: Hachette Littératures.

Sarat, A. (2001) 'Can Liberals Fight Crime? Review of 'The Culture of Control' by David Garland', *The American Prospect*, 30 July 2001.

—— (2002) *When the State Kills. Capital Punishment and the American Condition*, Princeton: Princeton University Press.

Savelsberg, J.J. (2002) 'Cultures of Control in Contemporary Societies', *Law and Social Inquiry*, 27: 685–710.

—— (2005) 'Book review: James Q. Whitman, Harsh Justice', *Punishment and Society*, 7(2): 228–31.

Scheff, T. (1990) 'A new Durkheim', *American Journal of Sociology*, 96(3): 741–46.

Scull, A. (1977) *Decarceration. Community Treatment and the Deviant—A Radical View*, Englewood Cliffs: Prentice Hall.

—— (1983) 'Community Corrections: Panacea, Progress or Pretence?' in D. Garland and P. Young (eds) *The Power to Punish*, London: Heinemann.

Sennett, R. (2006) *The Culture of the New Capitalism*, New Haven: Yale University Press.

Sessar, K. (1990) 'Tertiary Victimization: A Case of the Politically Abused Crime Victims' in B. Galaway and J. Hudson (eds) *Criminal Justice, Restitution and Reconciliation*, Monsey: Criminal Justice Press.

Sim J. (2002) 'Book review: David Garland (ed), Mass Imprisonment: Social Causes and Consequences', *Social and Legal Studies*, 11(2): 312–14.

Simon, J. (1993) *Poor Discipline. Parole and Social Control of the Underclass: 1890–1990*, Chicago: University of Chicago Press.

—— (1995) 'They Died with Their Boots On: The Boot Camp and the Limits of Modern Penality', *Social Justice*, 22(2): 25–49.

—— (1997) 'Governing Through Crime' in L.M. Friedman and G. Fisher (eds) *The Crime Conundrum. Essays on Criminal Justice*, Boulder, Colorado: Westview Press.

—— (2000) 'The "society of captives" in the era of hyper-incarceration', *Theoretical Criminology*, 4(3): 285–308.

—— (2001) 'Fear and loathing in late modernity. Reflections on the cultural sources of mass imprisonment in the United States', *Punishment and Society*, 3(1): 21–33.

Smandych, R. (ed) (1999) *Governable Places. Readings on Governmentality and Crime Control*, Aldershot: Dartmouth.

Smart, B. (2003) *Economy, Culture and Society. A Sociological Critique of Neo-Liberalism*, Buckingham: Open University Press.

Smith, D.E. (1974) 'The Ideological Practice of Sociology', *Catalyst*, 8: 39–54.

Snacken, S. (2006) 'A Reductionist Penal Policy and European Human Rights Standards', *European Journal of Criminal Policy and Research*, 12: 143–64.

—— J. Keulen and L. Winkelmans (2004) *Buitenlanders in Belgische gevangenissen: knelpunten en mogelijke oplossingen. Onderzoeksrapport: 1 november 2003–31 januari 2004*, Brussels: Koning Boudewijnstichting.

Sparks, R. (2001) 'Degrees of Estrangement: The Cultural Theory of Risk and Comparative Criminology', *Theoretical Criminology*, 5(2): 159–76.

—— (2004) 'Editor's note of thanks', *Punishment and Society*, 6(4): 355–56.

Spierenburg, P. (1984a) *The Spectacle of Suffering. Executions and the evolution of repression: from a preindustrial metropolis to the European experience*, Cambridge: Cambridge University Press.

—— (1984b) 'Introduction' in P. Spierenburg (ed) *The Emergence of Carceral Institutions: Prisons, Galleys and Lunatic Asylums 1550–1900*. Rotterdam: Erasmus Universiteit Rotterdam.

Steiker, C.S. (2002) 'Capital Punishment and American Exceptionalism', *Oregon Law Review*, 81(1): 97–130.
—— (2003) 'Why We're So Tough on Crime', *Boston Review*, October/November. Available at <http://bostonreview.net/BR28.5/steiker.html>.
Stern, V. (2006) *Creating Criminals. Prisons and People in a Market Society*, London: Zed Books.
Stones, R. (1996) 'Introduction: Society as More Than a Collection of Free-Floating Individuals' in R. Stones (ed) *Key Sociological Thinkers*, Houndmills: Palgrave MacMillan.
Taylor, I. (1999) *Crime in Context. A Critical Criminology of Market Societies*, Cambridge: Polity Press.
—— P. Walton and J. Young (1973) *The New Criminology. For a Social Theory of Deviance*, London: Routledge.
Tonry, M. (1999) 'Why are U.S. Incarceration Rates so High?', *Crime and Delinquency*, 45(4): 419–37.
—— (2004) *Thinking about Crime: Sense and Sensibility in American Penal Culture*, New York: Oxford University Press.
Traag, V. (2006) 'Brand in Frankrijk. Een sociologische diagnose van de Franse rellen', *Sociologisch Mokum*, 11(1): 14–15.
Van der Ven, C. (1998) 'De cultuur van het slachtoffer. Interview met Hans Boutellier', *Trouw*, 12 May 1998.
Van Stokkom, B.A.M. and P.B.A. Ter Veer (eds) (1995) 'Amerikaanse toestanden (thematic issue)', *Justitiële Verkenningen*, 21(9).
Van Swaaningen, R. (1995) 'Het confectiepak van product-manager Justitia. Acht verhalen achter een *law and order* beleid', *Recht en Kritiek*, 21(1): 13–37.
—— (ed) (2004a) 'De nieuwe veiligheidscultuur (thematic issue)', *Justitiële Verkenningen*, 30(7).
—— (2004b) 'Veiligheid in Nederland en Europa. Een sociologische beschouwing aan de hand van David Garland', *Justitiële Verkenningen*, 30(7): 9–23.
Van Zyl Smit, D. (2006) 'Humanising Imprisonment: A European project?', *European Journal of Criminal Policy and Research*, 12: 107–20.
Vaughan, B. (2002) 'Book review: David Garland, The Culture of Control', *Journal of Law and Society*, 29: 359–63.
—— (2003) 'Book Review, J. Pratt, Punishment and Civilization', *Theoretical Criminology*, 7(2): 242–45.
Verrijn Stuart, H.M. (1994) 'Via onschuld naar macht. Slachtoffers in het strafproces', *Justitiële Verkenningen*, 20(2): 94–114.
Vloet, C. (2002) 'Veiligheidsbevorderende kunst', *NRC Handelsblad*, 14 December 2002.
Voruz, V. (2004) 'Recent Perspectives on Penal Punitiveness' in B.A. Arrigo (ed) *Psychological Jurisprudence. Critical Explorations in Law, Crime, and Society*, New York: State University of New York Press.

Wacquant, L. (1986) 'Communautés canaques et société coloniale', *Actes de la recherche en sciences sociales*, 61: 56–64.

—— (1987) 'Différence ethnique et différences sociales dans les écoles primaires de Nouvelle-Calédonie', *Actes de la recherche en sciences sociales*, 70: 47–63.

—— (1988) 'Un mythe savant: la "modernisation" de la Nouvelle-Calédonie', *Actes de la recherche en sciences sociales*, 73: 77–84.

—— (1989) 'The Dark Side of the Classroom in New Caledonia: Ethnic and Class Segregation in Noumea's Primary School System', *Comparative Education Review*, 33(2): 194–212.

—— (1992a) 'Banlieues françaises et ghetto noir américain: de l'amalgame à la comparaison', *French Politics and Society*, 10(4): 81–103.

—— (1992b) 'Pour en finir avec le mythe des "cités-ghettos": les différences entre la France et les États-Unis', *Les annales de la recherche urbaine*, 54: 20–30.

—— (1993a) 'Urban Outcasts: Stigma and Division in the Black American Ghetto and French Urban Periphery', *International Journal of Urban and Regional Research*, 17(3): 366–83.

—— (1993b) 'De la "terre promise" au ghetto. La "Grande migration" noire américaine, 1916–1930', *Actes de la recherche en sciences sociales*, 99: 43–51.

—— (1993c) 'De l'Amérique comme utopie à l'envers' in P. Bourdieu (ed) *La misère du monde*, Paris: Éditions du Seuil.

—— (1994) 'The New Urban Color Line: The State and Fate of the Ghetto in PostFordist America' in C. Calhoun (ed) *Social Theory and the Politics of Identity*, Oxford: Basil Blackwell.

—— (1995) 'The Comparative Structure and Experience of Urban Exclusion: "Race", Class, and Space in Chicago and Paris' in K. McFate, R. Lawson and W.J. Wilson (eds) *Poverty, Inequality, and the Future of Social Policy. Western States in the New World Order*, New York: Russell Sage Foundation.

—— (1996a) 'Red Belt, Black Belt: Racial Division, Class Inequality, and the State in the French Urban Periphery and the American Ghetto' in E. Mingione (ed) *Urban Poverty and the Underclass: A Reader*, Oxford: Basil Blackwell.

—— (1996b) 'The Rise of Advanced Marginality: Notes on Its Nature and Implications', *Acta Sociologica*, 39: 121–39.

—— (1996c) 'La généralisation de l'insécurité salariale en Amérique: restructurations d'entreprises et crise de reproduction sociale', *Actes de la recherche en sciences sociales*, 115: 65–79.

—— (1996d) 'Quand le président Clinton "réforme" la pauvreté', *Le Monde diplomatique*, September: 16–17.

—— (1996e) 'L'*underclass* urbaine dans l'imaginaire social et scientifique américain' in S. Paugam (ed) *L'Exclusion: l'état des savoirs*, Paris: La Découverte.

Wacquant, L. (1997a) 'Elias in the Dark Ghetto', *Amsterdams Sociologisch Tijdschrift*, 24(3/4): 340–48.

—— (1997b) 'Decivilisering en diabolisering. De transformatie van het Amerikaanse zwarte getto', *Amsterdams Sociologisch Tijdschrift*, 24(3/4): 320–39.

—— (1997c) 'Les pauvres en pâture: la nouvelle politique de la misère en Amérique', *Hérodote. Revue de géographie et de géopolitique*, 85: 21–33.

—— (1998a) '"A Black City Within the White". Revisiting America's Dark Ghetto', *Black Renaissance*, 2(1): 141–51.

—— (1998b) 'Inside the Zone. The Social Art of the Hustler in the Black American Ghetto', *Theory, Culture and Society*, 15(2): 1–36.

—— (1998c) 'Negative Social Capital: State Breakdown and Social Destitution in America's Urban Core', *Netherlands Journal of Housing and the Built Environment*, 13(1): 25–40.

—— (1998d) 'L'emprisonnement des "classes dangereuses" aux Etats-Unis', *Le Monde diplomatique*, July: 20–21.

—— (1998e) 'La tentation pénale en Europe', *Actes de la recherche en sciences sociales*, 124: 3–6.

—— (1998f) 'L'ascension de l'État pénal en Amérique', *Actes de la recherche en sciences sociales*, 124: 7–26.

—— (1998g) 'Crime et châtiment en Amérique de Nixon à Clinton', *Archives de politique criminelle*, 20: 123–38.

—— (1999a) *Les prisons de la misère*, Paris: Raisons d'agir.

—— (1999b) '"Suitable enemies". Foreigners and immigrants in the prisons of Europe', *Punishment and Society*, 1(2): 215–22.

—— (1999c) 'Urban Marginality in the Coming Millennium', *Urban Studies*, 36(10): 1639–47.

—— (1999d) 'Ce vent punitif qui vient d'Amérique', *Le Monde diplomatique*, April: 1, 24–25.

—— (1999e) 'Traque des ex-délinquants sexuels aux Etats-Unis', *Le Monde diplomatique*, December: 25.

—— (2000a) 'The new "peculiar institution": On the prison as surrogate ghetto', *Theoretical Criminology*, 4(3): 377–89.

—— (2000b) 'Logics of urban polarization: the view from below' in R. Crompton, F. Devine, M. Savage and J. Scott (eds) *Renewing Class Analysis*, Oxford: Blackwell Publishers.

—— (2001a) 'Deadly symbiosis. When ghetto and prison meet and mesh', *Punishment and Society*, 3(1): 95–134.

—— (2001b) 'The Penalisation of Poverty and the Rise of Neo-liberalism', *European Journal of Criminal Policy and Research*, 9: 401–12.

—— (2001c) 'Moralisme et panoptisme punitif. La chasse aux délinquants sexuels aux Etats-Unis'. *Sociologie et Sociétés*, 33(1): 139–57.

—— (2001d) 'The Advent of the Penal State is Not a Destiny', *Social Justice*, 28(3): 81–87.

—— (2001e) 'Blairism: Trojan Horse of Americanisation?' in K. Rahkonen and T. Lausti (eds) *'Blairism'—A Beacon for Europe?*, University of Helsinki: Renvall Institute Publications (n° 11).

—— (2001f) 'Sur l'Amérique comme prophétie auto-réalisante', *Actes de la recherche en sciences sociales*, 139: 86–87.

—— (2002a) *Symbiosi mortale. Neoliberalismo e politica penale*, Verona: Ombre Corte.

—— (2002b) 'From Slavery to Mass Incarceration. Rethinking the "race question" in the US', *New Left Review*, 13 (January/ February): 41–60.

—— (2002c) 'Four Strategies to Curb Carceral Costs: On Managing Mass Imprisonment in the United States', *Studies in Political Economy*, 69: 19–30.

—— (2002d) 'The curious eclipse of prison ethnography in the age of mass incarceration', *Ethnography*, 3(4): 371–97.

—— (2002e) 'Taking Bourdieu Into the Field', *Berkeley Journal of Sociology*, 46: 180–86.

—— (2002f) 'The Sociological Life of Pierre Bourdieu', *International Sociology*, 17(4): 549–56.

—— (2002g) 'Scrutinizing the Street: Poverty, Morality, and the Pitfalls of Urban Ethnography', *American Journal of Sociology*, 107(6): 1468–1532.

—— (2003a) 'Penal truth comes to Europe: Think tanks and the "Washington consensus" on crime and Punishment' in G. Gilligan and J. Pratt (eds) *Crime, Truth and Justice. Official Inquiry, Discourse, Knowledge*, Cullompton: Willan Publishing.

—— (2003b) 'Towards a dictatorship over the poor? Notes on the penalization of poverty in Brazil', *Punishment and Society*, 5(2): 197–205.

—— (2003c) 'Pierre Bourdieu (1930–2002)', *American Anthropologist*, 105(2): 1–3.

—— (2004a) *Punir les pauvres. Le nouveau gouvernement de l'insécurité sociale*, Marseille: Agone.

—— (2004b) *Body and Soul: Notebooks of an Apprentice Boxer*, New York: Oxford University Press.

—— (2004c) 'Critical Thought as Solvent of *Doxa*', *Constellations*, 11(1): 97–101.

—— (2004d) 'Ghetto' in N.J. Smelser and P.B. Baltes (eds) *International Encyclopedia of the Social and Behavioral Sciences*, London: Pergamon Press.

—— (2004e) 'Decivilizing and demonizing: the social and symbolic remaking of the black ghetto and Elias in the dark ghetto' in S. Loyal and S. Quilley (eds) *The Sociology of Norbert Elias*, Cambridge: Cambridge University Press.

—— (2004f) 'Comment sortir du piège sécuritaire?', *Contradictions*, December: 119–33.

Wacquant, L. (ed.) (2005a) *Pierre Bourdieu and Democratic Politics. The Mystery of Ministry*, Cambridge: Polity Press.

—— (2005b) 'The great penal leap backward: Incarceration in America from Nixon to Clinton' in J. Pratt, D. Brown, M. Brown, S. Hallsworth and W. Morrison (eds) *The New Punitiveness. Trends, Theories, Perspectives,* Cullompton: Willan Publishing.

—— (2005c) 'Race as civic felony', *International Social Science Journal*, 57(1): 127–42.

—— (2005d) '"Enemies of the wholesome part of the nation". Postcolonial migrants in the prisons of Europe', *Sociologie*, 1(1): 31–51.

—— (2005e) 'Nothing Beyond its Reach', *The Chronicle Review*, 51(49): B14.

—— (2005f) 'Shadowboxing with Ethnographic Ghosts: A Rejoinder', *Symbolic Interaction*, 28(3): 441–47.

—— (2005g) 'Introduction: Symbolic Power and Democratic Practice' in L. Wacquant (ed) *Pierre Bourdieu and Democratic Politics. The Mystery of Ministry,* Cambridge: Polity Press.

—— (2005h) 'Het janusgezicht van het getto', *Agora*, 21(2): 37–41.

—— (2005i) 'Zur Militarisierung städtischer Marginalität. Lehrstücke aus Brasilien', *Das Argument*, 263: 131–47.

—— (2006a) *Parias urbains. Ghetto, banlieues, État,* Paris: Éditions La Découverte.

—— (2006b) *Straf de armen. Van de verzorgingsstaat naar de strafstaat*, Antwerp: EPO.

—— (2006c) 'Penalization, Depoliticization, Racialization: On the Over-Incarceration of Immigrants in the European Union' in S. Armstrong and L. McAra (eds) *Perspectives on Punishment: The Contours of Control*, Oxford: Oxford University Press.

—— (2006d) 'The "Scholarly Myths" of the New Law and Order Doxa', *Socialist Register*, 94–115.

—— (2006e) 'The Return of the Repressed. Riots, "Race" and Dualization in three advanced societies', *Monu: Magazine on Urbanism*, 5 (July): 6–18.

—— (2007) 'America as Living Laboratory of the Neoliberal Future' in Progress Lawyers Network (ed) *Syllabus Colloquium 'Veiligheidsbeleid: meer strafstaat, minder sociale staat? / Politiques de sécurité: plus d'État pénal, moins d'État social?' (16–3–2007)*, Antwerp: Progress Lawyers Network.

—— and W.J. Wilson (1989) 'The Cost of Racial and Class Exclusion in the Inner City', *Annals of the American Academy of Political and Social Science*, 501: 8–25.

Walgrave, L. (2002) 'Voorwoord' in I. Vanfraechem and L. Walgrave *Een wetenschappelijk onderzoek over de toepassing van Family Group*

Conferences (Herstelgericht groepsoverleg) in Vlaanderen, Leuven: Onderzoeksgroep Jeugdcriminologie.
Walters, R. (2003) *Deviant Knowledge. Criminology, Politics and Policy*, Cullompton: Willan Publishing.
Western, B. (2004) 'Politics and Social Structure in The Culture of Control', *Critical Review of International Social and Political Philosophy*, 7(2): 33–41.
Whitman, J.Q. (2003) *Harsh Justice: Criminal Punishment and the Widening Divide between America and Europe*, New York: Oxford University Press.
—— (2005) 'Response to Garland', *Punishment and Society*, 7(4): 389–96.
Wittebrood, K. (2007) *Slachtoffers van criminaliteit. Een inleiding in de victimologie*, The Hague: Boom Juridische Uitgevers.
—— and P. Nieuwbeerta (2006) 'Een kwart eeuw stijging in geregistreerde criminaliteit. Vooral meer registratie, nauwelijks meer criminaliteit', *Tijdschrift voor Criminologie*, 48(3): 227–42.
Young, J. (1999) *The Exclusive Society. Social Exclusion, Crime and Difference in Late Modernity*, London: Sage.
—— (2003a) 'In praise of dangerous thoughts', *Punishment and Society*, 5(1): 97–107.
—— (2003b) 'Searching for a New Criminology of Everyday Life: A Review of "The Culture of Control" by David Garland', *British Journal of Criminology*, 43(1): 228–43.
—— (2007) *The Vertigo of Late Modernity*, London: Sage.
Young, P. (1986) 'Book review: S. Cohen, Visions of Social Control', *Sociological Review*, 34(1): 222–25.
Young, R. (2002) 'Review: David Garland, The Culture of Control', *The Modern Law Review*, 65: 143–47.
Zedner, L. (2002) 'Dangers of Dystopias in Penal Theory. Review of D. Garland, The Culture of Control', *Oxford Journal of Legal Studies*, 22(2): 341–66.
—— (2003) 'Useful Knowledge? Debating the Role of Criminology in Post-war Britain' in L. Zedner and A. Ashworth (eds) *The Criminological Foundations of Penal Policy: Essays in Honour of Roger Hood*, Oxford: Oxford University Press.
Zimring, F.E. (1996) 'Populism, Democratic Government, and the Decline of Expert Authority: Some Reflections on "Three Strikes" in California'. *Pacific Law Journal*, 28: 243–56.
—— (2003) *The Contradictions of American Capital Punishment*, New York: Oxford University Press.
—— (2005a) 'Path dependence, culture and state-level execution policy. A reply to David Garland', *Punishment and Society*, 7(4): 377–84.

Zimring, F.E. (2005b) 'Capital punishment and hyper-incarceration: Does American exceptionalism have a future?', Paper presented at the 14th World Congress of Criminology, Philadelphia.
—— and G. Hawkins (1991) *The Scale of Imprisonment*, Chicago: The University of Chicago Press.
—— and G. Hawkins (1997) *Crime is Not the Problem: Lethal Violence in America*, New York: Oxford University Press.
—— and G. Hawkins (1998) 'Crime is Not the Problem: A Reply', *University of Colorado Law Review*, 69: 1177–1206.
—— G. Hawkins and S. Kamin (2001) *Punishment and Democracy. Three Strikes and You're Out in California*, New York: Oxford University Press.

Index